Agency of Change

Agency of CHANGE

ONE

HUNDRED

YEARS

OF THE

NORTH

CENTRAL

ASSOCIATION

OF

COLLEGES

AND

SCHOOLS

Mark Newman

THOMAS JEFFERSON UNIVERSITY PRESS

Library of Congress Cataloging-in-Publication Data

Newman, Mark, 1948–
    Agency of Change : One Hundred Years of the North Central Association of
Colleges and Schools / Mark Newman.
        p. cm.
    Includes bibliographical references (p.) and index.
    ISBN 0-943549-42-6 (alk. paper)
    1. North Central Association of Colleges and Schools (U.S.)—History. I.
Title.
LB2301.N62   1996
378.77—dc20   96-28885
                                                                      CIP

Published by Thomas Jefferson University Press at Truman State University in Kirksville, Missouri 63501 (*http://www.truman.edu/tjup/*).

The paper in this publication meets or exceeds the minimum requirements of the
American National Standard—Permanence of Paper for Printed Library Materials,
ANSI Z39.48 (1984).

Contents

Photographs

PHOTOGRAPHS

Preface

IN THE 1890S, BETTERING RELATIONS between secondary schools and colleges was a topic of much discussion among educators. A transformation of American education was occurring. The public high school had replaced the private academy as the basic secondary institution. The modern college and university with its formal, bureaucratic structure and professional administration had superseded the informally organized liberal arts college in higher education. In addition, the elective system had destroyed the prescriptive nature of the classical system, allowing curriculum planners to incorporate new fields of knowledge into courses designed to meet the differing needs of students. While many educators considered the changes long overdue improvements, many also felt the reforms had left the American educational enterprise in disarray, if not chaos. In 1898, Ohio State University president James B. Canfield suggested that the process of change was part of the problem: "It has all been done in a hurry, under great pressure, not always under the wisest leadership, and always without the most full and complete philosophic understanding of just what we wanted or how we were to get it."[1]

A number of factors contributed to the lack of coordination and, at times, direction of the educational transformation. As is the case today, one hundred years ago American education was less a systematically organized whole than a collection of independent, yet related, parts. In general, each college and school developed independently and individually to meet its specific needs, leading to a proliferation of institutional types. The diversity of types was further complicated by the substantial growth in numbers. In 1869, 563 higher education institutions enrolled almost 53,000 students. Thirty years later, 237,592 students attended 977 colleges and universities. High schools recorded even greater increases. There were an estimated 53 public high schools in 1860. By 1890, that number had multiplied almost fiftyfold to 2,526, and more than doubled again in the following decade to 6,005 schools. Where public high schools enrolled only 22,982 students in 1876, 375,000 attended them in 1898.[2] As a result, in the 1890s, it was not possible to develop a definition of a college or high school that fit all the existing institutions. One reason for seeking better relations between secondary and higher education was to define institutions and help to impose some order on the chaotic situation.

The disarray in the curriculum also motivated educators at different levels to form closer ties. For the most part, curriculum planning under the elective system had occurred independently and individually within a school or college. One problem in particular vexed educators: individualized college admission programs made the transition from high school difficult. High schools struggled with the almost impossible task of accommodating the numerous, specific requirements of each college's program.

Recognizing that the problems of institutional definition and of establishing uniformity in college admission, among others, transcended the ability of individual institutions to resolve, educators launched a large-scale organizational movement in the late nineteenth century. The founding of the North Central Association of Colleges and Secondary Schools in 1895 was part of that movement. The NCA aimed to improve relations between high schools and colleges by bringing together representatives from both levels to discuss matters of common concern. The underlying hope was that the new association would improve the quality of education in the United States. Emotions ran high at the first meeting of the North Central Association, held at the University of Chicago on April 3 and 4, 1896. "Never before, I think, has the interest in education been so widespread and profound as it now," observed James B. Angell, president of the University of Michigan. Noting that the conditions were favorable, Angell fired up the enthusiasm of the NCA delegates with a fervent call to action: "Let us, representatives of ten great states, do our utmost by the deliberations and discussions of the association, to make our secondary and higher education of the greatest service to these commonwealths and to the whole nation."[3]

Over the next hundred years, the NCA fulfilled Angell's expectations in ways and by means that exceeded his wildest dreams. At its inception, the North Central Association was the largest of the four regional organizations. Its territory included ten states in the middle of the United States, and in 1896 the membership numbered eighty-two high schools, colleges, and universities, and thirty-one individuals. In many respects, the NCA began as an elite debating society that sought to stimulate reform by the stature of its membership and the quality of its discussions. In its first five years of existence, the primary responsibility of the four officers was planning the annual meeting. They selected the topics for discussion and set the time and place.

Today, the NCA remains the biggest of six regional associations. Its territory covers nineteen states from Ohio to Arizona and North Dakota to West Virginia, plus the Navajo Nation, other Native American reservations, and the Department of Defense Dependents' Schools located around the world. Over seventy-two hundred elementary, middle, high, and postsecondary vocational-technical schools as well as almost one thousand degree-granting vocational-technical institutes, junior colleges, colleges, and universities enjoy North Central Association membership. Its work revolves around accreditation and encouraging institutional improvement. Its organization is highly functional and bureaucratic, structured around two commissions, one for precollegiate and the other for collegiate institutions. Both have independent, permanent headquarters and full-time, paid, professional staffs. The annual meeting is still the major event, but hardly the principal task of the staff.

In the development of accreditation, the NCA has played a preeminent role. It not only innovated the practice of voluntary regional accreditation, but in the 1930s, it transformed accrediting by switching from quantitative standards to qualitative criteria. This change implied assessment of schools and colleges on how well they met their own objectives. In a sense, it pioneered the idea of outcomes evaluation almost fifty years before this term became an educational buzzword.

As the NCA approached its centennial in 1995, its leaders decided that a history of the organization was an appropriate way to celebrate this milestone. In late 1992, I was commissioned to write the NCA story. The Centennial Committee did not want an in-house chronicle of the daily events of the organization, nor a warm, fuzzy promotional piece that just celebrated accomplishments. Instead, the Committee requested a social history that explored the internal culture of the NCA, but also connected its development to that of education and of the United States. The goal was to show that accreditation, this association, and education are important chapters in the history of our nation.

VOLUNTARY ASSOCIATIONS AS CONNECTORS

Voluntary associations, like the NCA, are an integral part of many societies. In the United States, they have served historically as basic building blocks of American society. Many readers of this book belong to a voluntary association, but most of these associations probably bear little resemblance to the North Central Association. Generally, "an association is a group organized for the pursuit of one interest or of several interests in common." It can be composed of individuals or organizations, or both. Initially, the North Central Association proposed to improve relations between high schools and colleges. It originally admitted individuals and educational institutions, but now only the latter are eligible for membership. According to sociologist David Sills, voluntary means that membership is not mandatory or acquired by birth, the majority of participants are part-time and nonsalaried, and the association is organized independently of the state.[4] Higher education professor Harland Bloland added two more qualifications. Following the basis of the American political system, the association is democratically organized and has a written constitution. Sills traced this democratic credo to the modern origins of associations in Europe, where the emerging concept of civil liberty in the sixteenth and seventeenth centuries influenced their development.[5]

Regarding the roles played by voluntary associations in American society, particularly after World War II, Bloland suggested they acted as connectors for their members and government.[6] Above all else, organizations founded voluntarily "connect" people and/or organizations to pursue a common purpose. The association provides a meeting place for contact and communication. It also supplies a mechanism for common action. The North Central Association connected high school and college educators, providing a formal, regular forum to discuss professional issues and forge personal relationships. In the process, they "connected" by identifying areas of common concern and by learning about their differences. As the NCA members gained a better understanding of each other, they proposed solutions to various problems.

On a larger scale, voluntary associations make connections far beyond the confines of their membership. Because the organizational purpose is typically narrowly defined, institutions and individuals often join numerous associations to address diverse concerns. For example, some of the same state universities that helped create the NCA had founded the Association of American Colleges and Experimental Stations in 1887 to gain increased federal funding. The National Association of State Universities, established in 1895, and the Association of American Colleges, organized in 1915 by liberal arts colleges, pursued objectives tied to their specific types of institutions. The overlapping memberships of these various organizations increased their connections and heightened the impact of the organizations. The decisions of the North Central Association exerted some influence on high schools and colleges nationwide, meaning it was "connected" to the American educational enterprise generally. Because the schools and colleges had public functions and these institutions accepted that NCA membership certified the quality of an institution, the Association also forged connections with students, parents, and local communities; in essence, to American society.

A unique characteristic of educational voluntary associations is their connection to the federal government. Throughout most of U.S. history, constitutional interpretations and tradition limited the role of the federal government in the development of education. As historian Hugh Hawkins has noted, many educators in the 1890s were skeptical of national government intervention in their affairs. These educators viewed the federal government as a source of funds and as an information agency that offered classification standards but opposed regulation. Voluntary associations allowed educators to address issues and to solve problems themselves.[7]

After World War II, the federal government assumed a much more active posture regarding education. Civil rights, foreign policy issues, and changing conceptions of the role of education led to vastly increased federal funding that required greater regulation of schools and colleges. The increasing intrusion of the federal government into societal affairs prompted officials in Washington to use nongovernmental organizations to perform public duties. In 1966, Alan Pifer reviewed the financial and policy problems delegated by the government to voluntary organizations. Noting it was rare before World War II, he concluded, "The use of nongovernmental organizations to carry out public functions is now accepted policy in most parts of government." Harland Bloland identified four major areas where government has relied upon associations. First, the need for information led to the use of "extragovernmental sources" to gain knowledge of the "functioning of American social institutions." In this respect, associations are "important channels through which information is transmitted to the governed as well as to the governors in the American system." Second, "[f]ederal agencies...must rely extensively on the technical expertise of nongovernmental specialists...to advise the policy process." Third, associations represent certain interests to the government. Lastly, associations provide government with new ideas and innovations for federal programs and new policy directions.[8]

Its increasing role in the funding of higher education prompted the federal government to use accrediting associations to certify the quality of the institutions receiving money. The resulting relationship determined that the NCA and other accrediting associations perform all four of the tasks Bloland identified above. They act as sources and conduits of information to provide data on quality educational institutions and to let the educational community know the requirements for federal funding. In requesting assistance from these organizations, the government relied on the technical expertise of "specialists" from accrediting associations to provide advice on funding policies. The stronger ties to government expanded and enhanced the connectedness of associations such as the NCA to all levels of society.

As connectors, then, voluntary associations help organize American society, often relieving a sense of isolation and alienation. In pursuit of the organizational purpose, all members gain a sense of belonging to a common cause. They also help open channels of communication to other organizations, individuals, and government.

THE HISTORICAL CONTEXT OF THE RISE OF EDUCATIONAL VOLUNTARY ASSOCIATIONS

The same general process of change that has characterized American history has affected the development of voluntary associations. Since the end of the Civil War, changes in society have caused two major alterations in these organizations. The first was the changed relationship with the federal government discussed above. The second occurred earlier as part of the process of modernization. Many scholars claim that a new organizational society emerged in the United States in the fifty years following the Civil War. Samuel P. Hays noted that, between 1865 and the beginning of World War I, scientific and technological advances profoundly altered American society, transforming the way America was organized and reordering human relationships. Kenneth Boulding narrowed the time frame of what he called the "organizational revolution" to the period between 1887 and 1918. It witnessed the rise of national and regional religious, labor, and business organizations, including the Federal Council of Churches (1905), the American Federation of Labor (1886), the Industrial Workers of the World (1906), and the Chamber of Commerce of the United States (1912), among many others. In general, the proliferation of associations in the late nineteenth and early twentieth centuries reflected a shift from "local autonomy and isolated institutional decision making toward national coordination and the common pursuit of interests."[9] In the process, the previous traditionally oriented, informal, often local modes of organization gave way to formal, bureaucratic, and functional groups that sought better control over environmental conditions.

Because they eschewed greater involvement by the federal government, educators formed their own organizations to seek improvement of their situation. Hugh Hawkins tied the rise of associations to a growing recognition that American society contained multiple centers of power. Organizations provided the necessary leadership and means of connecting these various power centers. However, while educators sought coordination and visibility on a national scale, they also believed that the pluralistic nature of society required a variety of organizations to pursue general and specific needs. The result was a proliferation of associations with either broad or narrowly defined functions.[10]

The North Central Association was founded in the midst of Boulding's "organizational revolution." It was part of a smaller movement that began in 1885 with the founding of the New England Association of Schools and Colleges and focused on organizing regionally to improve relations between secondary schools and colleges. Initially, the NCA pursued its goal of improving secondary-collegiate relations by employing an informal, deliberative structure that stressed discussion of issues of common concern. Five years after its founding, in 1901, it moved to a more active and modern stance by pioneering voluntary accreditation. As both a deliberative and accrediting organization, the Association has acted as a connector, occupying the middle ground between educational institutions of similar and different levels, schools and society, and schools and government. It has been a conduit of information and a lightning rod for action during one hundred years of fast-paced, deep-rooted, and ongoing change. Not surprisingly, the idea of change has been its consuming interest, indeed its passion.

CHANGE AND THE HISTORY OF THE NORTH CENTRAL ASSOCIATION

Because of the constant flux in educational thought and practice, the story of the NCA revolves around the organization's attempts to maintain its relevance and effectiveness by periodically re-creating itself to meet changing times. On three occasions, though the process took more than a decade, the Association re-created itself to remain in tune with ongoing change. In all these instances, the NCA not only reacted to change, but also promoted it. Between 1901 and 1916, it transformed itself from a traditional, deliberative to a modern, functional, accrediting organization. From the late 1920s to the early 1960s, it created and implemented a new modern theory of accrediting. During the 1970s and early 1980s, it devolved all power and operations to the two accrediting commissions, making the Association a symbolic shell. Thus, in different eras, the NCA presents itself as a very different organization, sometimes becoming almost the opposite of its previous incarnation.

Despite all the stress on change, the NCA's basic founding principles and beliefs related to its purpose, its attitude towards change, and its status as a voluntary association remained remarkably stable, indicating the NCA history is marked not only by change, but by continuity. For example, throughout all the revisions and re-creations, the thrust of Association activities has focused on helping members learn how to change themselves. In the process of adapting itself to meet new needs, the Association developed activities in a large variety of educational areas that stimulated alterations in its member schools and colleges.

In a variety of ways, then, the North Central Association has been an agency of change. This book examines how this agency of change attempted to reform education, and modernized its activities and organization in the process.

Studying change and continuity in the organizational and environmental contexts requires a multidimensional approach. From one perspective, there are the influences that affected the development of the organization, leading to questions about its nature, goals, policies, and procedures. There is also the issue of where these influences originated, raising questions about its role and place in society and education as well as regarding the parts played by external and internal forces in stimulating activity. Conversely, the idea that the organization initiated changes in education and society brings up very different questions about many of the above points. The interplay between external and internal influences, between acting as a respondent to or a stimulus of change, strongly influenced the development of the NCA.

The narrative itself combines a chronological and topical approach dictated by the various re-creations and the functional structure of the Association. The book opens with a brief look at the rise of education after 1865 that produced the conditions that stimulated the founding of the North Central Association. Chapter 2 explores the first five years of the organization, while the next chapter examines the first re-creation occasioned by the rise of accrediting from 1901 to approximately 1916. Chapter 4 chronicles the first phases of the second re-creation, the development of a new theory of accreditation, and also discusses the role played by the NCA as an educational reformer between 1916 and the early 1940s. World War II served as a temporary break that halted the implementation of the new accrediting theory and was a watershed in the history of education, ushering in a new era that required substantial adaptations by the NCA commissions. Because of the nature of educational change and the growing independence of the NCA commissions, chapters 5, 6, and 7 focus on developments in higher education, the schools, and the research commissions respectively between 1945 and the mid-1970s. The changes at the Association level are covered in chapter 7. The last chapter brings us to NCA's centennial, covering the impact of the post-1970 reform movement and the increasing intrusion of government in education on the two NCA accrediting commissions.

In writing this book, the author accumulated numerous debts of gratitude. Many people have contributed their time and energy to making it possible to tell this story. Thanks go first and foremost to my wife Kim and my daughters Jodi and Nicole for putting up with me over the last two and a half years. They provided the inspiration for undertaking such an arduous task, and so the finished product is dedicated to them. Second, thanks to Jerry Danzer, who as colleague and friend, has shown me how to be a better historian and person.

The ability to tell the NCA's story is due to the support and assistance of numerous people. The personnel at the archives of Northwestern University, the University of Chicago, and the Urbana campus of the University of Illinois offered much needed help in locating valuable records. Several graduate students in the Department of History of the University of Illinois at Chicago ably assisted in the research for the book, including Karen Ramsey, Tom Wolff, Diccon Ong, and Katja Stonebraker.

As was made clear by everyone interviewed for this history of the North Central Association, this organization is most of all about people. And it is those people involved with the NCA that made this book possible. My thanks to the NCA history subcommittee that gave me the opportunity to get to know the NCA. Similar gratitude is expressed to those who submitted to interviews. The support of Commission on Schools executive director Ken Gose is appreciated, as is that of his assistant director Cathy Baird. The NCA president for 1996, Mary Ann Carroll, has been a tower of support and continuous encouragement. My conversations with John Kemp, former NCA president and Illinois State Director emeritus, vastly expanded my knowledge and understanding of the organization and its development over the last thirty years. John has also reviewed the manuscript in its various stages. Thanks also to Myron Marty of Drake University and Bob Silverman, former editor of the *Journal of Higher Education*, for their thoughtful reviews of the manuscript.

My thanks to the staff of the Commission on Institutions of Higher Education come last. Because the office was located in Chicago, I had the most contact with them. The office staff proved extremely helpful, particularly Denise Branch, Marisol Gomez, and Leslie Logan.

Very special thanks are due two people who gave most generously of their time and energy. To Susan Van Kollenburg for all she did to make this book happen and for her friendship. To Patricia Thrash, executive director, who provided me with an office, offered unwavering support, and shared her profound insight into the NCA.

PREFACE

NOTES

1. James H. Canfield, "Presidential Address," *Proceedings of the Third Annual Meeting of the North Central Association of Colleges and Secondary Schools* (Chicago: University of Chicago Press, 1898), 17–18, hereafter referred to as NCA *Proceedings,* followed by the appropriate year.

2. Edwin G. Dexter, *History of Education in the United States* (New York: Burt Franklin, 1906), 172. Commissioner of Education, *Report of the Commissioner of Education for the Year 1893–1894* (Washington, D.C.: GPO, 1884), 37; Bernard Mehl, "The High School at the Turn of the Century," unpublished Ph.D. dissertation, University of Illinois, 1954, 18, 25; Richard Lykes, *Higher Education and the United States Office of Education, 1867–1953* (Washington: GPO, 1975), 32.

3. James B. Angell, "Presidential Address," NCA *Proceedings,* 1896, 12.

4. David Sills, "Voluntary Associations: Sociological Aspects," and Michael Banton, "Voluntary Associations: Anthropological Aspects," *International Encyclopedia of the Social Sciences* (1968), 357, 362–63; Harland Bloland, *Associations in Action: The Washington D. C. Higher Education Community,* ASHE-ERIC Higher Education Report number 2 (Washington, D.C.: Association for the Study of Higher Education, 1985), 1.

5. Bloland, *Higher Education Associations in a Decentralized Education System* (Berkeley: University of California Center for Research and Development, 1969), 39–40; Sills, "Voluntary Associations: Sociological Aspects," 363, 368.

6. Bloland, *Higher Education Associations in a Decentralized Education System,* 33; Bloland, *Associations in Action,* 3.

7. Hugh Hawkins, *Banding Together: The Rise of National Associations in American Higher Education, 1887–1950* (Baltimore: The Johns Hopkins University Press, 1992), xi–xii, 6, 8, 16.

8. Cited in David Sills, "Voluntary Associations: Sociological Aspects," 375; Bloland, *Higher Education Associations in a Decentralized Education System,* 28–30.

9. Samuel P. Hays, "Introduction—The New Organizational Society," in Jerry Israel (ed.), *Building the Organizational Society* (New York: The Free Press, 1972), 5–6; Hawkins, *Banding Together,* xi. See also Kenneth Boulding, *The Organizational Revolution* (New York: Harper, 1953).

10. Hawkins, *Banding Together,* xi–xii.

Chapter One

Education on the Rise

*Individualism plays a more prominent part today
in education than in the past. This same individualism is something which appears in our institutions as well as in our methods of instruction...
but after all we have at heart the same work, we
have in mind the same purpose, we are doing the
same thing.*

—William Rainey Harper,
in his welcome to the delegates attending the first
annual meeting of the North Central Association of
Colleges and Secondary Schools, April 3, 1896[1]

INDIVIDUALITY AND SIMILARITY: As the first president of the University of Chicago astutely observed, these two tendencies influenced
the development of education in the late nineteenth century, creating the conditions that prompted the founding of the North
Central Association. As many contemporary observers noted, the
late nineteenth century was a revolutionary period in education.
The changes were most evident in the sheer growth of the educational enterprise, in the development of basic institutions that fostered cohesion of the American system of schooling, and the
transformation of the curriculum that spurred individuality in that
same system.[2]

INSTITUTIONAL DEVELOPMENT

The post–Civil War era witnessed the rise of two basic educational
institutions, the high school and the modern university. Writing in
1900, Elmer Ellsworth Brown saw the emergence of the public high
school as the last of three well-defined stages of secondary education development. The first was the era of Latin grammar schools
during the colonial era. Between approximately 1789 and the mid-
1800s, the private academy dominated secondary education.

1

Though the first public high school was founded in Boston in the 1820s, only after 1840 did it become a factor in the American education system and then at a minor level.[3] After the Civil War, the public high school movement traveled a long, rough road to acceptance. In his 1954 doctoral dissertation on the history of the high school, Bernard Mehl explained, "The public high school...battled for its existence in the 1870s and established itself victorious in the area of secondary education. It fashioned gains in the 1880s, consolidated and increased these gains in the 1890s when it succeeded in becoming more and more diffused throughout the several states."[4]

Altered public conceptions of the role schools played in their lives and society fueled the rapid growth of the high school after the Civil War. James H. Canfield, president of Ohio State University, cited proof of public support in his 1898 NCA presidential address, observing that the school tax was the highest tax paid by Americans and that they rarely complained about it. Many parents saw education as a means of social mobility for their children. In addition, the settlement of the American continent, the rapid growth of cities, and the tremendous increase in foreign immigration, combined with industrialization, contributed to the rise of the public high school.

In the creation of new towns, high schools served as symbols of status, progress, and stability. "Attention has often been called to the fact that wherever a village arises, either on the prairie, or in the valley, or on a hillside, the most conspicuous building is likely to be the high school, to which the people point with satisfaction as evidence of their interest in this great and all-absorbing necessity," remarked University of Wisconsin president Charles Kendall Adams at the 1897 North Central Association annual meeting. James B. Angell, president of the University of Michigan, had noted, "In almost any western city, the finest building is the high school."[5]

In the cities, industrialization and immigration helped spur interest in a high school education. On one hand, the growing connection between education and the changing needs of the workplace created a movement to have the schools train workers for the industrial age. On the other hand, schools helped assimilate immigrants who were arriving from Europe in increasing numbers.

Concerns over the corrupting influences of city life on youth, the need to counter European political radicalism with American democratic ideas, and growing nativist sentiments also contributed to the urban high school movement.[6] The combination of all these forces led to the idea that the high school was the people's college, the institution that fit youth for life in American society by providing the education they needed to become productive, supportive citizens.[7]

The notion that high schools could prepare youth for adulthood dated back to the earliest public secondary institutions in the 1820s. But secondary schools had traditionally prepared students for college. These two opposing missions, fit for life and prepare for college, created difficulties for the high schools because they implied very different courses of study and were the source of much public criticism from proponents of both missions.[8] In practice, the college preparatory function dominated, most likely because its curriculum was better organized and traditionally practiced. The prescribed classical curriculum of the colleges offered a simple model for high schools to follow and, equally important, the colleges often educated secondary teachers. All students took the same course of study, focusing on a small number of subjects, with such foreign languages as Greek and Latin dominating. Instruction carried through from the first year of high school to the last year of college. The transition between grades and levels of education was smooth and straightforward.

Conversely, the fit-for-life course of study had no established tradition to draw upon in developing a curriculum. "The absence of definite standards for the organization of the curricula...is very evident," explained Northwestern University professor John Stout in his 1921 book, *The Development of High-School Curricula in the North Central States from 1860 to 1918*. The lack of curricula guidelines meant that "there is no apparent demand or complex of demands sufficiently clear in purpose or definite in influence to secure any sort of uniformity in length of course, organization, or subjects offered."

The prevailing belief among educators that a single knowledge base met the needs of all students further complicated the situation. It implied that a single curriculum could prepare students both for college and for life. In attempting to design curricula that served both purposes, schools overwhelmingly stressed the college side because most teachers had academically oriented training and the needed standards were available.[9] Though up to the present day, the debates over its purpose, organization, and curricula continue, by 1890, the public high school was the basic institution for secondary education.

The rise of the modern university also occurred during the late nineteenth century. While the roots of the university's emergence date back before the Civil War, it was primarily a post–Civil War phenomenon. According to historian Laurence Veysey, the university's basic organization was not established until approximately 1890.[10] Unlike the high school, higher education in America had a long history going back to early colonial days. The traditional antebellum colleges were largely exercises in orthodoxy that stressed two goals, mental discipline and piety. The first involved the training of such faculties as will, emotion, and intellect to develop mental abilities and morality through the memorization and recitation of classical works in the original Greek or Latin. As Veysey explained, students received identical training because educators believed that "college should equip its students with a series of underlying responses, applicable to all future situations, rather than with specific skills." This idea fit well with the piety goal since one of the traditional college's major purposes was to prepare young men for the ministry. Many college faculty and administrators were members of the clergy.[11]

By the middle of the nineteenth century, changing times stimulated reforms in the traditional American college. The economic development of the nation, including the rise of industrialism, the evolution of democracy, and the changing nature of knowledge had, as Veysey observed, made the thriving college of the eighteenth century outdated by the early nineteenth century. The prestige of the college degree was declining and enrollments remained static despite overall population growth. One problem was that many Americans had negative perceptions of the colleges because they knew so little about them. Recalling his own school days in the 1850s, University of Michigan president James B. Angell observed in 1895 that he had known little of what the college was or did. "People for the most part thought of college professors as harmless persons living in monastic seclusion disseminating useless knowledge to aristocratic and rather eccentric young men," he explained.[12]

Another difficulty was that many colleges resisted change. In *The American College and University*, Frederick Rudolph observed, "Resistance to fundamental reform was ingrained in the American collegiate and university tradition." He summed up the historic policy of change in higher education as "drift, reluctant accommodation, belated recognition that while no one was looking, change had in fact taken place."[13] Rudolph's views are somewhat misleading. While he accurately portrayed the attitudes of many educators and the experiences of numerous institutions, generally those promoting the status quo had counterparts who pushed for reform. Sometimes, the resulting conflict pitted one generation against another. Veysey explained that many of the college leaders who opposed reform in the 1850s were older men near the end of their careers. Those proposing changes in higher education were typically younger and discontented figures who recognized that enrollment problems required new approaches. Veysey called the 1850s and 1860s the seedbed of reform.[14] During those decades, forces were working to radically alter higher education in the United States, but the future course that led to the rise of the modern university was already apparent.

In many respects, the university was a product of a transatlantic encounter between Europe and the United States. A variety of connected and disparate forces combined in a complex, often confusing, fashion to create the modern university. The European Enlightenment triggered an explosion of human knowledge, including the creation of numerous new fields and the emergence of a scientific-technological worldview that clashed with the classically oriented, narrowly prescribed dictates of the traditional college. According to historians Alexandra Oleson and John Voss, in the first half of the nineteenth century, "the expansion of science and scholarship, the elaboration of analytic methods to specific fields, the concurrent need for new facilities and resources to advance research brought major structural changes in the learned institutions of Western Europe."[15] The rise of a new German university in the early 1800s was especially influential, because, between the 1830s and 1860s, many American educators went to Germany for their graduate education. They returned to the United

States with a new awareness of the evolving scientifically based scholarship, a model for integrating this scholarship into American institutions, and a willingness to pursue change.[16]

Developments in the United States worked to the advantage of those seeking to reform higher education. Perhaps, most importantly, the spread of higher education was tied to the settlement of the nation. Much as the land ordinances of the 1780s had set aside township sections to finance precollegiate schools, the same was true of colleges. In 1836, Congress strengthened the dictates of the ordinances, passing a law that required each territory seeking admission as a state to the Union to include provisions for establishing a state university.[17] Because of the federal statutes for public institutions and the growing number of private ones, colleges and universities played an important role in the settlement of the land. New and old communities waged fierce campaigns to land a college because it stabilized the community, providing a sense of permanence and a spur to growth. It also served as a source of local pride.[18] Equally important, public institutions had a commitment to their citizenry that became connected to a familiar dispute over purpose. Predating the debate in the high schools, the question of a utilitarian college education had arisen in the earliest days of the American republic. The evolving needs of an industrial society placed greater stress on science and technical education, and thus on utility. The state universities also were subject to democratic tendencies in society, leading to calls to open higher education to the populace.

Many of the forces working for change came together during Henry Tappan's presidency of the University of Michigan in the 1850s. Founded in 1817 on the French model, the University of Michigan was the capstone of the state's system of education and oversaw the development and operations of the other levels. However, collegiate education followed the prescribed, classical curriculum. Tappan instituted several reforms that profoundly altered the Michigan institution, making it, perhaps, the first modern university. Among other things, he diversified the curriculum by creating schools of fine and industrial arts. He established new courses leading to bachelor's degrees in science and civil engineering. He also set up a law school. Most important for the future development of the modern university, Tappan instituted electives for seniors.[19]

If the University of Michigan provided a model for reforming the traditional collegiate institution, events during the Civil War supplied the means. The war forced educators to recognize the professional respectability and the need for the engineer, natural scientist, and technician. This recognition and the requirements of the burgeoning industrial order created educational opportunities in these careers.[20] The conflict also showed the value of science and technology, bringing some prewar ideas on utility and scientific education into clearer focus. Because the war removed opposition to these ideas, an opportunity for change arose. The passage of the Morrill Act of 1862 helped set the tone for the future of higher education by tying land grant funding for colleges and universities to the sciences and utilitarian needs of society.[21] The Act set aside land for the creation of institutions of higher education that taught agriculture and the applied sciences along with classical and other studies.

The emphasis on science was shown by the curriculum of the University of Illinois, a land grant college. Originally called Illinois Industrial University, the institution was organized into four colleges: agriculture, engineering, natural sciences, and literature and science. These colleges, in turn, were subdivided into a number of different schools, including commerce, military science, and domestic science and arts. The influence of utility and the new developments in scholarship connected to the scientific-technological worldview were readily apparent at the Illinois university. To make instruction in these various programs possible, state superintendent of instruction Newton Daugherty noted, "The studies are elective."[22]

THE ELECTIVE SYSTEM AND CURRICULAR DEVELOPMENT

The idea of opening up the curriculum required altering or abandoning the idea that all students should take the same, prescribed course of study that focused primarily on classics and foreign languages. The providing of a choice, an elective system, was a simple idea that dated back to Thomas Jefferson's plans for the University of Virginia. Until the Morrill Act and the changed situation facing educators after the Civil War, however, it was an idea whose time had not yet come. After 1865, two champions supported the move to election. On an individual level, Harvard University president

Charles Eliot became the foremost advocate of the elective system. Institutionally, as historian Frederick Rudolph explained, "Unquestionably the large state universities of the Midwest and West, with their commitment to public service and learning were more friendly than any other group of institutions to the elective principle." The prewar pioneering of the University of Michigan certainly played a role in promoting support among western institutions, but the scientific thrust of the Morrill Act provided a stronger impetus for an elective system.[23]

The elective system opened up American higher education to expansion. It posited the theory that all subjects had scholastic importance, justifying the inclusion of scientific and utilitarian courses in the curriculum with the classics and humanities. The classical curriculum was not replaced or abandoned. Rather, it was supplemented by the new fields of knowledge. The impact was massive, creating a ripple effect that revolutionized almost every aspect of higher education from the organization of the institution to the training and status of faculty. "The elective principle was the instrument by which departments of knowledge were built, by which areas of scholarly interest were enlarged," observed Rudolph, "and therefore it was the instrument that enabled the colleges to become universities." Historian John Higham supported Rudolph's contention, suggesting the elective system opened higher education to the specialization that provided the basis for the development of a multi-institutional matrix for research that exists today.[24]

The expansion of the curriculum helped transform the traditional, informal organization of the college. The old organization had revolved around faculty chairs and disciplinary colleges, a president, and a board of trustees. Often a member of the clergy, the president was a paternalistic figure who not only administered the institution, but oversaw the moral training of students, probably taught classes, and answered to the board of trustees, whose qualification for governing a college varied widely.[25] The evolving university required a multitiered organization and a much more professional administration to fulfill its expanding functions. The rise of departments centered around specific disciplines that allowed professors to pursue research autonomously in an exponentially increasing number of fields. Because the department was the primary administrative unit for faculty, the number of departments could be expanded according to need. To provide further coordination and administration, colleges evolved within the university structure headed by a new figure, the dean. The college organized related disciplinary fields into a manageable whole, and reflected general tendencies of the late nineteenth century such as the departmentalization of corporations. The position of the president became more professional and followed the example of the emerging corporate executive. The personal touch that characterized presidential relations with students in the traditional college largely disappeared as the chief executive of the college became more removed from the classroom.[26]

Interestingly, the organizational changes followed the inclusive policy of the curriculum. The modern university "assimilated, rather than destroyed, the pre-existing college" by grafting German ideas onto the traditional English college.[27] This synthesis produced a multipurpose, comprehensive institution. It offered undergraduates the liberal course of study of the traditional college. Building upon the German model, it trained graduate students in scientifically oriented research and provided professional education in medicine, pharmacy, and law. In addition, many universities, public and private, offered a wide variety of community services.

The faculty also experienced a transformation as amateur teachers were replaced by professional scholars and scientists. The professionalization of the faculty was an ongoing process that helped raise academic standards and underscored the growing importance of research as part of a professor's duties. It also signified the ascendancy of science in higher education. The paramount importance placed on the Ph.D. degree helped certify the academic expertise of the college professor while supporting the equality of all fields of knowledge.[28] These developments facilitated the expansion of scientifically oriented graduate education to train scholars and scientists. In turn, the growing number of professional academics contributed to the more specialized organization of faculty into departments.

By 1890, the modern university had developed into a multifaceted institution. Just as the high school had organized the secondary levels of schooling, the university performed a similar function for the collegiate and professional levels. The institutional development of the high school and the university was part of a larger movement in education that, itself, was a component of a societal trend towards more formal organization of life that was connected to the process of modernization. Historian Samuel P. Hays has argued that after 1865 new organizational forms that "created new ways of ordering human relationships" helped transform the way "American society was put together." The organizational tendencies were evident in all aspects of life, and a major impetus was to reallocate functions once performed by the family and community to more formal, bureaucratic entities. Hays and other scholars have suggested that this organizational impulse helped define modernity.[29]

INDIVIDUALITY AND CURRICULAR CHAOS

In a sense, education in the late 1800s followed two different paths of development. The rise of the high school and the university aimed at greater, more efficient organization of the institutions of American education. Stimulated by the elective system, curriculum developments tried to effectively organize the expanding fields of knowledge. Despite the similarity of purpose, the stress on individual development worked against these tendencies. The absence of any coordinating organization or instrument meant that each institution developed independently and created its own curriculum, creating a disorderly situation due to lack of articulation of the various courses of studies in high schools and colleges.

Recognizing the severity of the problems created by the elective system, colleges and universities sought solutions by focusing on college admission programs, particularly entrance requirements. Two basic strategies emerged. The first was more prevalent in the East and involved entrance examinations, the traditional method of admission. More relevant to the purposes of this book, the second was the certificate system pioneered at the University of Michigan in the early 1870s. The admission by certificate program was adopted by many western colleges and universities and was the forerunner of voluntary accreditation later created by the North Central Association. Borrowing from a German model of admission, University of Michigan president Henry S. Frieze developed the program of basing admissions on the quality of the school, using the diploma rather than an examination to admit students. University examiners inspected high schools, and if they accredited the school, its graduates were assured admission to the state university.[30]

Neither entrance examinations nor the certificate system worked well. The institutional nature of the efforts meant that admission programs reflected the individual needs of each college, creating a sphere of influence that extended from a single college or university to multiple secondary schools. Because of the growth of higher education institutions, high schools became part of numerous spheres, many of which had differing requirements. So, while it proved possible to order relations down from a single college to many high schools, the connection up from the high school to the colleges remained jumbled and chaotic. In 1896, at the first NCA annual meeting, J. O. Leslie, principal of Ottawa, Illinois, Township High School, explained schools easily met one college's requirements, but "when it comes to meeting *all* the requirements of *all* the colleges, then we are in difficulty." Principal Henry L. Boltwood of Evanston, Illinois, Township High School agreed. He reported that "teachers in secondary schools are pretty unanimous in saying that the requirements for college are exceeding the hours at our disposal."

Collegiate administrators joined high school principals in calling for change. In 1897, President Charles Kendall Adams of the University of Wisconsin claimed high school administrators racked their brains to define their courses of study but, "in their doubt as to what they shall do, they do a little of everything," he noted, "and you will find in the high schools of the West a little of everything under the sun... with no logical order that can be deduced." A single high school could offer as many as twelve curricula to meet the differing demands of various occupations and the admission requirements of numerous colleges and universities.[31] Northwestern University president Henry Wade Rogers observed that secondary schools "have found themselves seriously embarrassed in their work of preparing students for college by the differing, and in some cases whimsical, conditions which have been established." He admitted, "The schools ask, and very properly, that the colleges reform the abuses that now exist respecting entrance requirements."[32]

The individuality of college admission programs thwarted institutional attempts to instill order into curriculum. Educators recognized that cooperative, concerted action was needed to provide more uniform entrance requirements. Cooperation required improved relations between high schools and colleges. This belief prompted the founding of the North Central Association of Colleges and Secondary Schools in 1895.

NOTES

1. NCA *Proceedings*, 1896, 8.

2. Laurence Veysey, *The Emergence of the American University* (Chicago: University of Chicago Press, 1965), 1; NCA *Proceedings*, 1902, 47.

3. Elmer Ellsworth Brown, "Secondary Education," in *Education in the United States*, ed. Nicholas Murray Butler (Albany, N.Y.: J. B. Lyon, Co., 1900), 3. In his study of American education, Edwin G. Dexter claimed only six public high schools existed before 1849. He estimated that 47 were founded between 1840 and 1860. Dexter, *History of Education in the United States*, 170–74. For a description of the first public high school, founded in Boston in 1821, see John Erle Stout, *The Development of High School Curricula in the North Central States from 1860 to 1918* (New York: Arno Press & New York Time, 1969, originally published 1921), 1–4.

4. Mehl, "The High School at the Turn of the Century," 22.

5. Brown, "Secondary Education," 51. For Adams' comments, see his "Presidential Address," NCA *Proceedings*, 1897, 3. Angell's remarks are from his 1896 "Presidential Address," 11.

6. Edward Krug, *The Shaping of the American High School, 1880–1920* (New York: Harper & Row, 1964), 1:10–11.

7. Ibid., 178, 212–16.

8. Richard Grant White, "The Public School Failure," *North American Review* 170 (December 1880): 541–42. For White, the issue was not inadequate schooling, but public education generally beyond the elementary level, which he opposed except for special situations, such as providing financial aid for poor students and supplying public secondary schools for students of exceptional ability.

See also Lawrence Cremin, *The Transformation of the School* (New York: Alfred A. Knopf, 1961), 3–7; David Tyack, "City Schools: Centralization of Control at the Turn of the Century," in Israel, *Building the Organizational Society*; and Maureen Flanagan, "Gender and Urban Political Reform: The City Club and the Woman's City Club of Chicago in the Progressive Era, *American Historical Review* 95 (October 1990); Stout, *The Development of High School Curricula in the North Central States from 1860 to 1918,* 51.

9. Ibid. On the consensual belief that a single course of study fit the needs of all students, see the comments of Chicago Public Schools assistant superintendent A. F. Nightingale, NCA *Proceedings*, 1898, 147.

10. Veysey, *Emergence of the American University,* 439.

11. Ibid.

12. Angell, "Presidential Address," 10.

13. Veysey, *Rise of the American University,* 9–10; Frederick Rudolph, *The American College and the American University* (New York: Alfred A. Knopf, 1962), 491.

14. Veysey, *Rise of the American University,* 9–10.

15. Alexandra Oleson and John Voss, *The Organization of Knowledge in Modern America, 1860–1920* (Baltimore: Johns Hopkins University Press, 1979), viii.

16. Veysey, *Rise of the American University*, 10.

17. Roger L. Williams, *The Origins of Federal Support for Higher Education: George W. Atherton and the Land-Grant College Movement* (University Park: Pennsylvania State University Press, 1991), 35; John S. Brubacher and Willis Rudy, *Higher Education in Transition*, rev. ed. (New York: Harper & Row, 1968), 154.

18. Williams, *Origin of Federal Support for Higher Education*, 62.

19. Brubacher and Rudy, *Higher Education in Transition*, 106–7. See also Peckham, *The Making of the University of Michigan, 1817–1967*.

20. Brubacher and Rudy, *Higher Education in Transition*, 109–10.

21. Williams, *Origins of Federal Support for Higher Education*, 1.

22. Commissioner of Education, *Report of the Commissioner of Education for the Year 1872–1873* (Washington, D.C.: GPO, 1873), 99.

23. Oleson and Voss suggest that Eliot's influence was so dominant that they characterize the university at the end of the 1880s as "Eliot's elective principle writ large." Oleson and Voss, *Organization of Knowledge in Modern America, 1860–1920*, x; Rudolph, *American College and the American University*, 303.

24. Rudolph, *American College and the American University*, 305; John Higham, "The Matrix of Specialization," in Oleson and Voss, *Organization of Knowledge in Modern America, 1860–1920*, 5; Brubacher and Rudy, *Higher Education in Transition*, 115.

25. Rudolph, *American College and the American University*, 169–72; Brubacher and Rudy, *Higher Education in Transition*, 25–28, 364–65.

26. Higham, "The Matrix of Specialization," 12; Letter, George MacLean to Andrew Draper, in Andrew Draper papers, box 9, University of Illinois (Urbana) archives.

27. Rudolph, *American College and the American University*, 305; Brubacher and Rudy, *Higher Education in Transition*, 143.

28. Oleson and Voss, *Organization of Knowledge in Modern America, 1860–1920*, xi; Rudolph, *American College and the American University*, 305.

29. Hays, "Introduction—The New Organizational Society," 1–2. Also see Louis Galambos, "The Emerging Organizational Synthesis in Modern American History," *Business History Review* 64 (Autumn 1970); Terreberry, "The Evolution of Organizational Environments," *Administrative Science Quarterly* 12 (March 1968): 601.

30. James B. Angell, *Reminiscences* (Freeport, N.Y.: Books for Libraries Press, 1971, originally published 1911), 237; Howard H. Peckham, *The Making of the University of Michigan, 1817–1967* (Ann Arbor: University of Michigan Press, 1967), 65–66; Allen S. Whitney, "Methods in Use of Accrediting Schools," *School Review* 11 (February 1903): 139, 147. By 1903, 250 schools participated in the program.

31. Adams, "Presidential Address," 117.

32. NCA *Proceedings*, 1896, 21–22; NCA *Proceedings*, 1898, 78.

Chapter Two

The Rise of the NCA

The time was ripe for the undertaking. It is for us to prove ourselves worthy of the opportunity which has been furnished us.

—James B. Angell, 1896

AT ITS FIRST MEETING in 1896, James B. Angell's presidential address probed into the origins of the North Central Association of Colleges and Secondary Schools. He hoped that future historians would highlight the role played by the members of the Michigan Schoolmasters' Club in the founding of the NCA. Secondary school educators not only initiated the movement for a regional organization, but they used their Michigan Club to found and partially build the new one. In commenting upon the influence of the Club on the fledgling NCA, Angell declared, "The life of this society was therefore rooted in a real experience."[1]

The real experience that led to the founding of the NCA had several dimensions. The culmination was the action taken by Michigan Schoolmasters' Club members. From a larger perspective, however, the creation of both organizations was part of a national impulse in education that began in the mid-1880s and continued for several decades. A growing recognition that reforming education required cooperative action not only stimulated the founding of new associations, but also changed the nature of some existing organizations. The NCA aimed to improve relations between secondary schools and colleges to address the curriculum chaos caused by diverging school missions and the elective system. In turn, the spread of educational associations was connected to a larger organizational reform effort that was part of the Progressive Era of the late nineteenth and early twentieth centuries.

In education and in society generally, the organizational tendencies had two major characteristics. First, there was a tremendous growth in the number of groups. Second, the nature of

15

James B. Angell. President of the University
of Michigan, Angell was the first president
of the North Central Association.

voluntary associations was transformed as older, personal, informal, and deliberative bodies gave way to modern bureaucratic,
functional, and active modes of organization. The changes allowed
for a more effective and efficient pursuit of reform agenda. The
North Central Association underwent modernization five years
after its founding, changing from a personal, informal debating
society to a functional accrediting organization.

During its first five years, the NCA developed its organizational foundations. It started creating what organizational development theorist John Kimberly has called "the rich fabric of norms,
values, and myths that help to shape and determine behavior in
the organization."[2] Both external and internal factors influenced
the developmental process.

THE CHANGING NATURE OF VOLUNTARY ASSOCIATIONS

Voluntary associations have been an integral part of American life
since colonial times. Many foreign observers have commented on
the associational character of American society. In the 1830s, the

French traveler Alexis de Tocqueville noted the popularity and influence of such organizations. After visiting the United States in the 1880s, English Lord James Bryce made a similar observation, as did German sociologist Max Weber, who in 1905 called the United States "the association-land par excellence."[3] The ubiquity of associations in the United States is due to a number of factors. Influenced by the American governmental tradition, voluntary associations are organized by a constitution and often employ democratic procedures. Traditionally, they have been defined by two criteria. Membership is a matter of choice and they are organized independently of the state. Though they perform a wide variety of functions, their nongovernmental status has led them to undertake tasks that are either beyond the purview of the government or that the American people prefer the government not undertake. In some cases, the assumption of tasks not considered the purview of the government prompted the founding of the association.[4]

Between approximately 1885 and 1910, the time was unusually ripe for the founding of associations because the educational revolution created a need for cooperative action that educators did not consider appropriate for the government. Some problems, such as school-college relations, required cooperative action to solve. In the case of college admissions, the solutions proposed by colleges and universities made matters worse. Because of the number and complexity of the issues confronting reformers, ideas and programs emerged from varying educational sources. Institutions, municipal governments, individuals, and associations tried to address the vexing problems.

Many new educational organizations followed traditional deliberation formats, but most quickly changed to a modern, activist approach more in tune with the emerging scientific-technological worldview. Initially, personal and informal relationships characterized these new groups as educators from a defined geographic area joined together to meet and discuss issues of common concern. Until about the 1880s, the local nature of schooling and the relative isolation of educators made communication a major function of associations. At times, these organizations passed resolutions on the issues of the day or even engaged in lobbying for specific actions. In the immediate post–Civil War years, educational associations waged a strong, successful lobbying campaign in Congress for a federal education agency.[5] But, generally, these associations were debating clubs.

By the 1880s, the increasingly chaotic conditions resulting from the industrialization and modernization of American society, combined with a growing inability to control the environment, created the need for a different type of organization. Two major organizational trends emerged in education. A major innovation was the creation of "republican" institutional associations. In this sense, "republican" indicated that while institutions were members, individuals in their employ represented their interests in various association activities. The rise of these institutional associations had profound implications. Historian Hugh Hawkins observed, "Educators chose to sacrifice a measure of institutional autonomy to gain the benefits of cooperation." Joining an association implied making such a sacrifice and reflected the ambivalent feelings of many educators toward reform. "Labeling change as progress did not keep it from being unsettling," Hawkins explained. "Among academic administrators, self-confidence often alternated with anxiety. Both emotions contributed to the creation of institutional associations."[6] He suggested that often the goal of the organization was to order the pursuit of progress by removing the unsettling aspects of change. Thus, individuals recognized the benefits of collective actions and combined in organizations to better control reform.

Related to the quest for control and order, the second trend was the narrowing of association interests to well-defined areas. The move from individual to group action did not expand reform efforts. Associations proliferated and duplication of memberships often occurred because many organizations had narrowly defined goals. These goals, in turn, influenced who joined and the activities undertaken. As a result, many educational associations became functionally oriented by specifically defining their membership and the focus of their activities. Such organizations restricted membership to certain specialized occupational, professional, and interest categories on a regional or national basis. By joining individuals with similar professions and interests, functional associations fostered relationships among equals in a common effort. The rise of disciplinary associations, such as the American Historical

Association, exemplified one organizational trend that focused on members of an academic discipline. Institutional associations provided a different orientation. They were grouped either by type and/or the pursuit of a very specific goal. For example, the land grant institutions formed their own organization primarily to secure greater funding from the federal government. State universities founded their own association, as did private colleges.[7] Another type of organization mixed specialists from different levels to pursue a common goal, such as the National Conference on Uniform Requirements in English.[8]

The associational movement in education followed various paths, reflecting the diversity of conditions it confronted. The early North Central Association does not fit comfortably into any of the above categories. In many respects, it bridged the gap between traditional and modern associations. The circumstances behind its founding and the organizations that influenced its initial form determined this transitional status.

THE BIRTH OF THE NORTH CENTRAL ASSOCIATION

Three organizations that exhibited old and new tendencies influenced the development of the North Central Association. As noted by James B. Angell, the Michigan Schoolmasters' Club was, in many ways, the force behind the founding of the NCA. Established in 1886, the Club's aim was to "to secure an opportunity to discuss matters that pertain to our common work, with particular reference to high school and collegiate training." Its constitution explained that the Club did not want "to antagonize any existing associations, but simply to obtain a large opportunity to discuss such topics as are necessarily and properly left untouched by associations that now exist." Membership was open to college and secondary educators in Michigan as well as anyone elected by a two-thirds vote of the members present at a regular meeting. Initially, the Club met for one day, three times a year. The sessions featured the presentation of papers and symposia. In 1892, the cost and time lost in traveling prompted a change to two meetings annually. Two years later, the meetings were extended to two days. Apparently, the Club filled an existing void as hundreds of educators from Michigan and other states attended its meetings.[9] In addition to providing a venue for educators to discuss the need for a regional organization, it also provided a model for the early NCA and supplied many of its founding members.

A different organization inspired the regional focus of the NCA, its overlapping secondary and collegiate membership, and the initial goal of improving school-college relations. Seeking greater uniformity in college entrance requirements, secondary school educators provided the impetus for the New England Association of Colleges and Secondary Schools founded in 1885. Membership consisted of "[p]residents and other authorized representatives of New England Colleges and the heads and other authorized representatives of New England schools that prepare for college."[10] The New England Association admitted only individual members, not institutions, and maintained this policy until 1927. It remained a traditional, informal, and personal debating society, but the Association also worked with various commissions in a more modern, "functional" manner to achieve greater uniformity in college entrance examinations. In this way, the New England Association combined a traditional structure with a modern approach. In assessing its influence, Edward Krug claimed, "As the first such group to be formed in the United States, the New England Association not only anticipated the organization of similar enterprises in other parts of the country, but also set the stage for a new era of study and discussion."[11]

The National Education Association also influenced the development of the North Central Association. What eventually became the National Education Association (NEA) emerged out of the National Teachers' Association (NTA) founded in 1857. At the 1870 meeting of the NTA in Philadelphia, a merger of several organizations created the National Education Association.[12] Joining the teachers under the NEA umbrella were the American Normal School Association, the National Association of School Superintendents, and the Central College Association. To cover all levels of schooling, a new elementary education department was established. Though divided into modern departments by profession and level, the NEA maintained a traditional deliberative format. In its early years, membership was extremely small for a national organization, averaging between two hundred and three hundred members until the mid-1880s.[13]

In the late 1880s, the NEA adopted a more aggressive, activist stance, experiencing substantial membership increases. At the 1887 NEA meeting, Principal Edward W. Coy of Hughes High School in Cincinnati observed that few high school students planned to go to college. He called for a curriculum adjustment to meet the seemingly different purposes of the high school, noting such a change required closer relations between high schools and colleges. In response, Principal James H. Baker of Denver High School introduced a resolution that led to the appointment of a committee to study the uniformity of the high school courses of study and college admission requirements. The first report proved "inconclusive and disappointing," but included a resolution that led to the 1892 appointment of the Committee of Ten on Secondary Schools. Harvard University president Charles Eliot chaired the committee.[14]

Published in 1893, the Committee of Ten report is the most famous document in curriculum history and exemplified a contemporary trend in designing model curricula. It outlined courses of study for the elementary and secondary grades. Besides suggesting what subjects be taught, the committee recommended the amount of time to spend on each subject and defined where it fit into the student's education. Claiming few schools implemented its recommendations, some scholars suggest the immediate impact of the report was relatively minor. However, the Committee of Ten report showed how associations helped schools manage change.[15] Gaining national recognition, it sounded a clarion call to educators for reform. Cited many times in various discussions on curricular topics, it motivated other reform efforts. In addition, the report provided guidelines to use in changing the curriculum. Reformers examined its specifics and then developed their own plans to meet local conditions. The letter inviting educators to the organizational meeting of the NCA specifically mentioned the Committee of Ten report.

The changing nature of the NEA also facilitated the creation of the North Central Association. The meetings of the NEA brought educators from all levels of schooling and all parts of the country together to discuss issues of common concern. The committees appointed to address these issues created a coterie of reformers whose activities eventually influenced a wide variety of other

organizations. Many educators active in the NEA became important figures in the North Central Association. The two men who
instigated the movement that led to the Committee of Ten, Coy
and Baker, became prominent figures in the North Central Association. Five of the ten on the NEA committee were influential NCA
members. A. F. Nightingale, a founding NCA member, chaired the
NEA Committee on College Entrance Requirements and was a
member of the NEA Secondary Department. Nightingale, Coy, and
Baker all served as presidents of the North Central Association. In
addition, NEA presidents James H. Canfield (1890) and Newton C.
Dougherty (1896) played important roles in the North Central
Association. Canfield was the third NCA president.[16]

Three different organizations, then, contributed to the birth
of the North Central Association. The Committee of Ten acted as a
motivating force, while the NEA provided a common ground for
the building of an informal reform circle that sought more formal
organization through the NCA. The Michigan Schoolmasters' Club
performed a similar function since its meetings brought together a
large number of reform-minded educators. The New England Association also supplied inspiration and provided models for development.

William Henry Butts combined all these strands together into
a single plan. Unfortunately, biographical information on Butts is
sketchy. He was born in Harmony, New York, on February 16,
1857.[17] He attended the University of Michigan, receiving a bachelor's degree in 1878 and a master's degree a year later. For his
advanced graduate training, Butts followed a familiar path for
American educators, studying in Europe at the Sorbonne in Paris,
the University of Zurich, and the University of Heidelberg, where
he earned a Ph.D. in mathematics. In 1886, he was principal of the
Michigan Military Academy, a private, college-preparatory secondary school in Orchard Lake, a small town outside of Pontiac and
about twenty-five miles north of Ann Arbor.[18] Given the emphasis
on public schooling in Michigan and the Midwest generally, it is
ironic that the head of a private academy thought of the idea for
bringing secondary and higher education figures together in a
regional organization.

As principal, Butts had to accommodate differing requirements of the various colleges and universities in the academy's

curriculum. In pursuit of the all-important certificate, he probably hosted the visits of several inspectors from different institutions. Thus, Butts experienced firsthand the chaos that college admissions policies created for secondary schools. The difficulties of preparing students for college possibly motivated him to pursue the idea of a regional organization though his goal extended beyond the north central states. He explained his plan in an aptly titled article, "National Uniformity in Secondary Instruction," published in the February 1895 issue of *The School Review*.[19] Stating his arguments in political terms, Butts declared, "The colonial days in educational development are fast passing away. The report of the Committee of Ten may be well called the first constitution of Educational America. What we need now is ratification and wise legislation." Referring to the results of a national survey conducted by the Michigan Schoolmasters' Club, he explained that the necessary legislation already existed: "It is evident that the plan which will most easily and quickly unite the East and West in a uniform system of admission to college will be based on Table IV of the Committee of Ten Report."

Butts wanted a uniform system of secondary education based upon equally consistent college entrance requirements. Most likely, the publication of the Committee of Ten report spurred him to act because it supplied viable guidelines that carried enough status to gain widespread acceptance. He strengthened his case by praising the well-coordinated and tightly structured Michigan school system. He claimed, "State control and state supervision, modeled on the Michigan plan, have created educational systems in a large part of the United States, more complete in many ways and more closely articulated than those of Germany or England." Given the great esteem accorded the German educational system, this was high praise indeed. But he tempered his enthusiasm and showed his willingness to compromise by suggesting, "The victories won and the lessons learned in developing these state systems only prepare the way for national unity and uniformity.... This is no time for states' rights and sectional interests to stand in the way of national development."

For Butts, the cornerstone of national development was cooperative action in educational associations. However, his idea was not for united action in a functional, active manner as had occurred with the Committee of Ten. Instead, he favored a traditional, deliberative format that maintained institutional autonomy. In outlining his path toward national uniformity, Butts explained:

> If the colleges and schools, after free discussion in inter-state associations, agree on elementary requirements, which all schools can meet while they are at the same time giving to a majority of their pupils final preparation for their life work—if they also name advanced requirements from which students preparing for college may have a choice according to the degree for which they are studying, basing this choice upon the utility of the subjects for future work, then the secondary schools can retain their individuality and teach those advanced studies for which they have the best facilities.

Butts' plan recognized the differing needs of secondary students and developed a core of uniform requirements that simultaneously met the needs of the fit-for-life and college preparatory missions. Other subjects relevant only to college-bound students supplemented this core. In addition, the core curriculum combined aspects of the older prescriptive course of study and the elective system. The required classes provided a basic education for all students, while the elective course supplements met individual student needs. Individual schools retained their autonomy because they would determine the advanced studies offered.

Equally important, Butts considered Table IV of the Committee of Ten report as a working guideline, rather than a dictate. "As soon as experience teaches that any study in Table IV is less valuable than some omitted subject, or that the arrangement of studies and the allotment of time are not productive of the best results," he explained, "changes can be agreed upon." He also posited the use of the certificate system of college admission in a very prescient way, noting, "With some certificate system of admission in states or *in larger sections*, uniformity can be hastened."[20] Even before the founding of the North Central Association, Butts presented the idea of regional certification.

Following reform trends in education, his plan called for the organization of interstate associations. Because of the sectional differences in both education and association development, Butts stressed regional organizations, noting the success of the New England Association. For a variety of reasons, he considered the north central region as most important to education and his plan. "With the largest percentage of school attendance of any sections in the United States, and with the closest articulation and most sympathetic relations between secondary schools and universities," he explained, "the North Central States are in a peculiarly favorable position to lead in establishing national unity and uniformity in educational matters." Before pursuing any national action, the East, West, and South had to agree on a common core of studies. Concluding in a rather patriotic way, he stated that "by the common experience and progress of all, an American ideal in secondary and higher education can be worked out with American methods on American soil."[21]

The first step was gaining support for his plan. He visited New England and interviewed several headmasters of academies and Charles Eliot of Harvard. All responded enthusiastically to his idea to form a regional association in the north central area. Upon returning to Michigan, he met with University of Michigan president James B. Angell, who at first rejected the idea, suggesting too many organizations already existed. However, Butts persisted until Angell concurred. The University of Michigan president also advised Butts to test out the idea with the presidents of the Universities of Chicago, Wisconsin, Indiana, Missouri, and Northwestern. They all supported his plan. Harper of Chicago purportedly interrupted Butts during their talk, jumped out of his chair, and cried, "Splendid, splendid, just what we need. We will soon outrank the New England Association."[22] Competition among educators worked to Butts' advantage.

Butts presented his idea to the Michigan Schoolmasters' Club at its fall meeting in Ypsilanti. Since many members already backed the idea for a standardizing organization, the movement towards founding the new association proceeded rapidly.[23] On December 1, 1894, Butts, who served as president of the Club the following year, sponsored a resolution calling for a conference of secondary school and college educators on college entrance requirements following the Club's Classical Conference, scheduled to meet in Ann Arbor in March 1895. He requested the appointment of a committee to call the entrance requirements meeting, suggesting it consist of three

Michigan secondary educators to represent the high schools, normal schools, and academies, and the presidents of Michigan, Northwestern, and Chicago universities. In his history of the Michigan Schoolmasters' Club, Leslie Butler reported: "The motion called for a very warm discussion on the part of friends of the Club, who thought this was not its province and that the Club was in danger of being swallowed up by side conferences." After being amended to instruct the committee to schedule the conference so it did not interfere with Club meetings, the resolution passed. The invitational committee consisted of Angell, Harper, Henry Wade Rogers of Northwestern, Butts, principal William A. Greeson of

Henry Wade Rogers. President of Northwestern University, Rogers signed original invitation to first organizational meeting, and he hosted organizational meeting of the Association, March 29–30, 1895.

Grand Rapids High School, and president R. G. Boone of Michigan Normal School. University of Wisconsin president Charles K. Adams later joined the committee.[24]

In December, the committee organized the meeting and wrote the invitation. Rogers agreed to host the conference scheduled for March 29–30, 1895, dates that overlapped with the Schoolmasters' Club meeting. "Prominent representatives of secondary and higher education in the ten states of Ohio, Michigan, Indiana, Illinois, Wisconsin, Minnesota, Iowa, Missouri, Nebraska, and Kansas," were invited to meet at 10:00 A.M. on March 29 in Rogers' office on the Northwestern University campus. The invitation also provided travel and lodging information, noting, "Trains for Evanston leave Chicago from the Union Station by the Chicago, Milwaukee, and St. Paul Railroad, and from the Wells Street Station by the Northwestern Railroad, about every half hour." The Avenue House in Evanston provided lodging for two dollars a day.[25]

Henry Wade Rogers arranged the meeting. An interesting sidelight is his correspondence with Andrew Draper, president of the University of Illinois. On March 15, 1895, Rogers wrote Draper. Certain the Illinois president had received the meeting notice, Rogers inquired, "I do not, however, see your name in the list [of attendees sent by Angell]. Are you not to be here?" Assuming the answer would be yes, Rogers asked Draper to attend a March 30 banquet honoring Angell given by the Chicago Alumni Association of the University of Michigan. Rogers added, "They would be pleased to have you respond to a toast and they wished me to write you to do so." Obviously, the gathering of educators provided an opportunity for a variety of activities beyond the founding of a new organization. A second letter from Rogers dated March 27 acknowledged Draper's affirmative response to the invitation for the conference.[26]

The invitation explained the purpose of the conference and included a list of six questions for discussion that covered the feasibility of the association, its organizational development, and its activities. The wording did not commit the educators to any action before the meeting. In fact, the first question was whether "[i]t is desirable and practicable to form an association." The next two questions concerned membership. The invitation specifically named "universities, colleges, scientific schools, normal schools, high schools, and academies," but omitted others such as business and commercial schools. Questions five and six addressed the nature of the proposed organization, following the ideas Butts had

Avenue House hotel. This is where attendees of the 1895 meeting stayed.

Andrew S. Draper. President of the University of Illinois and founding member of the Association, Draper was NCA president in 1904.

presented in his article. The fifth question asked: "Shall the association take steps looking to co-operation with the New England and Middle States Associations in securing greater uniformity in secondary instruction and in the requirements for admission to college?" Regional cooperation represented the first step to attaining the national uniformity Butts desired. To facilitate discussion, the last question suggested that, time permitting, the meeting address "some special subject, such as, (1) The requirements for admission to college in some branch, as, for example, science or English or mathematics; or (2) The best method for examination for admission to colleges; or (3) The modification, if any, to be recommended in the scheme of courses in secondary schools, set forth in Table IV of the Report of the Committee of Ten."[27]

Beyond listing the six questions, the invitation offered no agenda for the conference. There was no list of goals, no ideas as to any activities, or any ideas on the proposed structure of the association. The geographical boundaries of the north central region was also left open.

29

On March 29, 1895, at approximately 10:30 A.M., thirty-six educators convened on the Northwestern University campus in Evanston. The status of those attending attracted the local press, who provided good coverage of the conference. The *Chicago Tribune* called it "probably the most distinguished gathering of educators ever held in the West."[28] Seven states were represented: Ohio, Michigan, Indiana, Illinois, Wisconsin, Iowa, and Missouri. The presidents of each of the state universities and several other prominent colleges and universities attended. If normal schools, teacher-training institutions, are considered secondary, and they were at that time, school representatives came from Ohio, Michigan, Indiana, Illinois, Wisconsin, and Iowa. There were eleven high school representatives: three from Michigan, one from Indiana, and seven from Illinois. Four represented public high schools. One superintendent of high schools and two superintendents of schools attended. However, this high-level administrative gathering included no women and only one faculty member, Clarence A. Waldo, then of DePauw University.[29]

The delegates chose Andrew Draper as chair and Butts as secretary. Regarding the question of forming an organization, Principal Henry L. Boltwood of Evanston Township High School observed that the presence of those attending provided the answer. After formally voting to create the Association, the delegates discussed such matters as territorial boundaries and membership qualifications. According to John Grinnell, whose interpretation of events is uneven, problems arose because the delegates could not agree on a definition of a college and high school. There was also the issue of whether "only heads of colleges and such high schools and academies as prepared for college should be admitted." The *Proceedings* offer no insight into the discussion, just noting that the meeting was informal.

At the close of the morning session, Butts moved that a committee be appointed to draft a constitution, an essential step in forming a voluntary association. After naming the committee, the delegates attended a chapel service and a luncheon followed by "a drive about the beautiful city of Evanston." The nine-member committee that drafted the first North Central Association constitution was an all-star cast. William Rainey Harper was chair and Principal Edward L. Harris of Central High School in Cleveland served as secretary. Other members included President Richard J. Jesse of the University of Missouri; G. S. Burroughs, president of Wabash College; Charles F. Thwing, president of Western Reserve University; Oshkosh State Normal School president George S. Albee; Charles A. Schaeffer, president of the State University of Iowa; Augustus F. Nightingale, assistant superintendent of Chicago Schools; and Butts.[30]

Despite the difficulties in reaching agreements in the morning discussion, a draft constitution was prepared, discussed, and amended, and unanimously adopted in the afternoon. The name, North Central Association of Colleges and Secondary Schools, underscored the goal of the organization stated in Article 2: "The object of this Association shall be to establish closer relations between the colleges and secondary schools of the North Central States." The membership qualifications followed modern trends, stressing institutions though individuals could become members upon nomination of the Executive Committee and election by the Association. Because there were many more high schools than colleges, individual memberships helped meet the goal of equal representation of secondary and higher education that was a basic principle of the early organization.

The first resolution of the Association covered membership. President James W. Bashford of Ohio Wesleyan University moved that the number of members be limited to one hundred fifty. The 150-member limit reflected the disparity in numbers between high schools and colleges and the practical concern regarding the ability to achieve any results through deliberation at meetings.[31] A related problem skirted by the constitution was the territory of the Association. "North Central" was a rather unclear term left undefined by the committee and others at the meeting.

The function of the NCA also was an issue that divided the delegates. In keeping with the individuality of institutions and beliefs of autonomy, Article 4 on powers expressly stated: "All decisions of the Association bearing upon the policy and the management of higher and secondary institutions are understood to be advisory in their character." All agreed on this point but expressed differing answers to the question, "Shall this Association simply be another association that meets to listen to papers and discuss them, or shall we assume the responsibility of doing certain things besides talking?" Butts and some of his fellow Michigan School-masters' Club members likely desired an active organization, but Andrew Draper led the opposition. According to John Grinnell, the University of Illinois president "insisted that their duties were necessarily and primarily advisory," and that they should be very careful about assuming responsibilities.[32] Throughout his participation in the NCA, Draper strongly and often successfully opposed any incursion on institutional independence and autonomy. Pragmatic concerns possibly motivated Draper's caution. As the former head of the Cleveland school system and current president of a public university, he knew that public secondary schools already had governing bodies and boards of education, and were directly responsible to their local and possibly state governments. Colleges and universities had boards of trustees. Still, the ability to influence by resolution and example was potentially an effective method of achieving change.

The structure of the Association was well-defined, yet simple. There were a president, two vice presidents from each state, a secretary, and a treasurer. An executive committee comprised of the president, secretary, treasurer, and four other elected members ran the organization. It made all nominations for membership, arranged the logistics of the meetings, appointed "[c]ommittees for conference with other bodies, whenever in their judgment it may seem expedient," and acted "for the Association when it was not in session." The officers were elected for one year. The constitution called for one annual meeting and "such special meetings as the Association may appoint." One-fourth of the membership constituted a quorum. Each member had one vote and paid a $3 annual fee to meet expenses. Lastly, amending the constitution required a 3/4 vote at any regular meeting if each member received a printed notice of the proposed amendment two weeks before the meeting.[33] This provision ensured that changes in the Association were not undertaken in the highly charged atmosphere of a meeting.

The constitution did not address the content of the meetings or their procedures. The majority of delegates favored the debating format of the National Education Association and the Michigan Schoolmasters' Club. In addition, early disagreement on important issues made them aware of the potential for future problems. To facilitate agreement on the first topics to be discussed, a resolution was passed near the end of the meeting asking "that the Executive Committee be asked to submit for discussion at the next meeting the questions 'What Constitutes a Secondary School?' and 'What Constitutes a College?'"[34]

The resolution seeking discussion on definitions possibly reflected a reluctance among the delegates to proceed too quickly. The Association brought together a number of people who were strangers or who had only a slight acquaintance. Discussion would promote the exchange of ideas and opinions while helping members get acquainted and build relationships. The social aspect of the Association was especially important. At the first annual meeting, William Rainey Harper commented, "One of the most essential features after all...in an organization of this kind is the social side; the grasp of each other's hands, and the opportunity to look into each other's faces."[35] And, in what later became a standard though unwritten policy, NCA members acted very cautiously and conservatively when moving into previously unexplored fields.

University of Michigan president James B. Angell was elected president unanimously. Principal Frederick L. Bliss of Detroit High School became secretary and the treasurer was George N. Carman, dean of Morgan Park Academy in Chicago. The executive committee consisted of President Charles Kendall Adams of the University of Wisconsin, Assistant Superintendent of Chicago Schools A. F. Nightingale, Professor Clarence A. Waldo of DePauw University, and Edward L. Harris, principal of Central High School in Cleveland. By equally dividing the offices between secondary and higher education, the NCA founders recognized that improving relations between the secondary and collegiate levels required giving all members equal status and power. For secondary school representatives accustomed to college dominance, the policy of parity helped improve relations. For college representatives, it meant surrendering some of their status, but, given the advisory nature of the organization, the giving was more symbolic than real. The implementing of this policy at the very beginning of the Association certainly enhanced its appeal.

Draper suggested the first meeting be held around April 1, 1896, with the exact date to be determined by the Executive Committee. Charles Schaeffer of the State University of Iowa moved that Chicago be the site. Harper offered to host the meeting.

George N. Carman. Director, Lewis Institute, Ill., Carman was NCA treasurer, 1895–1901, and president in 1903.

The *Proceedings* of the meeting provide no record of a second day of the conference, possibly indicating that the North Central Association was founded on March 29, 1895.[36] Several factors probably accelerated the process. Those attending the meeting had extensive association experience and some participants had cooperated with other delegates on other committees. The correspondence of Andrew Draper shows that the higher education figures maintained close contact on a variety of professional and personal issues.[37]

In addition, several NCA founders had close personal or professional relationships. Obviously, the Michigan delegation built upon the ties made through the Michigan Schoolmasters' Club. Out-of-state educators such as George Carman and A. F. Nightingale had attended the Club meetings. The NEA also had brought many delegates together. Richard Jesse of the University of Missouri frequently appeared on NEA programs. Charles Thwing of

Western Reserve University, Henry Wade Rogers, and Andrew Draper were active NEA members. At the secondary level, Newton Dougherty of Peoria, Edward Harris, and Frederick Bliss served as officers of the Department of Secondary Education.[38] Nightingale was on the Board of Trustees of the University of Illinois and so had a working relationship with Draper.

Ironically, Butts played a diminishing role in the Association he fathered. His only official service was as vice president for Michigan from 1896 to 1898. He offered a paper at the 1897 annual meeting, but it largely rehashed his 1896 presentation at the New England Association on a high school program without Greek. Upon joining the mathematics department of the University of Michigan in 1898, his active participation in the NCA ended.[39] The disappearance of Butts from the NCA remains an enigma.

BUILDING THE ORGANIZATIONAL FOUNDATION

In 1915, James E. Armstrong, principal of Englewood High School in Chicago, and a member of the Association since 1896, celebrated the Association's twentieth birthday in his presidential address. He divided the history of the NCA into five-year periods. Referring to the early development of the organization, he suggested, "The first five years of the life of the Association seem to have been devoted chiefly to the discussion of resolutions which relate to foundation principles." This implied "clearing the atmosphere of the smoke of old battles," to reach tentative agreements on such outstanding issues as defining educational institutions, the elective system, and college entrance requirements.[40] During these founding years, the Association also raised questions regarding relations with other organizations and the role of the state in chartering degree-granting institutions. In his history of the NCA, John Grinnell came to a similar conclusion, observing that the early years were a feeling-out period that led to "the development of better relations between colleges and schools."[41]

In its first five years, the Association established itself on a solid footing. In many respects, the NCA's early development was influenced by "the interaction between situational factors and personal characteristics of founders." Situational factors included environmental and internal organizational aspects. The chaotic conditions in education and the tensions between the debating society and functional facets of its organizational models, combined with the diversity of its members, largely determined the building of the Association's foundations. From one perspective, the process of developing the organization centered around the "tension between innovation and institutionalization."[42] For the NCA, innovation involved moving from deliberation to action. The ability to act depended on several things, including having a method to implement change and also the ability to influence institutions to voluntarily adhere to any NCA actions. Both required a solid, respected organization whose existence was not in doubt. As a result, during the formative years of the NCA, the tensions between innovation and institutionalization favored the latter.

The early development of the NCA was steady and was facilitated by its growing appeal to educators in the region. The press coverage given the Evanston conference provided good publicity, as did the Michigan Schoolmasters' Club. By the opening of the first meeting on April 1, 1896, membership had grown to eighty-two institutions and thirty-one individuals from ten states. The additions included institutions from Minnesota, Nebraska, and Kansas. Schools from these states had been invited to the Evanston meeting but had sent no representatives. An interesting new institutional member was Hughes High School in Cincinnati. Its principal and NCA representative was Edward W. Coy, whose address at the National Educational Association had initiated the curriculum reform movement that culminated in the Committee of Ten report. Coy was NCA vice president for Ohio in 1896–1897 and later served as NCA president. Another prominent new, though short-term, individual member was John Dewey, professor at the University of Chicago.[43]

Coy, Dewey, and approximately one hundred of the region's top educational leaders gathered at the University of Chicago at 2:00 P.M. on Friday, April 3, 1896, for the first meeting of the North Central Association. James B. Angell delivered the Presidential Address and stressed the promise of deliberation, exclaiming, "Fired with enthusiasm, let us, representatives of ten great states, do our utmost by the deliberations and discussions of this association, to make our secondary and higher education of the highest service to these commonwealths and to the whole nation."[44]

In fact, the discussions served several important purposes for the NCA. They provided a focus for Association work by identifying major educational issues. The three topics for the first meeting followed those suggested in the invitation to Evanston. They included what courses in history should be required for entrance to college, how to define a high school and college, and college admission policies using the University of Michigan and the University Chicago programs as case studies. The topics discussed in the Association's first five years showed the diverse interest of members. They included using inexperienced teachers in first-year college classes, providing for individual differences among students, foreign language study, developing skills over content, the elective system, uniform college admission requirements, the curriculum in secondary schools and colleges, vocational education, and the duties of boards of education and superintendents of schools, among others.[45]

The Executive Committee chose the discussion topics in advance and recruited speakers to deliver papers and make prepared responses. Free discussion among the delegates followed. Between 1897 and 1900, the format changed to the debate of various resolutions prepared by the Executive Committee, but still followed the same sequence. The committee generally selected controversial topics because they fostered more spirited debate, or they addressed serious concerns. At the 1897 meeting, Charles Kendall Adams explained the reasoning behind a resolution calling the practice of having inexperienced teachers instruct first-year classes in colleges and universities a growing evil. He said, "When it came up in the executive committee there was a general consensus of opinion that it would be well to have the question discussed because complaints come from time to time from pupils that the grade of instruction the first year or two in the university is not equal in point of professional merit to that which they received before coming to the university." Observing that the committee agreed this feeling existed, Adams concluded that "it was thought best to present the subject here for discussion."[46]

The sessions also allowed for full expression of opinion that helped identify future topics. At the first meeting, the discussion on defining educational institutions touched upon a number of related issues to be pursued in the future. University of Missouri president Richard Jesse opened the two-hour session by delivering a paper entitled "What Constitutes a College and What a Secondary School?" Jesse observed that the great diversity of secondary and collegiate institutions made his task difficult. He attributed these conditions to the laissez-faire process of establishing educational institutions. "If we go by names and accept labels it does not take much to constitute either a secondary school or a college," he explained. The inability or unwillingness of the states to assume a greater responsibility in chartering institutions granting degrees exacerbated the situation by facilitating the founding of bogus institutions.[47] Over the next few decades, the NCA sought unsuccessfully to address this issue

The confusion over the character of higher education made defining institutions difficult. "Most of our universities, my own among the number," Jesse explained, "are doing much of their work in the college field." The resulting duplication also existed between high school and college, since "the first two years in college are really secondary in character." The previous discussion of history requirements also had noted this curriculum overlap. It remained a primary issue for the Association in the coming years.

Jesse's definitions showed that defining a high school and a college involved more than just identifying institutional characteristics. A secondary school had three basic criteria. It had "well arranged courses, the last four years of which are devoted to Latin, Greek, French, German, English, history, algebra, geometry, and science." The schools could add "music, drawing, manual training, bookkeeping, gymnastics, etc.," but the nine subjects Jesse listed provided the minimum "to establish the valid claim to the title of secondary school." He also favored a flexible, elective curriculum. The second requirement was "a sufficient number of well-trained teachers." The third point concerned facilities. The school needed "sufficient equipment, consisting of a library, suitable rooms, and a laboratory or laboratories." Jesse recommended greater use of the laboratory and library. Regarding the latter, he said, "A library in the charge of a librarian should be recognized as an essential part of every secondary school.... The library is the laboratory ... for work in language, literature, and history."[48]

Though citing general criteria, Jesse offered few concrete requirements, often suggesting that alternatives existed. He preferred a four-year course of study but considered three- and six-year courses viable options, reflecting the diverging opinions and practices of the schools themselves. His curriculum criteria largely neglected the fit-for-life mission. The nine subjects explicitly identified were college preparatory. His bias toward college-bound students was also shown by his observation that a school still fit his definition even if it did not have any nonacademic subjects, but included the nine he named. Though calling for greater training of teachers in college and universities, he did not require high school teachers to have a college degree.[49]

Jesse also provided a detailed definition of a college. Generally, a college was "an institution for academic instruction based upon the secondary schools," that had "respectable requirements for entrance to the Freshman class." He favored the Stanford system with some alterations so that it resembled the program of the University of Chicago. Personally, he noted, "I would require for all courses three years of English, three of mathematics and two of history. Then I would arrange the other units to be offered in groups suitable for the A.B., the Ph.B. [Bachelor of Philosophy], or the science course." The well-organized four-year courses of study should offer instruction in "Latin, Greek, French, German, English, mathematics, history, political economy, philosophy, physics, chemistry, and biology." He suggested that the subjects taken vary according to the course of study. Restating a point already made and one commonly cited in NCA discussions, he noted "the first two years are really secondary in character," and should reflect this fact. Regarding graduate study, he called for colleges to offer programs general in character and advised them to stay away from any professional academic preparation since that was the purview of the university.[50] Jesse initially stated that eight full-time teachers was the minimum for any college, but later admitted that six was enough in exceptional cases.

The quality of facilities was a major consideration. Jesse recommended "a good library, and suitable buildings, including three laboratories well-equipped, at least for undergraduate work, in the sciences named above." Last, the institution must possess "income enough to maintain well the instruction and the equipment."

Noting different economic conditions, Jesse said naming a dollar sum for income was difficult and warned that no minimum figure was safe. "In the view of the higher rate of interest and the smaller cost of living and of building in the West," he continued, "I am tempted to say that $250,000 amounts to as much for the establishment and maintenance of a college in any one of our ten states as $500,000 does in New York." However, he preferred $300,000 as the minimum. Somewhat apologetically, Jesse explained that he omitted the interior life of the college and secondary school and stressed "classification, organization, and management" due to time constraints.[51]

Jesse's definitions strongly influenced the development of the NCA. George Carman later claimed, "In determining what institutions may become members of the Association, the Executive Committee has followed in the main the definitions submitted by President Jesse." Carman also intimated that Jesse's ideas provided benchmarks to measure change though not necessarily progress.[52] James E. Armstrong suggested that Jesse's presentation fostered strong discussion on "the time-honored questions of classics vs. science and humanities vs. everything else."[53]

Edward W. Coy commented first on Jesse's paper. Observing that the ideas of primary, secondary, and higher education were borrowed from Europe, he concluded, "They hardly apply to our conditions." Coy also differed with Jesse on the length of a secondary education. Coy divided precollegiate instruction into two six-year courses, elementary and secondary, thus diverging from Jesse's idea of a four-year high school.

Building upon the idea that secondary and college work overlapped, Andrew Draper observed, "We cannot tell just where the high school is to end and the college course commence." He suggested the local character of education at all levels had created this dilemma. Draper offered a different plan of organization based upon the varying missions of school levels. He divided education into three stages. Elementary covered citizenship and self-reliance. The goal of secondary and college was "to train the pupil so that he may reach out and take hold of the higher things of life, and exert an influence upon people and affairs about him." The highest stage was the university, where scholars conducted original research that contributed to the world's body of knowledge and influenced instruction.

Principal J. W. Ford of Pillsbury Academy in Minnesota pursued yet a different line of thought. Regarding high school and college, he agreed, "It is a matter of common experience that these terms are not clearly defined." To pursue such definitions involved identifying the studies in the four years before college as well as the methods of study and instruction. Ford believed college entrance requirements provided a solution. Jesse had made this point, too. But where the University of Missouri president called for college and high school educators to collaborate on college admission policies, the Minnesota high school principal declared, "You, gentlemen of the colleges, will have to set the standard or you will never get the secondary school up to it." He advocated top-down reform. Closing the discussion, President C. A. Schaeffer of Iowa State University returned to the opening remarks by Jesse. He stressed the loose limits on establishing degree-granting institutions, indicating a need for a greater state governmental role in higher education.[54]

While NCA members identified the same issues, they approached them from differing perspectives and thus proposed various solutions. In examining the structure of schooling, Coy stressed educational philosophy and the unique American situation, while Draper emphasized instructional missions and outcomes. Ford and Jesse agreed on the critical importance of college entrance requirements but differed on who should determine them. Another issue was whether state boards of education should charter institutions. In this way, the NCA discussions provided an opportunity for members to identify three major issues: the nature of educational institutions, the composition of the curriculum, and college admissions programs.[55] With some additions and changes of emphasis, these areas remain primary concerns of the NCA.

THE MOVE TO GREATER ACTIVISM

The discussions also moved the Association toward a more active stance, in part, because some members consistently advocated such a course and used the deliberative format to pursue this goal. According to John Grinnell, a bloc of members moved the NCA towards activism. The leaders of this group were Northwestern

University president Henry Wade Rogers, Chicago assistant superintendent A. F. Nightingale, Morgan Park Academy dean and later
University of Chicago professor Charles H. Thurber, Cleveland
Central High School principal Edward L. Harris, and George Carman, director of Lewis Institute.[56] While some members pursued
activism by holding an Association office, others pushed for
change in the discussions. As treasurer, Carman served on the Executive Committee during the entire half-decade. Thurber was an
Executive Committee member in 1897–1898. Nightingale was
Association president in 1898–1899, and served on the Executive
Committee the following two years. Interestingly, neither Harris
nor Rogers held any Association office during the first five years of
the NCA. This group did not dominate Association offices but
often pushed for a more active posture by presenting papers and
participating in discussions at NCA meetings. Nightingale, in particular, effectively used the discussion format to advantage. As
editor of the influential journal, *The School Review*, Thurber pursued
his ideas in print.

In 1897, when the format changed from presenting papers to
debating resolutions, the Association took the first step toward
activism. Not every member applauded this alteration. Ohio State
University president James Canfield voiced his opposition, stating,
"Let me say, in passing, that I think no resolutions ought to 'pass'
here. We ought to remain a deliberative, not a legislative body."
However, as Calvin O. Davis noted, the debating of a resolution did
not necessarily result in legislation.[57] Between 1897 and 1899, the
Association discussed fourteen resolutions, including one that was
tabled for a year. Of these, the delegates unanimously adopted only
two as originally written. Five were either laid on the table or
referred to a committee. The other resolutions were revised or the
vote was postponed before the group took action.[58]

In its first five years, the Association also developed a mechanism for making decisions and implementing change that was
based on caution and conservatism. Influenced by the democratic,
egalitarian character of the Association and the deliberative format,
the process involved extensive discussion, study, and revision.
Though the resolution prohibiting more than 150 members made
the NCA an elite and highly selective organization in its early years,
all members were equal.[59] The custom of splitting the election of

officers and committee appointments among higher and second-ary education members fostered the equality idea. The sessions themselves were exercises in participatory democracy in that free discussion prevailed and each institution or individual had one vote. Typically, philosophical affinity rather than educational level created alliances that facilitated agreement or blocs that pursued a common agenda. The activist faction, for example, was comprised of two collegiate and three secondary representatives.

Whether intended or not, the democratic policy governing the Association and the resolution format promoted a more active stance. The ability to agree on issues showed that common ground existed while the influence exerted by these resolutions raised the stature of the Association. Though advisory, the resolutions affected member institutions. Davis explained, "The only way they ever became effective in practice was through their espousal by individual members."[60] However, some resolutions aimed to move beyond advice to mandate. In 1898, when Nightingale was presi-dent, one resolution sought uniform minimum college entrance requirements based upon a list of specific studies. A supporting res-olution recommended the appointment of a committee to prepare questions and conduct exams on these requirements, "the results of which shall be accepted by all members of this association; and that all colleges and universities in the association agree not to pro-mulgate changes in entrance requirements without first submitting them to this commission."[61]

The debate on the 1898 resolution to secure uniform entrance requirements illuminates both the working of the Association and the frustration some members felt because of the inability to agree on vital issues. Henry Wade Rogers opened the discussion. Predict-ing the eventual elimination of entrance exams and the exclusive reliance on admission by certificate by western colleges and univer-sities, he cautioned, "When that day comes we shall still be under the necessity of prescribing what the admission requirements shall be." He supported the resolutions, tracing the movement for uni-formity to the secondary schools. Citing action already taken by the New England Association to address this issue, he ruefully noted that "associations similar to this in other parts of the United States are at work on these problems. It is a matter of regret that the association has not before this seriously undertaken the work."

Identifying a major drawback of the deliberative format, Rogers admitted, "Uniformity cannot be established by simply resolving that it ought to be done." Some issues required more than talk. Rogers stressed, "The machinery must be provided by which the work to be done can be accomplished." Drawing upon the experience of the Committee of Ten and a New York conference, he recommended creating separate commissions for the various academic subjects. "The advantage of separate commissions over a general commission is that the uniform standard recommended will express the best judgment of the experts in the several departments," he explained, "and on that account will be more likely to be acceptable to the colleges and universities." He also noted, "With several commissions at work at the same time, conclusions can be reached with less delay."

Ironically, Rogers rejected the second resolution, for a commission to prepare exam questions that members had to accept. In explaining his reasoning, Rogers identified a general concern. "It is not at all clear what the attitude of the secondary schools in the north central states is likely to be, should a commission be established by an association in which so few of them are represented," he explained, noting only sixty were members. This logic also applied to colleges and universities. He then suggested students would take the exams only if required by institutions. Rogers cautioned, "To establish a commission before knowing whether any great number of the schools are likely to make such a requirement, seems unwise. It would be premature, therefore, to take at this time the action proposed."[62]

Many speakers supported the idea but disagreed with its specifics. Observing that "the idea of states' rights...has been pushed to its illogical extreme [in education]," Richard H. Jesse exclaimed, "Therefore, I, for one, welcome spontaneously every suggestion to introduce into our educational work more uniformity." Nonetheless, he opposed the specific requirements stated in the resolution. David Kinley of the University of Illinois voiced similar sentiments: "I am in substantial agreement with what the resolution intends to express, but much at difference with what it actually does say."[63] Others presented various ideas. Eventually, George Carman introduced a substitute resolution that made the requirements more general.

Recognizing the difficulty of agreeing on specifics, Rogers presented another, intriguing solution. His substitute resolution focused on setting up the curriculum commissions, because "it is utterly impossible to get the colleges represented in this association, or the colleges represented in any association to agree on a uniformity of subjects. We are simply wasting our time when we talk upon that line." University of Wisconsin professor Charles H. Haskin agreed: "We have practically come to the conclusion that we cannot agree upon a set of minimum requirements." Citing a similar path taken by eastern colleges, Rogers argued, "But I do think it is entirely feasible to determine the amount which is to be required, or which should be required for each one of the subjects."[64] By identifying the number of courses and defining the general content parameters, the Association preserved the freedom of institutions to select what subjects they required for admission. Colleges retained the freedom to decide individually the "what" of their entrance requirements, but the commissions would define "the requirement [that] shall be uniform in any particular subject." Agreeing on subject content promised to reduce the existing chaos. Uniform guidelines allowed high schools to develop courses that met all requirements.

Following the democratic ethos of the Association, the members agreed that the proposed commissions be composed equally of college and secondary school representatives. Charles H. Thurber broached this issue first, declaring that "if it is to be made of men who are to consider subjects as they relate to both colleges and secondary schools, I, for my part, should be glad to favor the resolution." Nightingale seconded Thurber, referring to the purpose of the Association as improving relations between educators at both levels. "I think that anything is out of order that tends to alienate the colleges and secondary schools," he commented, calling for equal representation on the commissions. Andrew Draper offered a solution, moving that each commission consist of ten members, five each from higher and secondary education.[65] Draper's amendment and Rogers' substitute resolution calling for the appointment of commissions passed by a vote of thirty to fifteen, but no commissions were created.

Rogers pursued the curriculum commission idea at the next two meetings with little success. Frederick L. Bliss later observed,

"Owing to a misunderstanding, these commissions were never appointed," but he claimed the deliberations on the resolutions had begun the movement toward greater activism. John Grinnell accepted Bliss's conclusion but interpreted the course of events differently. He said the failure to appoint these commissions involved more than the "forgetfulness" of the Executive Committee. "It is a supposition that lack of faith in the legislative or executive powers, so frequently denied, of the young Association might have contributed to the inertia on a matter which offered undeniable difficulties," he explained.[66] In his opinion, opposition to action doomed the commissions.

In reality, a variety of factors contributed to the commission failure. Initially, a misunderstanding over whether the outgoing or incoming president was responsible for making the appointments did postpone action. When Rogers noted this oversight at the close of the 1899 meeting, incoming NCA president William F. Slocum of Colorado College appointed a committee to study the curriculum commission idea, chaired by James H. Baker of the University of Colorado. At the 1900 meeting, the committee presented a series of resolutions. The first four covered admission requirements. One required completion of the equivalent of a four-year secondary course of study for admission to a college or university. It defined a year's work in any subject as a unit "covering at least four periods a week throughout the year." The committee suggested sixteen units for admission. They also prescribed requirements of two units each in English and math and one unit each in science and history. Electives in a variety of subjects comprised the remaining sixteen units. Resolution 5 contained a provision on school facilities. The last resolution repeated the original charge for various subject commissions composed of four members each. It mandated that the commissions "make the basis of their study and investigations the report of the committee of ten on college entrance requirements," chaired by Nightingale, who also served on this NCA committee.[67]

Again, no commissions appeared. At the 1901 meeting, Superintendent Edward Ayres of Lafayette, Indiana, asked about the commissions. NCA president George B. Aiton of Minnesota explained that the plan was impractical and required over forty commissioners, but many members had declined to serve. Apparently, they opposed the idea or perceived Rogers' plan as flawed.

Draper had pointed out defects in the plan during the initial discussion in 1898. Some members probably considered the workload too heavy. The voluntary nature of the NCA meant that the refusal of members to participate stymied any activity not strongly supported or considered poorly conceived. While refusal to serve helped to doom the commission idea, other factors also contributed. Henry Wade Rogers left the presidency of Northwestern University and relocated in the East, outside NCA territory.[68] His championship had kept this initiative alive and his departure diminished support. The NCA also lost one of its most influential and active members. In addition, the appearance of the Report of the NEA Committee on College Entrance Requirements temporarily co-opted the commission idea.

The failure of the commissions identified the obstacles Association members faced in promoting their projects, including the voluntary nature of the NCA. Beyond the problem of getting members to volunteer to serve on committees, completing the task also proved difficult. Already busy at their institutions, Association members sometimes required considerable periods of time beyond suggested deadlines to develop important programs. Where opposition was strong, a means of avoiding confrontation and possibly strong dissent without losing face was not to undertake an assignment. This strategy later proved effective in stalling the movement to accredit colleges.

Another point noted by Grinnell was the youth of the Association. Rogers' warning about acting without a large enough base probably led to inaction in many cases and that certainly occurred here. Requiring colleges to adhere to uniform requirements was both controversial and risky, possibly affecting the survival of the Association. If the NCA implemented a plan and institutions ignored the requirements, the integrity of the organization was threatened. The timing of discussion also hampered efforts. The Association typically discussed this commission idea near the close of the annual meeting when the crush of time seldom allowed for adequate consideration.

Despite the failure of the curriculum effort, it was one of the two major thrusts behind the rise of accrediting. The other was institutional integrity. Discussed at the same time as the curriculum commissions, the issue of controlling degree-conferring institutions aroused much interest.

The 1896 session on defining the college and secondary school raised the issue of institution charters. During the discussion, Andrew Draper raised the question of integrity, observing that conferring degrees was a primary criterion used in defining a college. He declared, "These degrees may well be made to form a common basis of operations and a bond of union between all branches of collegiate work throughout the state, or indeed throughout the world." State government had the power "to give or withhold from local institutions the right to confer these degrees, and thus to protect them from dishonor and establish the firm foundations of collegiate work." He recommended establishing state boards of education to charter colleges and universities. He also asked, "Cannot we take a long step forward in the way of leading the North Central States to take this course?" President Charles Schaeffer of Iowa State University seconded Draper's proposal, noting, "If we could control or limit the degree conferring power in the state which we represent we would accomplish a vast amount." The problem, he continued, was that "the condition of affairs is a very loose one at the present time." Suggesting a quick solution was possible, Schaeffer asked the Association to take a stand on the degree issue.[69]

Henry Wade Rogers prompted action with his 1896 resolution that created a committee to report on "possible legislation regulating the granting of academic degrees." Angell headed the committee that included Rogers, Draper, and Schaeffer. Interestingly, this committee was composed exclusively of higher education figures. A preliminary report at the 1897 meeting disclosed, "In no one of the states...is there any adequate restriction either upon the power to incorporate or upon the degree conferring power." The following year, Rogers reported that the NEA and the American Bar Association also were taking action on the matter. He condemned fraudulent institutions for impairing the value of American academic degrees and submitted a resolution to establish state commissions to confer degrees. He even offered a model procedure.

The report closed on a cautionary note. Acknowledging the difficulty of securing the desired legislation, the committee advised, "A reform so fundamental is not to be accomplished in a day. But in time it can be done. Meanwhile public opinion should be created favorable thereto." The committee suggested, "Let there be agitation and an exposure of the abuses that discredit American degrees abroad and at home." The recognition that change took time and the call for a persistent, patient movement reflected the conservative approach supported even by advocates of change.[70] The following year President Winfield S. Chaplin of Washington University, St. Louis, introduced a resolution renewing the recommendations of the previous year.[71] The failure of the Illinois legislature to pass the Rogers bill to regulate the conferring of degrees helped stimulate the rise of accreditation. If the state refused to assume the responsibility for regulating colleges and universities, the NCA would perform this function.

Though approaching the subject from a different perspective, secondary school educators also expressed concern over institutional and Association integrity. During a discussion of commercial schools at the 1898 meeting, A. F. Nightingale argued against a resolution that would admit commercial high schools with only a two-year course when the NCA required other schools to have four years. "Give us bona fide commercial high schools," he declared, pleading that passage of the resolution would lower the dignity of the Association. It was also unconstitutional, he claimed, observing, "We are breaking down these very sections in our constitution by admitting individual members through the back window, because they are not eligible to come in at the front door." To ignore admission criteria established by the membership threatened both the integrity of the Association and its ability to represent what Nightingale called "the highest interest of education in eleven states."[72]

During this period, admission requirements served a variety of purposes. They provided the Association with a method of setting a standard of excellence. They also helped in defining institutions, supplying a means of translating the ideas discussed into practice. Organizationally, entrance criteria defined the community of the fledgling association and also facilitated maintaining parity between the secondary and collegiate levels. In many respects, membership policies were the only instrument available for the NCA to pursue active improvement of education. Throughout the Association's first five years, the membership requirements were tightened. In 1896, Rogers of Northwestern proposed two resolutions the members unanimously adopted. The first stated: "That, in the opinion of this Association, no College is considered in good standing that confers the degree of Doctor of Philosophy or Doctor of Science, except after a period of at least two years of residence and of graduate study." The second restricted membership to institutions who met this qualification.[73]

Two years later, at the 1898 meeting, constitutional revisions tightened membership requirements even more by clarifying certain criteria. In explaining the need for the changes, Secretary Frederick L. Bliss commented that "for the most part, they put in form what already exists. There has been some little ambiguity in the wording of the clauses of the constitution." He also suggested that the passage of resolutions dictated constitutional amendments. The changes institutionalized the 1896 resolutions by Rogers regarding institutional requirements for students seeking the doctor of philosophy and the doctor of science degrees. Membership was limited to institutions that required "three years of graduate study, not less than two of which shall be years of resident study, one of which shall be at the institution conferring the degree." Nightingale's concern over admission of secondary schools was also addressed. Another amendment stated, "No secondary school shall be eligible to membership which does not have a four years' course of study." [74]

During the discussion on the amendments, an issue arose that led to the loss of one of the NCA's most active members the following year. Charles Thurber of the University of Chicago questioned the policy of admitting individual members. While not objecting to having individuals seek membership by themselves, he observed, "it seems to me we need some method whereby the institutions shall determine who shall be here, and not set us the delicate task of making a selection and electing individuals—or not electing them—as an association." The goal was not keeping people out, but admitting them "on a sound and equable basis." Thurber pursued his efforts to eliminate individual members without success. The issue prompted his departure from the NCA in 1899. Elected as an individual member, he acknowledged the honor, but declined it, explained that acceptance would compromise his strong opposition to this policy. By refusing, Thurber, in essence, resigned from the Association.[75]

Ironically, as the NCA stood on the threshold of embracing activism, two of the most fervent advocates for action, Rogers and Thurber, left the organization. The tightening of admission requirements signaled the NCA shift towards a more functional organization. The tightening of membership criteria to raise institutional standards and better control the environment is an early indication that an organization is moving toward a more functional approach.[76] Undertaking significant organizational change also indicates the NCA had established itself on a solid footing. By establishing policies and procedures, by building relationships among its members, the NCA had developed its institutional side enough so the tension between institutionalization and innovation began shifting toward the latter. In a sense, the members began to trust the wisdom of the organization. The implementation of the democratic credo and egalitarian policies had reduced the fears of educators from both levels. The discussion and voting on the resolutions demonstrated that neither the historical dominance of the colleges nor the numbers of the high schools created an imbalance in the voting on the resolutions. The experience of the deliberations also proved that agreement was possible even when differences of opinion existed.

TOWARD A PHILOSOPHY OF EDUCATIONAL AND ORGANIZATIONAL CHANGE

Equally important, the discussions had raised a number of ideas on change that were beginning to coalesce into an Association "philosophy." The dialogue opened at the first meeting in 1896. William Rainey Harper discussed the nature of reform in relation to the founding of the North Central Association. "Perfection in method is far beyond us. We must never hope to reach it, but we must strive for it, and in that effort the experience of our brethren will count for more than all other things combined," the University of Chicago president advised, noting, "We understand that this is the purpose of the Association."[77] Harper recognized that improvement of school-college relations was a never-ending quest that required the collective expertise of all NCA members. Deliberation, of course, implied a continuing, open-ended conversation, but as the discussion of issues and resolutions proceeded over the first five years, the dynamic character of reform also emerged.

In 1898, Charles H. Thurber claimed educational problems defied permanent solution. "Whoever thinks that any educational problem is permanently solved deludes himself and misleads others, for problems of education, like problems of philosophy, are, and always must be in the process of solution."[78] The continuing evolution of education stressed process over resolution because, as conditions changed, solutions applicable at a particular moment might lose their efficacy. A similar flux in educational thought affected innovative ideas. "What we consider radical ideas today will be conservative tomorrow," A. F. Nightingale observed, "and what is conservative today the wildest schemer did not dream of a decade ago."[79] The perception of reform ideas thus changed over time as implementation and familiarity converted innovations and experiments into the commonplace, institutionalizing them, so to speak. Once again, the emphasis on process was underscored.

The deliberations and experiences of the first five years of the Association had instilled in members the idea that change was the only constant in education and that stressing process mattered more than seeking resolution. This nascent "philosophy" had profound implications on the NCA's development. Since improving relations depended upon maintaining relevance in a world of changing educational conditions, thought, and practices, the Association's progress depended on its ability to change. Process, then, became the engine behind the Association's development. In a sense, the NCA has always been in the process of becoming. Its quest to remain compatible with evolving educational conditions has led the NCA to re-create itself periodically in its history by building upon the past to meet the present and plan for the future. The first re-creation occurred between 1901 and 1916, when the NCA transformed itself from a deliberative to a functional association and pioneered the idea of voluntary accreditation.

NOTES

1. James B. Angell, "Presidential Address," 9–10.

2. John Kimberly, *The Organizational Life Cycle* (San Francisco: Jossey-Bass, Publishers, 1982), 4.

3. James Bryce, *The American Commonwealth*, rev. ed. (New York: Macmillan, 1933, originally published 1888), 2:281–82; Cited in Sills, "Voluntary Associations: Sociological Aspects," 364.

4. Sills, "Voluntary Associations: Sociological Aspects," 362–63; Banton, "Voluntary Associations: Anthropological Aspects," 357; Bloland, *Associations in Action,* 1

5. Donald R. Warren, *To Enforce Education: A History of the Founding Years of the United States Office of Education* (Detroit: Wayne State University, 1974), 77–91; Charles H. Judd, *Research in the United States Office of Education*, the Advisory Committee of Education Staff Study, no. 19 (Washington, D.C.: GPO, 1939), 5–7; Harry Kursh, *The United States Office of Education: A Century of Service* (Philadelphia: Chilton Books, 1965), 10.

6. Hugh Hawkins, *Banding Together: The Rise of National Associations in American Higher Education, 1887–1950* (Baltimore: Johns Hopkins University Press, 1992), xi, 4.

7. Ibid., 7–10, on founding of the National Association of State Universities; and 16–19, on the origins of the American Association of Colleges. See also Hays, "Introduction—The New Organizational Society," 7–8.

8. On the origins of this organization and early NCA involvement, see NCA *Proceedings*, 1898, 52–54.

9. Leslie A. Butler, *The Michigan Schoolmasters' Club* (Ann Arbor: University of Michigan, 1957), 14, 115.

10. Krug, *The Shaping of the American High School, 1880–1917*, 1:1–3; John F. Nivens, *A Study of the Organization and Operation of Voluntary Accrediting Agencies* (Washington, D.C.: The Catholic University Press of America, 1959), 54–55, 57.

11. Krug, *The Shaping of the American High School, 1880–1917*, 1:3.

12. Edgar B. Wesley, *NEA: The First Hundred Years* (New York: Harper & Brothers, 1957), 20–25,43–45.

13. Ibid., 397. The largest increase in membership occurred in the years immediately following World War I, when membership jumped from just over ten thousand in 1918 to over fifty thousand in 1920 and rose to over two hundred thousand by 1929.

14. Krug, *Shaping of the American High School, 1880–1917*, 1:71.

15. Ibid. 71–74. Wesley held an unfavorable view of the Committee of Ten, suggesting it stifled the development of the high school and put the high schools under the domination of the colleges, but his view that no such domination existed prior to that time is belied by virtually every other source consulted. See also Krug, *Shaping of the American High School, 1880–1917,* 1.

16. Wesley, *NEA,* 71–72, 391–92.

17. Calvin O. Davis, *The History of the North Central Association* (Ann Arbor: NCA, 1945), 3.

18. Obituary, William Henry Butts, in *North Central Association Quarterly* 16 (July 1941): 3–4. Though Calvin Davis and John Grinnell interviewed Butts about his NCA experience, neither included much biographical information about Butts in their histories of the NCA.

19. William H. Butts, "National Uniformity in Secondary Instruction," *School Review* 3 (February 1895). This article intimates that the divergent college preparatory and fit-for-life missions of the high school influenced Butts' ideas.

20. Ibid., 69, 72–74. Italics added.

21. Ibid., 73–74.

22. Grinnell, "The Rise of the North Central Association of Colleges and Secondary Schools," 56. An alternate version of this meeting is presented by Davis. He also claimed Harper leaped from his chair, but claims he shouted, "Excellent! Excellent! A splendid idea." Davis does not mention any prediction of besting the New England Association.

23. Ibid., 55.

24. Butler, *The Michigan Schoolmasters' Club*, 114–15.

25. Reprinted in NCA *Proceedings*, 1895, 5–6. The invitation also raised various logistics issues, such as having each institution cast one vote, whether individuals holding important offices such as state superintendents of schools could join, fees, and meetings.

26. Letters, Henry Wade Rogers to Andrew Draper, March 15 and 27, 1895, Andrew Draper Papers, Box 6, University of Illinois (Urbana) archives. In 1994, this same train trip on the Metra commuter line takes about twenty-three minutes.

27. Reprinted in NCA *Proceedings*, 1895, 5–6.

28. *Chicago Tribune*, March 30, 1895.

29. Grinnell, "The Rise of the North Central Association of Colleges and Secondary Schools," 63–64. Illinois provided the most delegates, fourteen.

30. NCA *Proceedings*, 1895, 7–8. Existing sources provide no details on when the constitution committee met. The time frame makes it likely that they worked while the others took an Evanston tour. The general meeting resumed at 3:30 P.M. *Chicago Tribune*, March 30, 1895. An alternative scenario is intimated in a letter from Principal Parman of Matton, Illinois to Andrew Draper. He indicates that a meeting on the new organization was held, or at least discussed, in Ann Arbor on the day before the NCA conference opened in Evanston. Since Butts and Nightingale attended the Classical Conference in Ann Arbor, it is possible they and others discussed the upcoming meeting in Evanston. Letter, Parman to Andrew Draper, May 7, 1895, in Andrew Draper papers, Box 6, University of Illinois (Urbana) archives.

31. George Carman mentioned this point in his 1903 "Presidential Address." NCA *Proceedings*, 1903, 7

32. Grinnell, "The Rise of the North Central Association of Colleges and

Secondary Schools," 8–10.

33. Ibid.

34. Ibid., 12.

35. NCA *Proceedings*, 1896, 8. One hundred years later, the social side of the NCA remains a major function of the organization, and is often cited by members as a primary benefit of membership. It is also a facet of organizational life that too often is neglected.

36. NCA *Proceedings*, 1895, passim.

37. Draper papers in the University of Illinois archives show he maintained a regular correspondence with other college presidents, particularly Richard Jesse of the University of Missouri and George MacLean.

38. Wesley, *NEA*, 182, 215, 393.

39. Obituary, William H. Butts, *North Central Association Quarterly*, 3–4. Butts was recommended for individual membership in 1900, but apparently never joined. NCA *Proceedings*, 1900, 35.

40. James E. Armstrong, "Presidential Address," NCA *Proceedings*, 1915, 6.

41. Grinnell, "The Rise of the North Central Association of Colleges and Secondary Schools," 128.

42. Kimberly, *The Organizational Life Cycle*, 40.

43. NCA *Proceedings*, 1896, iii, v–vi.

44. Angell, "Presidential Address," 12.

45. NCA *Proceedings*, 1896–1901, passim. See also Davis, *A History of the North Central Association*, 16.

46. NCA *Proceedings*, 1897, 27.

47. Richard Jesse, "What Constitutes a College and What a Secondary School," NCA *Proceedings*, 1896, 24–25.

48. Ibid., 28, 33

49. The issue of the length of secondary education vexed the NCA for decades and became more complicated as junior high schools and junior colleges emerged.

50. Jesse, "What Constitutes a College and What a Secondary School," 32. Jesse expressed regret that the university had somewhat co-opted the college field.

51. Ibid., 29, 34. Interestingly, 1920s criticisms of NCA standards focused on their external focus. These criticisms are discussed in chapter 4.

52. Ibid., 5, 9. In his NCA presidential address that recounted sixty years of NCA history, Milo Bail also noted the influence of Jesse's paper. Reprinted as Milo Bail, "Six Decades of Progress," *North Central Association Quarterly*, 30 (October 1955): 196–97. Unfortunately, Bail gave the impression that Jesse's definitions were given as part of the debate over college accrediting during the NCA's second decade.

53. Armstrong, "Presidential Address," 7.

54. NCA *Proceedings*, 1896, 34–35.

55. The NCA activities expanded beyond these concerns to almost all aspects of education, including extracurricular activities such as athletics,

and relations with other organizations.

56. Grinnell identifies these members as the activist bloc. Grinnell, "The Rise of the North Central Association of Colleges and Secondary Schools," 77–78.

57. James Canfield, in NCA *Proceedings*, 1897, 23; Davis, *The History of the North Central Association*, 15.

58. The various resolutions, the discussions on them, and their resolutions take up most of the *Proceedings* during these years.

59. Carman, "Presidential Address," 7.

60. Davis, *The History of the North Central Association*, 15.

61. NCA *Proceedings*, 1899, viii.

62. Ibid., 75–76, 78–79, 82, 84, 87.

63. Ibid., 89, 94.

64. See Ibid., 101, 103, for Rogers' comments and 105 for Haskin.

65. Ibid., For Thurber, 107; Nightingale, 108; and Draper, 110. George MacLean and Rogers supported Draper's motion, 111.

66. Frederick L. Bliss, "Presidential Address," NCA *Proceedings*, 1905, 8; Grinnell, "The Rise of the North Central Association of Colleges and Secondary Schools," 104.

67. NCA *Proceedings*, 1900, 55–56.

68. The reasons behind Roger's dismissal from Northwestern University are unclear. Apparently, two factors contributed to his leaving, his strong antiwar stance regarding the Spanish-American War and the rapid rise of the University of Chicago. Henry Wade Rogers papers, Northwestern University archives.

69. NCA *Proceedings*, 1896, 40.

70. Ibid., 1897, 121; 1898, 117–18. These abuses prompted the first call for a list of approved colleges and came ironically from German universities seeking assurance of the quality of undergraduates applying to graduate school in Germany.

71. Ibid., 1899, 48–49.

72. Ibid., 1898, 89–90.

73. Ibid., 1896, 83.

74. Ibid., 1898, 1–14, 163–64.

75. Ibid., 1899, 23–24; NCA *Proceedings*, 1900, 121.

76. Hays, "Introduction—The New Organizational Society," 8.

77. NCA *Proceedings*, 1896, 8.

78. Ibid., 1898, 38.

79. Ibid., 1902, 40.

Chapter Three

The NCA Comes of Age

> *With us reforms in education...are effected by conference, by criticism, by discussion, by interchange of opposing views, by the weighing of arguments pro and con, until what seems best emerges and wins the day; whereupon we accept the situation and go on our way rejoicing.*
>
> —Edward W. Coy, 1909[1]

HUGHES HIGH SCHOOL PRINCIPAL Edward W. Coy's whimsical description captured the essence of the North Central Association decision-making procedure. The deliberative process provided more than a forum for expressing opinions. Discussion helped members reach agreements on difficult issues and supplied numerous safety checks on proposed actions. Deliberation also strengthened the NCA's democratic foundations. But Coy's suggestion that making a decision on an issue ended the discussion contradicts the NCA experience. Inevitably, decisions led members to identify other problems that initiated more deliberation and further reforms. The process was continual and progressive, building upon past efforts and sometimes resulting in substantial changes. The greatest transformation of the North Central Association began in 1901 and ended in 1916, after the NCA had re-created itself as a functional, accrediting organization.

The deliberations of the first five years paved the way for the pioneering of voluntary accreditation by the NCA. As University of Chicago professor Charles H. Judd explained, the movement toward accrediting began with University of Missouri president Richard Jesse's 1896 paper on defining institutions. "They didn't use the word 'standard' at all," Judd explained. "They used the word 'definition.'...It was that definition, mark you, not a series of standards at the outset, that was used in determining what colleges

Ella Flagg Young. Superintendent of Chicago Schools and first woman president of the National Education Association, Young was an individual member of NCA, 1910–16, and served on a number of committees.

should be approved." The definitions included basic characteristics of any college or secondary school. "It was obvious to...those who adopted an approved list that if certain characteristics belonged to a good college," he commented, "these characteristics must be found in any institution that went on the approved list." In this way, "the definition was transformed into a set of standards."[2] Though not mentioned by Judd, Henry Wade Rogers' plan to have curriculum commissions define the content of the subjects required for college admissions also influenced the rise of NCA accrediting. In addition, his failed campaign to strengthen state laws on chartering institutions showed that government would not act on the vexing problem of fraudulent institutions—a perennial

Charles H. Judd. Professor at the University of Chicago, Judd was NCA president in 1924; he was a leader of reforms, including standards revision of CIHE and COS in the 1930s.

plague of higher education—possibly influencing the NCA's more active posture.

A variety of factors thus contributed to the re-creation of the NCA and the rise of voluntary accrediting. The initiation of this change, of deciding to undertake what Englewood High School principal J. E. Armstrong called the "real work of the Association" occurred in the NCA's sixth year.[3] During the first five years, the organization had established its foundations. Over the next fifteen, it came of age.

THE MOVE TOWARD ACCREDITING

The same issue of college admissions that prompted the founding of the NCA also precipitated the formation of voluntary, regional accrediting. The turning point was a paper by University of Illinois dean Stephen A. Forbes at the 1901 annual meeting, entitled "The Desirability of So Federating the North Central Colleges and

Universities As to Secure Essentially Uniform or At Least Equivalent Entrance Requirements." Couching his argument in language familiar to social scientists, he suggested that progressive development involved two opposing elements. There was "always differentiation, with its gradual distinction and divergent growth of the parts of a system, and co-ordination, which brings each changing part under the limiting or the stimulating influences of all the rest—insures the subordinate action of each, the co-ordinate action of all, in the common interest." Differentiation allowed for adaptation to the environment, while inner unity and individual strength brought forth coordination. Forbes cautioned that "things highly differentiated but imperfectly co-ordinated are weak and easily disorganized. They tend to waste their energies by internal friction; to pull themselves in pieces in internal struggle, to succumb piecemeal to unfavorable conditions." Such conditions applied to social, physiological, educational, and political systems. He closed with an illuminating analogy: "It is as true of an association of colleges and secondary schools as it is of an association of ants or bumblebees. It is a law not merely of organisms or of groups of organisms, but of organization itself."[4]

In his analysis, Forbes summed up the history of educational development. While the idea of the high school and university promoted coordination in the system of schooling, the elective system and the local, autonomous development of institutions created differentiation. The NCA was founded to perfect coordination and thus avert the difficulties arising from high differentiation. His description of the interplay between individuality and uniformity also offers insight into the development of organizations. An organization's survival and development depended upon achieving a balance between these opposing forces.

Cautioning against any delays in seeking a balance between individuality and coordination, Forbes warned that the great diversity of educational conditions had created difficulties that "are already sufficient to tax the most ingenious and most experienced." In addition, the evolving state of education exacerbated the situation, making it impossible to plan for the future. The source of the problem was the elective system, and his solution was to "tie the elective courses of the high school to the elective courses of the college at so many different points that whatever high-school course is chosen the chooser may find a college course—yes, I will say *any* college course—open to him at the end of his high-school period."

Reversing the traditional practice of having the college dictate the high school curriculum, Forbes suggested the secondary school provide the benchmarks and that the uniformity be regional. He favored "a uniform standard of high-school graduation requirements, together with such an adjustment of college requirements to high school courses as may seem possible and desirable." This strategy followed the plan of the contemporary NEA Committee on College Entrance Requirements. That committee had concluded that linking the higher and secondary education depended on having the colleges begin where the best high schools ended. However, Forbes criticized the NEA Committee recommendations, explaining that the national scope of the work had made them incomplete and sometimes vague. He wanted the various regional associations to set up an apparatus that complemented the work of the NEA Committee. Early efforts in the Middle States and Maryland Association as well as in Iowa and Minnesota provided examples to follow.

Forbes offered suggestions on implementing his ideas, including building upon the efforts of other organizations. He recommended researching the organization of schooling to define a high school and a college, cataloguing existing courses of study and subjects, identifying college preparatory high schools and institutions that accepted Association decisions on admission requirements. Recognizing the temporary nature of any solution, he explained that changing conditions required that the NCA "be kept at work...year after year, probably making annual reports subject to approval by this association." Forbes suggested the committee organization follow the federal structure of the U.S. government, stating that "a thoroughly representative standing committee of this association would evidently be necessary, and to this I think we should add a sub-committee for each state represented in our organization." Since each state had "its own state teachers' association and its own state university, both of which should be utilized in this work," the proposed structure facilitated regional coordination without duplicating the work of the state systems of education.

Regarding the standing committee, it "might well be left the duty of acting upon the recommendations and suggestions of the Report of the National Committee of Thirteen; that of defining and describing high-school courses of study, ascribing to each its admission value, and dividing the list of such courses into constants, group electives, and general electives, to be accepted as such by all." The standing committee would also determine which colleges participated in the program. He offered options for determining eligibility. The first called for state subcommittees to report on high schools. The second employed existing secondary and higher education relationships by having the state universities send needed data to the NCA. Forbes also wanted the Association to form a working relationship with separate state agencies that evaluated high schools. Success depended upon coordinating efforts and having all members accept the results.

Shifting the activities to a special committee would create a bureaucratic layer in the organization, but would maintain the participatory and democratic decision-making procedure. The organization of the NCA required adjustment because "our present pressing need is a better co-ordination of our educational agencies in these North Central States, made with a view to organizing and unifying progress, which has lately gone too much along separate and disconnected lines." The committee provided the necessary connections to coordinate reform efforts. Where the existing organizational structure—general meetings and temporary committees—hindered resolution of difficult issues, the standing committee facilitated it. In this respect, the committee organization promised to resolve outstanding issues while better organizing the high schools and colleges. The high schools gained "one general standard of admission" understood by all. "High school students will not be forced to choose their colleges prematurely," Forbes noted, "or be left in doubt whether the high school curriculum preferred by them will serve for college admission." Colleges gained greater definition and uniformity in their high school relationships, resulting in "the consequent simplification and reduction of this part of their administration." They also realized "equal footing as to entrance conditions." Equally important, "colleges and high schools will be jointly benefited by an affiliation such that they will henceforth move together as one articulated organism."[5]

An extensive discussion followed Forbes' paper. Unfortunately, the *Proceedings* only summarized the various comments. A major concern was the small college's ability to meet tighter standards in a time of intense competition for students. Professor John J. Halsey of Lake Forest University noted such competition had led to great waste of effort in small institutions to the point that "they were...cutting each other's throats." He supported Forbes' idea of a cooperative college admissions system because it promoted reaching "a consensus of opinion as to what a college ought to be and as to what college entrance should require." Using the language of social Darwinism, Halsey observed, "Possibly if such an arrangement could be made some of the smaller institutions might be eliminated from the list of colleges by the law of the survival of the fittest." In this way, Forbes' plan addressed the problem of institutional integrity. Conversely, Northwestern University professor Thomas Holgate claimed the plan helped the small high school by raising its status to the same level as its larger counterpart. It provided "assurances to these schools that their certificates would be accepted everywhere at face value." Though affecting small colleges and high schools in opposite ways, the plan would raise the quality of education and the status of institutions. At the close of the discussion, the Association referred the matter to a committee of five chaired by Forbes and that included William Rainey Harper. The committee reported its finding the following day.[6]

Cautiously phrasing its recommendations, the committee explained,

> We have not attempted to reach conclusions, or even to raise questions, on any of the issues involved in the establishment of fixed and uniform relations between colleges and secondary schools, but have thought it best to leave the whole matter...to a permanent commission, whose appointment we recommend.

Perhaps recalling the criticisms lodged against the previous plan for curriculum committees, the members structured the commission to be "thoroughly representative, thoroughly responsible, and practically efficient." They predicted it "will prove to be a very influential and important agency of educational progress," and advised that "the Association do now proceed to the establishment of some definite form of affiliation and credit, as fixed, comprehensive, and uniform as may be, between the colleges and universities of this Association and the secondary schools of the North Central states."

Specifically, the committee recommended establishing a permanent Commission on Accredited Schools (CAS) consisting of twelve members, six each from the secondary schools and the colleges, appointed by the chair. Supplementing this core were "additional or delegate members one from each college or university belonging to the Association which has a freshman class of at least fifty members and which may appoint such a representative, together with a sufficient number of members from the secondary schools, to be appointed by the Chair, to maintain a parity of representation as between the secondary schools and the colleges." The committee suggested staggered terms for the twelve core members ranging from one to three years. The additional high school members served one-year renewable terms but the tenure of the extra college representatives was not defined. It also recommended the NCA president appoint a temporary chair until the commission selected its own officers. The relatively small number of core members addressed the concerns over size and practicality earlier raised regarding the Rogers' curriculum commission plan. The appointment of additional delegates on a large scale ensured full participation in making decisions and enhanced the likelihood of institutional acceptance. Among those appointed to the Commission were founding members and advocates of action George Carman, director of Lewis Institute, for one year, Chicago Superintendent of High Schools A. F. Nightingale for two years, and Cleveland Central High School principal Edward Harris for three years. Other important members were George MacLean, president of the University of Iowa; Dean Harry Pratt Judson of the University of Chicago; and Professor Allen S. Whitney of the University of Michigan. Whitney was the Michigan high school inspector and he played a major role in the development of accrediting policies and procedures.

Following Forbes' suggestions, the NCA Executive Committee outlined the duties of the commission. The NEA Committee on College Entrance Requirements was the "point of departure" for

Harry Pratt Judson. University of Chicago president, Judson was NCA president in 1912; he chaired the first Commission on Accredited Schools in 1901, which led to the NCA becoming an accrediting agency.

defining and describing units of study in high school subjects. The commission served "as a standing committee on uniformity of admission requirements for the colleges and universities of the Association." Its mandate included improving inspection methods to achieve greater uniformity. Most importantly, the commission was "to prepare a list of high schools within the territory of this Association which are entitled to the accredited relationship; and to formulate and report methods and standards for the assignment of college credit for good high school work done in advance of the college entrance requirement." To secure funds, the committee recommended each member's college contribute a sum "in proportion to membership in their freshman classes." The final point suggested that the commission meet at least once a year before the annual association meeting. The *Proceedings* omitted the discussion of the committee report, but noted it was considerable and led to adoption without any changes.[7]

By creating a permanent accrediting commission, the Association expanded beyond the deliberative tradition, extending its sphere of influence. Seeking greater control of the regional educational environment, the NCA became a functional organization that would use more than membership requirements to effect change. The tone of the committee recommendations, however, intimated action was not imminent. Following a cautious process of development, three years passed before the first list of accredited secondary schools appeared in 1904.

The first task was organizing the Commission. At a meeting on March 30, 1901, University of Chicago dean Harry Pratt Judson was elected chair. The Commission scheduled its next session for February 25, 1902, in Chicago to coincide with the meeting of the NEA Department of Superintendence. To reflect the functions of its work, the Commission established four committees: an executive and one each on unit courses of study, high school inspection, and college credit for high school work. Each committee developed a plan of action. At a meeting on March 27, 1902, in Cleveland, "the committees reported in full, and their reports were exhaustively discussed, amended and adopted by the Commission."[8]

At the 1902 annual meeting, members discussed the first Commission on Accredited Schools report. A. F. Nightingale called the report "eminently conservative." He praised it for accommodating the wide divergence of opinion among NCA members, claiming, "Those who are most radical in their demands for unlimited elasticity in programmes of study as well as those who still worship the fetich of the fifteenth century can safely unite in their endorsement of this report." He observed that the report had "nothing unique or novel, or, I may say, original in it." Instead, it incorporated elements from past efforts by a variety of organizations, including the NEA Committee of Ten, the American Historical Association, the NEA Science Department, and the Mathematical Association, among others. Following the idea of William H. Butts, Nightingale urged adoption and requested the various regional associations appoint a representative committee to develop "a report that shall have force and efficacy throughout the length and breadth of the nation."[9] Despite Nightingale's claim that the NCA conservatively followed educational reform, the Association was in the vanguard of regional accrediting.

Nightingale's praise was countered by skepticism. Anticipating later criticisms, University of Illinois president Andrew Draper questioned whether there was too much uniformity. Because it discriminated against smaller high schools, he objected to designating five faculty as the minimum required for NCA accreditation. The Association agreed with Draper's last point and adopted a motion striking out the specified number of teachers. Draper's resolution that the adoption of the Report was not binding on universities with existing systems of inspection passed by consent. After further discussion, a motion to adopt and print the report also passed.[10]

The report collected the findings of the various committees. Ironically, the committee on unit courses produced a curriculum study very similar to that proposed by Rogers. A unit of study was a "course covering a school year of not less than thirty-five weeks, with four or five periods of at least forty-five minutes each per week." High school graduation and college admissions required the completion of fifteen units. The various subjects and the suggested number of units required for each included: English (three), mathematics (four), history (four), Latin (four), Greek (three), French (four), German (four), Spanish (two), physics (one), chemistry (one), physical geography (one), botany (one), and biology (one). The unit courses committee report also discussed content, methods, textbooks, and teaching topics.

The recommended English unit course illuminated the thought of the committee regarding the high school curriculum. It covered four areas: grammar, reading, composition, and rhetoric. The committee recommended regular, progressive study and practice of grammar, leading to the ability to "point out the syntactical structure of any sentence" and "to state intelligently the leading grammatical principles." The reading curriculum used the book lists of the Joint Committee on Uniform Entrance Requirements in English and individual schools. There was a book list for reading and another for study and practice. Each had a revised version after three years. For reading, the committee suggested works by Shakespeare, "The Rime of the Ancient Mariner" by Samuel Coleridge, Sir Walter Scott's *Ivanhoe*, George Eliot's *Silas Marner*, and the works of several other authors. The study and practice list also included Shakespeare, as well as John Milton and Edmund Burke. The committee suggested that books read for study be "taught with reference to subject matter, form and structure," as well as grammar and the periods of English history in which they were written. The composition section required oral and written forms with regular, continuous instruction "to give practice in the four leading types of prose discourse: Description, Narration, Exposition and Argument." Beginning in the early high school years and connected to composition, rhetoric stressed such essential principles as "choice of words; structure of sentences and paragraphs," and the four prose types noted above.[11]

The committee on high school inspection presented four standards. Two standards focused on teaching. The first covered faculty preparation, recommending the "minimum scholastic attainment of all high school teachers be the equivalent of graduation from a college belonging to the North Central Association of Colleges and Secondary Schools," and that their education include "special training in the subjects they teach." The educational requirements were not retroactive. The second standard set five forty-five-minute class periods of instruction daily as the maximum teaching load. The third standard stated that library and laboratory facilities had to "be adequate to the needs of instruction in the subjects taught as outlined in the report of the Commission." The last standard examined the tenor of the school as a whole, specifying, "The *esprit de corps*, the efficiency of the instruction, the acquired habits of thought and study, and the general intellectual tone of the school are of paramount importance." To assess these qualities, the committee recommended "rigid, thorough-going inspection."[12]

This first list of NCA accrediting standards was narrowly focused and often vague in its language. The requirements for teaching preparation and load were quite specific and easy to evaluate. Assessing the general character of the school was more difficult because the standard was vague. In part, the uneven character of the standards reflected the equivocal aims of accrediting. The committee straddled the fence between seeking uniformity and preserving individuality and independence. In closing, the report advised, "Your committee believes that the Commission should refrain from any action which will lead to standardization of secondary schools and methods of instruction. It is our belief that the cause of secondary education will be best advanced by a somewhat free and natural development in the several states." Taking this credo into account, A. S. Whitney, chair of the inspection committee, wrote, "The Commission on Accredited Schools has an opportunity to assist immeasurably in strengthening secondary

education in the Northwest." The strategy initially involved com-
piling a list of accredited schools that "should be an honor list for
the North Central States."[13] Interestingly, membership was not a
requirement for approval, though earlier efforts at improving conditions had focused on this aspect. Nonetheless, the first NCA standards extended the Association's influence over the educational
environment of the region.

Though the Association accepted the report of the Commission on Accredited Schools, the battle over accrediting continued
at the 1903 annual meeting. The move into accrediting depended
upon all members supporting the idea, and this support rested partially on their understanding of how the NCA would act. To build
understanding and support, George Carman discussed the switch
from deliberation to activism in his presidential address, paying
great attention to the ideas of the founding members. Speaking
with the authority of someone who had attended the 1895 organizational meeting, Carman observed that the NCA founders had
planned a relatively small membership because "the Association
should be a working rather than, or as well as, a talking body," adding, "A comparatively small body, if truly representative of the
interests concerned, may act for a large territory and be more efficient than a larger body."[14] Following the admonitions of the
NCA's early years, he reiterated the basic premise of the Association: "We have no authority to act for the states or institutions
which we represent, for the state is the only authority in education." Though stressing that the NCA had only advisory powers, he
cited numerous instances where voluntary cooperation in an advisory capacity had yielded good results. The NEA Committees of
Ten and Thirteen reports, the newly founded College Entrance
Examination Board, and the NCA Commission on Accredited
Schools had all promoted cooperation between schools and colleges without resorting to coercion.

Carman's presidential address tried to persuade uncommitted
and opposing NCA members of the viability of regional accreditation. During the discussion of the report of the Commission on
Accredited Schools, an exchange between CAS chair Harry Pratt
Judson and Andrew Draper raised several concerns over the viability
of accrediting. When Edward L. Harris and A. F. Nightingale moved
the acceptance and adoption of the report of the Commission on

Accredited Schools, Draper objected, acknowledging he was a "doubting Thomas about this whole thing." He wanted to agree with the other members and did not want the University of Illinois hurt by his opposition, but needed some convincing. "I would like to get into this whole subject rather thoroughly," he explained, by asking questions of his colleagues, particularly Judson, "for whose opinion I have the highest regard and respect."[15]

Judson discussed the nature of action by the NCA and the purposes of accrediting. Supporting Carman's argument, he asserted that accrediting "is not legislation by the Association, in the sense of binding any of the members of the Association," but it was "a voluntary affair on the part of such colleges and secondary schools as see fit to take it up." He affirmed that "the fundamental principle of this Association is absolute freedom," and that this was the "sentiment of the entire Association." Judson suggested accrediting had several purposes. It aided the student by supplying a uniform system of high school graduation requirements that made entry into any college or university in the region likely. Accrediting gave collegiate institutions assurance about the academic preparation of the student. Secondary schools benefited because, "when this system is worked out and the whole thing is somewhat unified, a great deal of that inspection will become unnecessary, and will be dropped." Accrediting provided uniformity that eliminated multiplication of effort and expense. As a result, NCA accrediting simplified and strengthened relations between secondary schools and colleges, thereby meeting the primary goal of the Association.

Draper then shifted the focus to other concerns. He asked how accrediting would improve education. Judson answered that the standards provided motivation and guidelines for improving conditions. Draper inquired about schools whose resources did not meet the standards and observed, "I for one think that the great body of high schools are doing all they can." Judson drew upon his previous experience in Minnesota, noting that schools often believed they were doing all they could, but when pushed found more was possible. Draper then raised the issue of school inspection. Judson claimed the NCA plan would not interfere with existing institutional certification programs. Instead, where agencies existed the Association hoped to employ their inspectors. Only where no agency existed would the NCA fill the void. Questions were raised over the cost of accrediting and the Commission plan to assess levies by the size of the freshman class. Judson explained how the funding program would work, noting, "our secretary will write to President Draper requesting him to inform us how many freshmen he has." Draper replied that conditions varied in the colleges, and that his view might differ from other presidents'. At this point, the serious discussion turned briefly to a humorous exchange that helped ease the tension. Judson answered, "President Draper's view is law for the University of Illinois." Draper demurred, saying, "Very far from it. Now you've gone wrong. But then good men go wrong once in a while." Judson repeated his claim and Nightingale interjected, "As a member of the Board of Trustees of the University of Illinois, I want to say that Dean Judson is correct," leading to laughter from the members assembled.

The final topic of discussion was the proposed list of accredited schools. Some delegates complained about the embarrassing omission of some schools included on their state university's list. Draper's motion that the list be withdrawn passed. Professor Edmund James of Northwestern University then urged acceptance of the report, but claimed Draper's support was crucial. James asked if the University of Illinois president was converted. "Oh yes, I am," Draper answered, observing, "I want to make you all happy." The Association then unanimously adopted the report. However, the question of expenses was tabled after Draper suggested paying the small amount expended out of "ordinary revenues of the Association."[16]

The 1903 debate over accrediting showed how the town hall character of the early annual meetings allowed members to resolve differences of opinion. All delegates assembled were free to express their opinions in open session and enjoyed the same voting power. The CAS made no decisions, but instead presented a report for review and approval by the members at large. The prevailing spirit of participatory democracy made decision making difficult and time-consuming, but probably facilitated gaining a consensus when considering actions. By taking large programs and dividing them into more manageable parts, the sessions both enhanced understanding and reached compromises. The exchange with Judson and the ensuing discussion may not have totally allayed

Edmund J. James. University of Illinois president, James was NCA president in 1908.

the concerns of Draper or others. His questions regarding inspection, overtaxing school resources, and institutional freedom likely reflected those of other members. But the careful reiteration of basic Association principles regarding advisory functions, voluntary actions, and noninterference with the activities of institutions reassured members that neither legislation nor regulation was proposed. In addition, those participating in the discussion made sure it did not become too bitter and personal. Draper emphasized his reluctance did not imply any criticism of the work of Judson or the Commission.[17] The humorous dialogue among Judson, Draper, and Nightingale lightened up a potentially tense moment. Draper's later rejoinder about making everyone happy also reinforced the professional nature of his opposition. Interestingly, his motions solved the dilemmas over funding and the first list of approved schools.[18]

ACCREDITING SECONDARY SCHOOLS

After the 1903 annual meeting, the NCA moved from discussing the viability of accreditation to implementing its program of accrediting secondary schools. The first list of 156 approved secondary schools from ten states appeared in 1904. Illinois had the most schools with thirty-four, followed by Michigan (twenty-eight), Ohio (twenty-six), Wisconsin (twenty-four), Iowa (eleven), Colorado (nine), Missouri (eight), Indiana (seven), Minnesota (six), and Nebraska (three). In selecting the schools, the CAS commented that it had "been very conservative, believing that such action would eventually work to the highest interests of both the schools and the Association."[19]

Judson also noted that accrediting was an ongoing activity. Most immediately, he saw a need to strengthen weaknesses in the procedures for accrediting schools, suggesting the work of the Board of Inspectors and the definition of the units of study offered ways of addressing this concern. In 1904, a constitutional revision tied accrediting to membership by restricting membership to institutions meeting the 15-unit graduation and college admission requirements. In addition, an annual fee structure was established of $10 for universities, $5 for colleges, and $3 for all other members, presumably to help pay accrediting costs.

By 1906, the first large-scale revision of the standards was completed. The revised set of eleven standards covered more areas of school operations and offered details on requirements. Following earlier recommendations, the first standard mandated fifteen units for graduation. Other revisions advised rejecting schools that had more than thirty students per teacher or if doubts existed over a school's efficiency. In addition, schools with under five teachers were excluded from consideration. Several standards explained procedural matters, such as how to fill out the "blank," or annual survey that each school submitted to receive accredited status. Another set the term of accreditation at one year. The secretary of the CAS was identified as the "organ of communication" with the schools, while inspectors were defined as those individuals employed by the state university or state government in that capacity. Where no state authority existed, the NCA would appoint an inspector.[20]

Over the next several years, the Association periodically revised and expanded the standards. The revisions increased their specificity and reflected the growing functional character of the Association as it sought to improve secondary education. In 1907, a major addition addressed the quality of school buildings, stating, "The location and construction of the building, the lighting, heating, and ventilation, the nature of the lavatories, corridors, closets, school furniture, apparatus, and methods of cleaning shall be such as to insure hygienic conditions for both pupils and teachers." This standard reflected a growing societal concern for public health, particularly in the schools.[21]

In 1908, a detailed statement of Association aims prefaced the standards. The first three aims clarified the purposes of the NCA and showed the organization was expanding its influence on secondary schools. The general objective was: "to bring about a better acquaintance, a keener sympathy and a heartier cooperation between the Colleges and Secondary Schools of this territory." The Association would meet this objective by solving educational problems and promoting "the physical, intellectual and moral well-being of students by urging proper sanitary conditions of school buildings, adequate library and laboratory facilities, and higher standards of scholarship and of remuneration to teachers." The statement of aims also emphasized that the NCA was "voluntary, organized and devoted solely to the highest welfare of the boys and girls of this territory, and it bespeaks the cordial and sympathetic support of all school men."[22]

To assess the accrediting program, the Association sponsored several intensive studies, including one published in 1916 as a *Bulletin* of the U.S. Bureau of Education. George Counts, a major educational reformer of the 1920s and 1930s, conducted this "statistical study based upon 1,000 annual reports sent in by principals of 1,000 high schools of the North Central Association during the first semester of the school year, 1913–1914." The survey asked for general information on the school including enrollment, date of organization, and date of first accrediting by the NCA. It also probed into:

1. The composition and qualifications of the teaching staff and their workload

2. The length of the school year

3. Graduation requirements and numbers

4. Class size

5. Detailed aspects of enrollment

6. Equipment

7. Course of study

8. The library

9. Optional areas on the last graduating class, student standings, and teacher salaries.[23]

In general, Counts concluded, "The requirements of the association are not being met by all the schools of the association." He had expected problems with compliance because "no system of standards could be drawn up which would be met by so large a body of schools representing so large a section of the country and such varied conditions." His analysis of class size and teacher/student ratio illuminated some defects in the NCA standards that made compliance difficult and sometimes self-defeating. The median class size was twenty-one-and-a-half students, but great variation existed throughout the region. Almost 7 percent of the students had classes with more than the NCA maximum of thirty students. The ratio increased with the size of the school. In large schools with more than a thousand students, 13.3 percent of the classes had over thirty students. Counts considered the wide variations in class size and the number of schools exceeding NCA recommendations as serious problems because they affected the efficiency of instruction. He reported even wider differences in student/teacher ratios. Acknowledging that "the number of students that can be handled most efficiently by a teacher depends partly upon the teacher," he concluded the teacher/student ratio was far from standard, and that in many classes "there are either too many or too few teachers." Counts suggested the problem was with the focus of the standards. The NCA examined the number of students per teacher rather than the number per class. He claimed this was a "misplaced emphasis..., [because] it is in the class that the instruction is given. The number of students per teacher may be very low, and yet the number of students much too high for efficient instruction."

Another problem was that the NCA did not enforce the standards. NCA accrediting required member schools to meet certain standards for admission that were "not of such a character as to prevent the individual public high school from carrying out its peculiar mission to its community." Yet, the Association did not require strict compliance with its standards. Counts advised the NCA either to enforce the standards or to revise them. He also recommended the Association conduct more exhaustive studies of all secondary schools in the region. "Standards could then be set up on the basis of the known facts with regard to school practices," he explained, "and the methods of admission to the association could be determined on a strictly empirical basis."[24]

The study by Counts and an earlier one by Walter A. Jessup and Lotus Coffman that reached similar conclusions stimulated a major revision of the secondary school standards in 1916. Despite significant alterations, the standards retained many of the features in use ten years earlier. The biggest difference was an increasing stress on quantification. Standard 1 required fifteen units for graduation, but counseled against more than twenty class periods per week and set the school year at thirty-six weeks. A unit course of study consisted of a total of not less than 120, sixty-minute hours of classroom work, "two hours of manual training or laboratory work being equivalent to one hour of classroom work." The standard on teachers contained three subsections. It kept the college degree requirement, but required completion of a four-year or 120-hour course of study. Other sections covered professional training, mandating eleven hours of education that included both pedagogy and the "special study of the subject matter." Teachers new to a high school were exempted from the revised requirements. Regarding the teaching load, the desirable number of students per class was twenty-five, though the original designation of thirty remained the maximum. Other revisions showed that the standards finally acknowledged that not all high school graduates continued their education in college. A manual training provision was included, and one standard specifically recommended "the introduction of the so-called vocational subjects... where local conditions render such introduction feasible," and recommended employing an adequate number of teachers trained in these subjects.[25] Though initially geared solely for the college-preparatory curriculum, accreditation now encompassed all aspects of secondary schooling.

The revisions reflected contemporary societal trends, particularly the increasing attempts at quantification. During the late nineteenth and early twentieth century, a national movement for standards arose in American society. It stressed quantitative measurement to achieve better efficiency, the most famous example being the scientific management ideas Frederick W. Taylor applied to the workplace. In a 1908 article, LeConte Stevens traced the origins of the standards movement to efficiency sought in business through the development of corporations. "One of the real benefits to the public due to the existence of great corporations has been the development of a general demand for standardization," he observed, noting that "everything must be measured that can be bought or sold. The results of work must be numerically compared; new units of measurement must be devised as soon as needed; secondary units must be derived from them; and familiarity with these must be readily attained by the public."[26]

Education played a major role in the standardization movement. In a 1935 article, Max McConn of Lehigh University called the period from 1890 to 1915 the "Age of Standards." He suggested that "the ideal of high academic standards...seems to have come to the fore in American education in the late nineties. Certainly when those of us who are now in our fifties were learning our trade, 'standards' was the great word, the new gospel, in our profession." He observed that everyone from teachers and principal to officials in state departments of education and college presidents believed their duty was to set, enforce, and continually raise standards.

McConn tied the movement to the disorderly conditions prevailing in education in the 1890s, claiming standards "brought order out of that chaos." Contemporary authors made similar points. LeConte Stevens saw the uncontrolled growth and proliferation of schools at all levels as major aspects of educational development. In 1902, another author suggested that unrestrained growth had gone too far, stating that "it is generally agreed that there are already too many universities in America."[27] Stevens declared, "In the work of education the process of standardization is as inevitable as in other great industries, despite the fact that the training of the young is not directly merchantable and that industrial competition is not so conspicuous here as in transportation or manufactures." In his argument, Stevens covered many of the same points discussed at the NCA meetings, including defining institutions, articulation between secondary and higher education, adequate facilities, the nature of the curriculum, and diploma mills.[28]

The NCA accrediting program fit uneasily into the quantitatively oriented standards movement. Standardization contradicted the early beliefs of the Association and its CAS. In 1902, the committee on unit courses had specifically stated its position against standardization. Fourteen years later, the Association appeared more willing to embrace the idea. But, as the Counts study showed, the question of enforcement remained an issue. Changing standards is one thing, applying them is another, particularly given the laxity of enforcement evident previously.

The enforcement difficulty was not caused by the absence of an administrative apparatus. The NCA had adapted the certificate system of college admission, pioneered by the University of Michigan, to meet needs of voluntary regional accreditation.[29] Under the Michigan model, the university sent inspectors to various schools desiring to have their students admitted by certificate. If a school passed the inspection, the certificate was issued and its graduates were guaranteed admission. This program had gained wide currency in the North Central region. Departments of education in several states also had inspection programs to assess the quality of education at various schools. The use of university and state inspectors provided for an easy transition from institutional to association governance. Secondary school administrators and faculty were used to being overseen by municipal and state governments, and to undergoing inspection by representatives from colleges and universities.

The difficulty was balancing the dictates of the standards movement with the democratic nature and policies of the Association. In repeatedly asserting that its actions were advisory and voluntary, the NCA went against the theory of mandatory, rigidly applied quantitative standards. The NCA policy of preserving the individuality and autonomy of the institution thus clashed with the desire for uniformity in the educational community. The Association had to maintain its basic organizational beliefs and, simultaneously, maintain its relevance by keeping up with changing educational trends.

THE DEVELOPMENT OF HIGHER EDUCATION ACCREDITING

The accrediting of institutions of higher education was a much more daring innovation. Charles Judd called the NCA vote to accredit colleges "one of the most astonishing actions that had ever been taken by an association.... Nobody had thought up to that time that colleges could be subjected to inspection." Many members opposed college accrediting because it required surrendering institutional autonomy. University of Michigan professor and school inspector Allen S. Whitney observed, "There was a feeling that colleges would look upon it as an interference with their own private domain and would resent it." He added that opponents felt "it was too delicate a movement to enter upon without more careful consideration."[30]

George Carman first raised the idea of accrediting colleges in his 1903 presidential address. CAS chair Harry Pratt Judson added his support the following year, commenting, "I confess, the proposition seems to me to be eminently fair."[31] Yet the initial consideration of the subject produced an unfavorable response. Chaired by Western Reserve University president Charles F. Thwing and including James B. Angell as a member, a CAS committee researching the requirements for the bachelor of arts degree reported its findings at the 1905 annual meeting. Observing that there was an "almost amazing diversity of requirements" for the degree, the committee questioned the feasibility of drawing up a list of accredited colleges, because the undertaking was "beset by serious difficulties." Yet, it tempered this opposition by suggesting that the membership requirements for the Ph.D. and college admission had great value in considering such a list.[32]

The movement received a significant push at the 1906 meeting. In his presidential address, George MacLean urged a more active course. Following William Butts' reasoning, he saw NCA action as part of a larger effort to secure national standards and offered the College Entrance Examination Board as a model for an "American Federation of Learning." MacLean asked, "At this meeting of the association is not the time ripe to extend the work of the Commission on Accredited Schools to make a provision for a list of accredited colleges to co-ordinate with a list of accredited schools?"

MacLean suggested the earlier idea on membership provided a point of departure, as did the experience in accrediting secondary schools. "We have the machinery in our present Commission on Accredited Schools and Colleges in the points as to teachers, equipment, etc., in the blanks [questionnaires] of our board of inspectors, points which may be paralleled for colleges." Accrediting colleges involved adaptation of existing Association machinery. Though MacLean referred to the Commission on Accredited Schools and Colleges in his speech, when he delivered the address, the name change had not yet occurred.[33]

Two other papers seconded MacLean's request for college accreditation. Approaching the subject from the perspective of granting college credit for advanced high school work, George Carman suggested accrediting colleges would instill some order into the chaos of college admissions programs. He moved that the name of the Commission on Accredited Schools be changed to include colleges. He admitted that "from the time of the preliminary meeting for organization until the present time there has been a decided difference of opinion on this question." But, he asserted, "if, however, the Association serves the purposes for which it was organized, it must meet and overcome these differences." Carman concluded with four reasons to support college accreditation. Three addressed the issue of providing college credit for advanced work in the high school. The other stated that "the time has come when we ought to do systematically and consistently what we have done in a haphazard sort of way since the organization of the Association." The following presentation by Superintendent E. I. Coffeen of Marshalltown, Iowa, repeated many of Carman's points.[34]

The CAS report immediately followed the Carman and Coffeen papers, prompting the Commission to appoint a committee to develop "a plan for inspecting and accrediting colleges," that included Dean Harry Pratt Judson of the University of Chicago (chair of the CAS), University of Colorado president James A. Baker (vice chair), and Carman (CAS secretary). A. F. Nightingale then proposed a two-part motion. The first section, recommending that the Commission change its name to include colleges, passed. The second, requesting the Commission "set in motion the machinery for the inspecting and accrediting of colleges," was tabled.[35]

Developments at the 1906 meeting undoubtedly helped the advocates of college accreditation, but outside events both heightened and delayed the NCA move into college accrediting. The founding of the Carnegie Foundation for the Advancement of Teaching and the General Education Board by John D. Rockefeller marked the prominent entry of private foundations into higher education. In 1907, MacLean noted that the college accrediting committee had postponed deliberations to see what course these foundations would pursue. Established to provide pensions for faculty, the Carnegie Foundation had joined the attempt to define a college. Since many NCA members sought Carnegie funds, it exerted an influence on deliberations. Other organizations also entered this field, including the National Association of State Universities and the American Association of Universities.[36]

The Commission offered a report that received careful consideration at the 1908 meeting. Chairperson George MacLean explained the committee's approach to college accrediting:

> Your Commission has been so cautious that we have been two years in turning over this subject, and to-day I wish you please to notice that we come before you in a tentative and cautious spirit.... The Commission represents equally secondary school men and college men; that the Commission represents not state university or private college but every institution simply on the democratic basis of membership in this Association. It comes without suspicion of representing either this or that element, secondary school or college, public or private institution, and it comes, in candor, pushed upon us by great educational movements.

He also claimed the report lacked originality, citing the influence of NCA school accrediting and the work of other organizations on the report.[37]

The report had two parts. A preliminary draft was followed by amendments apparently made by the Commission at its meeting just prior to the annual meeting. In addition, the unfinished state of the report indicated the committee was seeking the advice and counsel of the members. In fact, when John R. Kirk, president of the First District Normal School of Missouri in Kirksville, apologized "for asking so many questions, but I am unable to understand whether the chairman is making a report which, in behalf of his committee, he recommends for adoption, or whether he is securing our criticisms with a view eventually to having a report written out," MacLean replied that he desired the latter.[38]

For the first time, the membership had something concrete to examine and the Association provided ample time for critical deliberation. Professor Clarence A. Waldo of Purdue University, a founding member, asked about the effectiveness of applying the system since it involved only those institutions inviting inspection. MacLean answered by drawing upon the voluntary nature of the NCA and referred to the high school program where some "magnificent high schools...have not bowed the knee to this Association." He stated, "This Association is nothing but a voluntary association, lifting up standards, and those standards are open before the eyes of all men, and those who wish to adhere can get fair judgment and adherence, and those who do not wish to we bless in the name of the Lord."[39] The volunteerism that underlay the Association also applied to accrediting, with the implied assumption that all NCA actions were advisory. Most of the remaining discussion focused on technical aspects that required explanation and possibly later revision.

Due to time constraints, the discussion on college accrediting was continued the following day. The lengthy discussion showed the value of deliberation. When questions arose about the composition of the inspector corps, MacLean presented a compromise amendment that the inspecting team consist of two college inspectors from each state, the high school inspector, and "the other a president or dean of an institution in this Association from outside the state, to be appointed by the Commission." This combination followed MacLean's admonitions on originality and the Association policy of building on the past by making effective use of the secondary school accreditation program. The standards also mixed the existing criteria with new requirements geared specifically for colleges and universities. The draft applied the first nine secondary school standards to colleges and added four specifically for higher education on income, number of departments, and requirements for admission and graduation. The amendments, however, led to substantial changes, resulting in fourteen separate college and university standards. In the end, the report was returned to the

Commission with instructions to report on the accrediting standards at the next annual meeting.[40]

Having received much momentum, the college accrediting movement stalled the following year, but gained impetus for the future. MacLean reported that the committee had failed to gather the institutional information needed to study the standards. The shoddiness of the committee's work was also evident in the sketchy report that presented "in the main general principles and a few recognized practices," but did include a revised list of ten standards.

The first standard defined a college and the various levels of collegiate education. "The Standard American College is a college with a four years' curriculum with a tendency to differentiate its parts in such a way that the first two years are a continuation of, and a supplement to, the work of secondary instruction, while the last two years are shaped more and more distinctly in the direction of special, professional, or university instruction." For students not seeking professional or graduate training as well as for those "who are willing to lay a broader foundation for their professions than is laid by those who specialize at the end of the sophomore year in the university, the four years' college work may be treated as a unit." For those who have chosen their professions, "the last two years in the best independent colleges should provide ample opportunity for training preliminary to the professions." A college education was both an end in itself and a transition from secondary to university work. Institutionally, the lines were blurred, for as the standard concluded, "the independent college may thus become a co-operative university college."[41]

By overlapping the levels of education, the standards provided a smoother flow to the schooling process. The definition also addressed concerns over the harmful effects of dividing education into distinct parts that broke the student's path from the elementary through the college grades. James B. Angell had mentioned this problem in the first NCA presidential address. Yet, the standards also maintained the distinctiveness of the college as an educational unit at a time when some educators believed the rise of the university threatened the college's survival.[42] In addition, the abstract nature of the definition allowed for significant institutional diversity and freedom.

The next seven standards covered areas similar to those of the secondary schools, though with different emphasis. The recommendation was that college teachers have graduate study and training equal to the Ph.D. However, the minimum was the "equivalent to graduation from a college belonging to this Association, and graduate work equal at least to that required for a Master's degree." Most important, the standard stressed "an instructor's success is to be determined by the efficiency of his teaching and not by his research work." Acknowledging that teaching load varied by department, the relevant standards offered no set requirement, suggesting instead that class preparation time, study needed to keep up with the subject, and the number of students determine how many courses an instructor taught. Admission to college required fourteen secondary units, and students needed twelve college units or 120 semester hours to graduate. The fifth standard identified the "chief factors in determining eligibility...," vaguely stated as "the character of the curriculum, the efficiency of instruction, the scientific spirit, the standard for regular degrees, the conservatism in granting honorary degrees, [and] the tone of the institution." A major factor noted in standard eight was the ability of colleges to prepare students for advanced training, meaning admission to graduate school without conditions.

The last two standards explained the administration of the accrediting process. Membership required the filing of a triennial blank, actually a survey form, a change from the annual blanks required from secondary schools. The last standards named the local inspector as "the organ of communication between the College and the Commission."[43]

A significant omission was the curriculum. Edward Harris defined a college unit course of study as "a course covering an academic year that shall include in the aggregate not less than one hundred and fifty sixty-minute hours of classroom work." Two hours of laboratory, drawing, shop or fieldwork equaled one hour of classroom time. The defining of a unit course represented a breakthrough. It offered a guideline for standardizing the length of undergraduate study, making graduation requirements and acceptance of college credit for high school work more uniform. But the content of the curriculum was not addressed. Though a major aspect of secondary school accrediting, the curriculum remained an institutional matter in the higher education program. The Commission also favored "the general principle" of awarding college credit for secondary school studies. Advanced credit required work done beyond the fifteen admission units and typically required a full year of study. A proviso softened this requirement, allowing credit where "half units are specified in the definitions of the unit courses, or for any study that is not pursued later than the second year of the high school course."[44] The college determined the amount of advance credit awarded. In this way, the NCA followed the practice of establishing general guidelines but not dictating their specific application to member institutions.

Acknowledging that more work was needed, MacLean asked that the Association continue the college accrediting work and approve the machinery. Apparently, no discussion ensued and no action was taken either on the report, on continuing the work of the committee, or on the accrediting machinery.[45] An interesting sidelight is that the NCA college accrediting program was prodded by outside influences. MacLean had reported that other organizations developing college standards, including the National Association of State Universities, the Association of American Universities, and the Carnegie Foundation, hoped "that within two years...we [the NCA] can have reasonable and fair standards for what will be called a standard American University." Thus, the NCA entry into college accrediting was not an isolated phenomenon, but was part of a national, though not a coordinated, effort.[46]

Perhaps in recognition of the lagging pace and the watchful eyes from outside, the Association passed a constitutional amendment that stated: "After April 1, 1912, no college or university shall be eligible to membership which is not on the list of accredited colleges of the Association."[47] This amendment gave the Commission a deadline of three years to develop an accrediting program that included a list of approved institutions. The alternative was the dissolution of the NCA because of the ineligibility of all its higher education members. Actually, by 1909, the Commission had made significant, albeit slow progress. Any accrediting program has three basic components: administrative machinery, measures of assessment, and a list of approved institutions. By 1909, the administrative apparatus was designed and awaiting implementation. The standards were complete enough to act as guidelines, and a timetable for implementation was established. Unfortunately, in the following three years, progress was slowed by resistance from state universities and a general dereliction of duty.[48]

Professor Charles H. Judd of the University of Chicago School of Education became involved with the NCA in approximately 1910. In the 1930s, he recounted the problems college accrediting encountered, acknowledging that opposition to the idea produced much stalling and dereliction of duty, leading to some very arbitrary and questionable decisions. In 1912, Judd was secretary for the Commission on Accredited Schools and Colleges. He recalled that the inability to develop a list in 1910 led the Commission to delegate the task to state university presidents. The following year they reported, in Judd's words, "that the state universities did not find it convenient to try to classify the various collegiate institutions in their territory and there was no list."[49] This failure, he continued, led to the appointment of a special committee of nine that actually meant adding two more members to the original committee, Harry Pratt Judson and Frederick Bliss. Both were well-respected and active members, but apparently they too had little success in constructing a list.

Judd's tale of the development of the first list of approved colleges is best related in his own words.

> I was Secretary of the Commission at that time, and it was my duty to address the chairman of these nine men who had been appointed. I told him he was chairman and asked him to please get his committee together and prepare the list. He started for Europe immediately on the presentation of that demand. I then took up the second individual on the list and asked him if he would please proceed to prepare the list. I have forgotten what he did—something along the Biblical line—whether he bought himself a farm or a new wife, I don't remember. The members of the group of nine disappeared one after another until I came to the last member of the committee. He couldn't disappear because he was President of the North Central Association. I asked him what was to be done and pointed out to him the history of these operations I have described. He said, "We have to do something, don't we?"
>
> I said, "Quite so."
>
> "Well," he said, "I think it would be a good idea to make

up an approved list of all those colleges that have ever been members of the Association." And that was the first approved list.[50]

ACCREDITING COLLEGES AND UNIVERSITIES

After ten years of continuous if uneven work, the first list of colleges accredited by the NCA appeared without any use of the standards or the machinery of inspection. Instead, because of the inability to gain any assistance, NCA president George Benton made an executive decision. Membership equaled approval, meaning admission requirements determined the institutions that appeared on the list. This bizarre conclusion epitomized an effort beset by opposition and inefficiency. The care and effort that characterized secondary school accrediting was missing at the college level. Once the list was assembled, however, the Association returned to its normal procedures and began the process of scrutiny, evaluation, and revision that typified implementation of change.

The following year, the standards were applied, resulting in a published list of seventy-eight institutions. Questions arose over where normal schools fit since NCA policy traditionally defined them as secondary schools. The Commission initially placed them on a separate, unclassified list, creating a problem that continued for many years. Interestingly, this first list also included a new type of institution, as two junior colleges were included. In addition, the list placed an asterisk by six institutions that met all the standards except the one on endowment. Of these, four were approved the following year.[51]

In 1914, the Commission recommended major revisions, including a substantial expansion of the list because the standards applied almost exclusively to colleges of liberal arts and sciences, either freestanding or within a university. The Commission criticized the traditional policy of keeping the membership small and exclusive: it admitted that the policy "seems at first sight to have certain advantages. The relation to high schools seems to be relatively simple. The Association promises to be fairly homogeneous. The standards are relatively easy to enforce." But, the seeming homogeneity masked an incredible diversity among those colleges and universities already accredited. In 1913, at least four different types of institutions appeared on the list: universities, colleges, junior colleges, and normal schools. The Commission concluded, therefore, "in range of courses and in point of size the institutions now on the list differ very widely, so that the effort to keep relations within the Association simple can hardly be expected to succeed."

The Commission recommendation would democratize the accrediting process by expanding and alphabetizing the list. However, a comprehensive study of member institutions was needed to assess the existing standards and to make the necessary modifications. Following the compilation of the data, "the list shall then be submitted to the Commission and the Commission shall determine its standards with the facts before it." This scientific approach facilitated identifying categories "deemed essential to admission to a classified list, and prescribing limits in each category." The procedure also involved an annual review that meant "the list shall then be made up automatically." One potential result was the inclusion of specific statistical information on accredited institutions, such as the faculty; students matriculating and degrees awarded; the number of elementary, advanced, and professional courses; salary expenditures; and equipment. The Commission anticipated that "the result of the adoption of this plan will be the ultimate development of a system of rating which may be used for high schools as well as for higher institutions."

The report also recognized that "the administrative system for carrying out the enterprise is not negligible." The Commission recommended charging new institutions a $25 admission fee. Each new applicant also had to "open its records to the officers of the Commission and fill out such blanks [surveys] as the officers shall prepare." Every three years, each approved institution had to supply information the Commission needed to update the accredited list. Those already accredited paid a $10 annual fee. The funds received from these two fees financed the inspection visits, any expenses incurred regarding the blanks, correspondence, and the printing of reports.[52]

The NCA was not alone in seeking a better classification of colleges and universities. In 1914, U.S. Bureau of Education higher education specialist Dr. Samuel Capen, later a strong critic of accrediting but not of the NCA, extended an invitation to the

Association to cooperate in the Bureau's plan "to publish from time to time a classification of colleges and universities with reference to their standards and equipment." This cooperative venture involved twelve other associations and foundations, including the NEA, the other regional associations, the Association of American Universities, the National Association of State Universities, the American Medical Association, an engineering organization, the College Entrance Examination Board, and the Carnegie Foundation. The Association appointed Horace A. Hollister of the University of

Horace Hollister. Illinois state director, NCA Commission on Schools, 1902–28, Hollister was instrumental in developing standards for accreditation.

Illinois as NCA representative.[53] The Bureau of Education effort showed that the movement to standardize institutions of higher education had national dimensions and had assumed various approaches. Accrediting was a method of standardizing education. Entrance exams, the Carnegie approach using funding and definitions, and classifying institutions—the legal purview of the education bureau—were other means.

In 1915 and 1916, the NCA published two studies of member institutions that also evaluated its higher education accrediting program. The first was an internal investigation while the second was conducted by Charles H. Judd of the University of Chicago and published as a *Bulletin* of the U.S. Bureau of Education. Both concluded that serious problems existed with the accrediting program. For example, a major difficulty was applying the standards for faculty preparation. The 1915 study reported that only six of the sixty-three institutions responding reported that 90 to 100 percent of their faculty possessed the master's degree, though this was the minimum NCA requirement. Two out of every three faculty had an advanced degree, but only one in three possessed a doctorate. In commenting on these findings, the Commission on Accredited Schools and Colleges concluded, "The scholastic preparation of college instructors... requires a very liberal interpretation," and that "the degree cannot be regarded as in any sense of the word a requirement."[54]

Despite problems in certain areas, the 1915 study found that many standards were met by institutions. Most colleges and universities exceeded the NCA admission requirements and complied with the required hours for graduation. The endowment standard had been "enforced with increasing rigor over the past two years," but indebtedness often counterbalanced the actual amount. Only junior colleges gained admission without the $200,000 minimum. The report recommended changing the endowment figures. "It should be pointed out that $100,000 annual income is a very much higher requirement for these institutions supported by the state than is the endowment requirement for private institutions." Municipal universities seldom met this standard and neither did many normal schools. As a result, the Commission recommended lowering the endowment figure for tax-supported institutions to $50,000. The institutions reporting easily met the minimum number of faculty standard, but many instructors taught more than the maximum of eighteen classroom hours per week. However, "it was repeatedly pointed out that this standard cannot be made to apply to members of the faculty who have laboratory courses."[55]

The NCA procedures to implement change allowed for quick identification of problems and equally rapid action to eliminate the difficulties. Only four years after applying the first collegiate standards, a comprehensive study of the accrediting program was conducted. Implementation followed by evaluation and revision were standard operating procedures to meet changing conditions or redress mistakes. The process of initial development involved a slow process of planning and development that reflected the voluntary nature of the work and the need to gain support for any new action. However, maintaining agreement implied accelerating the process to meet institutional objections swiftly, particularly in a new area like college accrediting where no guidelines, custom, or institutional experience existed.

THE IMPACT OF ACCREDITING

The transformation of the NCA into an accrediting association profoundly affected its development. Accreditation represented a direct, innovative attempt to control the educational environment by defining more clearly the region's school community. In pursuit of this goal, the Association largely redefined itself in a variety of ways leading to major alterations in some basic NCA policies. The policy of maintaining a small organization was abolished in 1908 and later reinforced by the Commission of Accredited Schools and Colleges' recommendation in 1914. Since accreditation was applied regionally to secondary schools and collegiate institutions, the idea of having a small minority dictate the standards clashed with the democratic philosophy of the Association. In addition, an accredited institution deserved the option of joining the organization. Initially, there was no connection between accrediting secondary schools and membership in the NCA. When higher education accrediting really began in 1913, accredited status was tied to membership. In 1916, the same provision was added to schools accreditation. As a result, by 1917, 598 institutions had joined the NCA; secondary schools outnumbered colleges and universities by a ratio of over ten to one.[56] Not surprisingly, the opening up of the Association led to tying accreditation to membership.

The changes in admission requirements showed that the organization was mature and confident enough not to fear domination by numbers. Expanding the Association also reflected the NCA's increasing influence over the region's educational community. The growing number of members increased its power while the high status achieved by accreditation enhanced its influence. In the process, the NCA was transformed from an exclusive club to a select but open association.

A related development was the substantial redefinition of the NCA territory. The original ten member states fit within popular conceptions of the north central region. However, factors beyond geography contributed to defining the region. Although the geographic core certainly was a criterion, the western states fit historian William Cronon's ideas on the sphere of influence of Chicago. In *Nature's Metropolis*, Cronon suggested that Chicago was the gateway for the West, exerting a major economic, social, and cultural influence on the region.[57] The centrality of the midwest metropolis made the initial inclusion of Minnesota, Kansas, and Nebraska quite natural. It also facilitated the later acceptance of Colorado, North and South Dakota, Wyoming, and Montana. However, the expansion into West Virginia, Oklahoma, New Mexico, and Arizona indicates another influence.

At the 1916 annual meeting, New Mexico State Superintendent of Education White argued for admission of his state into the NCA. He noted that the railroad system facilitated travel as it took less time to get to Chicago from Santa Fe than it did from Denver. He also noted, "our ideals have been molded largely from the state of Colorado, and we are in continuity there with Colorado." The Kansas and Missouri educational systems had also influenced New Mexico schools. Suggesting there was an interchange of teachers and students between New Mexico and the NCA states, White concluded, "Our relations are all with you people and this Association.... We are a part of you here." The NCA agreed and admitted New Mexico to its territory. In conjunction with this action, Horace Hollister proposed a change in the Constitution, leading to the inclusion of the phrase in Article II, "and such other territory as the association may recognize."[58] The NCA thus defined its region by compatibility of educational systems and interchange of students and teachers.

The tremendous increases in members and territory overtaxed the Commission on Accredited Schools, leading to constitutional changes that dramatically altered the organization's structure. The movement was initiated by the presidential address by James E. Armstrong, principal of Englewood High School in Chicago, at the 1915 annual meeting. Armstrong requested that the Association appoint a Committee to Revise the Constitution, comprised equally of secondary and collegiate representatives. Chaired by

Thomas Arkle Clark. Dean of men at the
University of Illinois, Clark was secretary of
the Association, 1906–15, and president in
1916.

Dean Thomas Holgate of Northwestern University, its members
included George Carman, Charles Judd, Deans James V. Denney of
Ohio State University and Thomas Arkle Clark of the University of
Illinois, University of Michigan professor Calvin O. Davis, Inspector
James Eliff of the University of Missouri, and Principals Henry E.
Brown of New Trier High School and Milo Stuart of Indianapolis.[59]

The revised constitution adopted in 1916 completed the re-
creation of the NCA begun by the move into accrediting. It established the structure of the organization for the next sixty years. The
major change was the creation of three separate commissions for
higher education accrediting, secondary education accrediting, and
curriculum and unit courses. The changes occurred rapidly because
the alterations institutionalized the ongoing, informal drift of

Calvin O. Davis. Professor of Education at the University of Michigan, Davis was first editor of the *NCA Quarterly* (1926–41) and Secretary of the Commission on Schools (1914–26); he wrote the fifty-year history of the Association.

development, and the need for better administration was so pressing. The accrediting functions, in particular, required a different organization. The centralization in one commission was unwieldy and inefficient, possibly contributing to the poorly managed development of the collegiate program. By raising the former accrediting committees to the commission level, the NCA enhanced their status and potentially increased their effectiveness. The curriculum commission connected the two accrediting bodies and maintained vital lines of cooperation and communication. Maintaining regular channels of communication became more important because the constitutional revisions lessened the collective, personalized nature of decision making. The annual meetings, of course, continued to serve communication purposes. Though dividing the previously united organization by level and function, the revisions kept the Executive Committee as the central Association authority.

The creation of a separate commission also reflected the special attention NCA had paid to the curriculum. Accrediting had ordered the college admissions process in a way that required defining the content of the high school course of study and had led to the fulfilling of Henry Wade Rogers' 1898 proposal for curriculum committees. In 1902 and in 1910, the Commission on Accredited Schools had expanded beyond the bounds of college preparatory courses, designing comprehensive programs of the secondary school curriculum development. Regarding the 1910 initiative, subject committees consisting of secondary and higher education representatives, roughly evenly divided, developed detailed descriptions of unit definitions and reading lists, offered advice on other resources, and suggested preferred instructional methods. The final report contained unit courses in thirteen subjects, offering combined descriptions of Latin and Greek, and French and Spanish. A committee designed nine commercial courses, including, interestingly, the "Economic History of England" and the "Economic History of the United States." The latter was "a study of American history with special attention to the economic factor." The manual training trend was recognized by twelve unit descriptions that fit into three general categories: "(1) the mechanic arts (shop work, drafting); (2) household arts (sewing, cooking); (3) freehand drawing and applied arts."[60]

The unit course descriptions differed from the standards in that they represented indirect attempts at improving education. Following in the tradition of the Committee of Ten and other similar efforts, the unit courses were guides that provided ideas on ordering the curriculum and making college admission requirements more uniform, both long-standing concerns of the NCA.

RE-CREATING THE NCA AND THE ASSOCIATION COMPACT

The re-creation of the NCA to meet changing needs is a major theme of its history. Over a course of one hundred years, the NCA undertook three major transformations. Accrediting was the first and the most important because it established the identity of the organization. The political character of voluntary associations allowed the Association to drastically change its nature, operations, and structure.[61] The NCA was created by a social compact that defined its organizational purpose. The Association constitution outlined the methods used to meet the purpose and also detailed the rights and obligations of members. They also enjoyed any benefits accruing from joining the NCA. In return, members surrendered a level of institutional autonomy and assumed various obligations, such as adhering to the organization's policies and participating in their determination. Involvement was both a right and an obligation. It also determined the viability of the organization. Too little participation in organizational activities meant little progress made in improving relations. Too little compliance with Association policies and procedures could doom any initiative, including accrediting. Commitment to the compact determined the fate of the organization.

The development of accrediting sorely tested the compact. The resistance of some higher education members to voluntary accrediting, along with the many deviations from the standards at the secondary and collegiate levels uncovered by Counts and Judd, threatened the success of accreditation and the viability of the NCA. In 1915, James E. Armstrong pointed out a specific instance of noncompliance with Association policies that made some institutions question the value of the organization. He reported that three large universities had accepted graduates from a large city high school recently dropped from the NCA for accrediting violations. Armstrong warned that breaking a basic Association policy tested the integrity of the organization. High schools asked, he noted, "Of what use is this Association if the universities accept the high school graduates whether the school is on the list or not?" The larger issue was whether the colleges and universities employed a double standard regarding accreditation. "The colleges have not regarded themselves as bound by the Association's standards or by any of the principles which they have enforced in their treatment of the secondary schools," Charles Judd complained in his 1915 study.[62] Interestingly, the high school violation of the standards was not as vociferously or as publicly condemned.

Given the noncompliance of many schools, a double standard apparently guided the enforcement of the NCA policies. The accrediting standards were not applied equally to all members because not every deviation led to expulsion. Another issue was whether expulsion was a fit penalty. Armstrong raised this latter point in his presidential address. He did not criticize the universities for accepting graduates from the dropped high school, but he suggested their action raised questions, in his words, about the sanity of some policies. He criticized a method that developed rules respected by neither the Association nor its members and that punished every offense with expulsion.[63] From Armstrong's standpoint, the problem was not with the members or their commitment to the NCA, but with the defects of the accrediting program and the Association policies. In this context, noncompliance identified problem areas that needed attention, and did not always imply resistance to the idea of accrediting or the purpose of the Association. For example, in his study, Judd had noted that few higher education institutions met the standards of requiring a doctoral degree for faculty. In his capacity as secretary of the accrediting commission, he also reported receiving many complaints from members about this provision.[64]

The real issue for the Association was how it responded to member complaints and noncompliance. Expulsion, as Armstrong indicated, was a questionable policy. Following the NCA philosophy and the constitutional tradition of voluntary associations, the recognition that the ongoing need for change meant all actions were imperfect and subject to revision provided a safety valve to relieve member discontent. The dynamic, evolving character of the NCA strengthened its compact. Since everything was open to alteration, members knew that opposition over time could produce revisions that removed objections. They also recognized that their participation played a part in securing redress. Protest, then, was another right of members. It opened up a channel of communication between institutions and Association officials to facilitate resolution of issues. But, rights incurred obligations.

In the final analysis, members seldom took the final step of withdrawing from the Association because their commitment to the social compact of the organization remained strong. But a fine line existed between exercising the right of protest to identify problem areas and not fulfilling one's obligations to the organization. A balance was needed between the standards imposed on institutions and the character of the standards. As Armstrong explained, "We need, then, to have a more complete and generous surrender of consent of the governed and at the same time a more carefully considered set of rules by which our list shall be regulated, if we are to strengthen our organization."[65] The development of the NCA has revolved around accommodating member rights and obligations while it pursued its goals.

NOTES

1. Edward W. Coy, "Presidential Address," NCA *Proceedings* (1909): 4
2. Charles H. Judd, "VIII. Discussion of the Report on the Revision of Standards," in "Reports Relating to the Revision of Standards for Institutions of Higher Learning," NCA *Quarterly* 9: 212–13.
3. Armstrong, "Presidential Address," 7.
4. Stephen A. Forbes, "The Desirability of So Federating the North Central Colleges and Universities As to Secure Essentially Uniform or At Least Equivalent Entrance Requirements," NCA *Proceedings* (1900): 11–12, 19.
5. Ibid., 13, 17–20.
6. For the comments of Halsey and Holgate, see ibid., 21–24.
7. Ibid., 70–71.
8. "Report of the Commission on Accredited Schools," in "Appendix" to the NCA *Proceedings*, 1902, 6–7.
9. Ibid., 39–40.
10. Ibid., 41–43.
11. Ibid., 8–11.
12. Ibid.
13. Ibid., 37–38.
14. George Carman, "Presidential Address," 7.
15. Ibid., 63–64.
16. Ibid., 67–68, 87–90.
17. Draper's praise of Judson was sincere. The two men apparently enjoyed good personal relations. When Draper left the region for a position in New York the following year, Judson wished him well and expressed a sense of loss in very complimentary terms. NCA *Proceedings*, 1904, 66.
18. Ibid., 43–44.
19. NCA *Proceedings* (1906): 125–26.
20. Ibid.
21. NCA *Proceedings* (1907): 56–57;
22. NCA *Proceedings* (1908): 75.
23. George Counts, "Accredited High Schools of the North Central Association of Colleges and Secondary Schools," in *A Study of the Colleges and High Schools of the North Central Association*, by Charles H. Judd, U.S. Bureau of Education *Bulletin* 6 (1916): 47–49, 53, 131–32.
24. Ibid., 127.
25. This was adopted in 1912. NCA *Proceedings*, 1912, 30.
26. W. LeConte Stevens, "College Standardization," *Popular Science Monthly* 73 (December 1908): 528.
27. Max McConn, "Academic Standards and Individual Differences—The Dilemma of Democratic Education," *The School Board Journal* (December 1935): 44. This article is the reprint of a speech given at the 71st Convocation of the University of the State of New York on October 18, 1935. Most of McConn's address criticized aspects of the standards movement and offered solutions to the abuses. Herbert Horwill, "A National Standard

in Higher Education," *Atlantic Monthly* 90 (September 1902): 329; Stevens, "College Standardization," passim.

28. For the views of two high school visitors, see Stephen D. Brooks, "The Work of a High School Visitor," *The School Review* 9 (January 1901): 26–33; Allen S. Whitney, "Methods in Use of Accrediting Schools," ibid. 11 (February 1903): 138–48. Brooks was a high school visitor for the University of Illinois. Whitney's article was a reprint of a speech he gave at the annual meeting of the Middle States Association.

29. Howard H. Peckham, *The Making of the University of Michigan, 1817–1967* (Ann Arbor: University of Michigan Press, 1967).

30. Judd, "VIII. Discussion of the Report on the Revision of Standards," 212; Armstrong, "Presidential Address," 8; Grinnell, "The History of the North Central Association of Colleges and Secondary Schools," 216. Grinnell's information came from correspondence with Armstrong and Whitney in 1934.

31. Charles F. Thwing, "Requirements for the Bachelor's Degree," NCA *Proceedings*, 1905, 46, 50; 15. George Carman, "Presidential Address," 7–18.

32. George MacLean, "Presidential Address," NCA *Proceedings*, 1906, 20–21. In what became a continuing pattern, the *Proceedings* provided no account of any discussion following the report at the meetings of the Commission on Accredited Schools or the Association, perhaps indicating that none occurred.

33. George Carman, "Shall We Accredit Colleges?" 82, 85–89, 95–96, and E. I. Coffeen, "The Inspection and Accrediting of Colleges and Universities," 96–107, in ibid.

34. Harry Pratt Judson, "Report of the Commission on Accredited Schools," ibid., 124, 130.

35. Interestingly, MacLean represented the National Association of State Universities, while Allen Whitney represented the NCA at the National Conference. NCA *Proceedings* (1908): 41.

36. George MacLean, "Report of the Commission on Accredited Schools," NCA *Proceedings* (1908): 94–96, 98, 101. The General Education Board and Carnegie Foundation histories and impact on higher education are briefly covered in Merle Curti and Roderick Nash, *Philanthropy in the Shaping of American Higher Education* (New Brunswick, N.J.: Rutgers University Press, 1965), 173–74, 223–25. See also, Raymond B. Fosdick, *Adventure in Giving: The Story of the General Education Board* (New York: Harper & Row, 1962); and Howard J. Savage, *Fruit of an Impulse: Forty-Five Years of the Carnegie Foundation* (New York: Harcourt, Brace, 1953).

37. Cited in ibid., 104, 107–108, 114.

38. Ibid., 121–22.

39. Cited in ibid., 104, 107–108, 114.

40. George MacLean, "Report of the Commission on Accredited Schools and Colleges," NCA *Proceedings* (1909): 50–51.

41. For Angell's comments, see his "Presidential Address," 12.

42. MacLean, "Report of the Committee on College Standards," NCA *Proceedings* (1909): 52–54.

43. Edward L. Harris, "Report of the Committee on Definition of Units," ibid., 58; "Report of the Commission on Accredited Schools and Colleges, NCA *Proceedings* (1908): 6.

44. "Report of the Commission on Accredited Schools and Colleges," NCA *Proceedings* (1909): 51–52.

45. For Harris' comments, see ibid., 58. On the amendment, see ibid., 17.

46. "Report of the Commission on Accredited Schools and Colleges," NCA *Proceedings* (1909): 51–52.

47. George MacLean, "Report of the Committee on College Standards," ibid., 52.

48. NCA *Proceedings* (1913): 63–65; 1914, 43–45.

49. Judd, "VIII. Discussion of the Report on the Revision of Standards," 212–13. The *Proceedings* for the 1912 annual meeting do not confirm Judd's account, but they do not refute it either.

50. Ibid.

51. NCA *Proceedings* (1913): 63–65; (1914): 43–45.

52. Ibid. (1914): 46–49.

53. Capen addressed the NCA Commission on Accredited Schools and Colleges on March 19, 1914. The *Proceedings* do not contain a transcript of his address. NCA *Proceedings*, 1914, 119–20.

54. Charles H. Judd, "Report on the Approved Colleges and Universities of the North Central Association of Colleges and Secondary Schools," in Judd, *A Study of the Colleges and High Schools of the North Central Association,* in *U.S. Bureau of Education Bulletin* 6 (1916), 20, 22–24. Compliance with the class size standard was a problem in large institutions.

55. Ibid., 13–14.

56. NCA *Proceedings* (1917): 166–78. There were also fifty-six individual members.

57. See William Cronon, *Nature's Metropolis: Chicago and the Great West* (New York: W. W. Norton, 1991).

58. NCA *Proceedings* (1916): 77–79, 230. Another factor that probably prompted the requests of the far western states like Arizona and Montana was the absence of any other association. The Northwest Association was founded in 1917 and the Western in 1924. After World War II, when the NCA began accrediting overseas schools, the full impact of Hollister's motion became evident.

59. James E. Armstrong, "Presidential Address, NCA *Proceedings*, 1915, 17. On the committee appointment, see ibid., 25. He also recommended hiring a permanent director and incorporating the Association, thereby seeking even greater formal administration and legal status. Interestingly, another recommendation focused on securing legislation on degree-conferring institutions, indicating the problem Henry Wade Rogers first brought to the attention of the NCA in 1898, remained an issue. Armstrong's suggestions for a permanent director and incorporation were rejected.

60. The later curriculum study appeared in the NCA *Proceedings* (1910): 76–146.

61. Sills, "Voluntary Associations: Sociological Aspects, passim.

62. Armstrong, "Presidential Address," 9; Judd, "Report on the Approved Colleges and Universities of the North Central Association of Colleges and Secondary Schools," 20.

63. Armstrong, "Presidential Address," 10.

64. Judd, "Report on the Approved Colleges and Universities of the North Central Association of Colleges and Secondary Schools," 22–23.

65. Armstrong, "Presidential Address," 10.

Chapter Four

The Midlife Change of the NCA

In the life of any organization, there are likely to come times when its usefulness and the need for its continued existence are seriously questioned. If in such critical periods the leadership fails to plan a program for continued usefulness and service, the organization is likely to cease to exist.

—Arthur W. Clevenger, Secretary
of the North Central Association, April 8, 1938[1]

THROUGHOUT ITS HISTORY, the North Central Association confronted critical times. Fortunately, its leaders responded with plans that allowed the organization to survive and often prosper. Between approximately 1916 and 1942, the Association experienced a prolonged period of crisis when its survival was in doubt and a creative response provided a new, strong path of development. Two events occurring in 1916 provide insight into why the Association successfully surmounted the challenges presented during a quarter century of change, questioning, and criticism. The first involved a group of high school principals who met to protest certain NCA actions. Jesse H. Newlon, later a prominent educational reformer, was principal of an NCA high school in Lincoln, Nebraska. He attended the meeting and is the sole source of information on the incident. Though the record is incomplete, apparently some members advocated forming a separate organization, but cooler heads prevailed. "We pointed out that the solution of the problems of articulation between the high school and college must be worked out cooperatively," Newlon related, "and that whatever the faults of the North Central Association might be, such an organization was indispensable to the solving of these common problems."[2] The common advantage the Association provided and the promise of its compact outweighed individual grievances. For most members, reform within the organization rather than secession became the preferred strategy for dealing with their complaints about the NCA.

How well the Association addressed the concerns of disgruntled members determined the strength of the compact that kept members within the organization. The second event was the 1916 constitutional revision that established the three-commission structure, enhancing the ability of the organization to change itself to meet member needs and to pursue the improvement of education. The changes were motivated by a crisis in the administration of the NCA accreditation program due to the expansion of accrediting to colleges, the growth in membership, and recognized flaws in the standards. Responding to calls for reform by NCA president James E. Armstrong in 1915, the constitution was amended so that accreditation responsibilities were divided between the Commission on Institutions of Higher Education (CIHE) and the Commission on Secondary Schools (CSS). Curriculum and other non-accrediting matters became the purview of the Commission on Unit Courses and Curricula (CUCC).

THE TRANSITION TO MODERN TIMES

The NCA's organizational overhaul came at a propitious time. The period between 1916 and 1942 was particularly turbulent, demarked by two world wars, a decade of relative prosperity followed by ten years of depression, and an underlying current of basic, permanent change in American society. Many contemporaries and later historians have considered the 1920s the advent of the modern age. Initially, World War I was seen as a watershed, sharply distinguishing two very different eras: a traditional time characterized by rural or small town values, informal organization, and a local orientation to life, and the emerging modern era of the national, mass society characterized by urbanization and formal, functional organizational tendencies backed by a scientific worldview and technological advances.

In his history of the 1920s, Ellis Hawley agreed it was hard to quarrel with those who felt "the war period constituted a great watershed in both American and world history.... In many ways the world of 1919 was a different world from that of 1914, and clearly the America of Warren G. Harding and Calvin Coolidge was not the America that had elected Theodore Roosevelt and Woodrow Wilson."[3] The widespread electrification of power in the home and workplace, the integration of the automobile and radio into everyday life, and the beginnings of commercial air travel heralded a revolution in technology that connected most Americans in new and intriguing ways. Technology also accelerated many aspects of life and work.

Socially, migration patterns changed radically between 1914 and 1919. The war and later government actions largely stopped overseas immigration into the United States, but the demographic mosaic of the country continued to evolve as hundreds of thousands of southern African-Americans left their rural homes seeking a better life in northern cities. The African-American migration helped the United States become a majority urban society for the first time in its history.

The economy also experienced a substantial shift in focus toward consumption, making the United States more a consumer than production-oriented society. The rapid rise of advertising reflected the consumption stress. A more subtle organizational movement sought to order society by creating more formal, functional, and impersonal modes of life and work.[4]

In education, too, many changes were evident. Historian David O. Levine claimed, "World War I proved to [be] the watershed in the history of American higher education." Among other things, Levine suggested that during this period colleges shed their elitist posture and became more democratic, citing the increased attendance of immigrant children as proof.[5] While college doors opened to a larger cross-section of the population, the high school evolved into a mass institution. Between 1920 and 1940, the number of young people between the ages of fourteen and eighteen attending high school increased by over four million. Where one in three attended in 1920, two in three were enrolled in 1940. Changing public perceptions of the role of the high school stimulated the dramatic enrollment increases. As upward mobility became tied to a high school diploma in the 1920s, "going to high school was increasingly the thing to do." The changing perception of the high school was connected to urbanization trends because as historian Edward Krug explained, "Particularly in cities and suburbs, it was accepted as one of the facts of life."[6]

Supported by trends in education, the high school was seen less as a preparation for college than an end of formal schooling, meaning that the fit-for-life function assumed more importance and the mission of schools became more comprehensive. The philosophy of former NCA member John Dewey gained great currency, stimulating the rise of the progressive education movement in the 1920s, a rather amorphous and motley collection of people and equally assorted, though often ill-defined, ideas that wanted to meet student needs better, including those beyond academics. Many progressive educators and other educational reformers believed the school was more than an institution of education. They considered it a community center that served varied needs of youth and adults, including some needs not connected to education, such as recreation. A related reform movement saw schools as instruments of social efficiency and suggested they should be the custodians of American youth.[7]

In some cases, educational goals and societal needs merged. For example, a major objective of secondary schooling during this period was the effective use of leisure time. Educational reformers were concerned with how Americans used their free time, as the idea of opening schools for recreational activities indicates. Several societal trends connected with modernity increased interest in leisure. The consumer society was based upon Americans' having free time to spend their money and enjoy their purchases. Technology provided various leisure activity opportunities, including travel by automobile or airplane, radio, and the movies. Another important factor was the rise of sports as major participant and spectator industries.[8]

In the 1920s, change was the watchword of the times. Many educators commented on both the fast pace and substantial impact of what they considered an ongoing transformation. In 1928, University of Chicago professor Charles H. Judd commented, "A generation has not passed since the world was transformed in its material and intellectual equipment." University of Buffalo chancellor Samuel P. Capen supported Judd's assessment, claiming that between 1914 and 1931, "The world has changed more radically than in any other seventeen years since man began to leave a record of his accomplishments." More soberly, he joined many others in predicting, "The process of change is going to continue."[9]

Connected to the frequent exclamations that the world was in the midst of a transformation were other prognostications on what impact these developments were having on the American people. Historian Roderick Nash has suggested that the perception of radical, massive, and fast-paced change created a sense of urgency or a nervousness that defined the generation of the twenties. This nervousness arose in part from the feeling of dislocation and lack of control over one's fate that accompanied the transition from traditional to modern society. "There has probably never been greater unrest in the world than today," observed Ohio State University professor D. H. Eikenberry in 1930. "The decline of traditional authority in our own day has plunged countless souls into the maelstrom of uncertainty, confusion, bewilderment."[10] The depression of the 1930s enhanced these feelings and the outbreak of World War II further increased the level of anxiety.

The reactions of Americans to the deep-rooted changes ranged from often violent rejection of change to fervent espousal of all things new and different. In the twenties, traditionalist opposition to modern trends fueled the rise of the Ku Klux Klan and animated the debate over the biblical and Darwinian explanations of creation that reached a zenith in the famous Scopes trial.[11] In education, the modernists pursued a campaign for change that was punctuated by strident criticisms of the status quo. In his 1972 history of the interwar high school, Edward Krug connected the reform movement in education to outside events, noting, "Social and economic upheaval called all traditions into question."[12] Jesse H. Newlon tied the educational reforms of the 1920s to a related scientific movement that reached a peak during that decade. He asserted, "The writings of social and educational philosophers, the discoveries of educational psychologists, and the researches and experimentation that have been carried out along scientific lines in every sector or field of education are bringing about far-reaching changes in the schools."[13]

THE NCA PHILOSOPHY OF CHANGE

The nature of post–World War I change and the responses to the rise of modernity place the history of the NCA in perspective because its survival and continued development depended on how well the organization adapted to remain in tune with contemporary educational thought and practice. Arthur Clevenger's comment at the beginning of this chapter speaks directly to the issue of changing to meet different needs. In 1926, Newlon directed a similar comment to institutions. He claimed that institutions unable to adapt to continuing change would lose their usefulness and become obstacles to progress.[14]

Given the widespread contemporary perception that World War I represented a break in time, the process of change and the relationship between past and present animated much discussion among contemporaries and later scholars. In his 1917 NCA presidential address, Principal Chester B. Curtis of Central High School in St. Louis offered a view that fit well with traditional Association thought. He suggested change did not involve sharp breaks between eras, but rather, "The present is always a time of adjustment between the best of yesterday and the prospective good of tomorrow." The process of change was stimulated by the almost intangible merging of generations, because "the interpretation of one age by another is subjected to a constant modification, and the needs of the future to as constant a revision." In education, Curtis concluded, the constant adjustment "produced a constant state of unstable equilibrium," leading to more study, progress, and ultimately new interpretations.[15] Curtis' idea that change is continual and that the past, present, and future are inextricably connected to an ongoing process was largely accepted by NCA figures.

The Association neither fulminated against the ongoing transformation to preserve tradition, nor wholeheartedly embraced everything new to the neglect of anything old. In 1920, Professor John E. Stout of Northwestern University headed a committee on revising the secondary curriculum. He prefaced a report on the project by noting, "Now, at the very outset, it need not be said that this is anything new." His committee operated under assumptions made as early as 1840 regarding the high school course of study. However, he also noted that the committee was using more modern, scientific approaches to curriculum development, such as intelligence testing, to determine individual student needs.[16] By 1927, the NCA had developed a more scientific and utilitarian method of inquiry. Referring to the same curriculum reform

John E. Stout. Dean of the School of Education at Northwestern University, Stout was
the first chair of the 1920s curriculum reorganization program and published "Standards for Reorganization of Secondary
School Curricula" in 1924 *Proceedings;* he
was active in NCA circles for many years.

project, Northwestern University professor L. W. Webb explained,
"Old material should be retained only when it has superior value to
anything which might take its place. New material, in many
instances, should be brought in but it should be subjected to most
careful scrutiny."[17]

The revisions made in the NCA philosophy of change helped
it remain relevant during a turbulent period in education. The Association was at the center of reform, contributing to the ongoing
development of education in two ways. On one hand, its activities
stimulated reform outside the NCA. On the other hand, the Association launched a significant reform effort in the late 1920s that
began the second re-creation of the Association. Though the second
re-creation continued into the 1960s, this chapter focuses on the
period from 1916 to 1942 when the new theory of accrediting was

developed. The implementation of the theory is the subject of chapters 5 and 6. Because it preceded the modernization of accrediting, the role the Association played as an agent of reform will be discussed first.

THE NCA AS REFORM AGENT: THE CURRICULUM REORGANIZATION PROJECT

One of the North Central Association's largest and longest reform projects was the reorganization of the secondary school curriculum. The effort expanded the work of earlier initiatives and was the last time the Association comprehensively addressed curricular issues. The NCA project was part of a national curriculum reorganization movement that responded to criticisms that the high schools were not meeting the needs of their students, in part because of the continued stress on college preparation. Critics claimed the college bias and other factors inhibited the ability of the schools to become custodians of American youth. Advocates of custodianship wanted to expand the responsibilities of the schools so they assumed socialization functions previously considered the purview of the family. The popularity of scientific management in educational circles and the continuing advocacy of "the nineteenth century idea of progress as the constant development of new techniques" also influenced the curricular reform efforts. The goals of custodianship and social efficiency as well as the use of scientific management principles were quite modern, but all had originated well before 1914 and so were hardly new. In other words, during the twenties and thirties, curriculum reform aimed at developing a modern high school course of study that built upon past ideas and practices to address present concerns about meeting the needs of all students.

As happened in the 1890s, a National Education Association commission triggered the high school curriculum movement after World War I. In 1918, the NEA Commission on the Reorganization of Secondary Education, chaired by Clarence Kingsley, issued the *Cardinal Principles of Secondary Education*. Hailed by some educators as the most significant study since the Committee of Ten report, *Cardinal Principles* reached very different conclusions. It recommended universal secondary education and supported a comprehensive curriculum organized around seven aims: health, citizenship, valuable use of leisure, home membership, ethical character, vocation, and the learning of fundamental processes. The *Cardinal Principles* served as a model for many other curriculum initiatives and influenced the NCA effort.[18]

The origins of the NCA Committee on Standards for Use in the Reorganization of Secondary School Curricula remains shrouded in the confusion that accompanied the setting up of the Commission on Unit Courses and Curricula. The curriculum project apparently began about the same time as the CUCC. Since the Commission experienced substantial organizational difficulties in its first three of four years, including the coming and going of several chairs, documentation on the founding of the curriculum committee is missing. The first progress report appeared in 1920 and indicates the committee had been working for some time. Committee chair Professor John E. Stout of Northwestern University explained that two old assumptions guided the work. The first was that certain subjects should be studied by all students. Reflecting the rise of the elective system and the *Cardinal Principles*, the second called for taking individual differences into account by providing additional subjects that met the diverse needs of students.[19]

The focus on the organization of secondary education was prompted by the high dropout rate. Only one of every four students entering high school in 1920 remained to finish their senior year. In 1921, Stout suggested part of the problem was that two classes of students entered the seventh grade, considered the beginning of secondary education. One group possessed the ability and disposition to graduate from high school. The other was unlikely to finish due to lack of ability, economic need, or lack of support and motivation. To address the retention problem, the committee developed the idea of two cycles of schooling based on a six-year period of secondary education. The cycles allowed for two stages of education, the first stage acting as a culmination of formal schooling for some students and as a gateway for the further education of others.[20]

Stout's 1921 report indicates that the committee possibly pioneered a new direction in serving NCA members. The project would not develop the ideal curriculum, but rather would identify basic considerations to guide schools reforming their curricula. As a result, the curriculum project was one of the first NCA efforts that specifically attempted to help schools learn how to change them-selves. While implicit in earlier curriculum initiatives and in the accrediting standards, the self-help aspect is much more clearly pronounced here. Reflecting the strategy of other projects prior to World War II, including the new theory on accrediting, the focus was on indirect contact through materials or special opportunities to engage in experimental projects.

The 1921 report also showed that the committee had made much headway in planning the project. The work was organized in three sequential phases: identifying educational objectives, relating these objectives to development of the curriculum, and suggesting an organization and administration for secondary education. Stout stressed the importance of the first phase, observing that "a clear determination of objectives is always fundamental in the process of curriculum making." They provided standards for evaluating exist-ing materials and also supplied criteria for developing new ones.

The committee actually developed two types of goals or aims. Stout explained, "Ultimate aims are stated in terms of disposition and abilities while the immediate ones must be thought of in terms of acquiring and developing." The ultimate goals organized the curriculum and showed the influence of the *Cardinal Principles*. They included maintaining health and physical fitness, using lei-sure time effectively, engaging successfully in vocational activities, and sustaining successful social relationships (civic, domestic, com-munity). The immediate goals explained how students would meet the ultimate aims. Acquiring fruitful knowledge came first and was subdivided into several areas: preparing for further learning, devel-oping dispositions, discovering and developing abilities, and learn-ing to control life situations. The second immediate aim was to develop attitudes, interests, motives, ideals, and appreciations, while the third stressed building skills in memory, judgment, imag-ination and the like. The fourth and last immediate aim was to acquire proper habits and useful skills.

The other two project phases were in the planning stages. The underlying assumptions of a core and elective curriculum promised guides that related the objectives to curriculum development. The committee planned to differentiate subjects and content as well as to organize and to sequence units to meet identified student needs, interests, and capacities. Though the college preparatory function did not dominate the thinking of the committee, it strongly influenced the selection of proposed common subjects. Though he named English, mathematics, and science as possible required subjects, Stout suggested that further research into common student needs would determine the prescribed curriculum.

By 1923, the committee had further refined its plans by organizing the work into four distinct stages. The first stage of developing objectives was in its final phases. The next step was using the objectives to define "the *qualitative* character of the units of instruction," defined by the committee as "the quality or kind of subject matter to be used and activities to be employed during a given period of the child's school career." It focused on the content and method of instruction, rather than its borders, the number of weeks, etc., because the committee reasoned, "units cannot be intelligently defined on a quantitative basis until their qualitative character has been determined." Defining the units quantitatively regarding the amount and kinds of materials to be included comprised the third stage. The final phase was organizing the units into curricula, ordering and sequencing them to "provide for the proper progress of pupils through the successive years of the secondary schools."[21]

Stout also reported that, following the procedures used in identifying the objectives, subject area subcommittees would develop the various units. Each subcommittee was chaired by a member of the larger curriculum committee, generally a university professor in education or a specialist in the teaching of a subject. R. M. Tryon of the University of Chicago, for example, was a professor in the teaching of history and headed that subject subcommittee. The subcommittee usually included members from higher and secondary education. However, some subjects were handled by one person. Olivia Pound of Lincoln, Nebraska, wrote the Latin unit, while Iowa State Teachers College professor W. H. Lancelot developed the one on chemistry. The work followed a general pattern of conducting special studies followed by the presentation of reports, often in the form of preliminary drafts that were reviewed by the entire committee. Upon receipt of the various comments, the reports were revised and presented to the Commission and NCA membership, especially secondary school teachers and administrators "to ascertain the best practice now available and also to secure the suggestions of these experienced administrators and teachers concerning revisions." Of particular interest, Stout explained, was information on the content of the units of instruction and the best types of materials.[22]

By 1923, the first units for development had been identified, focusing on "those subjects and fields... which seemed to be in need of rather fundamental reorganization." These were junior high school English, social studies, and general science, as well as ninth grade general science, physical education in various years, and vocational subjects. Other units developed for traditional academic subjects, included English, social studies, general science, chemistry, physics, mathematics, French, German, and Latin, as well as music, art, physical education, and vocational fields such as agronomy and home economics. A subcommittee also reported on extracurricular activities, showing that the curriculum extended beyond the traditional academic confines of the classroom. The coverage spanned the junior high and high school years but differed by subject.

Twenty-eight subcommittees had developed qualitative standards and had begun the quantitative stage of the work by 1928.[23] The preliminary report of the subcommittee on junior high social studies provides insight into the units. Noting its incomplete character, Chair R. M. Tryon of the University of Chicago commented, "It is hoped that the report as herein submitted might inspire some one to complete the job." Organized by grade level, the various social studies units showed differing levels of completion. The seventh grade covered only the social objective, and consisted of some detailed topics relevant to social studies and pertinent reading lists. The eighth grade included all four ultimate objectives—social, leisure time, vocational, and health—but it, too, was largely an organized list of detailed topics and relevant readings.

The ninth grade also spanned all four objectives and, more importantly, offered detailed descriptions of topics and student activities. The first section covered the social objective from the perspective of acquiring fruitful knowledge, focusing on the subheading, "preparative to acquiring other knowledge." Apparently, the goal of the section was to explore four basic ideas and practices regarding both the subject and its study. The dynamic quality of society was cited first with the observation that "the growth of our social institutions has been a long, slow process and even today they are constantly changing." As a result, the unit emphasized the fundamental historical theme of change over time. The second defined the learning process: "We grow by building on the past and by method of study we learn of past accomplishments." Next, books were identified as the means of securing knowledge and understanding.

The last topic provided students with a guide to using books effectively to gain knowledge. The social objectives section also listed pertinent readings that included texts such as Rowe, *Society, Its Origins and Development,* and novels. *Treasure Island* by Robert Louis Stevenson was on the list. The last part offered two student activity ideas. Students could write a report "on the growth of the city, school system, churches, industries, etc., of the locality." The other suggestion related to using books effectively. It required students to "analyze a number of books with respect to physical make-up and decide in which the work is done best." Other activities typically involved similar reports and research or answering questions related to the subject matter and objectives.[24]

The units were first published in the *Quarterly.* Their staggered completion meant that they appeared in various issues from 1927 to 1931. To achieve greater distribution, the Commission offered thirty reprints for sale at cost. By March 1930, 14,892 copies of the reprints had been sold, primarily in the north central region. Most cost ten cents each, but some units were bundled into sets. For example, for fifty cents, a school could order a single publication that included English, Latin, French, general science and biology, physics and chemistry, home economics, and physical education. The sales facilitated classroom testing of the units. The commission hoped that "teachers will try out the suggested materials in various kinds of situations, will offer constructive criticisms respecting the recommendations made, and will cooperate with the Commission in rewriting the proposals in the light of the experiences thus had."[25]

The committee received much feedback from schools. Unfortunately, the initial responses identified a problem with the testing program. Though the committee had warned against applying its standards too rigidly, misunderstandings arose over the nature and use of the units. Most recipients had evaluated the units "on the quantity of the material provided," but whether the term "quantity" meant the sheer physical bulk of the units, the amount of material to be covered, or something else was not explained. Apparently, the committee's instructions on evaluating the qualitative nature of the units were not understood by those responding.

The failure in communication may be traced to a number of different sources. Many receiving the units probably did not attend the annual meeting and so had no personal acquaintance with the committee's work. Low *Quarterly* readership levels probably meant that few read either the curriculum reports or the accounts of the annual meeting discussions on the units. In addition, the various reprints were not distributed with a brief explanation of the project and the evaluation goals. A lack of clarity in the units also contributed to the misunderstanding over their purpose. The incompleteness of the social studies unit and possibly others made evaluation difficult. More important, in reporting on the reaction of teachers and administrators, the committee emphasized flaws in the statement of the objectives. "The objections to the goals as generally stated is not that they are not proper objectives," the 1928 committee report observed, "but that they do not in themselves point out with sufficient clearness the more immediate objectives which must control educational practice." The committee provided revised versions, but the changes did not alleviate the difficulties. In 1929, John Stout again noted the persistence of misunderstandings of the committee's purpose.

Despite the various problems that hampered the project's evaluation efforts, the 1929 report indicated that the project was affecting high school teaching. Stout asserted, "Some evidence is available...to warrant the statement that substantial changes have resulted in the types of materials constituting the different subjects and fields." The following year, committee chair L. W. Webb presented the results of a survey that confirmed Stout's assessment. Questionnaires were sent to thirty-eight hundred people. Though only 15 percent returned their surveys in time for the report, the responses came from a wide variety of administrators and teachers. Forty-six percent of those responding agreed the materials were in use and had affected instruction. Only 18 percent were not using the materials. Administrators reported the materials had stimulated discussions at faculty meetings, facilitating their own curriculum revision efforts. Teachers commented that the materials gave them a new point of view and the reading lists helped in selecting books. They also had used some of the activity suggestions. The units apparently did provide guidelines to help schools develop their own curricula, indicating the NCA was helping institutions learn how to change themselves.[26]

While Webb did not report any criticisms from teachers or administrators, at the 1930 annual meeting, a critique of the reorganization project questioned not only the undertaking but the role played by the NCA in reforming education. Professor W. D. Cocking of Peabody College for Teachers in Nashville, Tennessee, complimented the Curriculum Reorganization Committee on the principles underlying the initiative, its methods, and the honest pursuit of answers in a tentative and experimental manner. However, he questioned some of the assumptions that guided the work and the results. The view that "curricula are to be almost exclusively determined by the needs of society" had led to a mechanical program that awkwardly tried to fit each unit into a prearranged pattern. Cocking called the reports impractical because they neglected to provide teachers with suggestions to improve classroom instruction. In particular, he noted the absence of a "careful articulation of the various units of instruction," both sequentially over time and in relation to other units being taught simultaneously. Questioning the research procedures, Cocking asked if any of the subcommittees seriously studied the secondary schools in the region before proceeding with their work. In concluding his criticisms of the project, he declared, "it is our belief that the Commission's pattern over-emphasizes subject matter without giving sufficient attention to procedure, as well as other means of education." Cocking also raised the issue of the NCA's ability to pursue educational reform. Citing the vastness of the region and its individual differences, he questioned how well the NCA served its member schools. He suggested that, in the future, the Commission confine itself to providing leadership and encouragement through the collection and dissemination of curriculum materials.[27]

L. W. Webb acknowledged Cocking's criticisms and outlined the committee's plans for the future. He claimed Cocking had misunderstood the purpose of the project, but did not dismiss his criticisms. Webb's outline of the next phases of the work showed that the committee was well aware of existing flaws and was seeking to address them. Breaking new, innovative ground in curriculum design, the general curriculum reform had shifted from reconstruction to function. Instead of using content areas or skills to organize courses, the committee developed functional units or courses that were organized around its general goals of health, citizenship, vocation, and leisure. These units were interdisciplinary, drawing from a number of subject areas. Recognizing the experimental nature of their new approach, the committee also recommended controlled experimentation of functional units in schools.

In 1933, the project reached a major culmination, though not an end. After revision, the various subcommittee reports were collected into a single volume entitled *High School Curriculum Reorganization*. Unfortunately, the type was destroyed. When the original print run of two thousand copies sold out in 1935, no other editions appeared. However, the work on functional units continued throughout the 1930s.[28]

The curriculum reorganization project was the longest and most significant Association effort to reform education in the interwar years. It was the only major initiative that did not seek outside funding and conceivably involved over three thousand people in various voluntary capacities. It probably pioneered the idea of helping schools learn to change themselves. The shift in project direction in the early thirties also showed how quickly the NCA could adapt to the changes in educational thought. Most important, the 1931 survey showed that the Association had succeeded in stimulating curriculum reform in the schools, thus contributing significantly to the development of education during this period.

THE NCA AS REFORM AGENT: ATHLETICS

Two other NCA efforts illuminate its role as a reform agent. Both relate more to higher education, though one also affected the secondary level. The first concerned athletics, an area where the NCA had a long tradition of involvement that dated back to 1902. The experience here showed the limits of Association power.[29] During the 1920s, severe and pressing problems arose in intercollegiate athletics, particularly football. NCA involvement began in 1922 when Lotus Coffman, president of the University of Minnesota, discussed the athletics situation in his NCA presidential address. He noted the all-encompassing nature of the difficulties. "There

Lotus D. Coffman. University of Minnesota president, Coffman was NCA president in 1922 and chair of the CIHE standards revision in the 1930s.

should be a concentrated attack on this problem," Coffman affirmed. "We must stamp out every effort at procuring players. We must eliminate professionalism and commercialism. We must reduce the number of intersectional games, and the desire for championships. We must make it very difficult for migratory players to play, and above all, we must make it [im]possible for illegitimate and unfair means to be used, in securing players."[30] To deal with the problem, the Commission appointed a committee "to study the athletic situation in higher education institutions, especially as it affects matters of accrediting, and to report at the next meeting of the Association."[31]

President H. M. Gage of Coe College chaired the committee on athletics. The authorizing resolution called for a cooperative effort and led the committee to work with the Carnegie Foundation, which provided a $10,000 grant. Using a method being developed by the Foundation, the committee proposed to "study the relations of athletics to scholarship in several typical North Central institutions," and requested any "president, principals, teachers,

Harry M. Gage. President of Coe College,
Gage was NCA secretary, 1919–25, and
served on or chaired several significant committees, including the committee on athletics and the 1933 committee on the revision
of standards.

and coaches...to write freely and in complete confidence to the
chairman of the committee."[32] In 1927, the committee reported
that Association members were coping with the problems in athletics as well as they could, but progress depended on making some
significant changes in the relationship of the athletics program to
the "general education program of the college." It made several recommendations for new standards to strengthen faculty control of
athletic matters, including awarding financial aid to students, out-
lawing payments to athletes or offers of special inducements to
prospective players, and making coaches full-time faculty members
with salaries determined by their academic rank. It also suggested
the institution's business office handle all athletic funds.[33]

To implement these new standards, another committee was
appointed in 1928, consisting of Gage, George Zook of the University of Akron, and J. L. Griffith, who was commissioner of the

George F. Zook. University of Akron president, Zook was secretary of the Commission on Higher Education, 1927–32, and a regular contributor to the *Proceedings;* he was a leader of NCA standards revision for colleges in the 1930s.

Western Intercollegiate Athletic Conference, or the Big Ten as it was more popularly known. The committee sought the cooperation of athletic conferences in applying the standards. Possibly because of the stature and cooperation of the Big Ten, twelve conferences with a total of 113 member institutions had passed resolutions supporting the NCA standards by 1933.[34]

Originally authorized in 1927, the study of the relationship between athletics and academic standards began three years later. The method of investigation followed the scientific trends evident in other studies. A questionnaire based on the NCA standards was sent to all collegiate member institutions. The committee selected a group of seven inspectors to visit selected institutions in every NCA state over a three-year period to uncover existing conditions and discuss their findings. The inspections involved meeting with various personnel at each college, including the president, director, coaches, students, alumni, business manager, and deans. The committee examined academic records of athletes and nonathletic students, scholarships and loans, employment, finances, etc. It also left a constructive report with the institutions related to the objectives of the study and visit. The goals of the visits were to "create good will founded upon an understanding of the procedure and objectives" and to gain institutional cooperation. The questionnaires were collected and analyzed with the inspection reports, and led to various conclusions.

In reporting on the findings of the study, the committee stressed the long-standing difficulties athletics had created for colleges and universities. While uncovering specific problem areas and places where institutions did not meet NCA standards, the general conclusion was that "the efforts of intercollegiate athletic conferences to eliminate some of the grosser evils that have developed from over-emphasis on athletics have resulted in much improvement." The Board of Review also received the questionnaires and the reports, taking action where needed on institutional accreditation. As a result of the 177 investigations made, the Board ordered 15 reinspections, summoned 26 administrators, and dropped 5 institutions from the accredited list. Each institution also received a copy of the report.[35]

Unfortunately, athletics problems persisted. In 1935, NCA president B. L. Stradley of Ohio State University observed that continuing well-known abuses had led the higher education standards revision committee to include athletics. He also advised that eliminating the abuses required a long-term commitment and recommended continuing the athletics committee. In addition, the Commission on Secondary Schools launched its own investigation under the auspices of a committee on athletics in the secondary schools. The secondary committee followed a procedure similar to that employed in higher education and developed new standards and recommendations to restrict competition to NCA members and to tie athletics to the larger educational objectives regarding health, leisure, citizenship, and character.[36] Unfortunately, none of these efforts solved the problem of athletics in education. In the late 1940s, scandals again brought intercollegiate sports to the attention of the NCA, but this time the large universities and athletic conferences blocked any action by the Association.[37] The

NCA quest to reform education in this area proved far beyond its scope, pointing out the limits of its power and authority.

THE NCA AS REFORM AGENT: EXPERIMENTAL PROJECTS

Another major reform effort promoted experimentation by institutions and was well in tune with modern trends. This action also aimed at helping institutions learn to change themselves by sanctioning institutional experiments that involved the NCA solely in an advisory or supervisory capacity. Colleges and universities, often in conjunction with secondary schools, developed curricular and administrative projects that sometimes violated accrediting standards. However, they also addressed long-standing issues, such as shortening the course of study for graduation or offering college credit classes in high schools. Some institutions tried out an innovative practice that promised to improve the institution's performance. But problems arose in determining whether the proposed experiments were to benefit education or the institution in some other way. In his history of the NCA, Calvin Davis commented that some so-called experiments "were instituted chiefly for advertising purposes or with the idea that they might serve to strengthen the institution's standing before its constituents and thus perchance help preserve its precarious existence." Davis claimed the practice began in the midtwenties in the CIHE, but the first record of an advisory committee is in 1929. Whatever the date, the experimental program thrived in the 1930s, involving a large number of institutions, including the University of Chicago, Stephens College, Cornell College, the Chicago Junior Colleges, Joliet College, and public schools in Kansas City, Tulsa, and Gary, Indiana. The experiments usually lasted from three to five years and were monitored by special NCA advisory committees. The advisory committee members visited the institutions, inspected the plans and procedures, and then periodically reported their findings to the Commission. In assessing the experimentation program, Davis claimed they produced a "number of general educational reforms."[38]

Both through internally generated projects and from the oversight of external programs, the NCA played a strong role in the educational reform movement of the interwar years. In most cases, the reforms contributed to the ongoing process of modernization in education and society. However, many of the reform initiatives did not reach their goals because of the outbreak of World War II, including the major undertaking of the North Central Association during this period. Responding to strident criticisms of the standards-based programs, the NCA completely overhauled its accrediting programs for higher and secondary education.

THE DEBATE OVER STANDARDS

As was true in education generally, between the end of World War I and the early 1940s, accreditation and the North Central Association were subjected to a strong barrage of criticisms. The attacks typically focused on some aspect of standardization, at times from opposite ends of the spectrum. In the early twenties, uniformity was a major topic of discussion and was approached from at least two different perspectives by critics. The newly formed American Council on Education (ACE) criticized the diversity of higher education standards, claiming a chaotic situation existed because no two agencies used the same measures. In 1921, the ACE and the National Conference Committee on Standards cosponsored a conference on the problem of uniformity. At the meeting, a founding father of NCA accreditation warned that a different sort of uniformity was causing a grave problem in education. Voicing a concern he had first raised in 1902 when the NCA was just beginning its venture into accrediting, University of Chicago president Harry Pratt Judson cautioned, "We are making it difficult to improve things from what they are to something better.... They [the standards] are too rigid." He urged a policy on standardization that was "flexible and responsive to thought from time to time, so we can change it any time." He closed by warning, "I think it needs changing right now tremendously."[39]

The ensuing debate over standards extended beyond the colleges, focusing much more on their rigidity than on their diversity. The attacks came from a number of different sources. In 1922, *School and Society* published an article by a concerned parent, who questioned whether standards allowed schools to meet the needs of their students. Frank Waugh related the problems his twelve-year old son Jerry faced in school because he disliked grammar. Jerry Waugh wanted to substitute the study of radio for grammar but neither he nor his father made much headway. In commenting on his experience, the disgruntled parent concluded, "I saw that the educational system was really standardized. Also that it was efficient, whether it met the needs of Jerry Boy in the sixth grade of the Pleasant Street school or not is another matter." Waugh's narrow vision and parental concern clouded his judgment, obscuring the value of grammar as a subject and also the probability that son Jerry would later change his mind about what to study. Radio was just becoming a household reality in 1922 and so it was a trendy school subject.[40] But the article raised the question of how schools could change to meet new conditions while having to comply with rigid standards.

Six years later, Jesse Newlon, a supporter of accrediting and a former NCA representative, defended the regional accrediting agencies, claiming they had been a constructive force in secondary education for twenty-five years. But he also reported that a prevalent complaint made by secondary school educators was that the standards had "a deadening effect on the schools which they standardize." He also identified the source of most attacks: "Advocates of modernizing high schools are undoubtedly the severest critics of the work of standardizing agencies." These advocates denounced the existing standards for being "based on an outworn philosophy."[41] Thus, the larger issue of the modernization of education lay underneath the debate.

Higher education figures expressed similar sentiments. Also in 1928, the higher education division of the Minnesota Education Association issued a scathing report on standards and the regional associations. Referring specifically to the NCA, the Minnesota group called the freedom to experiment the greatest need in higher education, but complained that NCA standards hampered rather than encouraged such efforts. Ironically, reversing the ACE critique of seven years earlier, the Minnesota report denounced the regional associations for their attempts to make the standards more uniform. It characterized the cooperation between the associations as a coercive technique designed to limit institutional freedom.[42] Apparently, times and attitudes had changed.

The Minnesota attack on the cooperation of the accrediting associations indicates that the standards were not the only object of criticism. The organizations, too, were targets of abuse. The severest critic of accreditation was University of Buffalo chancellor

Samuel Capen. Throughout the twenties and thirties, he waged a continuous campaign to abolish the accrediting associations. In 1931, he castigated these groups, suggesting they exercised more power than state governments and thus determined the survival of institutions. Interestingly, Capen never attacked the North Central Association. Instead, he paid the organization a strange compliment. Praising the NCA as a pioneer and constructive force whose efforts had improved education in the region, he, nonetheless, lamented its success because the Association had made standardizing respectable and impregnable.[43]

Though a very small minority adopted this course, some officials called for mass resignation from the organization or dropped out themselves. On May 4, 1927, President Smith of Iowa Wesleyan College delivered a vicious attack on education, focusing much of his attention on the NCA. "The North Central Association of Colleges and Secondary Schools, in my judgment, is manipulating plans and methods that are intended, if possible, to squeeze out every denominational college in its territory," he declared, predicting, "I think the colleges that have joined the association have put their heads into a noose that will strangle them." He called on all Iowa colleges to withdraw from the NCA and to affiliate with the Iowa State Board of Education so they could develop their own standards. The policies of the Association in administering accreditation, rather than the standards, seem to have angered Smith, for he also recommended that no Iowa college accept transfer credits from junior colleges that "do not meet the requirements and standards fixed for colleges by the North Central Association of Colleges and Secondary Schools." Secondary school educators also rebelled against what they considered to be "the demands of 'educational rings,'" as Gallatin, Missouri, High School board secretary F. M. Harrison phrased it in explaining why Gallatin had dropped out of the Association.[44]

Faced with what University of Minnesota president Lotus D. Coffman called a revolt, the NCA conducted several studies of its standards. In January 1927, the Commission on Institutions of Higher Education appointed a Committee on Cost of Instruction "to study the effects of the present financial standards of the Association." The Association of American Colleges also participated in the project. Committee members included Donald G. Cowling,

Lotus D. Coffman, and Floyd W. Reeves. They collected data from seventeen NCA liberal arts colleges. A preliminary report at the 1927 NCA annual meeting led to an expanded study to include thirty-nine colleges in fifteen states, including some non-Association members. The on-site visits usually lasted one to two days, but as University of Kentucky professors Floyd Reeves and Dale Russell, who conducted the study, explained in one report, "data from a considerable number of the institutions...were obtained as a part of more extensive surveys involving a stay of from one to three weeks at each institution." Thus, the NCA invested considerable time, energy, and presumably money to ensure that adequate and accurate information was obtained.[45]

The analysis combined scientific and more intuitive methods. Modern statistical analysis was used to organize the data, leading to some distressing conclusions. In a March 1928 *North Central Association Quarterly* article on financial standards, Reeves and Russell concluded, "The present financial requirements do not guarantee an expenditure per student for current educational purposes for an effective educational program." Since the financial standards were more assiduously applied than others, this finding struck at the very core of the NCA higher education standardization program.[46]

THE SPARK OF REFORM

Matters came to a head at the NCA annual meeting in 1928. Reeves and Russell's report was one of many presentations that indicated change was needed and soon. The turning point came on March 16, 1928, when Charles H. Judd delivered his paper, "A Method of Securing National Educational Standards." Sixteen years after his actions had produced the first list of accredited colleges, Judd's paper initiated a revolution in the standards—first for higher, and later for secondary education—that profoundly changed the future of the Association and accreditation. He originally had wanted to review the various criticisms against the standardization of education. However, an earlier speech by George Zook, then secretary of the Commission on Institutions of Higher Education, had covered that topic. Zook had agreed that some criticisms directed against the Association were valid and that the need for change was great. "Checking Up on Ourselves," the presidential address by NCA president W. W. Boyd, issued a similar call for action. As a result, Judd moved to the next logical level and presented a plan to effect the needed revisions. He noted that the NCA had already initiated action to address various concerns, including the revision of standards.[47]

Judd observed that the increasing complexity of the educational situation had made these "perilous" times. The chorus of criticism was so strident and frequent, he explained, because "education is evolving so rapidly and in so many different directions that it is almost unavoidable that gross misunderstanding should arise." Reforms were transforming many aspects of schooling. Judd noted that developments at the elementary level created a ripple effect felt in secondary and higher education while those occurring at the professional level had a similar impact on colleges and high schools. Because of the fast pace of change at all education levels, "misunderstandings are inevitable unless avenues of information are opened up and unless much energy is devoted to articulating the different institutions which make up our educational system." Though he did not mention this fact, the goal of the NCA was still to improve relations between secondary and higher education, making the Association a likely reform agent to improve communication and articulation. Contributing to the communication gap was the isolation of educators in their institutions. Judd observed, "Each of us sees the environment immediately around his own institution but is unable to look out on the remoter expanses of the educational system." The resulting limited vision of the field had created "an intellectual myopia" in many educators.[48]

The pace and character of change also made methods and practices that were adequate a few years earlier obsolete in the present. New studies indicated the rationales behind some standards were invalid. "Today no one has a right to say that a class of thirty is of the maximum size which can be safely tolerated," Judd commented, noting that some studies concluded class size was less a factor in promoting learning than previously thought. Other studies questioned the general efficacy of quantitative standards, including the 1927–1928 NCA effort headed by Floyd Reeves and Dale Russell. Besides noting difficulties arising from the quantitative nature of the standards, the two men concluded that the existing measures dealt "only with externals of excellence; they do not actually measure excellence." In a 1928 *North Central Association Quarterly* article, Jesse Newlon had commented that secondary standards suffered from the same flaw.[49] Judd also admitted that the NCA had not done enough to help itself. "We have been slow in making the studies which would standardize us from within," he claimed. As a consequence, "some of the ablest friends of education are beginning to call in question the standardizing activities of...regional associations."[50]

The perilous times also offered opportunity. Judd stated, "The time has come when a forward step can be taken; when this Association can become a sponsor for a new kind of standardization." He called for scientific studies of educational institutions and a scaling back of some reforms "until we can plan progress along lines that represent something far more deliberate than mere outbursts of enthusiasm." His rationale was that success required concerted action. "I am urging," he pleaded, "that we unite in a plan which is far beyond the possibilities of purely individual endeavor." He called for a cooperative effort of secondary school and college administrators, and also asked that those in the high schools and colleges acquaint themselves with the ongoing changes in the elementary and professional schools.

Before offering any details of his plan, Judd addressed the issue of funding, favoring a two-step approach. First, he recommended "collecting an adequate sum of money from the membership of this Association to show that we are genuinely prepared to finance at least a part of the studies which we ought to undertake." Second, referring to the successful example of the land grant colleges in securing an appropriation from Congress, he suggested the NCA join with other regional associations and the American Council on Education to apply for "support in a nation-wide study of high schools, colleges and their related institutions."[51] A national study offered many benefits, including the collection of accurate information to illuminate current conditions. National cooperation facilitated the selection of "certain crucial items on which institutions might be asked in the future to keep uniform and comparable records, particularly various financial aspects." A dire need existed for "a thorough national study of the sweeping changes which are taking place in the relations between the several institutions which make up the American educational system." Moving from the general study of education, Judd tackled the standards question. He asserted that general agreement existed on the inadequacy of current standards, but studies undertaken on a part-time basis by committees had severe limitations. Confronting the severe problems facing the NCA and other accrediting agencies required a cooperative effort, again financed by the federal government. Judd also noted the possibility of foundation funding. Though his paper is not totally clear on this point, he apparently supported two separate studies, one on education and another on standards.

The stakes were high and quick action was needed. "If this standardizing body is to continue to command the respect of the institutions in its territory, indeed if it is to survive at all," he asserted, "it will have to evolve out of the stage where its acts are based on the best guesses which can be made into the stage where its acts are defensible and rational." To accommodate the changing times, the NCA had to employ modern scientific methods of inquiry and analysis. In the modern era, analysis required accurate information. Collecting such data necessitated conducting extensive and intensive inquiries into existing conditions. Given the gravity of the situation, Judd concluded, "We are driven to adopt a program of inquiry whether we like it or not."[52]

Judd's paper elicited an enthusiastic response from many members. In the end, a founding father initiated the standards reform movement. Older but no less active, George Carman moved that Judd's plan be referred to the Executive Committee "with a recommendation that the suggestions made be put into effect." Carman commented that making the motion gave him great pleasure because, "It seems to me a logical outcome of what we have been doing."[53] The motion passed. Ultimately, the NCA became involved in two separate, though related projects: an Association effort to revise higher education standards and a cooperative, national survey of secondary education.

MODERNIZING THE ACCREDITING OF HIGHER EDUCATION

The Executive Committee authorized a committee to examine the standards for higher education, but the project was slow in getting started. Twice, on June 29 and September 13, 1929, George Zook wrote Charles Judd letters stressing the importance of the task but noting the committee had not yet been formed. At the 1930 meeting of the CIHE, Secretary Zook reported that ongoing studies had delayed action because of the obvious need to consult their findings. In addition, the other project, the national study of secondary education, had been seeking funding from Congress, and Zook explained progress on that effort "would affect our plans materially." Since Congress had authorized the secondary education study, "we can go ahead with the program for this committee." However, following Judd's urging of careful scientific study, he warned members not to expect a rapid change in standards.[54]

At a January 26, 1930, conference at the Hotel Windermere East near the University of Chicago campus, the process of modernizing the higher education accrediting program began. By this time, the Committee on Revision of Standards (also called the Committee of Fifteen) was organized. The fifteen members included NCA representatives and educators from outside the region, though not all on the committee actively participated. For example, prominent critic Samuel P. Capen was a member but he did not attend the Windermere meeting and later admitted he provided little input. Judd also played a diminished role as the work proceeded though he apparently helped get the committee rolling. Those attending the Windermere conference laid out many of the guidelines for the five-year project.

President H. M. Gage of Coe College, chair of the CIHE, served as temporary chair of the committee. The conference was a focused brainstorming session to discuss ideas on objectives and measures to be studied. The digest written by Zook noted that all attending recognized the present NCA standards had markedly improved the state of education. They also admitted that serious flaws existed. As a result, they identified two goals for the committee: "The problem of the Committee is therefore, first, to find new types of standards which will more accurately measure an institution in the new sense [of assessing the product of the institutions and student competence]; and secondly, to devise practical ways in which these new standards may be applied in the simplest possible manner." In this respect, the committee name was misleading. It aimed not to revise existing standards but to develop totally new ones.[55]

The discussion explored a variety of areas, including committee procedures and administration as well as new standards and developing the machinery to administer them. The first committee suggestion was to "require an institution to formulate a definite set of objectives for its various major divisions. In so far as possible, measure an institution in terms of the degree to which it succeeds or fails to attain these objectives." Just who proposed this idea is unknown, but it became the basis of NCA accreditation. Accreditation by objectives addressed several criticisms. Since approval depended upon achievement of institutional purposes rather than meeting a prescribed set of standards applied uniformly to all colleges and universities, individuality was accommodated and experimentation supported. In addition, the objectives approach provided a scientific and practical way of assessing an institution by seeing if it had done what it said it would.

The move from a uniform to a more individualized accrediting philosophy required an equally new accrediting machinery. Expressing dissatisfaction with the existing reliance on questionnaires, the committee noted the need for personal inspection by more than one person and for longer than one day. Equally important, they advised against "meticulous details," calling for a simple, flexible system that focused on "ten to twelve major characteristics of a good institution." They suggested the submission of annual, comprehensive yet compact, reports. The digest also reported another benefit of personal inspections that became more important as the project proceeded. "A secondary consideration in these visits would be to advise and counsel each institution." In this respect, the evolving idea of helping institutions learn to change themselves received greater momentum.

The committee's deliberations were influenced by the studies conducted by Floyd Reeves and Dale Russell. Their 1928 report on standards had extended beyond criticism to some suggestions to improve accreditation. They had concluded that appraising the effectiveness of a college involved developing "an independent criterion of excellence based upon observation and inspection." Reeves and Russell recommended that "standards should be applied to the individual institutions through a personal inspection rather than through the medium of statistical reports." This idea stood in direct contrast to prevailing practices. Their stress on the need for an expert to assess the situation scientifically and personally was a major innovation that the standards revision committee quickly adopted.[56]

Having identified some ideas on how to improve the standards, the committee organized the work. Two subcommittees were created at the Windermere conference. Headed by temporary committee secretary George Zook, one group would survey members of the committee for suggestions on modifying the existing standards until new ones were developed. The other subcommittee consisted of Zook, W. W. Charters of Ohio State University, President E. H. Wilkins of Oberlin College, Floyd Reeves of the University of Chicago, and University of Minnesota dean Melvin C. Haggerty. Their charge was "to digest the suggestions relative to a new type of standards and to formulate a program of procedure for the committee." Haggerty was not a committee member and did not attend the conference.

The committee also developed a preliminary plan of action. Because of the large workload, the members advised the subcommittee on standards to focus initially on two to four major studies and "attack others as progress is made." The general committee set up a three-stage procedure that began with identifying situations and characteristics that defined an excellent and effective institution. It suggested having a team of three visit fifty or more institutions to collect data on excellent institutions. Using these characteristics as the basis, the next step was developing a "new type of standards" that were scientifically based and phrased so they applied to the North Central accrediting situation. The final phase involved testing and revising the standards.[57]

After the Windermere conference, the committee made surprisingly rapid progress. In 1930, University of Minnesota president Lotus D. Coffman became the chair of the committee. Recognizing the need for "the services of experts with a considerable amount of free time," Coffman reported the creation of a subcommittee on ways and means, chaired by Melvin Haggerty. The ways and means subcommittee developed a pilot program to survey "a small group of colleges with a view of setting up a comprehensive program of investigation looking toward the revision of standards." This subcommittee evolved into the project's research staff.[58]

The pilot phase involved a preliminary investigation into conditions at eleven institutions in Ohio, Indiana, Michigan, and Illinois. Initially limited to four-year liberal arts colleges that comprised the largest number of NCA members, the test group was expanded to include two junior colleges, two private universities, and one teachers college. To facilitate their efforts, the research staff developed "a statement of principles of accrediting procedures that would guide its search for usable information." The principles identified several outcomes that served the purposes of accrediting institutions, the most important one being "guidance to students." Haggerty explained that accrediting helped students choose an institution to attend. Noting colleges prominently displayed their NCA membership status in catalogs, often on the front cover page, he claimed accredited status provided a "badge of respectability and a guarantee to prospective students that the college is qualified to offer a good college education." The NCA's responsibility was guaranteeing the soundness of its membership. Institutions also received guidance by being accredited. Accreditation improved relations among institutions on such matters as transferring credits, student activities, placement of college graduates, and recruiting faculty. Accrediting also stimulated institutional improvement. Acknowledging that the existing standards performed this function, Haggerty observed that "the locus of this stimulation is largely at the borderline of institutional competence and chiefly for colleges which hover at the threshold of acceptable status." He recommended developing descriptions of accrediting practices that described "desirable institutional ideals" and guaranteed "a wholesome flexibility to educational practices" to continually stimulate improvement.[59]

Using these outcomes as guides, the fieldwork began on November 17, 1930. Starting in November 1930, the staff, aided by Coffman, Gage, Zook, John Dale Russell, and President D. B. Waldo, made seventeen visits to DePauw University, Oberlin College, Ohio Wesleyan University, Shurtleff College, Knox College, North Central College, Joliet Junior College, LaSalle Junior College, Cedar Falls Teachers College, Kalamazoo College, and Battle Creek College. The visits generally lasted two days and were divided into half-day sessions. The first meeting was with the president and lasted from nine to noon, though there was a chapel break. The entire research staff interviewed the president on institutional objectives, administrative and educational organization, various financial aspects, institutional control, as well as matters pertaining to the students, faculty, and curriculum. The staff also examined a host of written documents, including college catalogs, reports from deans and other officials, and faculty record blanks provided by the NCA.

In the afternoon, the staff separated to meet with the business manager, deans, and the personnel officer, among other administrators. The following morning, the staff members went to various units of the college, "including visits to the library and a conference with the librarian, visits to classrooms and laboratories, and a general inspection of the plant, equipment, etc." They held informal and formal sessions with students and faculty, sometimes meeting faculty groups at lunch. The last session, where possible, was with the president. Though often asked to criticize and otherwise comment on the institution, the staff refused these requests because "the rather hurried examination of the institution would not warrant giving advice." Besides, problem-solving consultation was not considered a "legitimate function of the Research Staff."

A primary goal of the pilot project was to gain insight into the character and conduct of the institution. Another objective was "to learn the attitude of the president and others in the institution toward certain new modes of college accrediting which had been formulating in the minds of the staff during the period of visitation." Haggerty noted that as these ideas developed, "it became possible to state certain new proposals with a view to their applicability in the institution then being visited." In this way, the staff introduced college officials to "the trend of thinking concerning possible new types of accrediting procedure," potentially laying the foundation for future action and acceptance of the new NCA accrediting system. The feedback from the various officials also aided the staff in the further development of the system.[60] By employing this procedure of staff development and member consultation, Haggerty and his subcommittee made the process of revision a much more collaborative and extended effort.

The preliminary investigation enabled the staff to develop principles to guide future studies, though Haggerty stressed they were subject to revision. The underlying assumption was that "accrediting should...foster to the utmost the individuality of institutions." Haggerty asserted that "an accrediting association can not prescribe a single set of definitive standards for all...

institutions." NCA members differed sharply in purpose and the Association had to recognize and cherish these distinctions. He concluded, "It does not make for the improvement of higher education that they should all be crushed into a common mold."

Existing NCA policies and practices influenced the development of the new principles. Haggerty noted the CIHE did not maintain a single set of standards, but published a separate list for junior colleges and had vacillated over the years on those for teachers colleges. In addition, he claimed the Executive Committee often exercised independent judgment when evaluating institutions, using the idea of equivalency to get around the letter of the standard law, so to speak. The implication was that the existing standards presented problems in practice that led to widespread deviation from their stated intent. He noted the rise of a second method of classifying institutions by types offered a means of expanding the descriptions of standards and of inserting greater flexibility to promote institutional improvement. But the diversity of institutions within a single type also created problems.

Haggerty suggested the ideal accrediting plan not only recognized variations but encouraged "the enrichment of higher education through divergence." Returning to an idea first presented at the Windermere conference, he claimed that accreditation by objective would promote institutional individuality. Success depended, however, on institutions improving their own methods of stating their goals, "to re-define their purposes, to describe their natural clientele, to relate their aims to their curricular offerings, to give evidence that the institutional aims are shared by the faculty and understood by the students and the public."

The switch to individualized accreditation by objective did not eliminate the need for various criteria. Disregarding the original suggestion that the new accrediting process focus on approximately ten to twelve major areas, the staff listed thirty areas for future study. Standards revision had not simplified the process because the growing complexity of institutions and scientific thrust required greater sophistication and detail in the accrediting machinery. As a consequence, both institutions and the NCA faced a great deal more work. Another major change was in terminology. Negative connotations connected to the word *standards* made its use unacceptable. Haggerty explained that the term "has become associated with uniformity and in some quarters is looked upon as the enemy of educational experiment, variety, and progress." As a result, the staff suggested substituting a phrase such as criteria of excellence.

Regarding the future of the project, success depended upon several factors. The "scientific soundness of the study" required employing a variety of research procedures. Secondly, because the investigation aimed to discover "educational competence" rather than judge a single institution, the study had moved "beyond the usual survey procedures into more profound methods of educational research." A competently trained staff would pursue more active research procedures that employed "rigid statistical and experimental methods of study." Equally important, Haggerty concluded that the NCA "must prepare itself to accept the results of such investigation and to base its future procedures upon them." He claimed that "the degree to which member institutions share its purposes, its plans, and results" would determine success.

The strong stress on cooperation and support was basic to any undertaking by a voluntary association. The ability of the Association to transform its accrediting program depended upon the active participation of member institutions in developing it. The information needed by the study required a great expenditure of time and effort by the institution. Haggerty increased the burden, suggesting that institutions pay the costs of providing the required data. In addition, the structure of the Association made opening new lines of communication and cooperation important. The development of the first standards had benefited from discussion by the membership in general session at various annual meetings. Because the NCA no longer held such legislative meetings characterized by participatory democracy, and since decision making was far removed from most member institutions due to the commission structure, institutional cooperation at other levels assumed great importance. Members had to feel that they had participated in this momentous decision making instead of having the results of the new accrediting program imposed upon them.

In the process, the committee also gained from the expertise and experience of members. Noting the vast number of studies in various institutions, Haggerty called for the sharing of new ideas and practices. Another rationale for member involvement was that "the investigation will need their helpful criticism along the way, and by continuing cooperation its findings will in the end have found realization in institutional practices by the time they are given formal statement in accrediting procedures."[61] Among other things, change in the NCA required alterations in institutions for progress to occur. The staff had promoted communication and cooperation in its preliminary visits by using the interviews to ascertain attitudes, gain advice, and build support for the project, helping establish guidelines for future cooperative investigation. The visited institutions learned about the new accrediting program and gained valuable experience in self-examination.

A last requirement was funding. The magnitude of the project's scope necessitated a large expenditure of money over an extended period at a very unpropitious time, the onset of depression. In 1930, the NCA secured some funds by voting "to tax each of the colleges in the Association an additional annual fee of $25 with the understanding that this money would...be available for the conduct of these studies." Having gained the financial commitment of the Association and institution, the NCA appointed Coffman, Zook, and Gage to a committee to seek outside funding. They approached representatives of the General Education Board and held meetings in New York City and Chicago. Haggerty attended the Chicago session. His report on the findings of the preliminary investigation, Coffman noted, "helped materially in securing the funds we desired." But, Coffman continued, "the persuasive powers and convincing eloquence of Presidents Zook and Gage finally did the business." They "did not exactly picture a new collegiate millennium but they went as far as their reputations for truth and veracity would permit them to go," he explained, wryly observing, "and when you bear in mind that they belong to the species of academic animal who is not supposed to tell the truth you will understand that no matter how far they went their consciences weren't disturbed."

On January 27, 1931, the General Education Board granted the NCA $110,000, payable over five years in decreasing increments. The first year sum was $35,000 and in the following two years the NCA received $25,000 each, followed by $15,000 the fourth year and $10,000 the last. The grant required the NCA to continue its support by providing $5,000 per year over the funding period. Thus, a total of $135,000 was budgeted for the project.

Building upon the experience of the preliminary phase, the standards revision committee strengthened the project's organization. To plan and supervise the work, a Committee in Charge of the Study was appointed, chaired by Lotus Coffman and with Judd, Gage, Zook, and Charters as members. A smaller committee consisting of Melvin Haggerty, Floyd Reeves, and Zook would conduct the study.[62] The general committee divided the project into two phases: evaluation of existing standards for judging colleges and development of effective and flexible qualitative measures. Regarding the scope of activities, the advice of the Windermere conference was restated: concentrate on a few rather than many problems.

The study involved fifty-seven institutions that represented all types of NCA higher education members. A massive amount of information on various subjects was needed to allow institutions to be rated and then, solely for experimental purposes, compared. To facilitate the research, the committee of Haggerty, Reeves, and Zook drew up schedules for securing information from institutions and made some pilot visits to colleges to test these schedules and other procedures. In addition, representatives of most participating institutions attended an orientation meeting in Chicago in December 1931. The research strategy had several dimensions. Reflecting a contemporary vogue in education, intelligence and subject matter tests were administered to undergraduates. To help assess the results of a college education, Haggerty supervised a study on success in graduate school, using a previous project developed by the University of Minnesota. But not every area proved easy to assess. At the 1932 meeting of the Commission on Institutions of Higher Education, George Zook reported no progress in evaluating college teaching because it was "one of the most baffling problems to be solved." The research also extended beyond the classroom. For example, Douglas Waples of the University of Chicago conducted an inquiry into the library.[63]

The institutional visits provided other important benefits besides gathering needed information. The committee members believed that gaining a complete picture of an institution required more than objective data. Following the suggestions made initially by Reeves and Russell in 1928 and later shown in the preliminary program, the study emphasized the need for "evaluation through judgment." The committee added an experimental aspect to the research visits, seeking "to determine how closely the judgments of three men acting independently and with the various types of information in hand will correlate with one another and with the various types of objective data." The comparison of differing evaluation techniques promised to provide a more accurate, textured picture of an institution while testing potential accreditation procedures.

By summer 1932, the research was largely finished and the NCA executive committee authorized the development of "an entirely new set of standards or criteria for experimental purposes" to be tested at a small number of institutions. The economic depression influenced this action because it had created a financial crisis in many institutions that made meeting the NCA endowment standards difficult. The timetable for the development and testing of the new criteria was brief. The committee had less than a year to devise the criteria because all institutions applying for accreditation or up for reinspection prior to the 1933 annual meeting would receive a supplementary schedule requesting information that indicated how the institutions met the experimental set of criteria. However, only where clear deficiencies existed in meeting the existing standards were the new criteria applied. Following the return of the forms, the committee visited fifteen institutions to judge the quality of work. The Board of Review used the reports of these visits to consider accrediting institutions that did not meet existing standards because of the depression.[64]

In 1934, the committee published a statement on the "Proposed New Basis for the Accrediting of Higher Institutions" in the *North Central Association Quarterly,* showing that the work had proceeded much faster than the original estimate of five years. The new accrediting program was presented at the 1934 annual meeting. In describing the process of development, Lotus Coffman emphasized its scientific thrust, explaining, "We have moved along...in much the way that any group of scientists would move in the study of a problem they were sensitive about; we are not entirely clear as to the techniques that should be employed in studying our problem." As a result, the general committee and the subcommittee considered and tested every conceivable method, imparting an experimental quality to the work. In addition, Coffman claimed the committee members had no preconceived notions regarding results. While the members may not have articulated potential results, their conclusions addressed many criticisms voiced against the old standards and followed long-standing NCA ideas.

The new NCA accrediting program revolved around an equally new core of ideas regarding the character of standards and the role of the NCA. Coffman claimed the program represented "a fairly complete face-about policy." The overall stress shifted from quantitative to qualitative evaluation as the NCA focused on "the animating motive and spirit of a school." Addressing criticisms that the old standards were fixed and blocked educational progress, the new ones were based on old adages often repeated in the early NCA deliberations. In words strikingly reminiscent of William Rainey Harper's 1896 comment that achieving perfection was impossible but it should always be pursued, Coffman observed, "A standard that is alive and developing is never attained, and yet the effort to attain it stimulates constant achievement." As a result, the new standards were not absolute, but rather relative measures subject to revision. They were policy statements that served two purposes. They assessed whether a school met reasonable conditions, i.e. the accrediting standards, and also told the institution if it was improving. These purposes substantially changed the role of the NCA from that of a judge to an agent of improvement. Under the new system, the inspectors visited institutions in two guises: as evaluators for accrediting purposes, and as colleagues consulting with the faculty and administrators to improve the quality of the institution. In closing his introduction to the new accrediting program, Coffman used the political parlance of the time to emphasize the revolutionary nature of the committee report, suggesting the proposals represented "the new deal that we promised."[65]

Melvin Haggerty presented the new program, noting it had three parts. The statement of policy and a manual of accrediting procedures were completed, but the monograph that would explain the other two sections was not finished. In addition, the committee had developed an institutional pattern map to identify pertinent characteristics and to compare institutions with one another. The map's organization applied the principles of accrediting laid out in the statement of policy that formed the core of the new accrediting program.

The statement of policy presented a new philosophy and practice of accreditation based on institutional individuality. Instead of meeting a set of distinct standards where deficiency in one area could mean rejection, membership was based on the pattern presented by the institution as a whole. The NCA gained greater flexibility, because "superiority in some characteristics may be regarded as compensating, to some extent, for deficiencies in other respects." The institution benefited because the new program supported experimentation and other efforts at improvement, calling for continual study and revision of institutional operations. Membership requirements were also tightened. In addition, the NCA promoted the movement for a liberal education that became popular in the early 1930s. Either through course work taken at the college or admission requirements, a general education component was mandatory for Association membership. Another significant change was that the Association eliminated narrowly defined special purpose institutions from membership eligibility. Regarding the administration of the new accrediting program, the Association would continually assess its own efforts. The NCA secretary was "to conduct annually one or more detailed studies upon selected phases of the accrediting program." This information "will contribute to the procedures of accrediting and will reveal the changing character of these institutions."[66] The evaluation of the accrediting program created two levels of institutional assessment. Applicants for membership underwent a comprehensive study of all aspects of accrediting that included on-site visits. Existing members were annually evaluated on selected areas through surveys that provided feedback on the progress of the institution and the viability of the accrediting policies.

The need for a selected focus of accrediting related to the incredibly comprehensive and detailed institutional pattern map that was the heart of the new accrediting program. The map graphically depicted what accrediting the whole institution implied. The map also showed institutions where they stood in comparison with others at a single moment in time, allowing them to gauge their progress over time. The pattern map had two sections. Running horizontally across the top were the eleven major characteristics of an institution: faculty, curriculum, instruction, library, induction of students, student personnel service, administration, finance, plant, institutional study, and athletics.[67] These major categories were divided into various subcategories and, in some cases, the subcategories were broken down into smaller fields. For example, at the most general level, the faculty component examined competence, organization, and conditions of services. These were subdivided into smaller groups. Under faculty competence, the aspects were doctors and masters (indicating degrees earned), study, experience, books, articles, memberships, meetings, and program. The map contained eighty-one indicators of institutional quality.

The horizontal lines registered performance in the various categories in percentages. As recorded on the map, an institution's performance was expressed in comparison to all other NCA institutions. "Zero on this map is the point below which no institution falls," explained Haggerty. "One hundred is the highest point reached by an institution; fifty is the median point of all institutions."[68] Thus, the percentile ratings were not absolute in that an institutional ranking was not connected to an abstract quantitative formula. Instead, the scores achieved by the institutions determined the scale. In addition, the map did not determine accreditation, but hopefully it stimulated improvement.

The success of the innovative accrediting program, particularly its detailed inquiry into institutional operations, depended upon providing substantial guidance and training to inspectors, institutions, and reviewers. The study itself helped orient institutions and inspectors to the new criteria and procedures, but its scope limited participation to a minority of institutions. The goal of the other two publications was to expand this training and orientation. Appearing in 1934 after several revisions, the manual of accrediting was a massive work of several hundred pages that provided detailed descriptions and explanations of the new criteria and procedures. The third volume was to be a monograph that explained the profile map and the manual, but it never appeared.[69]

Testing and debate over the various components continued throughout the 1930s, but led to few changes in the basic idea and program. On April 8, 1937, George Zook, whose direct connection with the NCA had ended several years earlier, made a final recommendation for the standards revision committee. "I should like…

to suggest that the committee be continued to the first of July, 1937, and discharged at that time."[70] After almost a decade of study and experimentation, the project that had transformed NCA college accreditation ended.

Implementing the new program, however, had just begun. At the 1936 annual meeting, L. B. Hopkins, president of Wabash College, recounted his arduous experience as an inspector under the new system. Acknowledging the deficiencies of the previous standards and the many improvements in the criteria-based program, Hopkins offered some informed criticisms. After reviewing various aspects of the program, Hopkins concluded that "we have neither given up nor done away with quantitative measurements." He also questioned the validity of some of the indicators on the score cards given inspectors to record their findings on various institutional aspects. For example, he suggested few would disagree with his contention that not all books written by faculty "constitute a contribution to educational excellence or a proof of faculty competence," and neither did all the learned society meetings. Yet, the score cards were "based on the *number* of books written and the *number* of meetings attended in the last five years." Nonetheless, he praised the shift from specifics to general conditions that revealed the whole institutional pattern as "a very great advance over former methods." Hopkins claimed the greatest contribution of the Committee on the Revision of Standards was "that they realized the task was not completed when they turned the study over to the Association."[71] The 1930s witnessed the transformation of the basic philosophy, principles, policies, and procedures of NCA accrediting of higher education. But translating this idea into practice was delayed by World War II.

MODERNIZING THE ACCREDITING OF SECONDARY SCHOOLS

The Commission on Secondary Schools had a similar experience in modernizing its accrediting program. For reasons much like those in higher education, NCA school accreditation needed an overhaul in the late 1920s. But where the CIHE independently transformed its program as an internal Association project, though with outside funding, the CSS sought a greater impact. The schools commission strategy followed the general reform model William Butts had

presented in 1895.[72] In cooperation with the other regional associations and the U.S. Office of Education, the NCA secondary commission conducted a study of standards and developed a
comprehensive, revised accrediting program of national impact
and stature.

Several developments influenced the NCA secondary commission to revise its standards in a cooperative way. Prompted in part
by Charles Judd's 1928 paper, the national survey of secondary
education provided a successful example of cooperation between
the federal government and various educational associations, such
as the NCA, the Association of Colleges and Secondary Schools of
the Southern States, the National Committee on Research in Secondary Education, the American Council on Education, and the
National Department of Secondary School Principals. Congress had
appropriated $225,000 for the three-year survey and the U.S. Office
of Education had administered the project that then NCA president James Edmonson called "the most significant study of education ever undertaken in the United States."[73] The CIHE standards
revision project also stimulated interest in changing the secondary
accrediting program. By providing a successful example to follow,
the CIHE program also supplied answers to criticisms of NCA
school accreditation voiced in a 1932 survey of members. Edmonson had conducted the survey of 275 high school principals and
administrators who complained, among other things, of the quantitative character of the standards.[74] In response to these influences, in December 1932, the NCA Commission on Secondary
Schools authorized "a scientific study of the present standards of
the Commission."[75]

Simultaneously, another organization was preparing for a similar effort, though on a national, cooperative basis. Information is
sketchy on the origins and purpose of the National Association of
Officers of Regional Associations. However, the cooperative study
of secondary school standards originated at its meetings. The first
step was taken at its February 24, 1931, meeting in Detroit. Paul
Boyd, dean at the University of Kentucky and an active Southern
Association member, called for a shift from quantity to quality
standards. Citing the NCA initiative in higher education, Boyd suggested quick action. At a February 1932 meeting, a unanimous

resolution was passed proposing that the six regional associations cooperatively study secondary school standards.[76] The initiative went to the NCA. At the 1933 annual meeting, the Commission on Secondary Schools voted that the state committee chairs serve as ex officio members of a committee to develop a plan to study and revise the standards. The Association appropriated $1,000 to launch the study and authorized an executive committee consisting of George E. Carrothers of the University of Michigan (chair), Carl F. G. Franzen of the University of Indiana, J. T. Giles of the Wisconsin State Department of Education, University of Nebraska president A. A. Reed, and M. R. Owens of the Arkansas State Department of Education. The study's executive committee met on July 3, 1933, in Chicago. Representatives from the Middle States and Southern Associations also attended and "it was agreed that a cooperative effort on the part of all six regional associations, covering the entire United States, should be undertaken."[77] George Zook became U.S. Commissioner of Education at this time. Certainly aware of Zook's participation in the NCA and the higher education revisions project, those at the July 3 meeting asked Zook to call a meeting of representatives of all the regional associations to discuss revising secondary standards cooperatively.

On August 18 and 19, 1933, the association representatives met in Washington, D.C. They drew up a project proposal for "a Cooperative Study of Secondary School Standards and Accrediting Procedures," and established a general committee consisting of the five NCA members, five representatives each from the Middle States and Southern Associations, three from the New England Association, two from the Northwest Association, and one from the newly formed Western Association. In addition, four advisory members were named, including Zook and Carl A. Jessen of the Office of Education. Following Zook's suggestion, officers, an executive committee, and an administrative committee were appointed. Jessen was elected secretary, while Middle States representative E. D. Grizzell of the University of Pennsylvania and Carrothers became chairs of the executive and general committees, respectively. These last two men and Joseph Roemer of the Southern Association comprised the administrative committee. In addition, J. T. Giles served on the executive committee.

At a meeting in Cincinnati on November 4 and 5, 1933, the executive meeting posed four questions to guide the Study:

1. What are the characteristics of a good school?

2. What practicable means and methods may be employed to evaluate the effectiveness of a school in terms of its objectives?

3. By what means and processes does a good school develop into a better one?

4. How can a regional association stimulate secondary schools to continuous growth?[78]

Ironically, the Study began by addressing the same issue that the NCA had discussed at its first annual meeting: defining a good school. The other questions on connecting evaluation to objectives and advocating the doctrine of continual improvement indicated the influence of the NCA higher education standards revision initiative.

The project was organized into four phases. Between 1933 and 1935, a preliminary investigation into the scholarship on secondary education led to the reviewing and abstracting of almost twenty-five hundred books, articles, and graduate theses. In addition, tentative statements of philosophy and principles were developed. To coordinate the remainder of the Study, a central office was opened in Washington, D.C., on September 5, 1935. Soon afterwards, Dr. Walter C. Eells of Stanford University became project coordinator.[79]

The preliminary phases focused on building a foundation for the standards revision efforts. Initially, the committee identified fourteen areas for study. At a meeting in Montreat, North Carolina, in September 1935, the executive committee whittled the categories down to five: pupil, staff, plant, educational program, and administration. The criteria were further revised and checklists developed in the five areas. The committee recruited almost six hundred consultants to help evaluate the criteria, receiving mostly favorable reactions. The suggestions for improvement were published in a series of six pamphlets totaling seventy-six pages and were reviewed at a three-day meeting in St. Louis in late February

1936. In many respects, the St. Louis conference ended the preliminary stages of the Study.

The most pressing need was funding the experimental phase of the project. The regional associations contributed a total of $12,500, including more than $3,500 from the NCA. Following the funding precedent set by the CIHE standards revision project, the Cooperative Study received $25,000 from the General Education Board for the period 1935–1936. The committee again approached the General Education Board and secured a grant for an additional $116,000 for the period from 1936 to 1938. In spring 1936, the committee planned the experimental phase, estimating it would take a full school year and involve two hundred schools. The invitation to participate was well received and the target number was reached by September 1936. The printed draft criteria totaled 132 pages and contained about seventeen hundred separate items. The committee also considered "setting up tentative norms as a basis for the construction of a profile chart for each school, somewhat similar to the Institutional Pattern Map of the North Central Association."[80]

In preparing to test the criteria, the project staff trained surveyors and developed the survey procedures and instruments. The study employed eight full-time surveyors, including NCA members Paul Rhemus, principal of Battle Creek, Michigan, High School and president of the Michigan High School Principals Association, and J. E. Worthington, principal of Waukesha, Wisconsin, Junior-Senior High School and past president of his state's secondary school principals association. The surveyors attended a two-week training program in Washington, D.C., that included field testing of the draft survey procedures at four schools in Maryland and Virginia. Next, they visited four schools, two in Pennsylvania, and one each in Virginia and Delaware. They returned for a final conference with study personnel before beginning the study proper.

The survey phase had several components. The draft criteria were translated into a checklist of fifteen hundred items that addressed four hundred specific areas. Each participating school completed the checklist as part of its self-evaluation. The staff also administered a testing program to 100–110 pupils in the tenth through twelfth grades at each school in October and May. The first round involved intelligence, achievement, and social attitudes tests, while the second included only the last two. The achievement tests covered English, mathematics, science, social studies, and vocabulary, while the social attitude exams measured "changes in attitude toward war, the United States constitution, treatment of criminals, etc." There was also a series of focused studies on such topics as success in college of a school's graduates, parent and student opinions regarding school efficiency, follow-up on students not attending college, and "other similar evidences of school efficiency."[81]

The major activity was the visits to the two hundred schools by survey committees consisting of a minimum of three experts. Four committees divided the nation into sections, each of which started on October 1, 1936, in Maine, western Pennsylvania, Minnesota, and South Dakota. The heavy travel demands often extended an already grueling workday that surveyor Paul Rhemus described at the NCA annual meeting on April 6, 1938. The surveyors began their visit by examining paperwork, going to classes, and talking with administrators, teachers, and students in their junior and senior years. Next, they reappraised the checklist on the four hundred evaluations, adjusting school ratings as needed. Reappraisals took from about three hours to three evenings depending upon the completeness and quality of the reports. Rhemus observed that "most of the schools had actually rated themselves honestly and had rated themselves fairly." It soon became clear that generally the reports reflected the schools. "The better the school," he noted, "as a rule, the better the reports were made out." The final task involved a qualitative evaluation of the school because "we did not want to be lost in the total amount of detail which we had to cover in appraising each of those fifteen hundred items." In addition, they made a "qualitative evaluation of every school we had visited in terms of every other school we had seen before that time." In assessing the experience, Rhemus considered the job well done because "we had an honest picture of what we had set out to do in appraising these schools."

Principal Richard V. Lindsey of Pekin, Illinois, Community High School described the school's experience. He revealed that his staff had panicked at first because of the daunting task before them, but noted that their attitude changed as the work progressed. By the time the survey committee arrived in early April

1937, "all of our group were talking shop with a strictly professional attitude and enjoying it." This feeling extended to the students, who displayed a growing sense of pride in the school. He considered the weeklong visit of the team "as a most pleasant and profitable experience." In large part, the team added to the staff's comfort level by stressing they "were not with us to find fault, but rather to counsel and guide."

The survey experience increased staff awareness of problems and led to improvements, in part by energizing the faculty. Lindsey saw an increase in teacher pride and commitment. The study had helped stimulate instructional development because the faculty realized the "need for planning our work and objectives more from the point of view of the individual students." The staff had also become more aware of "the importance of always possessing very definite educational objectives." There was an increase in experimentation, resulting in more student activities in the classroom and greater interest among the faculty in teacher training. Lindsey concluded that participating in the study "gave us an incentive and impetus that is still present and shows no signs of abatement." He had learned that "the whole accrediting relationship can be made more interesting and beneficial to the individual schools when the technique for accrediting is developed in greater detail and on a more scientific basis." Other school officials offered similar praise of the study and the new accrediting program.[82]

After the experimental phase ended in July 1937, the staff developed a program that regional associations and schools could adapt to their individual needs. The core of the program was an innovative evaluation instrument that used educational thermometers. Like the institutional pattern maps employed in higher education, the thermometers were graphic devices with standardized calibrations that provided quantitative measures to evaluate a school. However, each thermometer approached an area from a different perspective, as Walter Eells explained. "Let us take, for example, the thermometer on the number of volumes in the library," he suggested. "Is that valid, or is it not?" In counting the number of volumes in a school library, if a specific school has only twenty-five books but the average for all schools was twenty-five hundred, then, he concluded, "For discriminative purposes...that particular thermometer is worthless." But, if the thermometer covered what he called "recency of publication," the validity changed. "Suppose it turns out that 75 percent of the books in one library have been published in the last ten years, and in another library only 12 percent," he explained, asking, "Isn't that pretty good evidence of discriminative value, something that helps differentiate a good school from a poor school?" The plan called for developing a large number of such thermometers that had the greatest discriminatory value. For libraries alone, he estimated over 1,032 different evaluation possibilities, or correlations as they were called then. Recognizing that the number of thermometers was overwhelming and impractical, the study staff assisted schools in selecting a much smaller number to meet their individual needs.[83]

The thermometers comprised one of three major products of the cooperative study. The others were the *Evaluative Criteria* that provided guidelines or criteria to use in evaluating a school, and an explanatory manual. All of these materials underwent long-term, significant review and revision. The first edition of the *Evaluative Criteria* was published in July 1935, and consisted of 13 pamphlets totaling 217 pages. Numerous revised drafts followed until a complete volume appeared in September 1939.[84]

If sales of materials are any indication, the Cooperative Study was well received nationally. As of May 15, 1939, the total sales for all three publications amounted to 16,405 copies. The Southern Association provided the best market followed by the NCA. In 1942, George Carrothers estimated that "a total of twenty-five hundred schools, forty thousand teachers, and one million pupils have had some contact with the Cooperative Study since its first use in 1936–37."[85] In addition, the Middle Schools Association recorded a high level of use by its members. By 1946, almost 70 percent of its members had used the criteria.

For a variety of reasons, including the size of the region and the number of member schools, the NCA rate of adoption was much lower. By 1946, slightly over 10 percent, or 401 of 3,031 secondary school members, had been officially evaluated under the new accrediting program.[86] The depression also hindered efforts. As Commission on Secondary Schools secretary G. W. Rosenlof explained in his 1938 report, "Until there is a return of economic prosperity and until the time when there is restoration of stability in our social, political and moral status, our schools will continue to confront the many significant difficulties characterizing our times in recent years." The NCA confronted these same problems in its activities. World War II made a bad situation much worse.

Internal Association developments possibly slowed adoption, too, though their goal was just the opposite. In 1938, the Commission on Secondary Schools launched a major, two-pronged organizational revision to accommodate the new system. The Committee on Standards substantially revised the accrediting policies for secondary schools, but there is some question as to whether the changes were implemented.[87] The introduction to the published revisions cautioned that "until the final recommendations of the Cooperative Study of Secondary School Standards are available for careful study no radical departures from present accreditation should be undertaken." The committee suggested clarifying and simplifying the existing program, making the criteria of evaluation more flexible, placing more stress on continuous evaluation, and shifting to a more comprehensive effort of stimulating improvements.[88]

Also in 1938, the Commission radically altered its organization, by dissolving all standing committees. In their place, the CSS members unanimously approved the creation of a new Administrative Committee of nine people whose major task was "to discover ways and means for adopting forthcoming proposals growing out of the Cooperative Study and directing such other responsibilities as they pertain to the evaluation of schools."[89] In his 1939 report, G. W. Rosenlof noted the Committee of Nine had arranged for field representatives from the Cooperative Study to visit almost every state and offer leadership and training in using the new system. The Commission also had approved a series of four recommendations. The first created a Committee on Policies consisting of seven members to continue the work of the Committee of Nine, while the second reaffirmed the policy of approving schools under the existing system, but continuing the process of clarifying and simplifying the program. The third and fourth recommendations dealt explicitly with the evaluative criteria.

The committee urged continued use of the criteria to stimulate improvements in schools. They strengthened adoption efforts by agreeing, "State Committees may, at their discretion, require that schools seeking membership in the association apply the evaluative criteria." The committee also expressed the hope that within five years all member schools would have used the evaluative criteria. The last recommendation suggested using trained personnel in various states to help implement the Evaluative Criteria, approving an advisory committee on its use. With expenses paid by the Association, these advisors would provide assistance to state committees upon request.

The 1939 report also expressed the Commission's enthusiasm for the Cooperative Study, declaring, "The challenge is there and the Commission is ready to accept it." But, the Committee of Nine recommendations had reduced the power of the CSS to face this challenge and possibly sent confusing messages to schools. By placing the decision-making power in the State Committees, it decentralized and possibly lessened Commission control of the adoption process.[90] The CSS had recognized that successful implementation of the modernized accrediting program depended on providing expert assistance to schools. Trained consultants were in short supply when compared to the potential numbers of schools using the new evaluation methods. Responding to these conditions, the policy statements intimated the need for a slow, studied transition, and thus affirmed use of the old program while promoting the new one.

The actions taken by the schools commission in the late 1930s represented the culmination of the initial phase of the second re-creation of the NCA. The outbreak of World War II temporarily stopped the process at the point where the modern accrediting theory had been developed and tested, but not implemented. The transformation of accrediting as well as the Association continued after the war, when education itself underwent a tremendous change that also influenced how the NCA re-created itself.

NOTES

1. Arthur W. Clevenger, "The Association—Some Suggestions for a Continued Program of Service," *North Central Association Quarterly* 13 (July 1938): 182.

2. Jesse Newlon, "How Can Standardizing Agencies Best Serve the Cause of Education in the Future?" *North Central Association Quarterly* 3 (September 1928): 208–9.

3. Ellis Hawley, *The Great War and the Search for a Modern Order: A History of the American People and Their Institutions, 1917–1933*, 2d ed. (New York: St. Martin's Press, 1992), 1–2.

4. See ibid. on the organizational movement. On African-American migration and urbanization, see James R. Grossman, *Land of Hope: Chicago, Black Southerners, and the Great Migration* (Chicago: University of Chicago Press, 1989), and St. Clair Drake and Horace Cayton, *Black Metropolis: A Study of Negro Life in a Northern City,* rev. ed. (New York: Harper & Row, 1962). On the rise of the consumer society, see Warren I. Susman, *Culture as History: The Transformation of American Society in the Twentieth Century* (New York: Pantheon Books, 1973), and Rolland Marchand, *Advertising the American Dream: Making Way for Modernity, 1920–1940* (Berkeley: University of California Press, 1985).

5. David O. Levine, *The American College and the Culture of Aspiration, 1915–1940* (New York: Cornell University Press, 1986), 23.

6. Edward Krug, *The Shaping of the American High School,* vol. 2: *1920–1940* (Madison: University of Wisconsin Press, 1972), xiii–xiv.

7. Lawrence Cremin, *The Transformation of the School: Progressivism in American Education, 1876–1957* (New York: Alfred A. Knopf, 1961) is largely a history of the progressive education movement. See also Krug, *The Shaping of the American High School,* vol. 2: *1920–1940,* 4–9, on the custodian idea.

8. On the impact of the automobile, see James J. Flink, *The Car Culture* (Cambridge, Mass.: MIT Press, 1975), and Peter J. Ling, *America and the Automobile: Technology, Reform, and Social Change* (New York: Manchester University Press, 1990). On radio and the movies, see J. Fred MacDonald, *Don't Touch That Dial!* (Chicago: Nelson-Hall, 1979), and Robert Sklar, *Movie-Made America: A Cultural History of American Movies,* rev. ed. (New York: Vintage Books, 1994). For contemporary views, see Robert S. Lynd and Helen Merrell Lynd, *Middletown: A Study of Modern American Culture* (New York: Harcourt, Brace & World, 1929); and Frederick Lewis Allen, *Only Yesterday: An Informal History of the 1920s* (New York: Harper & Row, 1959, originally published 1931).

9. Charles H. Judd, "A Method of Securing National Educational Standards," *North Central Association Quarterly* 3 (June 1928): 46–48; Samuel P. Capen, "The Principles Which Should Govern Standards and Accrediting Practices," *Educational Record* 12 (April 1931): 93. See also Newlon, "How Can Standardizing Agencies Best Serve the Cause of Education in the

Future?" and Lura Blackburn, "Applying North Central Standards to the Reorganization of a Curriculum in High School English," *NCA Quarterly* 4 (September 1929): 267.

10. Malcolm Cowley, *Exile's Return* (New York: Viking Press, 1951, originally published 1934), 309. Cowley rejected the idea his generation was lost. Roderick Nash, *The Nervous Generation: American Thought, 1917–1930* (Chicago: Rand McNally, 1970). See also D. H. Eikenberry, "How Can the Unit Courses and Curriculum Commission Develop Its Plan of Curriculum Construction to Serve Best the School Systems in the North Central Association," *North Central Association Quarterly* 5 (December 1930): 407. The rather esoteric source of this quote indicates how widespread such sentiments were. On life in the twenties, a particularly interesting work is the collection of primary sources edited by George P. Mowry, *The Twenties: Fords, Flappers & Fanatics* (Englewood Cliffs, NJ: Prentice-Hall, 1963). See also Allen, *Only Yesterday: An Informal History of the 1920s* for a contemporary and astute analysis of the decade.

11. See George M. Marsden, *Fundamentalism and American Culture: The Shaping of 20th Century Evangelicalism, 1870–1925* (New York: Oxford University Press, 1980); Kenneth T. Jackson, *The Ku Klux Klan in the City, 1915–1930* (New York: Oxford University Press, 1967); and Ray Ginger, *Six Days or Forever? Tennessee v. John Thomas Scopes* (Boston: Beacon Books, 1958).

12. Krug, *Shaping of the American High School, 1920–1940*, vol. 2, xiii–xiv.

13. Newlon, "How Can Standardizing Agencies Best Serve the Cause of Education in the Future?" 208, 210.

14. Jesse H. Newlon, "Practical Curriculum Revision in the High Schools, *North Central Association Quarterly* 1 (September 1926): 254.

15. Chester B. Curtis, in NCA *Proceedings*, 1917, 36–37. Curtis' opinion is supported by many later historians on change in the two decades following World War II. Ellis Hawley suggested that all post–World War I developments were rooted in the prewar experience and did not represent "anything approaching complete breaks with the past." Much of the advent of the modern age was less concerned with the invention of something new than innovative and mass application of phenomena created before 1914, or a culmination of an ongoing initiative. To cite just two examples, the technological innovations connected to electrification, the automobile, radio, and air travel all grew out of decades of development before the war. The big change was availability and use due to widespread application. Similarly, the high school's new status as the people's college represented the culmination of a movement that dated back several decades. Hawley, *The Great War and the Search for a Modern Order*, 2. Also see William Leuchtenberg, *The Perils of Prosperity, 1914–1932* (Chicago: University of Chicago Press, 1958), 4–6.

16. John Stout, "Report of Committee on Curriculum Problems," NCA *Proceedings*, 1920, 37.

17. L. W. Webb, "Report of the Committee on Standards for Use in the Re-Organization of Secondary School Curricula," *North Central Association*

Quarterly 1 (March 1927): 430–431.

18. Krug, *The Shaping of the American High School, 1920–1941*, vol. 2, 24.

19. John Stout, "Report of Committee on Curriculum Problems," NCA *Proceedings*, 1920, 37.

20. John Stout, "Curriculum Problems," NCA *Proceedings*, 1921, 43–57; John Stout, "Curriculum Problems," NCA *Proceedings*, 1923, 36–37. See also NCA *Proceedings*, 1896, 37; 1897, 1; NCA *Proceedings*, 1913, 13–14; 1916, 175; Calvin O. Davis, "The Special Study respecting the Junior High Schools in North Central Association Territory," supplement to NCA *Proceedings*, 1918, 6, for other discussions on the structure of secondary school.

21. John Stout, "Curriculum Problems," 43–57; John Stout, "Report of Committee on Objectives and Definition of Unit Courses of Study," NCA *Proceedings*, 1923, 34–36.

22. Stout, "Curriculum Problems," 36–37.

23. "B. Committee of the Commission on Unit Courses and Curricula: I. Committee on Standards for Use in the Reorganization of Secondary School Curricula," *North Central Association Quarterly* 3 (September 1928): 158. According to Calvin O. Davis, the Commission had created a new committee on Quantitative Studies in 1925, but this was somewhat premature as the committee on Qualitative Definitions of Units had only completed its work in three subject areas: English, general science, and physical education. There is a question of whether these committees actually existed as named, or represented the various stages of the curriculum reorganization work. No reports appeared under these committees' names, save for Davis' article, but rather the various and different permutations of the Committee on Standards for Use in the Reorganization of Secondary School Curricula offered its reports. On the early involvement of the NCA in athletics, see NCA *Proceedings*, 1902, passim.

24. R. M. Tryon, "Report of Sub-Committee on the Social Studies in the Junior High School," *North Central Association Quarterly* 2 (March 1928): 420–44. The ninth grade unit is on pages 436–44. This report was rather late. The March 1926 NCA *Quarterly* contained nine reports.

25. "Curriculum Reprints," *North Central Association Quarterly* 2 (June 1927): 3.

26. John Stout, "An Interpretation of the Work of the Committee on the Reorganization of Secondary School Curricula," *North Central Association Quarterly* 4 (September 1929): 258, 260–61; L. W. Webb, report to the Commission, in *North Central Association Quarterly* 5 (December 1930): 358–59. For a committee member's evaluation of a unit, see Lura Blackburn, "Applying North Central Standards to the Reorganization of a Curriculum in High School English," *North Central Association Quarterly* 4 (September 1929): 267–71. This article covers the experience in Oak Park–River Forest, Illinois, High School where Blackburn taught.

27. W. D. Cocking, "The Commission's Pattern and a Practical Program

of Curriculum Making," *North Central Association Quarterly* 5 (December 1930): 399–408.

28. "Curriculum Reorganization," in "Association Notes and Editorial Comments," *North Central Association Quarterly* 8 (June 1933): 7; "Sold Out," in "Association Notes and Editorial Comments," *North Central Association Quarterly* 10 (July 1935). On functional units, see Will French, "I. What Initiative Shall the North Central Association Take in Relation to the Secondary School Curriculum?" in "Curriculum Responsibilities of the North Central Association," *North Central Association Quarterly* 9 (January 1935): 317–21; "Functional Health Teaching," *North Central Association Quarterly* 12 (April 1938): 415–23. This is a series of articles on this project component.

29. NCA *Proceedings*, 1902, 90–103.

30. Lotus Coffman, "Presidential Address," *Proceedings*, 1922, 41. The athletic issue came to a head in 1926 and led to swift action by the Association. To help alleviate the problem, the CIHE voted that institutions provided financial aid and other free services were ineligible for accrediting under standard 9. "Aid to Athletics," *North Central Association Quarterly* 2 (June 1927): 33.

31. "Notes from the Annual Meeting," *North Central Association Quarterly* 1 (June 1926): 2.

32. H. M. Gage, "Committee on Athletics," *North Central Association Quarterly* 1 (December 1926): 335.

33. H. M. Gage, J. S. Nolen, L. W. Smith, "Report of the Committee on Athletics to the Commission on Higher Education of the North Central Association," *North Central Association Quarterly* 2 (September 1927): 217–18.

34. Gage, Zook, and Griffith, "Report of Committee on Athletics," *North Central Association Quarterly* 4 (December 1929): 321; W. P. Morgan, "II. General Report of the Committee on Physical Education and Athletics," in "Report of the Committee on Physical Education and Athletics," *North Central Association Quarterly* 8 (June 1933): 65.

35. B. L. Stradley, "I. Athletics and Physical Education in Higher Institutions," 26–28, 55, and W. P. Morgan, "II. General Report of the Committee on Physical Education and Athletics" in "Report of the Committee on Physical Education and Athletics," *North Central Association Quarterly* 8 (June 1933): 59.

36. See E. E. Morley, "Report of the North Central Association Committee on Athletics in Secondary Schools," *North Central Association Quarterly* 5 (December 1930): 332–39; 6 (June 1931): 21–30; Morley, "Athletics in Secondary Schools," *North Central Association Quarterly* 7 (December 1932): 287–90; "Proceedings of the COSS," *North Central Association Quarterly* 9 (July 1934): 72–74.

37. Louis G. Geiger, *Voluntary Accreditation: A History of the North Central Association, 1945–1970* (Menasha, Wis.: George Banta, 1970), 35–37.

38. Davis, *The History of the North Central Association*, 101.
39. A. Fox, "Unified College Standards Proposed by American Council of Education, *Proceedings*, 1922, 15. Fox was vice president of Marquette University and reported to the NCA on a 1921 conference on standards. See also William S. Harper, "A History of 'Extra-Legal' Accrediting of Higher Education in the United States from 1890 to 1970," unpublished Ph.D. dissertation, University of Missouri, Columbia, 1972, 68–69. Harper's dissertation surveys the various criticisms against accrediting of higher education, offering great insight into this often overlooked subject. For a summary of the Minnesota report, see Kenneth Holmes, "The Fixing of Standards in Higher Education," *School and Society* 27 (March 31, 1928): 396. See also Harry Pratt Judson, "Dangers of the Standardization Movement," *The Educational Record* 2 (July 1921): 114–15. Judson also noted he had not been active in the NCA recently.
40. Frank A. Waugh, "A Standardized World, *School and Society* 16 (November 4, 1922): 527.
41. Newlon, "How Can Standardizing Agencies Best Serve the Cause of Education in the Future?" 208–210. See also J. V. Yawkey, "The Validity of Regional Accrediting Standards for Secondary Schools," *North Central Association Quarterly* 8 (April 1934): 495; George E. Carrothers, "A Cooperative Attack on Secondary School Standards," *North Central Association Quarterly* 11 (April 1937): 273.
42. Holmes, "The Fixing of Standards in Higher Education," 396.
43. Ibid., 395; Samuel P. Capen, "The Principles Which Should Govern Standards and Accrediting Practices," *Educational Record* 12 (April 1932): 94–97. He recommended abolishing accrediting agencies and setting up "sanitary" organizations to combat fraud that bizarrely would result in the exercise of even more arbitrary power.
44. Copy of paper by President Smith, College Presidents Association, May 4, 1937, Des Moines, Iowa, dated April 30, 1927, in Charles H. Judd papers, Box 19 in University of Chicago Archives; Krug, *The Shaping of the American High School*, vol. 2: 1920–1941, 65.
45. Floyd W. Reeves, "Financial Standards for Accrediting Colleges, *North Central Association Quarterly* 2 (March 1928): 372; Floyd W. Reeves and John Dale Russell, "Standards for Accrediting Colleges," *North Central Association Quarterly* 3 (September 1928): 214–15. Both the NCA and the AAC provided funding, but Reeves did not mention the amount. Samuel P. Capen, "College Efficiency and Standardization: Certain Fundamental Principles," *Bulletin of the Association of American Colleges* 1 (1915): 149. In 1915, Capen was with the U.S. Office of Education. In the 1920s, Capen became chancellor of the University of Buffalo and was the most prominent critic of accreditation, though he sometimes omitted the NCA from his charges.
46. Reeves, "Financial Standards for Accrediting Colleges," 368. See George F. Zook, "Proceedings of the Commission on Institutions of Higher Education: IV. Annual Report of the Secretary," *North Central Association*

Quarterly 5 (June 1930): 70.

47. Judd, "A Method of Securing National Educational Standards," 43. Though Judd did not mention this fact, the Committee on Cost of Instruction had already published some reports that pinpointed problem areas and also offered some solutions.

48. Judd, "A Method of Securing National Educational Standards," 43–44, 46.

49. Newlon, "How Can Standardizing Agencies Best Serve the Cause of Education in the Future?" 208; Reeves and Russell, "Standards for Accrediting Colleges," *North Central Association Quarterly* 3 (September 1928): 228. The issue of providing accurate measures had been raised in 1922 by University of Akron president George Zook, who noted the dilemma faced by standardizing agencies. He commented that a discrepancy existed between the goal of standards to guarantee superior quality and the use of quantitative measures to meet this objective. At that time, he considered measuring the quality of work impossible. George F. Zook, "The Movement toward Standardization of Colleges and Universities," *School and Society* 16 (December 23, 1922): 710.

50. Judd, "A Method of Securing National Educational Standards," 43–44, 46.

51. Ibid., 46–48.

52. Ibid., 49, 51.

53. Carman's statement is included in the discussion section the *North Central Association Quarterly* added to the transcript of Judd's speech, Ibid., 55.

54. Letters, George Zook to Charles Judd, June 29 and September 13, 1929, in Charles H. Judd papers, Box 19, folder 9, University of Chicago archives. George Zook, "Proceedings of the Commission on Institutions of Higher Education," *North Central Association Quarterly* 5 (June 1930), 71.

55. "Digest of Conference," Committee on Revision of Standards, North Central Association, Hotel Windermere East, Chicago, Illinois, January 26, 1930, in Charles H. Judd papers, Box 19, folder 18, University of Chicago archives.

56. Reeves and Russell, "Standards for Accrediting Colleges," 221, 227.

57. Digest of Conference," January 26, 1930.

58. Lotus Coffman, "Part I. Introductory Statement," in "Improvement of Accrediting Procedures," *North Central Association Quarterly* 6 (September 1931): 200; Melvin Haggerty, "Part II. The Report of the Research Staff," in ibid., 201.

59. Haggerty, "Part II. The Report of the Research Staff," 201–8.

60. Ibid.

61. Ibid., 203, 205, 206.

62. Coffman, "Part I. Introductory Statement," 199–201. D. H. Gardner, John Dale Russell, and Hugh Gregg contributed much time and effort to the work.

63. George P. Zook, "Work of the Committee on Revision of Standards

for Higher Institutions in the Association," *North Central Association Quarterly* 7 (December 1932): 291–95; Douglas Waples, "Progress Report of the Committee on Library Standards," *North Central Association Quarterly* 5 (September 1930): 199–208, and *North Central Association Quarterly* 6 (December 1931): 245–51.

64. Zook, "Work of the Committee on Revision of Standards for Higher Institutions in the Association," 293–94.

65. Lotus Coffman, "I. Report for the Committee on the Revision of Standards," in "Reports Relating to the Revision of Standards for Institutions of Higher Learning," *North Central Association Quarterly* 8 (September 1933): 175–76.

66. Melvin Haggerty, "III. Accrediting Institutions of Higher Education," in ibid., 177–88.

67. Ibid., 182–83.

68. Ibid., 181.

69. No record exists of the unnamed third monograph's appearance and no copies have survived to my knowledge. It is possible that this publication was subsumed into the manual.

70. Cited in *North Central Association Quarterly* 12 (October 1937): 171.

71. L. B. Hopkins, "Scoring the Score Cards," *North Central Association Quarterly* 11 (January 1937): 315, 319. The italics are Hopkins'.

72. See chapter 2.

73. J. B. Edmonson, "The Influence of the Survey," *North Central Association Quarterly* 7 (September 1932): 216–17. See also Leonard V. Koos, "The National Survey of Secondary Education," *North Central Association Quarterly* 5 (September 1930): 219. This is a reprint of a paper Koos presented to the NCA at its 1930 annual meeting.

74. J. B. Edmonson, "The Newest Crisis in Education," *North Central Association Quarterly* 7 (June 1932): 18–19.

75. "Association Notes and Editorial Comments," *North Central Association Quarterly* 7 (December 32): 254.

76. Paul P. Boyd, "Shifting the Emphasis from Quantity to Quality in High School Standards," *North Central Association Quarterly* 6 (March 1932): 344–50; E. D. Grizzell, "The Cooperative Study of Secondary School Standards," *North Central Association Quarterly* 12 (July 1937): 34. See also Vernon Pace and Donald C. Manlove, *The First Fifty Years: Five Decades of Service to Education* (Falls Church, Virginia: National Study of School Evaluation, 1983). This is a commemorative, 50th anniversary volume.

77. George E. Carrothers, "Progress Report of the Committee on Study and Revision of Standards of the Commission on Secondary Schools," *North Central Association Quarterly* 10 (July 1935): 156.

78. Grizzell, "The Cooperative Study of Secondary School Standards," 34; George Carrothers, "A Cooperative Attack on Secondary School Standards," *North Central Association Quarterly* 11 (January 1937): 272–73. Reprint of an April 23, 1936, address before a joint meeting of the COSS and CIHE at the annual meeting in Chicago.

79. Pace and Manlove, *The First Fifty Years*, 5; Grizzell, "The Cooperative Study of Secondary School Standards," 35.

80. Carrothers, "A Cooperative Attack on Secondary School Standards," 273–76, 277.

81. "The Cooperative Study of Secondary Education," Walter C. Eells, "I. Some Significant findings of the Study," *North Central Association Quarterly* 13 (January 1939): 258, 260; Paul Rhemus, "II. Techniques of Visitation," ibid., 265; Grizzell, "The Cooperative Study of Secondary School Standards," 36, 43. Initially the number of items was eleven hundred.

82. Grizzell, "The Cooperative Study of Secondary School Standards," 36–37; Paul Rhemus, "II. Techniques of Visitation," 265–68; "The Cooperative Study of Secondary Education," Richard V. Lindsey, "III. Practical Values Arising from the Study, *North Central Association Quarterly* 13 (January 1939): 268–70.

83. Eells, "I. Some Significant Findings of the Study," 262, 263.

84. Pace and Manlove, *The First Fifty Years*, 7–9.

85. Ibid., 10; George Carrothers, "The Cooperative Study in Action," National Association of Secondary School Principals *Bulletin* 26 (April 1942): 26.

86. The figures come from a study by Joseph Roemer of the Southern Association cited in Geiger, *Voluntary Accreditation*.

87. G. W. Rosenlof, "I. Report of the Commission," in "Proceedings of the Commission on Secondary Schools," *North Central Association Quarterly* 13 (July 1938): 96.

88. "II. Policies, Regulations, and Criteria for the Approval of Secondary School," "Proceedings of the Commission on Secondary Schools," ibid., 98.

89. Rosenlof, "I. Report of the Commission," 97–98.

90. G. W. Rosenlof, "I. Report of the Commission," in "Proceedings of the Commission on Secondary Schools," *North Central Association Quarterly* 14 (July 1939): 68–69; Geiger, *Voluntary Accreditation*, 41.

Chapter Five

The Higher Education Commission Charts Its Course

The experience of the years that have passed points to a number of respects in which our practices are not consistent with the theory.

—Norman Burns, 1953

In the rapidly shifting higher education scene one thing is certain: new problems will emerge at least as rapidly as existing ones can be solved.

—Norman Burns, 1965[1]

THE HISTORY OF THE NCA from 1945 to the mid-1970s revolved around two themes: putting theory into practice and solving problems. To continue the re-creation that began in the 1930s with the development of the modern theory of accrediting, the Commission on Colleges and Universities and the Commission on Schools had to implement that theory. They accomplished this task and, at the same time, accommodated a widespread, deep-rooted revolution in education. Fortunately, the needs of fulfilling past organizational promises and addressing present environmental changes proved surprisingly compatible. The Association and both accrediting commissions introduced a new level of organizational bureaucracy by adding professional staff and establishing a central headquarters in Chicago. Though the commissions followed different paths, the policy of helping institutions learn how to change themselves became ingrained into accrediting procedures.

The higher education commission's development was so closely identified with Norman Burns that his tenure defined the era. He became involved with the NCA in 1945, when he was an assistant professor of education at the University of Chicago. After

Norman Burns. Executive secretary of the
Commission on Institutions of Higher Education, 1946–75, and secretary of the NCA,
1960–75, Burns was a leader of the post-
WWII NCA reform movement.

assisting then Commission secretary John Dale Russell, Burns
assumed this office in 1948. He remained with the NCA until his
retirement in 1974. His involvement spanned the era of educational revolution and commission reform. A combination of personal qualifications and circumstances allowed Burns to play such
a pivotal part in shaping the course of the higher education commission. He was a private man and very little is known about his
personal life. Patricia Thrash, executive director of the Commission
from 1988 to 1996, worked with Burns during his last few years
with the Association. She remembered him as a soft-spoken, gentle
man with a sharp intellect and dry sense of humor. His early writings, however, portray a vigorous, strong, and aggressive leader
with deep convictions and a creative mind. He also possessed a
pragmatic bent and an inclination toward cooperative action.
Thurston Manning, who succeeded Burns as Commission director,
noted his predecessor acted as a "formulator of policy alternatives."

In other words, his leadership qualities fit the voluntary association culture, an environment where, Manning noted, "Staff do well
when they develop policy alternatives and refrain from policy decisions."[2] Commission members make decisions and staff assist in
the process. Burns acted as a spearhead of change, an organizational entrepreneur who led a widely supported and well-organized
reform effort. Using the voluntary and collaborative features of the
NCA to advantage, he innovatively helped the higher education
commission move to higher levels of productivity. His success
rested on matching his ideas with those of the Commission, facilitating the process of change by offering guidance in making decisions, and then overseeing their implementation. Given the
turbulent higher education environment of the post-World War II
era, this meeting of an individual and the Association was fortu-
itous.

THE RISE OF THE POSTSECONDARY EDUCATION COMMUNITY

Between approximately 1945 and 1975, the massive changes
accompanying the educational revolution greatly increased the
need for institutions and the Commission to manage change better. Not only was there tremendous growth in the number of institutions and students, but the nature of schooling beyond the
secondary level changed markedly. Traditional colleges and universities experienced many changes, including the rapid rise of graduate degree programs and a phenomenal increase in the number of
two-year community colleges. The rise of community colleges was
stimulated by the emergence of a wide variety of programs and
institutions that did not fit into the traditional parameters of
higher education. Many of these programs and institutions occupied what University of Michigan professor Norman Harris called
"the 'twilight zone' between secondary-level trade schools and col-
legiate-level technical colleges and universities." Their programs
had an occupational orientation and the course of study ended
with a certificate rather than a degree. In addition, some institutions were proprietary.[3] As a result, by the late 1960s, the term
"postsecondary education" was used to refer to schooling beyond
the high school. The more restrictive adjective "higher" described
academically oriented degree-granting institutions, though some

were community colleges that offered two-year associate of arts degrees.

Three major environmental forces stimulated the ongoing changes. First and foremost, the realization of mass education provided Americans with equal access to a college education. Throughout most of U.S. history, attending college had been open to a small minority of the population. During the Progressive Era, the idea of using higher education for economic and democratic ends gained currency and was a prominent subtheme of early NCA discussions. The opening of the college doors was a slow and uneven process. Prior to World War II, higher education remained a privilege enjoyed by few Americans. The doctrine of equal educational opportunity gained greater credence during World War II and was first applied to the returning veterans through the Servicemen's Readjustment Act of 1944, or GI Bill. A major report on education sponsored by the Truman administration led to the official espousal of the goal of educational democracy in 1948. Other federal legislation and actions supported this position. By the 1970s, the idea of mass education had yielded to an even more inclusive notion: universal education. In 1973, K. Patricia Cross, a research psychologist with the Educational Testing Service, explained the rationale behind this "fundamental change in the purpose of higher education." She noted that contemporary conventional wisdom claimed, "The way to raise the standard of living in this country is no longer to train a few leaders but rather to educate the masses to their full humanity."[4]

A variety of forces coalesced to promote the idea of universal education. Business and industry advocated a better-educated workforce, and the public saw education as providing a step up the economic ladder. Many of the parents of children born after 1945 had come of age during the depression of the 1930s and the world war of the 1940s. They saw a college education less as a luxury than as an integral part of their children's formal education. In addition, the changing nature of work and technology created the need for continuing education for individuals beyond the traditional eighteen–to–twenty-two age group. The vocational and often specialized character of this schooling required different venues than those provided in traditional, academic classrooms. Arising from a very different perspective, the Cold War raised fears about the future of American democracy that sometimes translated into educational action. Americans generally believed education provided the United States with an edge in the struggle with the Soviet Union and the fight against the spread of Communism. The National Science Foundation Act of 1950 helped stimulate scientific research, while the National Defense Education Act of 1958 improved educational efforts in science, engineering, foreign languages, and mathematics. The latter was a response to the Soviet launch of the first space satellite.[5]

Government's growing presence fueled both the democracy movement and the growing public interest in postsecondary education. After having avoided much direct involvement in higher education for 175 years, the federal government became intimately and intricately involved in the future of collegiate institutions. In support of the equal access doctrine, it used legislation, funding, and even force to open colleges and universities to minorities. The courts and federal enforcement of legal decisions and legislation also helped make education more democratic and egalitarian. Culminating with the 1954 *Brown v. Board of Education* ruling, the National Association for the Advancement of Colored People (NAACP) used the courts to break down the system of legalized racial segregation, opening schools to African-Americans and other minorities. To enforce the new interpretation of the law, President Kennedy later deployed national guard troops to open southern universities to African-American students.[6]

Funding also stimulated change. Prior to 1963, federal funding followed a tradition of supporting specific groups, particularly during periods of national crisis.[7] The passage of the Higher Education Facilities Act of 1963 and the even more influential Higher Education Act of 1965 (HEA) ushered in a new era of federal funding for higher education. The facilities act was a legacy of the Kennedy administration passed after his assassination. It pioneered the idea of direct general aid to higher education by providing funds for construction of new facilities to meet the burgeoning enrollments. The second bill followed in the groundbreaking path of general funding legislation for elementary and secondary education. The HEA consolidated previous federal legislation for higher education to include providing student financial aid, extending the land grant idea to urban areas, and aiding African-American colleges. The HEA was amended in 1968 to cover the growing vocational sector of education. An astonishing sixty education bills were passed during the Johnson administration, raising the level of federal funding to higher education from $1.8 billion annually at the beginning of the decade to over $12 billion annually by 1970.[8]

Backed by favorable economic conditions, the combination of the democracy of education idea, the changing needs of society, and the federal government stimulated phenomenal growth in numbers and diversity of both the student body and the institutions serving this population. In 1940, almost 1.5 million students attended an institution of higher education. Over 3.2 million were enrolled in 1960. The student population more than doubled in the following ten years as 8.5 million Americans sought a higher education in 1970. By 1980, this number had increased by another one-third, to over 12 million.[9] The massive growth in the number of students meant that those seeking a collegiate education came from increasingly diverse backgrounds, possessed varying levels of ability, and had differing interests and goals. In the late forties, the appearance on campuses of veterans taking advantage of the GI Bill was an early sign of diversity. Their numbers overwhelmed the facilities of many institutions and also presented some unique challenges. The veterans tended to be older, often more experienced due to their military background, and often had families. They required different instructional approaches and facilities than those offered the eighteen–to–twenty-two-year-olds who comprised the traditional student body.[10]

Soon after the veterans of World War II and the Korean conflict left the campuses, the first members of the baby boom entered college. Beyond their overwhelming numbers, the baby boom generation expressed new attitudes and opinions that they translated into forms of activism that violently shook the foundation of higher education. In addition, equal opportunity dictates meant that more minorities sought a college education. Institutions had to accommodate disadvantaged individuals, adult learners, low academic achievers, and part-time students. In 1964, Norman Burns observed that one of the demands made on higher education was "the continually rising percentages of our youth and adults who go to college." A decade later, K. Patricia Cross observed that adult learners had different goals and needs. "The traditional academic fare of the social, biological, and physical sciences does not rank high in adult preferences." They overwhelmingly desired "occupational and career education." The same was also true of many students with poor academic records who sought a post-secondary education. In addition, by 1972, an estimated one-third of American adults attended school on a part-time basis, and that meant adjusting class schedules and possibly degree require-ments.[11]

The growing numbers and diversity of students stimulated a large increase in the number and variety of institutions and pro-grams. In 1940, there were 1,708 universities, colleges, professional schools, teachers colleges, junior colleges, and U.S. service acade-mies in operation. By 1960, that number had increased slightly to 2,008. By 1980, the number of institutions of higher education stood at 3,200. This growth rate translates into an average of 500 new institutions per decade. Two-year community colleges experi-enced the greatest growth. Existing and relatively new institutions also expanded their programs to accommodate various needs. In his 1948 report to the NCA higher education commission, Burns reported on the rapid extension of master's degree programs in many institutions. In later years, doctoral studies also expanded greatly.[12]

One of the fastest-growing sectors was vocational-technical education. Federal funding of vocational education had a long his-tory, dating back to the Smith-Hughes Act of 1917. In 1945, the federal government budgeted $15 million for vocational educa-tion. By 1964, this funding had more than tripled to $55 million. Following the passage of the Great Society educational programs between 1964 and 1970, federal funds for vocational programs soared to $300 million. Between 1964 and 1965 alone, funding increased by over $100 million to $157 million. In 1968, Univer-sity of Michigan professor of technical education Norman C. Harris claimed that federal funding under the Great Society program of President Lyndon Johnson was stimulating a boom in vocational-technical schooling. The financing of construction and work-study programs fueled much of the increase. Total state and local funding experienced similar rates of increase. The growing demand for vocational training fueled an increase in programs and institu-tions. The number of students in vocational programs rose from just over 2 million students in 1945 to almost 8.8 million in 1970. During the 1960s and early 1970s, Harris suggested the Vietnam War and military selective service requirements provided an added incentive for enrolling in these programs. By 1969, Norman Burns acknowledged the phenomenal increase in this area, claiming that "vocational-technical education beyond the high school is among the fastest growing parts of the educational system." He also noted that many of the new vocational institutions were seeking accreditation to establish themselves in the educational community.[13]

Yet another growing sector in postsecondary education was nontraditional learning. Though some aspects of nontraditional education had long been part of university extension programs, others were new and experimental. In a 1975 *North Central Association Quarterly* article on the subject, Patricia Thrash, then associate executive director of the NCA higher education commission, explained why defining the nontraditional sector was difficult. She cited Samuel B. Gould, chair of the Commission on Nontraditional Study, who had defined the term as an attitude that "puts the student first and the institution second, concentrates more on the former's need than the latter's convenience, encourages diversity of individual opportunity rather than uniform prescription, and de-emphasizes time, space, and even course requirements in favor of competence and, where applicable, performance." Thrash observed that nontraditional encompassed a wide range of ideas and practices, including "off-campus programs, grading innovations, no-major degrees, credit by examination, credit for life experience, credit for work experience, competency-based learning, individualized instruction, external degree programs, and programs offered in consortial arrangement with other institutions and agencies."[14]

All of the above developments were part of the revolution in education that resulted in the greater integration of higher education into the lives of Americans. The movement succeeded because institutions adapted to meet the needs of an increasingly diverse constituency, the federal government provided the funding, and the public desired the expanded educational services. Thus a combination of private and public interests fueled the revolution and dictated its course. In this process, accreditation played an important role. The educational revolution profoundly affected the development of the North Central Association, in large part because the NCA was a willing participant in the process of change.

An important part of the context of Association involvement was a basic alteration in its relationship with the federal government. The GI Bills had a direct impact on accrediting policies. Seeking to curb abuses that had occurred under the World War II legislation and to insure the quality and integrity of institutions participating in the Korean War program, the Veterans' Readjustment Act of 1952 required the states and the U.S. Office of Education to approve courses taken by eligible participants. To facilitate the approval process, the legislation stated, "For the purposes of this title the Commissioner [of Education] shall publish a list of national recognized accrediting agencies and associations which he determines to be reliable authority as to the quality of training offered by an educational institution and the State approving agencies may, upon concurrence, utilize the accreditation of such accrediting associations or agencies for approval of the courses specifically accredited and approved by such accrediting association or agency."[15] In other words, accreditation provided institutions with the seal of approval needed for participation in the GI Bill funding programs.

The connection between funding eligibility and accreditation was later extended to other federal funding programs. As a result, a new dimension was added to the NCA's service to its members. Accreditation provided access to money that, because of the increasing role of Washington as a funding source, could determine the development—indeed, the survival—of an institution. In addition, the Association and the federal government forged a new, more intimate relationship. In 1953, Norman Burns observed, "There are other forces operating to increase the magnitude of the task faced by the Association. Federal government agencies, for example, are looking more and more to the regional accrediting agencies for the certification of the quality of higher institutions." In an article published in the October 1953 *North Central Association Quarterly,* Burns tied the reliance of the government on accreditation as quality assurance to the increasing importance of institutional evaluation to the NCA, its members, and the public. He explained, "The listing of institutions bearing the accrediting agency's stamp of approval has come to be accepted by various governmental and nongovernmental agencies and by the general public as evidence their educational tasks are at an acceptable level. In this respect, the accrediting agency serves to protect the public interest."[16]

Serving the public interest was also a result of the democratization of education. The increase in students, programs, and institutions combined with rising costs made parents and adults question whether they were actually getting their money's worth. The trend toward nontraditional education brought up the issue of consumer protection in education. In his 1974 article, "Bad Apples in Academe," George Arnstein discussed the dilemma faced by all involved in the educational process. He returned to a long-standing educational problem—degree mills that defrauded their students. He also noted that ongoing innovation had created difficulties in assuring the quality of educational programs. Parents and students, along with officials in postsecondary institutions, government agencies, and accrediting associations had to distinguish "between the legitimate and the spurious within the context of educational pluralism." They also had to make "the baffling distinctions between innovation, openness, and unconventionality on one hand, and humbuggery, corner-cutting, and duplicity on the other."[17]

Confronted by challenges on all sides, the higher education commission of the NCA faced a daunting task between the midforties and midseventies. In 1961, Norman Burns posed the question on the minds of many NCA members throughout this period: "Does this Association possess the power of adaptability to changing times?"[18] The answer came in two interrelated thrusts by the Association's higher education commission: putting the reform theory of the 1930s into practice, and reorganizing the Commission and its procedures both to accommodate the practice of this theory and to adapt to the ongoing educational revolution.

PUTTING THEORY INTO PRACTICE

The reforms developed in the 1930s never really had a chance to be implemented due to the continuing economic depression and the ensuing global conflict. The postwar era proved equally turbulent, but the character of the tumult was different, being marked by prosperity and growth. However, implementing the ideas of the standards revision movement of the thirties remained problematic. Modern accrediting theory called for qualitative evaluation of the total institution in a way that stimulated self-improvement while preserving institutional individuality. The core of the process was evaluation by institutional objective. For existing members, maintaining accreditation in the late 1940s and early 1950s involved periodically filling out written forms that probed into selected areas of the institutional pattern map. New applicants underwent a more thorough procedure described by Norman Burns in 1951:

> An institution submits its application for accreditation. If it is the kind of institution which falls within the purview of our Association, its application is accepted and it is asked to provide a large amount of detailed information on schedules provided for that purpose. If it continues with its application, the institution is then visited by an examining committee which checks on the data that have been submitted, gathers additional information, makes its judgments and reports its findings to the Board of Review.

He also noted that the procedures stressed the judgments of the examiners. This corps of individuals received informal training through an apprenticeship under an experienced examiner. In assessing these practices, Burns suggested the institution played a passive role in the process and that "the emphasis is still largely on policing rather than the stimulation of self-improvement." There also was the difficulty of accommodating different types of institutions. In 1948, Burns had criticized the existing accrediting procedures for being inappropriate for evaluating junior colleges, concluding, "The North Central Association has been largely without constructive influence on the junior college movement." Similar inadequacies were identified in accrediting new graduate programs. Burns had also noted problems in the examiner corps, due to increased applications for membership and an insufficient supply of qualified personnel to conduct team visits.

To place his 1948 assessment in context, Burns cited the Statement of Policy Relative to Accrediting of Institutions of Higher Education that called for ongoing study to adjust and improve commission procedures. He warned that the failure to be flexible and adaptable to changing conditions could mean that "the

Association may act as a retarding influence on the appropriate development of higher education rather than as a force for the stimulation of soundly conceived educational programs designed to meet the emerging needs of a changing society." His comments ironically recalled similar criticisms voiced in the 1920s that had spurred the 1930s reforms. The need to maintain relevancy by being in the mainstream, if not the vanguard, of educational trends remained a basic Association policy. In part due to his continual prodding, the higher education commission continued the re-creation process by implementing many innovative changes.[19]

In the early fifties, Burns focused on the inability to implement the 1930s reforms, The quote that opened this chapter summed up his message: NCA practices were not always consistent with its theory. As for the problem, he explained, "Primarily, our difficulties stem from the questionable validity of some of the assumptions we have made in translating theory into practice." Some of these misconceptions reflected the transitional state of the Commission's accrediting program. "We have continued to assume, as we did under the former procedures," he argued, "that quality can be engendered by requiring institutions to conform to a set of practices laid down by the accrediting association." Burns also refuted the idea that "we can evaluate a particular institution, at least in part, in terms of practices found to be characteristic of quality institutions in general." This latter idea he attacked as being "in direct contradiction of the philosophy of accrediting enunciated twenty years ago."

One problem was that in attempting to implement the new theory, more attention was paid to the letter than the substance of the criteria. Citing this practice as a "persistence of standardization," Burns explained that some statements in the *Revised Manual of Accrediting* "which were doubtless intended merely as guides to institutions and examiners became prescriptions when translated into the directions given the examiners."[20] The result was a distortion of the rationale developed by Melvin Haggerty, Floyd Reeves, and others. But, the continuing practice of applying general standards to be met by all institutions also highlighted one of the problems the Commission faced in implementing its theory. The old and familiar ideas and practices were difficult to replace and implementing the innovations was equally hard.

The examining visit also raised important issues. Burns suggested the time allotted the visit was too short to accurately appraise an institution. Admitting the competence of the NCA examiners, he explained that assessing the intangible aspects of institutional quality was difficult for an outsider, and the time constraints further inhibited the gaining of insight into the institution. The resulting evaluation by "subjective judgments" was fallible and open to variable interpretations. To overcome these defects in visitation, "our criteria tend to stress organizational or structural aspects and other tangibles that can be readily determined rather than the actual results obtained in the various aspects of the institution's activities." Again, the old and familiar made implementing the reforms difficult.

The various criticisms notwithstanding, Burns concluded, "we have had some success in putting our theory into practice." He noted significant improvements in weaker institutions as an example. However, an important omission lessened the record of the Commission. Examinations were scheduled solely for institutions that required the visit, such as new applicants or in cases where problems were identified. Because the overwhelming number of members have not needed an examination, Burns suggested, they have "derived little direct benefit from membership in the Association other than the prestige of inclusion in the list of accredited institutions." Some founding member institutions, in fact, had never been visited by a NCA team in the forty years of higher education accrediting.[21]

Burns' 1953 assessment of the ills of NCA higher education accrediting was part of a five-year crusade for reform he spearheaded. In reports to the Commission and in articles published in the *North Central Association Quarterly*, he pursued a consistent and, most likely, well-received argument that aimed at making certain the NCA did adapt to changing conditions. However, he did not just point out defects and deficiencies in the NCA accrediting system and organization. Rather, reflecting the historical tradition of criticism, he affirmed, "Consciousness of our shortcomings is not new to us." As had been true in the past, the public airing of faults prefaced the presentation of problem-solving ideas. For Burns, the solution was to practice the reform ideas of the past.

In 1951, two years before his assessment of accrediting conditions, he had presented the seeds of a plan to reform the NCA. Reflecting the tendencies of the times, he called for "a democratization of the accrediting process which would permit the institutions being appraised to play an active role in the process." His democratically inspired activism required revising the accrediting criteria and procedures to include more institutional involvement in the approval of any recommended changes. The four-step procedure he outlined had already been approved in principle by the Commission and was to be experimentally tested. The major change was the first step. "When an institution applied for accreditation it would be asked to submit evidence that it had been engaged in a program of self-evaluation," he explained. A comprehensive report was required that offered a detailed analysis of the institution's operations. It also defended the "appropriateness of their avowed objectives," identified the areas of strength and weakness, and explained the reasons why the institution should be accredited. The second step was a visit by examiners, who would use the institutional report as a guide. The examiners' report followed and appraised the institution according to NCA criteria. The recommendations of the Board of Review and the Commission completed the process. In addition, Burns noted that a similar procedure would be used for member institutions requiring reappraisal. Over the next two years, this initial plan underwent some changes, particularly the institutional self-evaluation requirement.

By 1953, the nascent reform effort required improved administration that necessitated greatly increased funding. By raising member fees, the Commission increased its annual budget from $14,000 to $50,000. The extra money paid for the full-time employment of a Commission secretary and support staff as well as various studies related to the proposed reforms. In defending the fee increases, Burns exclaimed, "We may again, as we were twenty years ago, be at the beginning of a new era in accrediting." In October of that year, the movement began anew with Burns' proclamation: "We are about to reform. We are now engaged in a full-scale, critical examination of our present procedures and of the assumptions underlying them, and in planning for an extension of our program to the end of greater service of the higher institutions in our territory."[22]

The employment of full-time professional staff was one indication of the new accrediting era. A paid staff broke with earlier tradition. On prior programs, consultants had received payments for their services, but most had volunteered their time by gaining leave from their institutions for the duration of a project. The switch from a voluntary to a professional staff would solve a long-standing difficulty by bringing "a larger measure of uniformity and consistency into the program of accrediting than has been possible in the past. This lack of consistency and uniformity in the accrediting activities has been one of our major problems."[23] In 1953, Norman Burns became the first full-time professional NCA staff member.

Clarence B. Hilberry. President of Wayne State University, Hilberry was a prime mover and committee chair for the reorganization of the Association in the 1950s.

The goal of the reform program was to increase the effectiveness of the Commission's work. C. B. Hilberry of Wayne University in Detroit identified four factors that hampered Commission activities. The first problem was size, and referred not only to the vastness of the region but the number of members, too. As Hilberry explained, "There are nearly 400 of us spread thinly over nineteen states." From a different perspective, size related to the increasingly diverse types of members, including the proliferation of junior colleges and the expansion of institutions into graduate programs. The other difficulties concerned problems arising from the size issue. Hilberry claimed, "We have failed to provide a working mechanism through which like-minded schools could get together for the study and resolution of common problems." This failure, in turn, was accompanied by the inability to systematically "make available to individual members of the association the know-how and the wisdom which we have as a group." As a result, he concluded, "we have failed to inform each other adequately about the techniques and the results of such studies and explorations which are being carried on both within and without our membership."

To address the mounting concerns, the Commission had set up three committees that approached their tasks in customary NCA fashion. To organize their efforts, they posed three sets of questions. The first question asked: "Is our present organization adequate?" The second inquired into whether the commission structure needed revising to make it more representative, to enhance the active participation of member institutions, and "to bring members with common interests and problems together for a better common attack upon them." The last question asked about extending the accrediting function to assist "each other to make the greatest possible growth in strength and vitality of which we are capable." The underlying thrust of reform was to better help institutions learn how to change themselves through cooperative action.

The posing of questions facilitated the development of assumptions and the devising of "a series of working hypotheses" to guide the actual work. The two basic suppositions were (1) NCA members as a group were "committed to providing the finest opportunities for higher education of which we as a group are capable," and (2) "within the North Central institutions themselves lie all the basic skills and all the wisdom necessary to meet our up-coming problems, insofar as they can be met." Basing their actions on these assumptions, the committees revived a 1930s idea that Norman Burns had also suggested: include an institutional self-evaluation component in the accrediting process. The self-study became the core around which the implementation of the 1930s theory revolved. The committee hypotheses all focused on the self-study. The first hypothesis stated, "That self-study (both for the capacity for productive self-study and the consistent pursuit thereof) is the best single evidence on institutional vitality and growth." The second observed that a self-study was "seldom carried out in isolation." The third suggested groups of similar institutions could better conduct such studies than a single college. The last dealt with sharing the fruits of these studies.[24]

The development of the hypotheses identified the basic components of the reform program. Each committee set about completing its assigned task. The Planning Committee was to develop, coordinate, and conduct "studies of fundamental problems facing higher institutions." Its members recognized the limitations and the standardizing effects of relying on outside examinations to evaluate and stimulate improvement. They also realized that only a small number of institutions benefited from this experience. The self-study offered a more effective approach so the committee suggested having institutional staffs study assorted facets of their work. One idea was to "sponsor a series of institutional studies of various aspects of the administrative process." Among the numerous topics available for scrutiny were the operation of boards of control, the determination of institutional policies, and solving problems of communication and coordination. To help the institutions participating in such studies, the committee recommended developing a consultant service. The hope was that a program of self-studies would redirect Commission efforts toward "stimulating institutions in general to study their problems in the light of their objectives and the particular set of conditions in which they operate." In the process, the Commission would "encourage institutional individuality, innovation, and differentiation in objectives and methods." It would also help institutions learn how to solve their problems better.

Where the planning committee's focus was on improvement, the Committee on Reorganization of Accrediting Procedures dealt with evaluation and implementation. It was to develop "procedures under which the institution would play a much more active part in the accrediting process," bearing the responsibility of showing "why it should be accredited." In practice, the Commission requirement that institutions must conduct a self-study prior to examination lessened the difficulty of this task. The Committee was also to develop better methods for conducting self-studies, possibly expand their use, and address the implications the new evaluation approach might have on the visitation component. Any change promised to alter the role of the examiners substantially. "They now play the part of the medical practitioner who examines a patient," Norman Burns explained. But, he continued, "their proposed role would be that of the examiners before whom the candidate for a graduate degree defends his thesis." The examiners would use the institutional self-study as a guide to evaluation.

The reorganization committee had to restructure the organization of the Commission to accommodate the proposed new program. The existing method placed "complete responsibility for the accrediting process up to the point at which the Board brings its recommendations to the full Commission" on the Board of Review and the Commission secretary. The mounting workload and the emphasis on institutional individuality created the need for an intermediate, decision-making, bureaucratic layer. The creation of a set of committees was suggested as a possible solution. Two possible approaches were organization by geographic area or by type of institution.[25]

The Committee on Professional Accrediting Problems tackled the general problems in the accreditation sector. After 1945, the number of professional accrediting agencies that focused upon one program or area of an institution's work increased greatly. These agencies typically employed quantitative evaluation to achieve standardization. Large, complex institutions attacked the proliferation of agencies and their work as a usurpation of the power of authorities legally mandated to govern higher education. In response, they founded the National Commission on Accrediting in 1949. This organization proposed combining all accreditation under the auspices of the regional associations and discontinuing the accrediting activities of the professional agencies. The latter would only be concerned with improvement. Changes in this plan made its implementation unlikely, but did not eliminate many other problems in the accrediting sector. The Committee on Professional Accrediting Problems was to develop ways for achieving better cooperation and coordination among the various agencies, so "they can work together in the best interests of higher education and of the society it serves."[26]

The success of the reform program depended largely on realizing the promise of the self-study. A versatile instrument, the self-study, provided the means to implement the 1930s theory that accrediting should be qualitative and that it combine evaluation and improvement while preserving institutional integrity. In addition, the self-study promoted active institutional involvement in the accrediting process and the Association. The experience of conducting the self-analysis offered a number of benefits, including the integration of a self-evaluation mechanism into institutional operations to stimulate continual improvement and help institutions learn how to change themselves. In the process, the prevailing top-down approach to accrediting would give way to a grassroots effort that enhanced the voluntary character of membership and possibly increased NCA involvement. Last, the self-study would alleviate the reliance on subjective judgment in evaluation by changing the role of the visitor from that of a diagnostician to an examiner.

To realize the promise of the self-study, both institutions and the Commission had to solve various problems. Institutions faced difficulties in conducting competent self-studies because of lack of expertise and experience. The newness of the practice had the potential of falling flat due to poor efforts, and failure could lead to a lack of confidence, motivation, and commitment among member institutions that might doom the Commission's reform efforts. Since the reform program rested on the quality of the self-study, the Commission's major task was ensuring success by facilitating effective use of this evaluation instrument. Institutions had to understand the value of the process, and their experience had to be rewarding and exhilarating, leading to recognized improvements. The Commission also had to accommodate the growing number and variety of members. In addition, the question of effective use extended beyond the actual administration of the proposed program to its frequency. Because they called for one-time use of the self-study for admission purposes, existing procedures worked against the reform goals of continual self-evaluation and improvement. To involve all members in the self-study process on an ongoing basis, the accrediting program had to be expanded.

But implementing change required the endorsement of the members. Over the years, the NCA had employed different strategies to build agreement on proposed changes. In the early years, the participatory democratic nature of the annual meetings facilitated discussion and acceptance, as did the credo that even new policies and practices were subject to revision. The 1930s standards revision effort benefited from the institutional involvement and cooperation during the pilot stages, when the new program took shape. In the 1950s, reformers built upon these traditions and added some new ideas. Following a strategy successfully used in the 1920s to spur the standards alteration, the Commission launched a five-year meeting and media campaign to persuade members of the need for change and to convince them of the direction reform should take. Papers at the annual meetings, combined with articles in the *Quarterly* and other Commission publications, continually pointed out the problems with the current system. Reform advocates, with Norman Burns as primary spokesperson and leader, claimed the changing nature of higher education required a NCA response and offered ideas for potential courses of action. A new Association effort to improve communication provided a regular way to promote reform. In the early 1950s, the Association began publishing a newsletter entitled *NCA Today*. Burns published articles in the newsletter to further the reform cause.

The campaign for reform reached its zenith at the 1955 annual meeting. Certainly, the celebration of the Association's sixtieth birthday that year was not lost on the reformers. A number of speakers delivered the message that change was needed and pushed for acceptance of the proposed plan for reorganizing the Commission and its activities. Planning committee chair C. S. Hilberry prefaced his remarks at the first general session of the meeting by noting that the heavy promotional campaign meant, "I am to re-tell, not a twice-told, but at least a thrice-told tale and keep you all awake for twenty minutes." He mentioned that the activities of the three committees "have been so widely discussed that I'm sure every college administrator, even those of us who find it impossible to keep up with our mail, have been indoctrinated somewhere."[27] Hilberry intimated that the Commission kept members aware of the ongoing developments through various mailings so that action could be taken at the meeting.

In pushing for reform, Burns, Hilberry, and their colleagues used a vehicle that had successfully stimulated reforms in the past, the presidential message. Milo Bail celebrated the sixtieth birthday of the NCA by chronicling its history, recalling

> some of the enduring values, mountain peak experiences, out-standing leaders, significant committees and commissions, important terms and standards, outstanding studies and reports, magic numbers, and parliamentary decisions which have exerted tremendous influence not only upon the second-ary schools and higher institutions in some twenty midwestern states during the past half-century but to the national scene as a whole.

In placing the current situation in context, he repeated an often cited theme: "Every problem facing us today is but an extension of the problems which have faced educational institutions through-out the whole history of the North Central Association." Bail iden-tified "the needs of the NCA, in the seventh decade based upon six decades of progress." Among the proposals he cited, the fourth dealt with training individuals to conduct self-studies. Supporting an idea by a speaker at a regional meeting in Omaha, Bail recom-mended a pilot study in training evaluators.[28]

In many respects, Milo Bail's strategy and message were strik-ingly reminiscent of the presidential address given by James E. Armstrong in 1915 that resulted in the three-commission structure. Just as the problems facing the NCA remained similar to those of the past, so the strategy to propose solutions also had a long tradi-tion.

Hilberry described the proposed five-year project. The core activity was developing and evaluating "a program for training consultants for service in self-studies." The second component called for the "carrying forward of a growing number of self-studies in which the consultants-in-training would participate." Part of this effort involved developing "the many instruments, tests, and manuals necessary to carry such studies forward," including a revi-sion of the *Manual of Accrediting*. The last element was the presenta-tion of progress and final reports that "would provide a sound

Milo Bail. University of Omaha president, Bail was NCA president in 1953 and was actively involved in the reorganization of the Association in the 1950s.

beginning for the clearinghouse." The clearinghouse would supply institutions with various materials to help them improve their operations. Underlying these components was the implicit goal of making self-studies central to accrediting activities. The project would achieve this end by developing a "corps of trained consultants and a large accumulation of data and conclusions as well."[29]

THE LEADERSHIP TRAINING PROJECT

The Commission plan was approved on Friday, March 25, 1955. The first phase of training self-study consultants required funding. The next day, a subcommittee of the planning committee formulated the "first proposal which it will then lay before a Foundation." Apparently, securing funds took some time, because not until 1957 did NCA secretary Charles W. Boardman report that the Commission had received a five-year grant for $147,000 from the Carnegie Foundation.[30] As a result, the Leadership Training Project (LTP) was born. On July 30, 1957, Norman Burns sent a letter, a brochure explaining the project, and other materials to the chief administrative officers of the higher education members of the

NCA. Editor Harlan Koch announced the project in the October 1957 *Quarterly* and reprinted the project brochure. The LTP was under the purview of the Committee on Leadership Training and Studies. The objective of training general consultants was tied to a long-range purpose of the committee, developing future leaders for higher education. In this respect, the Commission connected its needs to those of its member institutions.

Admission to the program was restricted to administrators or faculty members in their early to middle thirties who "through positions held, administrative or scholarly activities engaged in, give promise of being future leaders in education." The candidates had to be in a NCA institution and be nominated by the institution's administrative head. Possession of a Ph.D. was preferred, but not required. An obvious by-product of the focus on the best and the brightest was that these people would also provide the Commission with high quality examiners, while the youth emphasis promised long tenure. The participants retained their positions during the training period, but needed release time, estimated at fifty-five to sixty days over a one-year period. Apparently, the LTP met a major need, because the committee received a hundred nominations for the fifteen slots open in the first year's class.[31]

The activities were spread over a calendar year. The fifteen enrollees began their training by attending a three-day conference in November 1957. They discussed major problems in higher education, learned about evaluation techniques and procedures, and planned institutional visits. The remainder of the school year was spent visiting five institutions for four days each. The visits were scheduled at different types of institutions to help the candidates gain a general understanding of higher education institutions. The diversity strategy also helped combat the limited vision that, in 1928, Charles H. Judd had suggested created a myopia that hampered educational progress. As Harlan Koch explained, "One may paraphrase the basic purpose of this project by saying it is designed to guard against the provincialism which flows from experience wholly contained within a single institution."[32] The candidates were paired with an experienced consultant and divided into teams of three. Two Commissioners comprised the remainder of the group. Before each visit, they reviewed the materials prepared by the institution and met with the supervisor to discuss these studies and further plan the visit.

The field experience involved the candidates in assisting institutional staff members in developing appropriate, but not ready-made solutions. The idea was to enhance the individual character of each college or university by devising solutions unique to their situation. This strategy overcame any uniform or standardizing features and promoted institutional initiative in seeking change. In the first year, candidates conducted institutional surveys during their visits. Following the visit, they wrote reports of the experience that served as evaluative devices for the project and provided guidance for the institution. During the first year, 1957–1958, nine institutions were visited by LTP teams.

The final component was a summer, follow-up workshop for candidates and supervisors. It was "seen as a device for integrating and making meaningful the experiences that the enrollee will have had and for further broadening his outlook through relating these experiences to the larger scene." The workshop also provided an opportunity for evaluating the project. Originally it was planned for two weeks, but was later reduced to four days. The first follow-up session was held in August 1958.[33]

As the project developed, the LTP revised its training program. In the second year, the focus of the institutional visits changed so that the candidates explored problems in-depth. The following year, examiners attended a series of conferences to discuss educational problems and reach agreements on aspects of evaluation, as well as to interpret their observations of the project. The conferences also allowed those attending to prioritize institutional elements for evaluation purposes. In the process, the Commission created a follow-up component to the training program that continued the process of education and evaluation of both accrediting and the LTP. By 1959, enough graduates were available that a College Field Service was established to provide consultants for institutions and project coordinators. In assessing the Leadership Training Project, Norman Burns reported that the Commission viewed it "not as a terminal program, but rather as the foundation for further growth of the participants, first, as generalists to be used as consultant-evaluators, and, looking a little more to the future, as leaders in higher education." After only three years, the project had

CHAPTER FIVE

already met its primary purposes. In 1960, the Commission received a supplemental grant of $61,000. When that money ran out, it funded the program internally.[34]

Between 1963 and 1965, the Commission transformed the LTP into a larger Consultant-Examiner Program. The C-E component, in turn, was integrated into Commission operations, as several name changes indicated. The designation of those participating in the training component changed from candidate to associate, with the result that the LTP was sometimes called the Associate's program. In addition, the consulting arm of the Commission, the College Field Service, was subsumed under the new Consultant-Evaluator (C-E) Corps that provided evaluation and consulting services. By 1965, examiner had replaced evaluator in the C-E equation, greatly altering the connotation of what this individual did.[35]

Both environmental and internal organizational factors led the Commission to reorganize the LTP. The environmental influences reflected the changing conditions in higher education and in the role played by accreditation. A major theme of the development of higher education after World War II was the addition of graduate programs by existing and new institutions. In 1950, the NCA added a requirement that accreditation of new programs required an examination visit, substantially increasing the need for trained visiting team members. Equally important, membership in the NCA increased steadily during this period. Most likely, the primary incentive for seeking NCA accreditation was the access it provided to federal funding programs. For example, in 1965, Commission vice-chair Albert Pugsley reported that ninety-two visits had occurred in the previous year. He cited the eligibility requirements of the recently passed Higher Education Act as stimulating interest among institutions previously indifferent to the NCA. For funding and other reasons, the NCA membership jumped from 312 institutions in 1945 to 432 in 1960, and to 554 in 1969. The growth in numbers was accompanied by a similar increase in diversity, particularly the appearance of many community colleges.[36]

To adapt to the increased demand and the evolving higher education scene, a series of changes occurred in the LTP. In 1963, admission requirements to the program were expanded to reflect the increased workload and, even more importantly, the depletion of the ranks of older, more experienced consultant-evaluators. Noting that it had "strengthened that segment of the group of field representatives which is composed of young men of promise," the Commission explained the current need was "to strengthen that segment of its evaluating corps which is composed of scholars and administrators of distinction." The admission of senior administrators and scholars ensured that a complementary mix of age and experience was present in the C-E Corps.[37] The following year, seven junior college representatives were included for the first time. Their participation was part of a cooperative project with the Midwest Community College Leadership Program, funded by a Kellogg Foundation grant.

In 1964 and 1965, the training program was overhauled. The enrollees first came together at an orientation session in Chicago on September 21, 1964, where they learned about the history and activities of the NCA, present policies and procedures, and the LTP plan of operation. The participants then went on several visits as members of the team and wrote parts of the various reports. But the types of visits differed from those under the original program. The associates participated in diagnostic examinations at institutions working toward accreditation. They also served on preliminary accrediting teams, meaning they visited member institutions seeking to expand their graduate programs and gain NCA approval of these new efforts.[38] Associates went on full accrediting visits for potential new members, and on periodic review examinations. To discuss their experiences, they attended a Midway Conference at the annual meeting and the orientation session the following autumn, where they became C-E Corps members.[39]

Annual consultant-examiner conferences were also instituted "to provide opportunities for continuing conversations among those who are serving as consultants or as examiners." The Commission felt that "the meeting of minds that can be accomplished through such conversations is important in the interest of developing a consistency of approach to the problems of consulting and evaluation." The diversity of institutions and the strategy of evaluation by objectives through a self-study threatened to create a very chaotic and problematic accrediting process. Consistency of procedure and approach helped alleviate such conditions by providing order to the process, and facilitated drawing upon prior experience in solving institutional problems. It might also have lessened the likelihood of litigation in cases where an institution felt wrongly served and complained of unfair treatment. The conferences served an additional purpose in that they allowed for "a systematic analysis of the field experiences "to identify areas that needed revising. They also helped determine whether the program required modification to meet changing conditions.

As the consulting and evaluation program expanded, funding became a major consideration. The fee charged for institutions undergoing visits had been raised from $300 to $400 in 1957. In 1964, rising costs and demands prompted another increase to $600 per visit. The Commission justified this action by claiming it placed NCA "rates a little more into line with current rates for professional services." The rate increase provided for an increase in the honoraria paid to evaluators. At the same time, the Commission's Executive Board approved higher charges for consultant services. They estimated this increase would produce $35,000 annually, "an amount sufficient to pay for the consultant-examiner conferences, for the Leadership Training Program," and other needs.[40]

The formal training program for the C-E Corps was ended in 1975. Over the next five years, attempts at using informal training efforts proved unsuccessful. In 1980, a new annual meeting workshop program was started.

In many respects, the major innovation of the NCA higher education commission after World War II was the training and maintenance of an expanding body of professional volunteers whose role was basically to implement the policies of the Association. As such, the Leadership Training Program and the C-E Corps represented the logical continuation of the 1930s reform initiatives and, like the self-study, should be considered as part of this earlier movement, rather than as a distinct element or a separate response. The reform of higher education accreditation facet of the NCA re-creation was a long-term effort that began with Charles Judd's 1928 speech and ended in the early 1960s with the formal establishment of the corps of consultant-examiners. The 1930s witnessed the development of theory and much of the implementation strategy. The depression, the war, and, to a certain extent, the adjustment to peace and prosperity after 1945 delayed applying these theories and testing out the plans.

Because of the extended time span, the practice of qualitative accrediting by institutional objectives mixed the ideas of the 1930s with new concepts developed after 1945 to meet changing conditions. The idea of a self-study was implied in the institutional pattern map idea of the thirties, but got lost in the plethora of details. After the war, the self-study emerged as the cornerstone of the new practice of accrediting. Similarly, the notion of experienced consultants was mentioned in the 1930s, but post–World War II consulting transcended the conceptions of Melvin Haggerty and his committee. If the self-study became the way to apply the new accrediting theory, the LTP and the C-E Corps provided the means for it to play this role. Through the LTP and the C-E Corps, the higher education commission institutionalized the recruitment, training, and maintenance of a large number of volunteers from member colleges and universities to perform its activities.

After 1957, the Leadership Training Project also served as the primary entryway into Commission activity. The C-E Corps allowed for wide representation of member institutions. However, the parameters for NCA involvement narrowed as experience in the C-E Corps activity became a prerequisite for future participation in Association affairs as a Commissioner or officer. Thus, individuals serving in NCA decision-making positions had extensive experience in the Association and higher education, often at the grassroots level.

In a very different sense than originally conceived, the LTP also fulfilled the early, abandoned promise of training future leaders of education. The experience as a consultant-examiner benefited the institution and the individual. The gains related to the multidimensional educational aspects of the LTP and C-E work. In the process, the Commission provided a great service to members. The ability of institutions to change themselves depended in part upon the expertise of the personnel undertaking the task. By having people participate in the Commission evaluation program, they were supplied with experienced, in-house staff for the self-study and other change processes.

Individuals who received this informal education often realized unexpected benefits. The NCA experience helped their careers and increased their competence. Paul C. Reinert, S.J., chancellor emeritus of Saint Louis University, was that institution's NCA representative from 1944 to 1974. Reinert also served on the NCA Board of Review, as chair of the higher education commission, and NCA president. During fifteen years of this tenure, he served on a C-E team at least once a year. "From these visits, I learned at least as much, if not more, than I did from my classes in the School of Education at the University of Chicago," he noted.

> Not only did these visits provide me with personal acquaintance with the educational leaders in the North Central geographic area, but I learned what leadership qualities are most effective in a chief executive who is to be truly an internal leader of his faculty, staff, and students and at the same time an influential civic and community leader.

However, the insight gained was not always as constructive as he intimated. Retired University of Nebraska president Ronald Roskens became involved in the Association while he was at Kent State University in Ohio. He remained active as his career progressed and he became chancellor of the University of Nebraska at Omaha and later president of the University of Nebraska system. During this period, Roskens served in a variety of NCA capacities, including visiting team member and chair, member and chair of the higher education commission, and president of the Association. Regarding the visits, he recalled,

> There are gains from both ends of the spectrum, in that one witnesses some outstanding program thrusts which inspire revitalization at one's home base, and on the other hand one sometimes see conditions which are less than desirable and which one would not want to replicate.[41]

As indicated by Reinert and Roskens, the C-E experience offered a number of rewards. In part, the gains were by-products of the changing character of accrediting. In pursuing the idea that evaluation and stimulation would strengthen higher education, the Commission had adopted aspects of modern learning theory. "One aspect of this theory involves recognition of the importance of having the learner actively involved in the learning experience," explained Norman Burns. As a result, "We now view accreditation as a learning experience." This learning experience impacted most on the individuals involved, especially the consultant-examiners whose visits provided a wide variety of such encounters.[42] The C-E participants forged personal and professional bonds with other individuals and the Association. In many cases, serving on examination teams instilled a deep commitment to the NCA and its work. The experiences of Reinert and Roskens offer just two of many examples of how involvement with the Association spanned the greater part of an individual's career.

THE EVOLUTION OF PEER REVIEW AND TOTAL INSTITUTIONAL EVALUATION

The perception that accrediting was a learning experience redefined the voluntary character of the higher education commission. Its service functions became connected to the successful implementation of the new accrediting program. In the process, the Commission reshaped its relations with members in ways that enhanced, and profoundly altered, its voluntary aspects. In general, the Commission changed from a top-down agency imposing standards to a service-oriented organization that placed primary responsibility for policy making and administration on the representatives of member institutions. The development of Commission policy, procedures, and practices had always rested with the membership. However, the 1950s reform movement added significant new components to the accrediting process, including the self-study and evaluation by peer review. The idea of having representatives from similar member institutions examine a college or university applying for membership dated back to the creation of accreditation by the NCA. Beginning in the 1920s, the higher education commission required site visits for applicants.

However, the peer review process did not apply to all members until adoption of the ten-year periodic visit policy in 1957. The original purposes of the periodic examinations were to aid weaker institutions, hopefully initiate ongoing institutional self-evaluation and improvement, and to provide a venue for the mutual stimulation of the examiners and the institutional staffs. The failure to meet the original goals prompted an overhaul of the visitation program in the early 1960s. In 1963, the institutional self-study was made the core of the periodic visit and the purpose was changed to evaluation along the lines of a regular accrediting inspection.[43] Eventually, different types of visits evolved to meet varying purposes.

The implication of employing peer review universally through the C-E Corps meant that the first and most important phase of evaluation was conducted by peers. Their recommendations provided the basis for Commission and Association action. Consulting followed a similar procedure, meaning that institutions seeking help were not confronted by outside, professional experts, but by colleagues who might have confronted similar difficulties at their college or university. As a result, both evaluation for accreditation purposes and consulting for improvement were grassroots activities performed by peers who volunteered their time and expertise for a modest honorarium. In this guise, *voluntary* meant implementing the goals and policies of the Commission by direct, representative member participation. The professional staff and, to a lesser extent, the Commission facilitated the process by managing the various activities and giving them sanction.

The C-E Corps provided the human resources to perform various services, but peer review required ancillary materials. The Commission anticipated such needs. The mid-1950s reform effort developed a *Guide for the Evaluation of Institutions of Higher Education* to replace the *Manual of Accrediting*. Initial versions of the *Guide* were tested by the first LTP class in 1957–1958, and a complete version appeared soon afterward. The *Guide* was "designed to assist (1) institutional faculties engaged in self-study, (2) consultants working with institutions, and (3) examiners assessing the quality of an institution for accreditation purposes."

Seven questions that structured the evaluation process indicate what the Commission wanted a self-study to include. The first was: "Is the educational task of the institution clearly defined?" Citing the growing diversity in higher education, the *Guide* stressed that each institution had to define its tasks to provide a frame of reference for making decisions about curriculum, instruction, financing, and faculty, among other things. Clarity of definition necessitated developing clear and concise goals so that all involved understood what the institution was attempting to achieve. Without a clear conception, the institution had no way to plan for further development and improvement. The second question asked whether the institution possessed the necessary resources to carry out the defined task. These resources included "financial stability, sources of support, size and competence of the faculty, adequacy of the library and other instructional facilities, adequacy of the physical facilities" and, if research was part of the mission, any special facilities required. Suggestions on evaluating these various areas often recommended using subjective judgment. For example, evaluating faculty implied not only collecting data on educational background, experience, and scholarly interest, but on assessing "the general tone of the institution, the zest with which faculty and the students pursue their work." Another concern was whether the institution's organization facilitated carrying out the educational tasks. Institutional strength was tied to the effectiveness of the administrative organization. Evaluation involved "not only an analysis of institutional structure but also a study of the administrative processes." One indicator was the "provisions made for the institutional self-study." The quality of the self-study not only demonstrated the institution's expertise, but reflected its attitude toward the NCA and its own operations.

The remaining four questions dealt with specific aspects of the institution, such as the connection between the curriculum and the instructional program, and the institutional goals. The central issue was whether the institution enrolled students who could best benefit from its program. Assessing this match required examining the appropriateness of instructional procedures, the course offerings, and student services. Faculty morale influenced the quality of teaching and involved such factors as "adequate salaries, equitable service loads, satisfactory provisions for retirement, insurance, and other fringe benefits, opportunities for professional growth and encouragement to take advantage of these provisions." Faculty morale was also affected by recreational opportunities, and the soundness of the policies governing recruitment, appointment, promotion, and tenure. The other questions evaluated the facilities for students and student achievement. The *Guide* observed, "The general effectiveness of the student personnel program will be reflected in the attitudes and actions of faculty, student, personnel staff, and students." Regarding student performance, the emphasis was on "the progress made by the student during the time spent in the institution in the direction of achieving the goals set by the institution."

Structuring of accreditation around seven questions changed the direction of NCA collegiate accrediting. In many respects, the questions resembled the first accrediting standards. In addition, the inquiry model of asking questions reflected the revised philosophy of accreditation. The *Guide* was not a manual presenting standards, but rather identified areas "deemed important in the assessment of quality, and indicates in some detail the kinds of questions that should be asked about the several aspects of the institution's work." The subjective nature of the peer review process rejected quantitative, fixed minimum standards, claiming "that there is no substitute for good judgment, arrived at objectively, by knowledgeable persons."[44] In addition, following the position of the 1930s reforms, the totality of the institution was the subject of evaluation—based on the assumption that the college or university was more than the sum of its parts.

Modern psychological theory applied to learning provided the rationale for accreditation of the total institution. As Burns explained, "We view the institution, not as the blank slate of the earlier psychology upon which the accrediting agency wrote its standards, but rather as a Gestalt—a living organism of interrelated parts reacting with its environment and growing continually in educational effectiveness." While this philosophy meshed well with the conception of the Commission as a facilitator stimulating improvement, it also created problems in the late fifties and early sixties. Burns observed that lack of understanding as to the meaning of "accreditation of an institution as a whole" plagued regional accrediting associations. "The fact of accreditation of the institution as a whole does not permit us to assert that any particular part or program of the institution is of good or even acceptable quality at any given point in time," he explained. "What we can say is that an accredited institution is basically of such quality that it will not permit any aspect of its work to continue for long to be below a minimum level of acceptability—that appropriate steps will be taken to correct the deficiencies."[45]

Evaluating the total institution represented a refinement of the 1930s idea of accrediting a college or university by using the scores recorded in numerous categories on the institutional pattern map. Both versions placed the burden of performance on the institution and stressed the ability to solve internal problems independently. The 1950s policy had two bases of evaluation. It assumed that as a whole and in all of its parts, the institution maintained a recognizable benchmark level of quality that served more as an indicator for solving problems than evaluation. More important for accrediting purposes under the self-study system was whether or not the institution had an internal mechanism for diagnosing and correcting defects. In essence, the minimum level of quality acted as a red flag for problem solving. Burns and others also recognized that the dynamic character of an institution meant that, at any moment in time, not all areas ran at as high a level as desired. Differences in performance were expected and natural. Evaluating an institution by its parts distorted the accrediting process because it failed to consider the dynamism evident in all institutions. Examining parts put more stress on the tree individually or on the sum of many trees than on the forest. Just as there was much more to a forest than a collection of trees, so a collegiate institution was more than a collection of its parts. By stressing the ability to correct deficiencies, the NCA could accredit an institution that was generally sound but had some problem areas. The understanding was that as these problems would be corrected, others would arise to be solved. A quality institution was characterized by a continuing cycle of problem diagnosis and solution leading to improvement. In this respect, accreditation was based on the ability of the institution to improve itself.

The connection of accrediting to institutional improvement also had other implications. The new program modified the NCA image, answering the long-standing criticism that the Commission performed a policing function. However, the application of accrediting the whole institution philosophy also raised concerns about how well the NCA could assess institutional quality, because total evaluation served as the measure of assessment. Standards had pinpointed areas that lent themselves to quantification, such as facilities and resources. Improvement implied extending the scope of evaluation to processes. Burns saw dangers in this approach, too. He warned, "We have looked for evidences of concern in the institution with the improvement of instruction rather than the actual quality of instruction." He suggested that the Commission do more in evaluating the product as well as the processes. For example, he explained, "We would look at the administrative arrangements, not in terms of some kind of standard or accepted practice, but in terms of whether the arrangement seemed to facilitate or retard learning."[46] This perspective extended the dimensions of accrediting to include not just what an institution was, but also to address how and why it worked, and what the results were.

But accrediting processes and results were subjective exercises that required guidelines to be meaningful. The institution's objectives provided the needed measures of evaluation, because the ability of a college or university to meet its own goals very objectively showed how well it had developed its processes to use its resources to obtain designated results. The reasons behind its success or failure in this effort offered insight into the specific areas of strength or weakness, again providing clear assessments of quality. However, institutions also needed advice and counsel on how to conduct a qualitative self-evaluation that provided evidence to measure how well its objectives were met. In this regard, the consultant-examiners provided expert assistance, while the *Guide* offered "a basis on which the observer may formulate judgments and draw conclusions."[47]

The combination of three components—self-study, training of consultant-examiners, and the publication of a handbook of accrediting—provided the means to apply the 1930s theory of accrediting. This implementation was based on the refinement of existing ideas on having accrediting conducted on a peer review basis and on looking at the total institution, particularly its ability to improve itself. The remaining question was whether the Commission itself could implement its new accrediting program.

REORGANIZING THE COMMISSION

The development of practices to implement the 1930s theories on quality accrediting was one of two major themes of the post–World War II history of the NCA higher education commission. The other was the reorganization of the Commission itself. The two efforts were intimately connected, representing a two-pronged attempt to modernize accrediting. Reorganization efforts altered the structure of the Commission so it could successfully perform its vastly expanded duties and responsibilities. The catalyst behind the reorganization movement was the Commission's willingness to accommodate the changes that were transforming higher education into a new postsecondary educational community. Unlike many other momentous choices, the decision-making process did not involve a conscious, concerted deliberation and study of prevailing conditions and opinions that led to the passage of a statement on inclusion. Rather the Commission responded piecemeal to specific aspects of change as they arose. These responses, in turn, came together over time to form a general policy of incorporation. To a great extent, the development of postsecondary education offered the NCA little choice but to extend the boundaries of its community.

In 1961, Norman Burns commented on the growing diversity in higher education, relating it to NCA accreditation. Observing that "diversification of programs both within and among institutions has come to be a major characteristic of the American educational enterprise," he suggested, "Only through diversification can education serve the many functions assigned to it." He tied the increase in the number and variety of tasks to the equally multiplying needs of society, including the expansion of educational opportunities to all Americans. He observed that the result was a proliferation of programs and institutions. In some cases, the growth was among colleges and universities historically included in the Association accrediting program. In other cases, the institutional trends were outside the traditional NCA community, including "schools of engineering, schools of business, schools of medicine, schools of art and schools of music, theological seminaries and schools of cosmetology." Burns also noted, "We have various combinations of these, as well as some admixture of liberal arts." He concluded that "institutional quality cannot be thought of as an absolute," but had to relate to institutional function.[48]

Many of the 1950s reforms facilitated the evaluation of these programs and institutions. After all, the assessment by institutional objective based upon a self-study was easily applied universally. Similarly, the seven basic questions used to guide the accreditation process were abstract enough to allow any institution to answer them. However, successful consulting and evaluation leading to accreditation required accommodating the specifics of the accrediting process to these diverse institutions. A major difficulty involved the peer review system. Successful peer review required trained examiners from similar types of institutions and relevant ancillary materials to guide the self-study, to facilitate the training of consultants and examiners, and to help with the accrediting visit. A partial solution to these difficulties accompanied the development of the new *Guide*. Noting the general nature of the *Guide*, the Commission recognized that "from time to time, it appears to be desirable to prepare statements of policy which deal with particular problem areas in higher education at a higher level of specificity." As such, it developed various statements of policy to address these specific areas. The role of the statements was "to explicate the more general *Guide*." The various statements covered general education, the junior or community college, graduate programs in education, accreditation of doctoral programs, off-campus programs of instruction, and specialized institutions and programs.[49]

The added statements eased, but did not solve, the problems arising from the expansion and increasing variety of programs and institutions. In 1965, Burns noted the tradition of voluntary accreditation made it "incumbent upon those of us who are engaged in accrediting activities to be continually alert to the need for keeping our policies and practices relevant to the requirements of the times." He observed, "Increasing numbers of specialized institutions are coming into being and virtually all of them are seeking accreditation." Other issues included reviewing complex universities and accommodating "the growing numbers of off-campus programs of various kinds." The Commission had already addressed some of these concerns. For example, in response to the rise in specialized institutions, the Commission had "broadened our eligibility requirements to include them."[50]

Expanding membership affected all aspects of Commission operations, influencing the reorganization efforts. By the early 1950s, the increasing workload and growing complexity of the tasks prompted the switch from an all-voluntary to a professional, full-time administration headed by a secretary and supported by clerical and other staff. However, throughout the fifties, operations still remained disjointed and temporary because, prior to 1961, the Association and the Commission were housed at various institutions, depending upon the affiliation of the secretary. Thus, when Norman Burns became Commission secretary, its office was located at the University of Chicago, but the NCA headquarters was at the University of Minnesota where Association secretary Charles Boardman lived. For much of the 1950s and early 1960s, the Commission on Secondary Schools was housed in the West Virginia State Board of Education, where Secretary Alva Gibson worked. In 1957, the Association's long-range planning committee recommended consolidating all the offices in one place.

Three years later, NCA president Stephen Romine, then dean of the University of Colorado School of Education, vigorously supported professionalizing the operations of the Association and the commissions. "The educational power structure is much more complicated today than in years past and... the struggle for the control of educational standards is at an all-time high," he explained, concluding, "The conditions are not conducive to the continuation of regional accreditation as traditionally viewed." Romine suggested establishing a central NCA office. "The absence of this has long served to retard the proper development of cooperative projects involving the Commissions and has contributed to some misunderstanding that has reduced the effectiveness of the Association," he argued. "Proper facilities would enhance the opportunity for the Association at large and the Commissions separately and jointly to operate more effectively and more efficiently than is now possible."[51]

In 1961, Norman Burns became NCA executive secretary and the Association moved its headquarters to the University of Chicago. Soon afterwards, space for the Association and Commission on Colleges and Universities was rented at the Shoreland Hotel on Chicago's south side, several blocks from the university's campus. The Commission on Secondary Schools moved to the Shoreland in 1963.[52]

While the NCA centralized its administration, the increasing number and diversity of institutions created the need for decentralization of the accrediting program. In 1954, the Committee on the Reorganization of Accrediting Procedures recommended decentralizing Commission operations by dividing the region into districts and grouping institutions by type. In justifying this proposal, Norman Burns claimed, "This arrangement would recognize differences in the needs of the different kinds of higher education in our Association and provide a channel for them to express their ideas and to present their common problems." Association secretary Boardman observed that the general idea resembled the organizational structure of the schools commission, "which had been operating in a highly decentralized way for many years." Boardman praised the plan, observing it provided for "greater democratization...in conducting the affairs of the Commission," and also noted it gave "greater authority and responsibility to the colleges in the various areas of the Association." Equally important, decentralization promised to better acquaint college faculties with the Association.[53]

The division of the Commission by district committees was abandoned in the early 1960s. The committees by type, however, proved more successful and enduring. The pre–World War II classification was more strictly defined by type in that the four membership categories were liberal arts college, teacher's college, university, and junior college. The revised definition of type was based on highest degree offered, and separate committees were assigned to each. They examined the pertinent reports of examining teams and made accrediting recommendations to the Board of Review. The committees by type provided an intermediary administrative step in the accreditation process that divided up the mounting workload and helped overcome difficulties of understanding and adequacy, as had happened with junior colleges in the late 1940s. In addition, the focus on degree rather than a specific name allowed for the inclusion of other types of institutions, a factor that became increasingly important in the 1960s and 1970s. By the late 1960s, the committees by type had evolved into review committees, though institutional type continued to influence their jurisdiction.[54]

CHANGES IN MEMBERSHIP REQUIREMENTS

Reorganization went beyond administrative makeup and structure. Reflecting developments in higher education and the needs of the federal government, the Commission significantly transformed membership and accreditation status policies and practices. The question of membership arose in the 1950s and prompted the development of a basic policy on curriculum and purpose to define the boundaries of NCA operations. The NCA had always supported a liberal education. The pre–World War II policy eliminated single-purpose institutions from membership consideration because such institutions seldom had liberal education offerings. During the late 1930s and 1940s, reformers renewed their interest in a general, comprehensive education, leading to various programs and even new institutions that offered a liberal course of study in an innovative way. In 1950, the NCA voiced its continuing support for a general education component. The Board of Review of the Commission on Colleges and Universities ruled that only institutions with acceptable general education programs could apply for membership. This policy was reaffirmed periodically and remains a major requirement for admission today.

The imposition of a general education component did not conflict with the corresponding policy on protecting institutional individuality. The requirement was later redefined to accommodate the increasing specialization and variety of institutions and programs. In 1968, the Commission developed criteria on general education for vocational-technical programs. Robert C. Bartlett, assistant secretary of the Commission, explained, "The Commission expects the institutions offering vocational and technical programs to develop specific approaches to providing general education experiences for their students." He recognized that "the general nature and pattern of general education in such programs has been and will continue to be a subject of discussion in the Commission." To aid institutions, the Commission outlined several guidelines to connect the general and vocational-technical curricula so that graduates attained "reasonable competencies both in areas of general education relevant to the modern world and in their field of major specialization and that they see these as mutually reinforcing rather than disparate."

The guidelines mandated a clear distinction between general education and specialty courses, the disciplinary stress determining the distinction. Mathematics and physical science classes were not part of the general education component in engineering-oriented programs, but would fit in that category for those in business. Conversely, economics was part of the business curriculum in the latter schools, but was a general education class in engineering. In general, "courses which provide basic theory for direct support of the specialized studies will not be considered as primarily general education in nature." The second guideline tied the rigor and content of the general education course work to the ability level of the students. Success depended upon providing "the same degree of support as the technical or vocational specialization courses," to ensure that general education was "a viable part of any program." The last point suggested that about one-fourth of the total instructional program be devoted to general education. Bartlett added that the proper allocation of courses should follow a sound rationale developed by the institution.[55]

By tailoring the policy to the general theory and practice of accrediting, the problem of requiring a general education component was easily solved. The Commission set the requirement and provided general guidelines to help institutions in the design of their curriculum. A sound rationale based upon goals influenced the content and context of the curricular organization. In this way, institutional individuality was preserved and even used to facilitate the structure of the general education program.

Some issues were not easily resolved. Membership requirements and accreditation status were transformed to accommodate fast-paced change in education and federal government funding programs. As originally conceived, institutions were either accepted as members and accredited, or not. The increasing importance of government funding necessitated a more flexible, multi-tiered structure to accommodate the expanding membership. Broadening admission criteria required refining existing accrediting levels and ranks as well as adding new status categories. The earliest change related to the development of new graduation programs by member institutions. Accredited at a certain degree level, many colleges and universities added advanced degrees that required altering their accredited status. For more effective evaluation of new graduate programs in member institutions, the Commission had developed a policy requiring "that there be graduates from a new program before the Association would consider an application for the accreditation of the program." Initially instituted in 1950, the policy was strengthened in 1961 by adding a new category, preliminary accreditation, which applied to a previously accredited institution that was "inaugurating a new program in an accreditable manner."

On several levels, the preliminary status addition was innovative. Accrediting a program ran counter to the Association emphasis on the total institution. In addition, the 1961 revision allowed approval of a new development prior to its being proved in practice, but was based on the traditional NCA belief that an accredited institution would maintain a desirable level of quality in all its operations. Preliminary accreditation thus adapted an existing idea for a new purpose to improve productivity. The concept of development in an "accreditable manner" provided the NCA with needed flexibility to respond to changing conditions. At the same time, the Commission added new services for its members. By defining accreditable manner as assuming that "the quality level of the institution and the planning which has gone into the new program are such that the Association is convinced the new program will develop satisfactorily," the NCA expressed its confidence in the ability of members to expand their operations, in their capacity to learn how to change themselves. In the process, it promoted, indeed certified, improvement to enhance the chances for success.[56]

Preliminary accreditation accommodated the rapid growth in graduate programs, but later category additions proved more problematic and risky since they involved institutions seeking membership, rather than those already accredited. Federal funding eligibility influenced the addition of questionable "membership" categories. Following the passage of the Higher Education Facilities Act, and in response to a request in 1964 by the U.S. Office of Education, the Commission strengthened the candidacy status originally established in 1961. Candidacy applied to institutions seeking membership. Following a diagnostic examination similar to a regular accrediting visit, an institution became a Candidate for Membership, and received "a letter from the Association indicating that, with reasonable progress, they may be expected eventually to achieve accreditation." This letter made the institution eligible for federal funding. In the late 1960s, the Commission added an even more preliminary level—correspondent status—that applied to institutions that were working toward becoming accredited and planned to apply for candidate status within two years.[57]

Reorganization of membership involved more than adding new accrediting status levels. The emergence of postsecondary education, particularly the phenomenal rise of vocational-technical education in the 1960s, precipitated major changes in membership qualifications. The theories and practices of the NCA higher education commission were revised to accommodate an additional level of schooling that often overlapped, yet stood apart from, the traditional secondary and collegiate realms. In 1967, an ad hoc committee recommended that a separate commission not be established to accredit public vocational schools, and that no institution fall under the purview of both accrediting commissions. The NCA action was well-timed. Two years later, Norman Burns reported that "vocational-technical education beyond the high school is among the fastest growing parts of the educational system," and that this growth was evident in the expansion of programs as well as the creation of new institutions. As a result, "these newer institutions are seeking the endorsement of regional accrediting agencies as part of their effort to establish themselves in the educational world." Federal funding eligibility also provided an incentive for applying for accredited status. But accommodating these new schools required a basic change in the higher education commission's membership policies. Previously only degree-awarding institutions were eligible for admission to the NCA. In 1969, the Commission opened up membership to institutions that had been chartered by the government to award "a certificate or diploma or an associate degree."[58]

As the response to vocational-technical education indicated, the higher education commission adapted to changing educational conditions by modifying its policies and programs, but maintained its basic structure, organization, and philosophy. The Commission substantially altered its policies regarding accrediting new types of institutions, but incorporated them into the existing structure of the organization. In other words, the NCA either changed or added new spokes instead of creating a totally new wheel. But, in adding these spokes, the character of the membership changed dramatically, leading the Commission to change its name. In 1970, the Commission on Colleges and Universities became the Commission on Institutions of Higher Education. Burns explained that the name change would "accommodate these institutions which, though clearly of post–high school grade, are not necessarily degree-granting institutions and therefore may not properly be considered collegiate, at least in the traditional meaning of the word." Implied in his explanation was another significant revision, expanding accreditation to programs and schools that granted certificates instead of degrees. The actions of the Commission indicate that a more appropriate name might have been Commission on Institutions of Postsecondary Education.[59]

The expansion of NCA membership was not trouble-free. Serious problems arose that had severe repercussions on Commission activities. Abuses occurred as the Association responded to government requests for information on institutions following the passage of the Higher Education Facilities Act in 1963. Initially, upon receipt of a letter stating the intent to begin working toward accreditation and to apply for candidate status within two years, an institution became eligible for federal funding. Possibly an honest mistake, some institutions cited NCA approval in their public relations and marketing efforts in ways that misrepresented its true meaning. Such claims went against the philosophy and practice of NCA accrediting, and damaged the Association's reputation. In 1966, the Commission issued a disclaimer that institutions were required to use in their public statements. The disclaimer clarified the relationship as one that was working toward NCA membership, and also emphasized the Association's cooperation with the federal government. To avoid misrepresentation, it stated, "This is not to be construed as an accrediting action."[60]

The membership problems often were caused by the accelerated pace of educational change. As occurred with the vocational-technical field, fast-paced growth necessitated equally quick responses from the Commission because the federal grants sparked this growth. The eligibility turn-around time worked against the steady, measured pace of the normal self-study, examination visit, evaluation routine. The crush of applicants also overburdened a consultant-examiner corps that did not have enough competent examiners to assess the new types of institutions.

In addition, the burgeoning federal eligibility programs created confusion in the accrediting field, leading to jurisdictional disputes between regional and specialized accrediting agencies that had profound repercussions. Relations between the general and more specialized accrediting organizations vexed institutions throughout the post–World War II era. In the late 1940s, large universities founded the National Commission on Accrediting to combat what they felt was needless duplication of effort, among other things. In the early 1950s, this group had proposed eliminating all specialized, or program accreditation and making it the responsibility of the regionals. The plan failed and difficulties in the accrediting community continued. In the mid-1960s, problems arising in the eligibility program led to stronger government oversight and new regulations. An Accrediting Review Committee was appointed to oversee the eligibility programs. By 1969, it was called the Advisory Committee on Accreditation and Institutional Eligibility. The U.S. Office of Education also conducted a study that questioned the connection of accreditation and funding eligibility. In 1969, the Accreditation and Institutional Eligibility staff prepared new guidelines for approving accrediting agencies that could certify institutions for eligibility. The NCA higher education commission protested against the increased workload the new guidelines required and protested against government interference in its internal affairs.[61]

The government's actions of the late 1960s initiated a new pattern of interaction with the accrediting agencies that often strained relations. The relationship became more formal and restrictive. As both parties questioned its viability over the next twenty-five years, frequent conflicts arose. But, the government had no practical alternatives to relying on accreditation as a certification of institutional quality, and the importance of the eligibility programs offered accreditors few ways out. Many of the changes made by the NCA higher education commission were geared to helping institutions establish themselves on a more solid footing or expand their operations. In almost all cases, development depended upon federal funding. As a result, the loss of accreditation could prove disastrous, and became a life or death matter for many institutions, and not just because of funding eligibility.

THE PARSONS COLLEGE CASE

Ironically, the most celebrated example of how NCA accrediting could affect an institution's survival did not involve a new institution or one seeking to add programs; nor did it involve federal funding. The controversy concerned an old Presbyterian college whose president claimed to be experimenting with a new type of educational endeavor. Parsons College in Fairfield, Iowa, was on the first NCA list of accredited institutions of higher education in

1914. The college later ran into difficulties. In 1948, enrollment had dropped to two hundred students, the college faced bankruptcy. Parsons lost its NCA accreditation, but was reaccredited two years later, in 1950. In 1955, Parsons hired a new president, Millard G. Roberts from New York. In his history of the NCA between 1945 and 1970, Louis Geiger described Roberts as "a dynamic minister-promoter-president."[62] Under Roberts' leadership, Parsons became a laboratory for two experimental ideas. The first involved enrolling students who had dropped out of other collegiate institutions to provide them with a second chance. The second suggested that more effective and efficient use of an institution's faculties and resources could reduce dependence on outside funding and still return a profit.

Supported by aggressive marketing and advertising, Parsons had constructed a new campus and enrolled almost five thousand students by the early 1960s. During this period of growth, the Commission exercised cautious oversight of the college. In 1959, Parsons submitted a review report that was followed by an examination visit in 1960. At the meeting of the NCA Executive Board in March 1961, the admission and retention policies of the institution were discussed. The Board agreed that providing a higher education for less able students was laudable, but expressed concern "if students of low ability were being prepared for teaching." However, mention was also made of the excellent quality of the faculty and the high salary level, as well as some success "in developing the potentialities of poor students because of the time devoted to them." Obviously aware of the experimental nature of the Parsons program, the Commission adopted a wary, patient stance. Besides, though the sponsoring church advised against such a course, Parsons planned to initiate master's degree programs and so would be subject to NCA procedures regarding preliminary accreditation. It "would come under our new procedures [preliminary accreditation] and would be subject to a thorough examination."

In April 1963 and December 1964, examination teams visited Parsons and found serious problems. After the 1963 visit, the college was placed on probation. Both reports "stressed the importance of careful study by the College of the effectiveness of its program but noted the absence of such studies." They claimed that the information needed to support claims of student progress "were not available or were assembled in such a fashion as to make valid interpretation difficult if not impossible." Among the problems identified were careless handling of statistics and inconsistencies in the data. Despite the persistence of these problems, the 1964 visit noted progress in other areas, so, in March 1965, the probationary status was removed. However, the Association "notified the College that another examination would be made within three years."

A number of sources, including professional organizations, soon voiced concern about Parsons, prompting the NCA to schedule an examination visit in February 1967. In justifying this action, the Association Board of Directors noted, "The North Central Association took the position that the public interest, the institution's interests, and the Association's responsibility" required swift action. The team reported some improvement, but also cited the college for the "same shortcomings in data gathering and analysis noted in the earlier reports—lack of data which should be used to support the college's claims, inconsistencies in the data that were available, carelessness in the use of data, and excessive exaggeration." Such conditions raised grave doubts about the adequacy of the institution's education program. Having exercised patience with the institution, and having accepted the rationale that improvement would take time, the Association had postponed action in 1965. The Board of Directors later claimed that already many felt the college had failed to correct its faults. By 1967, the Association felt enough time had been allowed for Parsons to have addressed these problems. "Its failure to do so has become a matter of such grave concern to the Association," the Board of Directors noted, "that at the meeting of the Association of April 6, 1967, the College was dropped from membership in the Association, effective June 30, 1967." An appeal by Parsons was unanimously denied.[63]

Parsons lost its accreditation because the college failed to improve the collection and presentation of information that had created problems of inconsistency and exaggeration in its reporting. These defects indicated a lack of performance and possibly an attempt to hide damaging data from the NCA. The continuing problems also suggested that the quality of the organization and administration had dropped below an acceptable level, and that the institution had permitted the decline to occur without taking action. The response of the Parsons trustees to the NCA action showed that the defects identified in the examination visits were just the tip of a mismanagement iceberg. On June 9 and 10, 1967, the board of trustees of the college agreed on a plan to regain accreditation. They asked for a meeting with NCA representatives and offered to fire Roberts in return for regaining accreditation. In commenting on this proposal, Robert G. Collins, professor of English and comparative literature at Parsons, ruefully wrote, "The board of trustees did just the wrong thing." Hired as the provost of Parsons during a one-year leave from Indiana University, higher education professor Raymond C. Gibson condemned the NCA action, but agreed with Collins. "But the NCA would not play the Parsons brand of poker. Acceptance of such a proposal would have brought about the disintegration of the association, because other colleges might offer presidential heads for less significant results."[64]

Having erred once, the trustees sought legal action that also backfired. Gibson explained, "Parsons' resort to legal action to maintain NCA membership was the final step in a comedy of errors. It was like going to court to maintain one's membership in a country club after breaking all the rules." The NCA easily surmounted the legal challenge. The loss of NCA accreditation proved fatal to Parsons, though it should be noted that bad press also contributed to its demise. The college's responses to its problems further exacerbated a deteriorating situation. In June 1967, the college had enrolled five thousand students. The following September, that number dropped to twenty-two hundred.[65]

The *Parsons* case was the only major policing incident that involved the higher education commission between 1945 and 1970. The court ruling was important because it reaffirmed the earlier *Langer* decision (see pp. 281–84). The experience of the college also showed that innovation and experimentation, in and of themselves, are not guarantees of quality education. Accreditation depended on implementation, too. The precipitous drop in enrollment following the loss of accreditation indicated just how powerful and pivotal accrediting had become. It also showed the growing public recognition of the NCA and the increasing role the NCA played in society. The public interest, for example, was cited first among the reasons for dropping Parsons from the NCA membership.

REORGANIZING THE REGIONAL ACCREDITING COMMUNITY

The reorganization of the Commission not only affected the internal structure and operations; it also extended to relations with other voluntary associations. Again, Norman Burns spearheaded the program for change. In a paper delivered at the 1962 annual meeting, Burns raised a problem related to the regional scope of accreditation. In discussing the origins of accrediting associations, he agreed that to meet their purposes of defining and organizing American education required building "relationships among institutions which, at least at that time, could most readily be effected on a regional basis." The regional approach still had value, but changing conditions required a national effort. He explained, "Developments in business and industry, advancing technology, increased speed and ease of transportation and communication, the growing interdependence of segments and regions of our society arising out of increased specialization, and the growing mobility of our population tend to blur the lines of regional difference." Societal concerns, including those in education, had become "national in scope and are dealt with at the national level." The various professional accrediting agencies were also national organizations, as were the major foundations. In addition, "The federal government has come to play a role of tremendous importance in education." In citing examples of this role, Burns listed the National Institute of Health, the National Science Foundation, and the National Defense Education Act, but not the eligibility function performed by accrediting agencies.

Burns concluded, "General accrediting carried on through regional organizations is at a real disadvantage in establishing and maintaining relationships with other agencies concerned with educational matters, but operating at the national level." General accrediting needed "a strong voice," because associations involved in this type of accreditation were the only organizations that "speak for education in its institutional form.... Most other agencies and groups in our society are interested not in the totality of the educational process and the integration of the fields of knowledge but, rather, in the promotion of their particular field." He considered functional specialization inevitable, but suggested its growth increased the importance of "countervailing forces pressing for understanding of and the promotion of relationships among the fields of knowledge." He suggested that the regional accrediting association brought the various institutional programs together.

Burns advocated collaboration among the regional agencies, not unification. He cited the various cooperative efforts over the years, including the development of the evaluative criteria and the existing National Committee of Regional Accrediting Agencies. He characterized the latter as a discussion group. He also cited the NCA Commission on Research and Service for extending some of its activities beyond regional boundaries. But more cooperation was needed. "The time has now come for a truly coordinated, interregional attack on some of the crucial problems with which we are faced in the field of general accrediting," he declared, citing the rapid growth of doctoral programs as an example. The National Committee of Regional Accrediting Agencies already had passed a resolution calling for a coordinating committee comprised of representatives from the regional accrediting associations that "would speak for general accrediting at the national level in evaluation of programs leading to the Doctor's degree." He suggested that success in that current effort could lead to further coordination of activities on other common issues.[66]

Coordination did lead to organization. On March 2, 1964, the Federation of Regional Accrediting Commissions of Higher Education (FRACHE) held its first meeting. Burns heralded the day "as an important date in the history of accrediting." The national organization was a federation. Its founding articles of agreement reaffirmed the responsibility of each regional commission for the evaluation of institutions in its territory, and for any other services it offered. As for FRACHE, its "general aim is to establish a national consensus for regional application." As an agent of the member commissions, it would codify and develop "general principles and procedures for institutional evaluation and accreditation and generally for strengthening and increasing the effectiveness of higher education." FRACHE would also promote coordination, communication, and cooperation among its members. One of the first efforts of the new organization was a directory of regionally accredited higher education institutions that contained a variety of information about the institution and its accredited status.[67]

The founding of FRACHE came at a propitious time. The Great Society programs and the corresponding explosive growth in higher education created common problems with the federal eligibility programs. One of the areas that the Federation investigated was the burgeoning field of vocational-technical education. In 1967, a National Committee for Occupational Education was proposed, and soon afterward FRACHE began coordinating efforts to accredit vocational-technical education. In 1972, a policy statement on graduate education that the NCA higher education commission was adopted. FRACHE pioneered in the renewal of outcomes as part of the accrediting process. In 1972, a common guide was published on institutional self-study for use by all the regional associations. During this period, Norman Burns served in several capacities for the Federation including secretary and director.[68]

FRACHE represented the first phase in a movement to coordinate all accrediting activities on a national level. Changing conditions in education prompted more organizational efforts. On October 14, 1971, the Executive Committees of FRACHE and the National Commission on Accrediting met to formulate plans for a merger of the two groups. Representatives of specialized and professional accrediting agencies noted their willingness to participate, leading to the creation of an ad hoc committee to represent their interests. Over the next three years, the planning proceeded. Bylaws were approved on July 24, 1974. On January 15, 1975, the Council on Postsecondary Accreditation was founded "to foster and facilitate the role of these accrediting agencies in promoting and ensuring the quality and diversity of American postsecondary education."[69]

CHANGING CONDITIONS CREATE INCREASING STRAINS AND PRESSURES

The rise of national coordinating organizations for the accrediting sector are significant in their right. However, the national combination of autonomous groups also represented an attempt to accommodate the changes caused by the rise of the postsecondary education sector and to relate more effectively to the federal government. The forces of change had strained the resources of the regional accrediting associations. In fact, *strained* accurately describes the NCA situation from approximately 1965 to 1975. The explosion in education combined with the changing government relationship placed new pressures on the higher education commission that neither the reform nor the reorganization efforts alleviated. The provisions of the 1972 amendments to the Higher Education Act intensified the strains. The 1972 Act legitimized the expanding postsecondary world by extending the legislation to vocational and proprietary schools, hospitals, museums, and a variety of other adult educational venues. A further complication was the founding of state higher education boards. Richard Millard claimed there were twenty-three state boards in 1960 and forty-seven in 1970.[70] For the NCA, the state boards created more tasks and involved another level of government in accrediting, exacerbating the existing strains and stresses on the organization.

A variety of other forces also contributed to the increasing pressures on the NCA and its commissions. The Vietnam War and the growing turbulence on college campuses and in American society contributed to the nation's divisive and anxious mood. Another important factor was that, between the late sixties and early seventies, education was in a transition period. Clark Kerr claimed the "Golden Age" of higher education that had begun in 1945 ended in 1970. He saw the seventies as a time of slower rates of growth, if not declines, and "an enforced choice of new directions, a dogged effort to retain the best of the old conditions in the face of new circumstances." Kerr predicted slower enrollment increases of traditional college students. Financial funding would follow a similar pattern, in part because of the end of federal dominance over new programs. The initiative had passed to the states, and he believed they would exercise greater control. He concluded a need existed "for careful advance analysis and more sophisticated application of policies" to survive in an age of controversy and competition. In 1974, Kerr suggested that the theme of the new "Age of Controversies" was "survivalism."[71]

Others offered even gloomier predictions. In his early 1970s study for the Carnegie Commission on Higher Education, Earl F. Cheit erroneously forecast a depression in higher education.[72] Instead, enrollments grew throughout the 1970s, but largely in nontraditional areas, such as adult and part-time students. Kerr, however, accurately predicted the decline of funding and the need for more effective planning and policy development. As the nation experienced a cycle of recession and inflation in the 1970s, post-secondary education confronted the dilemma of serving more students with less, due to declining budgets. In many universities, the financial situation became very tight, leading to hiring and other freezes.

An integral part of the transition in higher education during the 1970s was the rise of a new accountability movement that threatened to shake the very foundations of accreditation. In 1971, University of Colorado professor of higher education and long-time NCA figure, Stephen Romine discussed the "new accountability." He warned, "The emergence of the new accountability not only asserts that something is wrong with higher institutions; it also implies that the warranty of accreditation is subject to question." He identified cost consciousness and control as two major goals of the new movement, tying them to the rising trend toward retrenchment and the violent activism on the college campuses. The accountability movement demanded that higher education and accreditation officials prove their effectiveness and efficiency. For institutions, this proof included showing "a demonstrably significant dividend on the investment in people which they represent." For the NCA and other accrediting associations, proving effectiveness implied justifying their existence by verifying "that conditions of membership have a positive influence on the effective and efficient achievement of outcomes by member institutions." As part of the accountability movement, the old issue of fraudulent institutions was raised again, leading to a campaign for consumer protection in education.[73]

The various external forces that bombarded the NCA higher education commission in the late 1960s and early 1970s were complemented by growing internal initiatives for reform that, in part, were responses to the increasingly turbulent environment. To a great extent, the internal reviews of Commission operations were part of the traditional self-study procedures that had characterized NCA accrediting since its inception. For example, as early as 1960, within three years of the inauguration of the program, Donald MacKenzie, associate secretary of the Commission on Colleges and

Universities, suggested changes be made in the periodic visits to members to give greater stress on evaluation and improve its effectiveness. In 1967, Paul Dressel reported on a study of examiners' reports made by the Committee on Revision of Standards. He pointed out several deficiencies, but judged them overall as being insightfully written. Similarly, Commission staff member Joseph Semrow assessed the accrediting process in 1974, noting the influence of the accountability movement on the ongoing review process. Semrow believed that many difficulties could be alleviated by emphasizing the "outcome of product evaluation" of the accountability campaign. Semrow also noted, "This approach is not new to the Commission," but he explained it previously had been applied in limited fashion.[74]

The combination of external and internal forces stimulated an Association reform movement in the 1970s that led to another re-creation of the Association. In some ways, the 1970s reforms were different from those of previous eras. For one thing, they came as a changing of the guard occurred. On June 30, 1975, Norman Burns retired. He was replaced the following year by Thurston Manning, a physics professor and former president of the University of Bridgeport, Connecticut, whose philosophy and working style contrasted with Burns in many ways.[75] Similarly, the mass level of operations created a higher degree of complexity and difficulty than was true in the past. In addition, the accrediting world was much more connected to other aspects of society. Throughout much of its history, the Association, its members, and the college and university community comprised the higher education commission's world. After 1945, this world expanded to include various components of society. The expansion reached a peak in the 1970s.

In part, the forces spurring reform were by-products of the expanded roles and responsibilities of accrediting agencies that created some difficult dilemmas. In one of his last contributions to the *North Central Association Quarterly*, Norman Burns commented on the predicament organizations like the NCA faced. "Created, controlled, and supported by institutions of postsecondary education, regional accreditation is obliged to operate in their service," he explained. "In these activities, it plays a supportive role to individual institutions." However, because accreditation had become accepted by governmental and other agencies as well as the public as certifying that "institutions so listed are performing their educational tasks at an acceptable qualitative level," the Association played another equally important, but not always compatible role. In the latter guise, it served "to protect the public interest."

The dilemma arose when an accredited institution was unable to maintain the acceptable level of quality. Burns asserted, "This fact must be made known to the public." But, he acknowledged, "the disclosure of serious weakness in an institution can hardly be regarded as supportive of the institution." He suggested that during the preceding twenty-five years of growth, institutions had successfully responded to change, thus obviating the issue of what interest to serve. The predicted trends in lower growth levels and the declining economy threatened to raise serious problems for the Commission regarding its responsibilities and to create hard choices. His advice followed his long-practiced philosophy of placing the responsibility on the institution: "So long as the present unfavorable conditions that threaten educational institutions exist, the Commission must be even more vigilant in protecting the reputation of postsecondary institutions through public disclosure of institutions in which the requisite level of quality, despite all efforts, is not being maintained." He concluded, "To do otherwise will discredit the Commission and destroy its usefulness."[76]

Because Burns ended his career with warnings of the future rather than predictions of future successes, he ominously presaged the turbulent future of the NCA higher education commission. His words of warning also closed a distinguished career and marked the end of an epoch in NCA history. Burns was the most visible and probably the central figure behind the reform movement of the 1950s and sixties. He was able to stamp this era with his imprint for several reasons. He was the first full-time professional staff member. In addition, he had a clear direction to follow. His task was to apply the theories of the 1930s. Their compatibility with the trends on educational development facilitated his efforts. In pursuing this objective, however, Burns did not make the decision to implement the idea of quality accrediting by objective, though he lobbied long and hard for such a move. Initially in this lobbying, he acted as a volunteer representative of the University of Chicago, not a paid staff member. As secretary of the Commission, Burns' tenure depended upon his performing his tasks efficiently by serving the members. If he voiced the need for reform, his voice was not a solitary cry. Rather, his position made him a likely spokesperson, and that was the role he played.

In his NCA career, Norman Burns played a number of different, yet related roles. He was a spokesperson for reform and for the Commission, a catalyst for action, an entrepreneur formulating ways to implement innovative decisions, an intermediary in disputes over what choices to make, and, most of all, a leader. But always, he acted within a service capacity, not so much imposing his will as seeking consensus. While his position as executive secretary enhanced his power and effectiveness, the goal was not to be the leader. Instead, the central office he ran implemented and influenced policy.

Therefore, the NCA experience of Norman Burns was unique yet typical. His personal and professional experience was unique, because of the longevity of his position. The roles he played were typical, fitting well within the traditional confines of employment in a voluntary association. Regarding his heightened influence, his role was enhanced because of the status of the Commission. When he began his tenure, its administrative structure and the underlying philosophy no longer met the needs of the membership. Such conditions provided an opportunity for this entrepreneur to pursue an innovative strategy to construct a new structure and philosophy. Working cooperatively with representatives of institutional members who recognized that a combination of internal and external forces created the need for change, the re-creation of the NCA proceeded at the higher education level.

NOTES

1. Norman Burns, "Some Thoughts on the Theory and Practice of Accrediting," *North Central Association Quarterly* 28 (October 1953): 206; Norman Burns, "Proceedings of the Commission on Colleges and Universities," *North Central Association Quarterly* 40 (Summer 1965): 21.

2. Thurston E. Manning, "Regional Accreditation at the Crossroads: Challenges and Directions for the Future," in *A Collection of Papers on Self-Study and Institutional Improvement* (Chicago: NCA-CIHE, 1991), 105; interview, Patricia Thrash, Chicago, Illinois, December 14, 1994.

3. Norman Harris, "The Accreditation of Technical Schools—An Analysis of Some Major Issues," *North Central Association Quarterly* 42 (Spring 1968): 316.

4. Hawkins, *Banding Together*, 3; K. Patricia Cross, "Serving the New Clientele for Postsecondary Education," *North Central Association Quarterly* 48 (Fall 1973): 255.

5. On the Sputnik's impact on education, see James Kirby Martin, Randy Roberts, Steven Mintz, Linda O. McMurry, and James H. Jones, *American and Its People*, 2d ed., vol. 2: *From 1865* (New York: Harper Collins Publishers, 1993), 2:947–48.

6. Hugh Graham, *The Uncertain Triumph: Federal Education Policy in the Kennedy and Johnson Years* (Chapel Hill: University of North Carolina Press, 1984), xvii–xviii.

7. The best account of the legal aspects of the civil rights movement is Richard Kluger, *Simple Justice: The History of Brown v. Board of Education and Black America's Struggle for Equality* (New York: Alfred A. Knopf, 1976). The issue of desegregating precollegiate schools is covered in chapter 6.

8. Graham, *The Uncertain Triumph*, xix, 80–82, 191. Title V created a national teacher corps. Ralph W. Tyler, "The Federal Role in Education," *The Public Interest* (Summer 1974), 164.

9. *Statistical Abstract of the United States*, 1962 (Washington, D.C.: GPO, 1962), 11; 1970, 104; 1993, 147.

10. Keith W. Olson, *The G.I. Bill, the Veterans, and the Colleges* (Louisville: The University of Kentucky Press, 1974), passim.

11. Clyde Vroman, "The Role of the North Central Association: Improving Education through the Accreditation Process," *North Central Association Quarterly* 37 (Summer 1963): 23–24; reprint of a series of papers delivered at the 1962 annual meeting. Norman Burns, "Changing Concepts of Higher Education," *North Central Association Quarterly* 38 (Spring 1964): 296; reprint of an address given at the University of Akron's Founders' Day, December 11, 1963. Cross, "Serving the New Clientele for Postsecondary Education," 256–57, 259. In instances where students, adult, and youth, with low academic abilities desired the customary liberal arts and sciences undergraduate experience, they also required substantial assistance to succeed.

12. *Statistical Abstracts of the United States*, 1962, 111; 1993, 147. Norman

Burns, "II. Report of the Secretary to the Commission on Colleges and Universities," in "Proceedings of the Commission on Colleges and Universities," *North Central Association Quarterly* 23 (July 1948): 20.

13. Norman Harris, "The Accreditation of Technical Schools—An Analysis of Some Major Issues," 316–17; Norman Burns, "Implications of By-Laws Revisions," in "Associations Notes and Editorial Comment," *North Central Association Quarterly* 44 (Fall 1969): 221.

14. Patricia Thrash, "Nontraditional Institutions and Programs: A Challenge for the Accreditation Process," *North Central Association Quarterly* 49 (Winter 1975): 322, 326. See also Patricia Thrash, "Evaluation of Nontraditional Learning Forms: The Extended Campus Program," *North Central Association Quarterly* 51 (Fall 1976); and Edward C. Moore, "Some Forms of Nontraditional Higher Education," *North Central Association Quarterly* 49 (Winter 1975). The last article examined the British Open University, showing the nontraditional movement was not just an American phenomenon.

15. Public Law 550, Chapter 875, HR 7656, July 16, 1952, 675.

16. Norman Burns, "I. The Report of the Commission," in "Proceedings of the Commission on Colleges and Universities," *North Central Association Quarterly* 28 (July 1953): 15; Burns, "Some Thoughts on the Theory and Practice of Accrediting," 211. Norman Burns, "The Accrediting Dilemma," in "Association Notes and Editorial Comments, *North Central Association Quarterly* 49 (Fall 1974): 261.

17. George Arnstein, cited in Thrash, "Nontraditional Institutions and Programs," 323. See George Arnstein, "Bad Apples in Academe," *American Education* 10 (September 1974). The issue of degree mills was a constant problem throughout the postwar period, leading to the publication by the federal government of a list of fraudulent institutions in April 1960 and some correspondence between the NCA and the Department of Health, Education, and Welfare. See the news releases, Department of Health, Education, and Welfare, April 11, 1960, March 1961, announcing the list and then providing the names of the offending institutions. The above materials were included as enclosures in a May 6, 1971, letter to Norman Burns from John Proffitt, Director, Accreditation and Institutional Eligibility Staff, Bureau of Higher Education, U.S. Office of Education.

18. Norman Burns, "Report of the Secretary of the Association," *North Central Association Quarterly* 36 (Summer 1961): 12.

19. Norman Burns, "I. The Report of the Secretary," in "Proceedings of the Commission on Colleges and Universities," *North Central Association Quarterly* 26 (July 1951): 10–11; Norman Burns, "II. Report of the Secretary to the Commission to the Executive Committee," in "Proceedings of the Commission on Colleges and Universities," *North Central Association Quarterly* (1948): 17, 19–21.

20. Burns, "Some Thoughts on the Theory and Practice of Accrediting," 206.

21. Ibid., 206–9.

22. Burns, "I. Report of the Secretary," *North Central Association Quarterly*

1951, 10, 12. Junior college fees were raised to $65, bachelor's degree-grant-
ing institutions to $135, and masters and doctoral institutions to $235 and
$335 respectively. Burns, "I. Report of the Commission," *North Central
Association Quarterly* 1953, 17; Burns, "Some Thoughts on the Theory and
Practice of Accrediting," 209.

23. Burns, "I. Report of the Commission," 1953, 17.

24. C. S. Hilberry, "Future Program of the Commission on Colleges and
Universities," *North Central Association Quarterly* 30 (January 1956): 274–76.
For all intents and purposes, the Commission passage of the 1951 proposals described above made constructing a self-study of some sort an official
part of the admission process. That the later committees stressed the role of
this instrument is not surprising.

25. Burns, "Some Thoughts on the Theory and Practice of Accrediting,"
209–12.

26. Ibid., 212–14. On the National Commission on Accrediting and its
proposal to eliminate duplication of accrediting programs, see also William
S. Harper, "A History of Criticisms of 'Extra-Legal' Accrediting of Higher
Education in the United States from 1890 to 1970," 155–57, 168–71; Wil-
liam K. Selden, *Accreditation: A Struggle over Standards in Higher Education*
(New York: Harper & Brothers, 1960), 76–81.

27. Hilberry, "Future Program of the Commission on Colleges and Universities," 274.

28. Milo Bail, "Six Decades of Progress," 194, 206–7.

29. Hilberry, "Future Program of the Commission on Colleges and Universities," 276–77.

30. Charles W. Boardman, "The Report of the Secretary of the Association," *North Central Association Quarterly* 32 (July 1957): 12–13.

31. A copy of the letter and brochure are in the NCA archives. In addition, the brochure was reprinted in the *Quarterly*. See "Leadership Training
Project," "Association Notes and Editorial Comment," *North Central Association Quarterly* 32 (October 1957): 158; Norman Burns, "The Task of Accrediting in Higher Education Today," *North Central Association Quarterly* 34
(January 1960): 224.

32. Harlan C. Koch, "Broadening the Competence of Leadership in
Higher Education," in "Association Notes and Editorial Comment," *North
Central Association Quarterly* 32 (October 1957): 157.

33. Donald M. MacKenzie, "Suggestions for Strengthening the Review
Program," *North Central Association Quarterly* 35 (October 1960): 199;
"Leadership Training Project," 159; Burns, "The Task of Accrediting in
Higher Education Today," 224.

34. Burns, "The Task of Accrediting in Higher Education Today," 224;
Louis Geiger, *Voluntary Accreditation*, 83.

35. "Proceedings of the Commission on Colleges and Universities,"
North Central Association Quarterly 32 (July 1957): 16; "Proceedings of the
Commission on Colleges and Universities," *North Central Association
Quarterly* 39 (Summer 1964): 13; Norman Burns, "I. Report of the Secre-

tary," in "Proceedings of the Commission on Colleges and Universities," *North Central Association Quarterly* 40 (Summer 1965): 20. The term *examiner* was in use before 1965, but seems to have gained consistent employment by that year. Given the change, *examiner* will be used from now on.

36. Albert Pugsley, in "Proceedings of the Commission on Colleges and Universities," *North Central Association Quarterly* 40 (Summer 1965): 14–15.

37. "Proceedings of the Commission on Colleges and Universities" (1964), 13.

38. These visits reflected new degrees of accreditation status that are discussed below.

39. "1964–65 Class Leadership Training Program," *North Central Association Quarterly* 39 (Fall 1964): 173–74.

40. "Proceedings of the Commission on Colleges and Universities," 13.

41. Letters to author, Paul C. Reinert, December 21, 1993; Ronald W. Roskens, December 14, 1993. In virtually every response to a questionnaire sent to various people with NCA experience and in every interview, the respondents praised the visits for their professional and personal benefits.

42. Norman Burns, "The Task of Accrediting in Higher Education Today," *North Central Association Quarterly* 34 (January 1960): 221. In 1994, higher education commission executive director Patricia Thrash also asserted accrediting was a learning experience. Interview, Patricia Thrash, December 14, 1994.

43. On the initiation and development of the periodic visitation program, see Charles W. Boardman, "The Report of the Secretary of the Association," *North Central Association Quarterly* 32 (July 1957): 13; Donald M. MacKenzie, "Suggestions for Strengthening the Review Program," *North Central Association Quarterly* 35 (October 1960), a reprint of a paper delivered at the 1960 annual meeting; "Proceedings of the Commission on Colleges and Universities," *North Central Association Quarterly* 38 (Summer 1963): 15; Albert Pugsley, in "Proceedings of the Commission on Colleges and Universities," *North Central Association Quarterly* 40 (Summer 1965): 14–15.

44. "II. Guide for the Evaluation of Institutions of Higher Education," *North Central Association Quarterly* 38 (Summer 1963): 16–18.

45. Burns, "The Task of Accrediting in Higher Education Today," 221; Norman Burns, Some Basic Problems of Accrediting," *North Central Association Quarterly* 35 (July 1960): 193–94; reprint of a paper given at the 1960 NCA annual meeting.

46. Ibid., 197.

47. "II. Guide for the Evaluation of Institutions of Higher Education," 16. Though revised over time, the *Guide* remained the major reference for accreditation until 1975, when it was replaced by a new handbook.

48. Norman Burns, "Accrediting and Educational Diversity," 257.

49. "III. Statements of Policy," *North Central Association Quarterly* 38 (Summer 1963).

50. Norman Burns, "I. Report of the Secretary," in "Proceedings of the

Commission on Colleges and Universities," *North Central Association Quarterly* 40 (Summer 1965): 20–21.

51. Stephen A. Romine, "The North Central Association—A Look to the Future," *North Central Association Quarterly* 35 (October 1960): 177–79. Romine's other suggestions for improving Association operations are discussed in chapter 7.

52. Geiger, *Voluntary Accreditation*, 69. The Shoreland remained the headquarters until 1975.

53. Burns, "The New Role of the Commission on Colleges and Universities," 166; Charles W. Boardman, "Report of the Secretary, *"North Central Association Quarterly* 30 (July 1955): 13.

54. The by-laws of the Association approved in 1970 retained wording reflecting the original decentralization plan, though in a different context. They stated that the higher education commission "shall group the member institutions of higher education by geographic districts and type of institution." Reproduced in Geiger, *Voluntary Accreditation*, 171.

55. Robert C. Bartlett, "Accreditation As It Relates to Technical-Vocational Programs in Institutions of Higher Learning," *North Central Association Quarterly* 42 (Spring 1968): 313–15.

56. Cited in "Proceedings of the Commission on Colleges and Universities," North Central Association Quarterly 38 (Summer 1963): 20.

57. "1964–1965 Class: Leadership Training Program," 174; Albert L. Pugsley, cited in *North Central Association Quarterly* 40 (Summer 1965): 14. See also Joseph Semrow, "Activities of the NCA Consultant-Examiner Corps," *North Central Association Quarterly* 41 (Fall 1966); Geiger, *Voluntary Accreditation*, 85.

58. Plan for Vesting Responsibility for Accreditation Activity in the Vocational Education Area in the Commission on Colleges and Universities of the North Central Association, March 27, 1969.

59. Norman Burns, "Implications of By-Law Revisions," in "Association Notes and Editorial Comment," *North Central Association Quarterly* 44 (Fall 1969). The changes were approved in 1970. Burns also noted that the secondary commission was considering equally important changes to accommodate vocational-technical schools. These are discussed in the following chapter. The impact of the vo-tech and general postsecondary explosion on the Commission on Research and Service is discussed in chapter 7.

60. The disclaimer is cited in Minutes, Commission on Colleges and Universities Executive Board, November 1966. The approval policy developed into the official correspondent status initiated in 1967.

61. John R. Profitt, "The Federal Connection for Accreditation," *Journal of Higher Education* 50 (March/April 1979): 146–47; Semrow, *In Search of Quality*, 121. In addition, a 1917 study by David R. Trivett concluded that accrediting agencies should be relieved of their eligibility function. (David R. Trivett, *Accreditation and Institutional Eligibility* (Washington, D.C.: American Association for Higher Education, 1971), 87, cited in Fred Harcleroad, *Voluntary Organizations in America and the Development of Educational Accred-*

itation (Washington, D.C.: COPA, 1980), 23, 82. Cited in Proffitt, "The Federal Connection for Accreditation," 153.

62. Geiger, *Voluntary Accreditation*, 95.

63. Minutes, Commission on Colleges and Universities Executive Board meeting, March 18, 20, and June 22–23, 1961; Reprint of letter to Parsons College, in Minutes, NCA Board of Directors meeting, June 23–24, 1967.

64. Robert G. Collins, "Notes on the Parsons Experience," *Education Digest* 33 (January 1968): 34 (Reprinted from the *Journal of Higher Education*); Raymond C. Gibson, "The Scholarch of Parsons and the NCA," *Phi Delta Kappan* 49 (June 1968): 589. Gibson criticized the NCA for being inhumane, but he seemed unaware of the reasons why the institution was dropped. In addition, his own article brought up so many bad moves made by the trustees after Roberts left that his own words actually supported the NCA decision. Both the Collins and Gibson articles show astonishing practices and policies that worked against the process of education. Faculty seldom stayed for the length of their contracts. Failing students for excessive class absences was prohibited. Perhaps most damaging was the inability of administrators and trustees to listen to friends of their experiment, such as John Emens, president of Ball State University and longtime NCA member, who counseled them against several courses of action taken, as noted by Gibson.

65. Gibson, "The Scholarch of Parsons and the NCA," 589.

66. Norman Burns, "The Role of the North Central Association: Improving Education through the Accreditation Process," *North Central Association Quarterly* 37 (Summer 1962): 19–20.

67. Norman Burns, "Higher Commission Federate," *North Central Association Quarterly* 38 (Spring 1964): 273; "Articles of Agreement of the Federation of Regional Accrediting Commissions of Higher Education," reprinted in ibid., 274–75; "New College Directory Issued by Federation," *North Central Association Quarterly* 39 (Fall 1964): 173.

68. For a discussion of FRACHE activities, see Geiger, *Voluntary Accreditation*, 93, 113; Semrow, *In Search of Quality*, 118, 136, 191, 198, 201, 250.

69. Minutes of Special Committee on Planning for Structure of National Board of Accreditation for Postsecondary Education, August 18, 1972; "Bylaws and Finance Plan for the Council on Postsecondary Accreditation," July 24, 1974.

70. Richard M. Millard, "Postsecondary Education and 'The Best Interests of the People of the States,'" *Journal of Higher Education* 50 (March/April 1979): 124.

71. Clark Kerr, "The Future Course of Higher Education: The Age of Controversies," *North Central Association Quarterly* 48 (Spring 1974): 350, 351, 354.

72. Earl F. Cheit, *The New Depression in Higher Education: A Study of Financial Conditions at 41 Colleges and Universities*, A Report by the Carnegie Commission on Higher Education (Berkeley: Carnegie Commission on Higher Education, 1972).

73. Stephen Romine, "Accreditation and the New Accountability in Higher Education," *North Central Association Quarterly* 46 (Fall 1971): 257–59.; Millard, "Postsecondary Education and 'The Best Interests of the People of the States'"; Bender, "Accreditation: Uses and Misconceptions, 74.

74. Donald MacKenzie, "Suggestions for Strengthening the Review Program," *North Central Association Quarterly* 35 (October 1960); Joseph Semrow, "Toward Maximizing the Analytical Aspects of the Evaluating/ Accrediting Process," *North Central Association Quarterly* 49 (Fall 1974): 286.

75. "Norman Burns Retiring after 28 Years with the NCA," *North Central Association Quarterly* 49 (Spring 1975): 351.

76. Norman Burns, "The Accrediting Dilemma," in "Association Notes and Editorial Comment," *North Central Association Quarterly* 49 (Fall 1974): 267–68.

The Commission on Secondary Schools Charts Its Course

Change is the marching order of the day in American education. It is not sufficient for any professional organization merely to seek to survive in today's turbulent educational world. It must make a positive contribution to the solution of these problems perplexing our schools, or it should not endure.

—John Stanavage, executive secretary,
NCA Commission on Secondary Schools, 1971[1]

AS WAS TRUE for the higher commission, the NCA schools commission not only confronted massive changes after 1945; it also fanned the fires of reform. Because the two commissions played similar roles in the development of education after World War II, their experiences were similar. Both commissions had to implement the modern accrediting theories of the 1930s during a period of massive and deep-rooted change in society and education. Their responses to this challenge followed the same basic outline. In each case, the need for stability and continuity in a time of flux resulted in a professional, stable administration. Both commissions expanded the bounds of Association membership, often severely straining traditional policies and practices to accommodate the proliferation and diversity of educational institutions. However, the particulars of the conditions encountered and the details of their ongoing reform programs differed substantially, as did their organizational philosophy and structure.

John A. Stanavage. Executive secretary of
the Commission on Schools, 1969–74.

THE CHANGING FACE OF SECONDARY EDUCATION

Secondary education experienced revolutionary growth and increasing diversity after World War II. In 1940, over 7 million students attended high school. This number increased to 9.6 million by 1960, but the massive influx of the baby boom generation led to a doubling of the high school population by 1970. The enrollment surge leveled off by 1980 as the number of high school students declined slightly from 19.7 million in 1970 to just over 18 million a decade later. The rise in population was not paralleled by a similar increase in the number of schools. In 1942, there were 28,691 high schools. Twenty years later, there were 29,810, and, in 1970, students attended 29,200 schools. Nine hundred more high schools were added by 1980, bringing the total to 30,100.[2] While these figures do not include junior high schools, the growth rate seems surprisingly small. Actually, the statistics on the number of schools hide more than they illuminate trends in secondary education after 1945. "In hundreds of communities, grim old structures that had served generations of pupils were replaced by attractive, well-lighted, modern buildings," explained Arthur S. Link and William B. Catton in their history of the United States between 1945

Santa Fe Indian School, 1980 Annual Meeting. Richard Whitmore (top left), NCA president, 1979–80, and president of Kellogg Community College pictured with representatives of the Santa Fe Indian School, the first tribal school to be accredited by the COS.

and 1973. In addition, they noted, "Thousands of one-room county schoolhouses and inadequate small-town facilities gave way to new district-wide elementary schools and county union high schools."[3]

Trends among NCA secondary schools support Link and Catton's assessment that the growing student population was accommodated by enlarging existing institutions and, perhaps, consolidating smaller ones into a single large, but not necessarily new institution. Just over 70 percent of NCA member schools enrolled less than 500 students in 1945–1946. The average enrollment of all member schools was 493. By 1964, the number of NCA schools enrolling under 500 students had declined to 43.7 percent. Average enrollment had increased to 832 students by the latter year. Behind these statistics stood an unmistakable trend. In 1964, secondary commission executive secretary Gordon Cawelti observed, "In 1945–46, one-third of all students in member schools were enrolled in schools with fewer than 500 students whereas today this is estimated to be about 18 percent." Cawelti suggested much of the change was due to a strong decline in schools with under 200 students.[4]

Though all levels of education experienced phenomenal growth, diversity of the institutions was not as dramatic at the secondary level as it was in higher education. However, the restructuring of precollegiate education that had continued throughout the

William E. McVey. Superintendent of Thornton Township High School, McVey was NCA president in 1944 and treasurer, 1946–51.

twentieth century. For example, the junior high school attained the status of a separate, viable level of schooling by the early sixties. However, by the late sixties, a movement emerged that sought to transform junior highs into middle schools. Its impetus was "the new school approach being shaped for the emerging adolescent."[5] In addition, this era witnessed the rise of secondary vocational-technical and occupational programs as well as adult high schools. Another interesting development was connected to the larger presence of the United States in global affairs after World War II. The stationing of military personnel in Europe and Asia, and later other areas of the world, created the need for schools for the dependents of those people serving overseas. The NCA became the official accrediting agency for these far-flung schools.

Interestingly, the overseas schools represented one of the first instances of growing government involvement in education after

Gordon Cawelti. Executive secretary of the
Commission on Schools, 1962–69, Cawelti
was a leader of the COS reform movement
in the 1960s.

1945. At the federal level, first desegregation and later direct funding under the Great Society program vastly increased Washington's
role in elementary and secondary schools. As was true of higher
education, an underlying principle of this government involvement was the democracy of education movement. Between 1945
and 1980, equal opportunity was the goal of postwar educational
reform. By the mid-1940s, high school administrators viewed
expanded enrollment as a special democratic mission. For example,
the theme of the 1948 annual meeting of the NCA was "Effective
Education for All Youth." The 1948 Truman Commission recommendations also supported the democracy movement.[6] In addition, the focus of the NAACP desegregation campaign was on
education, with the pivotal 1954 *Brown v. Board of Education* ruling
providing constitutional sanction for integration. Reluctantly but
vigorously, President Dwight Eisenhower enforced this law with

Earl Sifert. Superintendent of Proviso Township High School, Ill., and director, Dependents Education Organization, Sifert was
NCA president, 1953–54.

the forced desegregation of Central High School in Little Rock, Arkansas, in 1956.

The NCA was involved with school integration in Arkansas and other states. In 1958, the Commission on Secondary Schools (CSS) reviewed the situation of three member high schools in Little Rock. Apparently, the schools had not desegregated and were closed by federal action. The closing meant that they could not meet the NCA requirements on length of term. Though dropping the Arkansas schools was discussed, the Commission allowed them to resign their membership. When the schools were integrated and reopened in 1959, they had to apply for accreditation as new applicants. According to Louis Geiger, the secondary commission never formulated an official policy on schools that refused to integrate and thus defied the law. Apparently, the law itself comprised the policy since the Commission did not accredit institutions opened to evade the integration ruling of the Supreme Court. Later, federal legislation tied funding to integration.[7]

The government's entry into precollegiate education extended beyond civil rights. The passage of the Elementary and Secondary Education Act in 1965 provided a strong stimulus to the growth and development of schools. But, unlike the situation in higher education, no eligibility function was required, meaning the impact of the legislation on secondary accreditation was often indirect. The NCA did not perform any official functions for Washington, nor did it have any direct, working relationship with the federal government connected to the funding. Instead, the Association responded to Washington's influence on the schools.

However, the increasingly active roles played by state departments of education impacted strongly on the work of the secondary commission. In 1963, Commission on Research and Service chair Herbert W. Schooling commented on the intrusion of the states into areas previously the purview of the NCA, noting, "Accreditation of secondary schools had become the legal function of State Departments of Education." He overstated his case since conditions differed in each state. In his 1965 report on proposed accreditation procedure reforms, Donald Manlove, Indiana NCA state chair and professor of education at Indiana University, did report that his committee considered the possibility of leaving the quantitative aspects of evaluation to the state education agencies and having the NCA secondary commission focus solely on qualitative facets. The growing presence of the state in the schools created a need for cooperation and coordination between the NCA and state education departments.[8]

THE ROAD TO REFORM

The responses of the Commission on Secondary Schools to the ongoing process of educational change differed from the higher commission because the CSS stressed a decentralized, democratically oriented approach to reform that reflected its organizational structure. Following constitutional provisions that mandated the states as the governing bodies of education, and acknowledging differences in the various state systems, the CSS decentralized its

Donald C. Manlove. Indiana state director
for the Commission on Schools, Manlove
was chair of the NCA Committee on
Accreditation Procedures and executive
director, National Study for Secondary
School Evaluation; he was a leader of the
Commission on Secondary Schools standards reform in the 1960s.

operations, giving much autonomy and responsibility to the state
chairs and committees. The Commission belief that it worked best
at the local level contributed to this philosophy and administrative
framework. As a result, decision making often involved referenda
to members and, in the early 1970s, the NCA annual meeting
began featuring an informal business session of the CSS to gain
feedback on proposed actions that harkened back to the general
sessions of the first annual meetings. In addition, the process of
change often was slower than that of the higher commission
because the accelerating agent of funding eligibility was missing.
The relationship with government also differed because it involved
the states. Relations with the federal government, as in the case of
the overseas dependents' schools, bore few similarities to the
higher commission situation.

However, the specific reform actions taken paralleled those of the Commission on Colleges and Universities. The CSS modernized accrediting by applying the theories of the 1930s, reorganized its operations by professionalizing the administration and setting up a permanent central office, and expanded its membership by changing entrance requirements. There also was a movement toward a national federation of secondary commissions, though this effort was much less a priority than it was for the higher commission. In addition, as the CSS expanded its boundaries to encompass all precollegiate education—save for preschool—it, too, underwent a name change. On July 1, 1974, the Commission on Schools became the official designation.[9]

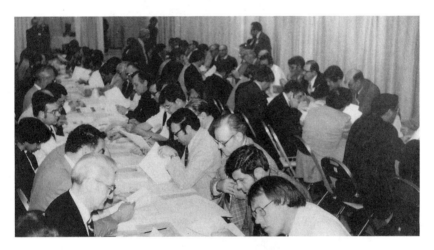

Commission on Schools. Reviewers evaluating Annual Reports, 1974 Annual Meeting.

The name change symbolized the reformist tendencies of the secondary schools commission. The roots of the reform movement extended back at least to the 1930s, but the stimulus for the post–World War II phase quite possibly was a 1954 survey of the membership conducted by the CSS Cooperating Committee on Research, chaired by Stephen Romine of the University of Colorado. The survey goal was to "discover strengths and weaknesses of state committees and the Commission on Secondary Schools as regards: (1) aims and means; (2) activities, procedures, and services; (3) report forms and reporting procedures; (4) trends on accreditation." The

K. Forbis Jordan. Executive secretary of
Commission on Schools, 1969–74.

John Vaughn. Executive secretary of COS,
1976–86.

Kenneth F. Gose. Executive director of COS, 1986 to present.

Stephen A. Romine. Dean of the School of Education at the University of Colorado, Romine was NCA president in 1961 and a leader of many reforms in the 1960s.

importance of the state committees in Commission operations was underscored by their inclusion in the survey. For many members, the state committee was the Commission, just as for many others the Commission represented the Association. A major task was "to make suggestions for improvement based upon the findings."

The grassroots, democratic philosophy of the CSS and the traditional policies that stressed careful planning, review, and revision in program development guided the development of the survey instrument. The entire process from initial design to final version took fourteen months. Over 150 administrators as well as the state chairs contributed to the final product. Replies were received from 2,083 administrators, representing 65 percent of the total secondary membership. Beyond the expression of general satisfaction with the state committees and the Commission, Romine reported eight major findings. Three are particularly relevant to this discussion. Many respondents recommended "careful study of the interpretation and application of policies, regulations, and criteria" to achieve greater uniformity and to focus more on "the total pattern of the school." Another suggestion was for "more self-appraisal and greater use of visiting survey committees." In interpreting this request, Romine explained, "It is possible that member schools are at their highest level of performance at the time they are surveyed for membership, and that without periodic resurvey activities they may not remain at that level of service." The third noted the need for more leadership at the state level. Schools visits, consulting services, and conferences were named as possible solutions. Recognizing that increased services of this sort presented problems in funding, personnel, and time, Romine observed, "Greater cooperation of the NCA with other agencies offers one approach to meeting this demand."[10]

In a later commentary on the survey results, Romine saw six trends affecting the future of secondary accreditation. Of these, three are most pertinent. He observed a change in attitude among NCA members that showed less concern for accreditation details and a greater stress on stimulation and leadership. The current administrative structure of the Commission hampered responding to the changing needs. Romine explained, "We probably cannot, with voluntary part-time workers, increase leadership and consultative services in the NCA without a decrease in the time and energy given to the details of reporting, inspection, and related activities."

In commenting upon the trend toward more self-appraisal and other improvement initiatives carried out at the local level, he suggested that members had changed their perceptions of the NCA. They had recognized that "the NCA was not an outside pressure which conforms and imprisons, but an inside force and drive which expands and frees." Romine claimed this new attitude was "the key to the future of NCA leadership and service." Declaring that the Association was "your organization and composed of the schools you represent," he tied the altered view of the NCA to its voluntary character, declaring that "our Association functions best, if at all, on the local level." Apparently, the image of the NCA as a policing agency had been replaced with a more friendly view as an organization that provided members with a sense of ownership and camaraderie. The philosophy of working at the local level through helpful state committees had effectively rebutted the police perception that generated much criticism in the 1930s.

The last trend was a movement toward more qualitative standards. Romine counseled that success depended "in some degree upon the nature and effectiveness of state accreditation programs and the cooperative working relationships which we can establish between these programs and ours." The interest of state government and the move to coordinate efforts with public education agencies acknowledged the greater involvement of the states in schooling. More importantly, the shift from a quantitative to a qualitative accrediting approach had a ripple effect that altered the mind-set of educators and the operations of the Commission. As Romine observed, the change meant that "mere numbers, for example, as of books, do not make a library." As a result, he continued, "It appears that we shall, therefore, be increasingly concerned with the actual functioning of a school and with the influence it has on boys and girls and on the school community as well." The Commission had to shift the "emphasis from what we include under 'Regulations' to what we specify under 'Criteria.'"[11] Here, too, the CSS moved away from policing, and from a standardized accreditation that made schools adhere to a universally imposed quantifiable measure. Accrediting schools involved more than just facilities and resources; it also required looking at processes and results. The difference between a regulation and a criterion is not subtle or small. The first seeks to control conduct by imposing a principle, rule, or law. The other is also a standard or rule, but in a very different context. Because it serves as a basis for judgment and can act as benchmark or even a goal, a criterion was more in tune with the reform thought of the 1930s and 1950s. A regulation could be inhibiting, while a criterion could prove stimulating.

The survey and the interpretation by Romine indicated that the membership would welcome attempts to apply the ideas and program set forth in the Cooperative Study of the 1930s and the *Evaluative Criteria.* Yet, no concrete action was taken until the 1960s. And, then, the first CSS initiative was not a trend mentioned by Romine, though he did intimate its need. The stimulus for change was the voluntary, part-time administration of the Commission. In 1961, the Administrative Committee established two committees to study reorganization. Each had an $800 budget. The purpose of the Committee on the Study of the Position of Executive Secretary was obvious, but possessed tremendous significance. It promised to professionalize the administration of the Commission by employing a full-time executive secretary. In 1962, this committee recommended the hiring of an administrator "who can give dynamic leadership to an expanded program." It also suggested setting up a permanent headquarters in Chicago.[12] Both recommendations showed that while decentralization was the basic organizational philosophy, a certain level of centralization was needed if change was to be implemented effectively.

In making these recommendations, the executive secretary committee worked closely with the Committee on Fees. Chaired by Harold Metcalf, principal of Bloom Township High School in Chicago Heights, Illinois, the latter had a more expansive purpose. Depending upon the source, it was either "to study the fee structure, general organization, and service of the Commission," or to study "the philosophy, obligation, and needs of the Secondary Commission in relation to the adequacy of the present schedule of fees."[13] While the distinction between the two descriptions may seem small, the second interpretation implied a much more expansive mandate touching upon the totality of the Commission. Equally important, both accounts show that the stimulus for reform was directly connected to financial resources. In one sense, cost effectiveness was the engine that made change possible. In 1962, an increase in the annual fee to $35 was recommended with this caution: "The Fees Committee does not propose the Secondary Commission go on a spending spree; the Committee does recommend sound financial underwriting of expenses necessary to the future development and good work of the Secondary Commission."[14]

The decision on a fee structure underscored the democratic philosophy of the Commission. The initial recommendation was for a graded scale based on size, but the Administrative Committee rejected that idea and asked for a standard fee between $25 and $50 per year. The proposal was made for a $50 annual fee, but the committee reduced it to $35. In explaining the rationale behind a single fee for all members, the committee stated, "The single fee is advantageous...because it is generally agreed that the contribution to the NCA by a single school cannot be differentiated on the basis of size and location." A single fee also simplified administrative procedures.[15]

During its deliberations, the Committee on Fees identified several other needs that required attention. Most were older concerns, such as providing more active leadership for member schools, making more school visits, and using more consultants. Others expanded upon these ideas by proposing research studies and applying the results in the high schools. Another recommendation was for greater use of the *Evaluative Criteria*. The statement of needs indicated that the underlying rationale for the fee increase was to provide greater service to members, in part, by implementing the proposals of the executive secretary committee. On July 1, 1962, the Commission on Secondary Schools ushered in a new era as Gordon Cawelti became the first full-time, paid executive secretary. That same day, the CSS opened its offices at 5454 South Shore Drive, Chicago, thus bringing the administrations of both Commissions and the Association under the same roof.[16]

MODERNIZING ACCREDITATION

Having expanded its financial base and with the administration on a secure, professional footing, the CSS inaugurated its reform movement, seeking to modernize its accrediting program. The opening salvo came from a familiar voice for reform. At the 1962

NCA annual meeting, Stephen Romine pointed out the dilemma the Commission faced. "Seldom has regional accreditation pointed the way to new directions or dimensions. At times the administration of criteria has discouraged exploration and experimentation.... On the other hand, there are pressures that must be resisted and protection that regional accreditation must provide. Not all the banners on the educational pole are worthy."[17] As the 1955 survey had indicated and Romine intimated, the issue facing the secondary commission was how to use accrediting to evaluate and stimulate schools.

The existing procedures seemed inadequate. Member schools were evaluated indirectly through the review of annual report forms that dealt mainly with quantitative matters. For example, on Tuesday, March 27, at the 1962 annual meeting, 515 volunteers screened thirty-six hundred reports in six hours. For many members, the annual reports and review represented the only contact with the NCA on evaluation. In assessing this program, Indiana state chair Donald Manlove noted, "Our evaluations have largely been unplanned, incidental, fragmentary, or nonexistent." As a result, he concluded, "Thus, the opportunity for stimulating members schools to improve, to innovate, to experiment, and to be creative has not been as extensive as we would wish."[18]

At the sixteenth annual conference of the Administrative Committee and state chairs held at the Coachman's Inn in Little Rock, Arkansas, from October 17 to 20, 1962, the issue of evaluation arose during the discussions on relations with members and the Commission's role in secondary education. On Friday morning, October 19, "the question was raised as to what the proper role and function of the Secondary Commission should be in the years to come." Various groups had criticized the Association and "perhaps some rethinking was in order." CSS chair L. A. Van Dyke prefaced the discussion by commenting on the historic role the NCA had played in helping bring order out of the chaotic situation in secondary education at the turn of the twentieth century. He suggested redirecting Commission efforts away from quantitative standards and toward "providing real educational leadership by working cooperatively with member schools," repeating again the calls made by the respondents to the 1955 survey. While some members supported Van Dyke's position, others complained that most efforts at using qualitative measures failed. It was also noted that even though the secondary standards were minimal benchmarks, they did represent marks of quality.

The free-flowing discussion then turned to "the adequacy of the reviewing procedures." Most CSS officials supported the existing practices and suggested that the best way to avoid the growing national influence in education was "to improve regional accrediting agency cooperation." The minutes of the conference provide no insight into what cooperation was desired or at what level. However, it probably implied more active involvement between members and the Commission, because the next topic discussed was the feasibility of periodic self-evaluation and committee visitations. A Committee on Accreditation Procedures was appointed "to make a thorough study of the possibilities of some type of periodic self-evaluation and visitation to supplement our current procedures." A report with findings and recommendations was due at the March 1964 NCA annual meeting. The next day, Van Dyke named five state chairs—Donald Manlove, Indiana (committee chair); Harold Bowers, Ohio; John E. McAdam, Iowa; Clarence Brock, West Virginia; Lawrence R. Simpson, Kansas; and superintendent Harold Fern of West Aurora, Illinois—to the committee.[19]

The review of accreditation procedures was "part of the progress the Administrative Committee is making on the long-range, expanded role of the Secondary Commission." The goal of this expansive reform movement was to realize the Commission belief that "accreditation should be based increasingly upon overall quality rather than on quantitative factors." Other efforts included the professionalization of the CSS administration and a simultaneous revision of accreditation standards. Reflecting this larger interest, the Association newsletter, NCA Today, reported that the committee's mandate had been enlarged beyond the narrow function outlined in the conference minutes. The committee's had to formulate a plan for periodic revaluation. Two more tasks were added. The committee was also to review procedures on how member schools became accredited and maintained that status, and to study ways that state departments of education, universities, and school personnel within a state could help member schools improve their program. Though the minutes do not provide a rationale for the new tasks, the committee possibly was trying to devise a means to meet the heavy personnel needs a visitation program required.[20]

In discussing their charge, Manlove and the other members realized that accreditation procedures encompassed virtually all the Commission did. This recognition led to a number of far-reaching and expansive questions on the scope of the work. They asked whether the annual report review should be made less frequent or eliminated. The idea was raised of leaving all quantitative aspects to the states. Were the accrediting procedures and criteria too detailed in laying out the quantitative requirements? But, in the end, the committee narrowed the focus to evaluation, because it had "no wish to attempt the impossible and to completely revolutionize our present procedures, many of which serve an important purpose." Existing procedures were not necessarily ineffective or bad. The problem was that they did not meet the current needs of the Commission and member schools. As a result, expansion of effort, not reconstruction, was the strategy employed by the committee.[21]

In addition, as Manlove explained, no major overhaul was needed because "within the framework of our current policies and criteria lie the very means to stimulate schools to improve." Policy III: Evaluation of the Composite Effectiveness of Schools, criterion IIF, read: "Each member school shall make a planned and continuous evaluation of the effectiveness of its educational program in accomplishing its objectives or outcomes upon which its staff and board have agreed." This criterion probably represented an unsuccessful attempt to implement the theory of the Cooperative Study. "State chairmen, members of our state committees, and administrators of our member schools have long been aware that the criterion has been largely disregarded," commented Manlove. To a great extent, the same had been true of the *Evaluative Criteria*. NCA member schools had been much slower to employ the *Criteria* than those in other regions, though size and numbers probably hampered implementation.[22]

A number of factors hampered widespread acceptance and use of self-evaluation programs, including the belief that qualitative measures tended to turn into quantitative assessments. Another problem was that the application of the Commission's standards was inconsistent. Stephen Romine claimed the decentralized philosophy of the Commission contributed to this lack of uniform enforcement. He suggested that an extreme states' rights stance had resulted "in great variations in the interpretation and administration of many requirements, frequently reducing the all too minimal existing standards," and obviously not applying others. This practice caused "widespread and mounting dissatisfaction among school principals," and possibly prompted the criticisms that led to the creation of the accreditation procedures committee.[23] In addition, though the *Evaluative Criteria* offered an instrument for self-evaluation, the Commission had no procedures to promote its use specifically, or school self-evaluation generally. Recognizing a growing need, the 1955 survey findings and the various discussions in the Commission focused on a periodic visitation program for member schools.

At the April 6, 1964, meeting of the Administrative Committee, Manlove recommended that the Rules of Procedure be changed to include the policy that "each member school shall be reevaluated at least once every seven years, using the materials of the *Evaluative Criteria* or some other instrument approved by the Commission." He suggested beginning the program in September 1965. The Commission approved the plan at the 1965 NCA annual meeting.[24] The next step was ensuring that reevaluation visits were acceptable to members. Following a referendum of its members, the Commission changed item 4 of policy 3 of the Policies and Criteria so that it repeated verbatim the initial recommendation for a school self-study and visitation every seven years. To help members obtain the *Evaluative Criteria*, the last sentence of the revision noted, "These materials may be secured by writing to the National Study of Secondary School Evaluation, 1785 Massachusetts Avenue, N.W., Washington, D.C. 20306."[25]

Though the groundwork was laid for the new program, effective implementation required overcoming a variety of difficulties. CSS chair Elmer Weltzin observed, "This new procedure is going to take a tremendous amount of voluntary help and schools must be willing to assist each other." Manlove agreed, claiming that the effort would involve thousands of faculty and evaluators in hundreds of schools. "The majority of administrators of member schools, as well as perhaps another member or two of the professional staff," he explained, "may expect to serve as a member of a visiting committee for another school once every year or two." Beyond the need to provide enough evaluators was the more critical matter of gaining cooperation and support inside the schools. The self-study was the core of the program, and "the greatest barrier to self-study is an unenthusiastic faculty that fails to accept the values of the evaluating process." Regarding both the evaluators and those being evaluated, the Commission had to allay the fears of many people regarding something new. They also had to prepare the way for the acceptance of change. One solution was making sure all involved knew what they were doing, how to do it, and why.

In promoting the self-study/visitation program, Manlove stressed the local, democratic approach to change. "It is a principle of democracy that those affected by judgments or decisions should understand and participate in making them." Using this logic, he suggested that faculty participation was a "sound democratic practice." Faculty involvement made the self-study a grassroots, cooperative effort and not a top-down administrative one imposed either by the NCA on administrators, or by administrators on teachers. Citing research studies, he explained that when faculty defined the goals of work their productivity increased, their morale was higher, their interest was maintained—and they accepted change better. A 1953–1954 survey of 613 teachers who had used the *Evaluative Criteria* provided a good example. Eighty percent reported the experience had benefited them and seven out of eight claimed it had helped their school. As a result, Manlove concluded, "The self-study then must be a group endeavor involving faculty, supervisors, administrators, and, in many instances, students." He also suggested including community figures to improve public relations.

The success of the program depended on effective planning. If the self-study was hurried, unplanned, and "assigned to teachers as extra duty to do at the end of a long school day, it would surely fail." A pivotal aspect of the planning process was to ensure the faculty understood the purpose of the evaluation and what outcomes were expected. But, equally important, they needed sufficient time to complete the self-study.[26]

The Administrative Committee had recognized that the changes in accrediting practices required substantial support to succeed. To assist member schools undergoing the new evaluation process, Manlove and his associates were to develop an "Evaluation Guide for Secondary Schools, which would outline the basic steps to be followed in the self-study and visitation process and would be used by administrators in helping them to carry out the evaluation." The initial draft was written by Manlove and David Beggs III of Indiana University. It was then reviewed by the other committee members.[27] Elmer Weltzin's 1965 report to the Association included information on the status of the new guide that shows that, even under a short deadline, Association procedures regarding change were followed. The Commission maintained a careful, though in this case hurried, process of development that included extensive review before preparing the final product. "The tentative guide has been circulated among the state chairmen and members of the Administrative Committee for their recommendations and criticism," Weltzin explained, noting that afterward "the Committee will review all suggestions and then hopefully ready the guide for publication in the spring issue of the *Quarterly*. Reprints will also be made available to schools." The fourteen-page *Evaluation Guide for Secondary Schools* appeared in the Spring 1965 *North Central Association Quarterly*. At its June 1965 meeting, the Administrative Committee decided to publish seventy-five hundred reprints.[28]

The *Guide* offered a brief and succinct explanation of the program, stressing the constructive nature of evaluation and how the self-study/visitation process fit within the operations of the North Central Association. The development of the new accrediting program was tied to the situation in secondary education: "These are years of accelerated and fundamental change in instructional practice. New content, improved methods of instruction, and an urgency for comprehensive quality in secondary school education made periodic school-wide evaluation mandatory." As was true of the higher commission, accreditation on the secondary level followed the Association philosophy of focusing upon the totality of the institution. In this context, the *Guide* affirmed that "effective school program evaluation is a dynamic, vital foundation for school improvement. Educators undertaking a school evaluation are taking inventory of all phases of the school program." In addition, those conducting such a program had to recognize that evaluation was not just a search for problem areas. "Evaluation does not imply that something defective exists," the *Guide* claimed. "Quite the opposite, evaluation is a form of insurance that good practice will be nurtured and continued. School evaluation makes good schools even better." In the course of assessment, the school would identify areas of strength to maintain and places of weakness that required change. The Commission goal was for schools to engage in continuous evaluation both to sustain a level of quality and to adapt to the changing conditions in education.

Drawing upon contemporary scholarship, Manlove and Beggs briefly discussed the different types of evaluation. They noted the past stress on quantitative criteria. "These kinds of criteria are also known as 'presage' or 'predictive' criteria, so-called because of a conjectured relationship to indices of quality, notably such things as desired changes in pupil behavior which may be attributable to the school experience." As examples, they included the number of volumes in the library and the length of class periods and school days. Evaluation, however, had other measures, too. Product criteria focused on pupil behavioral changes, assessing such things as "growth in achievement test scores, shifting of students' attitudes toward art forms, from one of simple awareness to one of valuing certain forms over others," and changes in motor skills. Another category was process criteria, such as the ability of the teacher to establish rapport with students and maintain discipline or the overall social climate of the school.

The *Guide* explained that the large increases in the numbers of schools and teachers had forced the NCA to focus upon predictive criteria. To strengthen evaluation efforts and to fulfill the Commission goal of stimulating school improvement, the self-study/visitation program aimed at expanding the emphasis to the product and process. "Membership in the North Central Association has come to mean a commitment to continual improvement of the educational program," Manlove and Beggs asserted. Drawing upon numerous studies, the *Guide* identified four generalizations that led to successful implementation of innovation and change in a school. The key ingredient was a principal who provided informed and active leadership for teachers to "initiate changes and innovation." In addition, "the major structural elements of the learning situation include teachers, subjects, students, methods, time, and place." Following this line of reasoning, faculty had to be involved in and empowered by the evaluation process. The last generalization outlined the first stages of change, namely, "the emergence, recognition, and definition of need." Summing up the Commission's position, the *Guide* reaffirmed the scientific bases of evaluation espoused by the NCA in the 1920s, claiming, "Solid improvements can and should come about on the basis of evidence relating to the program rather than having program decisions made because of tradition, rationalization, or pressure."

Manlove and Beggs described the evaluation program in detail. They estimated that the entire process took parts of two school years. They also named the person or persons most responsible for each stage. The principal began the process by notifying the NCA state chair, the board of education, and the school staff of the upcoming evaluation. The self-study followed, taking from six months to a full school year. It involved the organization of various committees, including a steering committee, by the principal and faculty to study each aspect of the school and prepare reports. The steering committee then compiled the reports, conducted general staff discussions on the findings, and wrote the self-study. The school visit had three stages. The steering committee arranged the school visit by the NCA team. Manlove and Beggs suggested spending a minimum of two days at the school.

The selection of the visiting committee underscored the cooperative, friendly, and improvement-oriented character of the evaluation program. The *Guide* recommended a minimum of five visitors, including the chair. Possibly in consultation with the principal, the state chair appointed two people from other schools in the area to serve first as consultants on the self-study and later as members of the visiting committee. Selection of the other members was decided by the chair of the visiting team and the principal. These procedures fostered a cooperative attitude while imparting a collegial feel to the committee. The Commission wanted the school personnel to feel they were being visited by colleagues familiar with the community and the school who could assess strengths and weaknesses as well as offer suggestions for improvement.

The total institutional approach required that the visiting team be representative of school operations as a whole. Evaluation tasks were defined by the experience and expertise of the various members. There were two areas of focus. The first areas of focus were the school plant, administration, and staff; philosophy and objectives, school and community, and school program; guidance and health services; instructional materials; and student activities. The second part concentrated on subjects. For example, a team member might look at art and music, while another examined social studies and health or physical education. Other members could look at math and science, English and foreign languages, or aspects of vocational-technical education, respectively.

The *Guide* also provided a sample visit schedule for a two-and-a-half day visit. The evaluation visit began after school at an informal coffee hour with the faculty to explain the purpose and procedures of the visit. The visiting committee then met from 4:30 to 6:30 P.M. to review materials (most materials, including the self-study had been gone over previously) and to finalize the visit schedule. A dinner with the Board of Education followed. In this way, the committee and the school personnel became acquainted and made certain that all involved knew what was going to occur before the official visit began. In the morning, the team examined documents and conversations with teachers, students, and administrators. This format continued in the afternoon and led to the reviewing of the *Evaluative Criteria*, the beginning of the writing of reports, and initial classroom visits. At the end of the school day, the committee met for an hour in small groups with faculty of the subject matter departments. They then convened to hear reports on the various general areas, followed by dinner. On the last day, the morning was devoted to classroom visits. In the afternoon, the team reviewed the *Evaluative Criteria* materials and wrote the report. At three o'clock, the committee met to hear subject area reports. Two hours later, the sample visit outlined in the *Guide* concluded with an exit interview, actually an oral report, with the principal and superintendent that was "concerned with broad, general conclusions," and constructive recommendations. A written report followed.

In addition to providing an easy-to-read, brief outline of the self-study/visitation program, the *Guide* also acted as an instrument of persuasion. It included numerous references to the cooperative nature of the evaluation program and the need for planning. "Quality education does not result from chance," it affirmed. "Careful, cooperative planning is required."[29] One thing the Committee on Accreditation Procedures probably did not plan for was a critical study of the *Evaluative Criteria* that appeared in the Winter 1965 *Quarterly*, pointing out potential problems with the use of the *Criteria*.

In *"Evaluative Criteria*—Let's Improve Our Use of It," Dr. Charles Edwards, an associate professor of education at Illinois State University, offered some advice. Since the CSS was initiating an "extensive program of revisitation among North Central schools," and since this program "will greatly increase the use of the *Evaluative Criteria*, it may be appropriate at this time to raise questions about its effectiveness." He also observed, "Not since the original study in the 1930s has any major attempt been made to validate the use of the *Evaluative Criteria* as an instrument for rating schools." The *Criteria* had been revised a couple of times, but it had not been assessed in the gestalt sense of examining it as a whole. Costs prohibited such an undertaking and so did the "lack of confidence by most people in the instruments that would be used to validate it."

Drawing upon the recent scholarship of educator Ralph Tyler, Edwards identified three kinds of evaluation used to judge schools. They reflected the categories described in the CSS *Evaluation Guide for Secondary Schools*, but used a somewhat different terminology. Structural evaluation was easy because it focused on facilities and was easily quantifiable. Process assessed "the way in which the school carries out its stated aims," and was more difficult because of the difficulties in developing units of measurement and in determining if the process used in the school, even if effective, was the best. The most difficult and most desirable evaluation assessed product, or how well the school accomplished its tasks. Edwards called product the "ultimate evaluation." Again, questions arose over the validity of the instruments used in the evaluation.

In his study, Edwards examined eighteen Iowa schools, trying to relate the findings of their use of the *Criteria* to other external measures. These schools had used the *Criteria* as part of their evaluation by NCA committees over the previous four years. They also

249

had used the same testing program on their students. By studying the results of the tests, the costs per pupil in the various schools, grade point averages in post–high school education, and attitudes of graduates who did not continue their schooling, Edwards correlated the results with ratings achieved on the *Evaluative Criteria* scales as assigned by the NCA visiting committee. He concluded that the *Evaluative Criteria* was not sufficient to use as an instrument to evaluate the total quality of a school. He also noted that it was difficult to know whether the problem was with the instrument or how it was used. Drawing upon the experience of users, Edwards believed that the *Criteria* was "most helpful when employed as a *guide* for the comprehensive evaluation of high school rather than an established set of criteria." His findings confirmed the opinions of the people who had designed the instrument in the 1930s, and the strategy of use suggested by the Committee on Accreditation Procedures.[30]

As the new CSS *Guide* advised, "The *Evaluative Criteria* is a relatively complete and systematic guide which facilitates the work of the faculty and the visiting committee. By using a guide which has been refined through years of use in hundreds of schools, valuable staff time can be directed toward the self-study rather than developing a design for the study."[31] The emphasis was on *guide* not *dictate*, and this stress indicated how the Commission viewed the *Criteria*. Edwards' article brought up a serious issue. Not everyone shared this view of the *Evaluative Criteria*, meaning a danger existed that schools and visiting committees could see it as a set of standards to reach. Such misuse threatened to retard school improvement rather than stimulate it, and seriously detract from the effectiveness of the self-study/visitation program.

Recognizing that misperceptions regarding the use of the *Criteria* and a host of other problems could arise with the initial implementation of the new accrediting program, the CSS offered a series of clinics and workshops to help schools prepare for their visits. In Wyoming, forty administrators from member schools attended a three-day workshop from June 28 to July 2, 1965, at the University of Wyoming. Participants examined simulated materials that contained information typically available to visiting committees and listened to tape recordings of conversations to study the conduct of these committees. They discussed the various types of recommendations and evaluative statements that might be submitted. They also prepared reports based on the simulated materials that "were subjected to group critique." On September 28 and 29, 1965, at a two-day clinic in Missouri for principals, Gordon Cawelti outlined the purposes of the program of revisiting schools periodically, or revisitation, as it was called. Iowa state chair John McAdam described procedures developed in his state, and Missouri state chair Neil Aslin offered the recommendations of his state committee. In addition, "simulated materials were used to facilitate discussion on the responsibilities of the visiting teams." Similar workshops were planned for other states.

Apparently, the new evaluation was welcomed by NCA members as *NCA Today* reported that "many schools volunteered for inclusion in this year's program and these schools are already engaged in the self-study phase of the project."[32] Some states and school districts developed their own evaluation programs and requested NCA sanction. Kansas designed a program for the entire state, while the Cincinnati Public Schools offered a plan that focused on an in-depth evaluation of one major area every year.[33]

As the program proceeded, the CSS continued to improve its effectiveness. For example, schools and individuals participating in various aspects of the process needed more support. In 1966, the Committee on Accreditation Procedures developed a packet for schools participating in the self-study that included the *Evaluation Guide*, an informational brochure for faculty, reprints of pertinent articles, other information, and *Evaluative Criteria* order forms. By 1967, the Commission had produced other resources to aid schools in self-evaluation, including overhead transparencies and an instruction handbook for school steering committees. In addition, Gordon Cawelti wrote an evaluation guide that provided an alternative to the *Evaluative Criteria*. Another major development was the creation of a Commission Training Program for prospective visiting committee chairs that evolved from the original workshops offered to school administrators. One hundred sixty-three people from ten states participated in three clinics in 1967 and 1968.[34]

The new emphasis on quality and improvement influenced a major revision of the *Policies and Criteria* in the late 1960s. John McAdam, the NCA Iowa state committee chair, headed the Criteria Revision Committee. Its goals were: "(1) raise those criteria that are most defensible indicators of quality, (2) eliminate any present criteria that are of marginal importance or seem to restrict experimentation, and (3) establish some new criteria believed to be descriptive of good schools." The timetable reflected the democratic philosophy of the Commission regarding change. The committee first held meetings with national leaders in secondary education to consider ways of improving secondary education. Next, they drafted revisions that were presented at the 1967 annual meeting and then distributed to member schools during the following summer. In the fall of 1967, state chairs held meetings with administrators. Their suggestions were reviewed at a meeting of the criteria committee on December 1 and 2, 1967. Two weeks later, the Administrative Committee reviewed the changes and prepared the final versions that were submitted to members for a referendum vote in May 1968. After passage, application of the new high school criteria was delayed until September 1969 to allow schools a year to make any adjustments in their operations.

One of the more interesting changes was in how the criteria were presented. The format stressed the qualitative nature and improvement orientation of accreditation. A qualitative principle introduced each criterion, describing "its general significance and the required provisions." The second section identified the minimum standards required of all member schools, while the third part described "Optimal or Exemplary Conditions" that offered "directions or objectives for those member schools that meet or exceed the minimum requirements." Though not required for membership, the suggestions did recommend areas of improvement. The new format of the criteria strengthened CSS efforts at school improvement through self-study and visitation by providing a context, a benchmark, and ideas on moving beyond the minimum that stimulated further change.[35]

Another area that required attention due to the rigorous nature of the revised accrediting program was the issue of admitting newly opened schools. At the 1966 annual meeting, Donald Manlove recommended the establishment of provisional accreditation status that delayed the self-study and visit for certain applicants. Provisional membership allowed new schools to become NCA members for not more than two years if they met all the qualifications listed in the *Policies and Criteria*. The committee recognized that new schools needed to stabilize their program and faculty before undergoing the accreditation process. Full membership could only be granted following the self-study and visit.[36]

In a variety of ways, then, the NCA Commission on Secondary Schools supported the program to implement the 1930s theory of accrediting. As was true in higher education, success in instituting the self-study and visitation component allowed the Commission to adjust to the ongoing transformation of secondary education. The general theory and practice of accrediting proved remarkably adaptable to almost any educational situation, resulting in a significant expansion of the NCA community. As the higher commission moved upward into programmatic accreditation of proliferating graduate programs and downward into the emerging postsecondary realm, so the secondary commission expanded upward into adult education at the fringes of the postsecondary level and, more significantly, downward to encompass all of precollegiate education.

EXPANDING THE MEMBERSHIP

The provisional membership category allowed the NCA to accommodate newly opened schools. Representing a marked departure from traditional policies, the provisional and other membership initiatives allowed the Commission to respond to the changing conditions in education. In most cases, membership expansion programs followed the same general pattern.

The NCA schools commission addressed junior high school membership first. Responding to numerous requests by junior high principals, in 1960 annual meeting, the Administrative Committee authorized a committee "to explore the possibility for accreditation of junior high schools by the NCA."[37] The committee conducted two surveys. The first was in the winter of 1960, but its findings proved inconclusive, except for ascertaining that junior high administrators generally favored accreditation. Approximately two-thirds of the principals responding were favorable to accrediting junior highs, as were 62 percent of the superintendents. In terms of state returns, NCA accreditation proved most popular among South Dakota and Kansas principals. Ninety-three percent favored the idea. In addition, Kansas superintendents recorded the highest approval rating, with 95 percent saying they favored accrediting.

However, 20 percent of all respondents objected to accreditation, and 14 percent of the principals and 18 percent of the supervisors were uncertain. In Nebraska, the idea was soundly defeated as 70 percent of the principals and 91 percent of the supervisors opposed accreditation. Given the large number of fears, cautions, and objections expressed, a second, more in-depth, survey was conducted than in the winter of 1961.

The results of the second survey were flawed because the lists of schools provided by the NCA state chairs included many institutions that were not junior highs. Thus, while the committee sent out two thousand questionnaires, only 48 percent of the returns were usable. However, the responses proved illuminating. A majority of principals desired accreditation to focus on "minimum quantitative and qualitative standards, guidelines for self improvement, research and its publication, articulation of elementary, junior high and senior high school levels, the status and security of the junior high school and its personnel, and resistance to adverse factors and forces." Answers to open-ended questions identified such concerns as more "attention to teacher and/or administrator preparation for junior high school personnel" and the need to consider the curriculum and instruction "including grade placement of subjects." Regarding the proposed process of accreditation, the number of responses was small, but illuminating. They focused on three concerns: "[to] maintain flexibility in the program to encourage experimentation, to avoid imposition of senior high school accreditation on the junior high school and to utilize junior high school personnel."

The survey identified two important issues. The results indicated that junior high school administrators misunderstood what traditional accreditation was, and that, despite its long history dating back to the turn of the twentieth century, the junior high was still evolving. Its needs circa 1960 seem very similar to those of the senior high school in the 1890s. The survey also uncovered several problem areas that could negatively impact on accrediting efforts. In general, educators disagreed on the nature of junior high school education. The organizational structure of the schools varied. Of the 950 schools responding to the second survey, 684 had three-year programs that covered grades seven through nine. A total of 253 were two-year schools that encompassed grades seven and eight, while 13 had some other configuration. Diversity also existed in the organization of the educational program. The trend was towards greater departmentalization of instruction and less core, self-contained classroom work as the grades progressed, but the best format remained a subject of debate. A third issue was the continued employment in junior high schools of teachers trained for the elementary grades.

Romine connected many of the problems in the junior high school to its uncertain status. He suggested the junior high was the "stepchild in the educational family." His terminology had wide implications, beyond the traditional neglect implied by the word *stepchild*. "It is a known fact that in some school systems this level is a 'stepping stone' to senior high schools for faculty and administrators as well as students," he explained, concluding that the junior high needed to be "regarded as an organizational level in its own right." Even among administrators, the status problem was evident. While 673 respondents considered the junior high school as a "separate & distinct" level, 81 perceived it as an upward extension of the elementary school, 76 as a downward extension of the senior high school, and 79 as a combination of both. If one-third of the junior high principals and superintendents did not consider their level of schooling as an independent organizational component, elementary and senior high school administrators probably had similar feelings. Accreditation would legitimize the junior high school.[38]

Romine recommended the NCA accredit junior high schools, but advised that development be slow "and with due regard to subsequent observations and continued counsel of junior high school principals." This recommendation fit the findings of the survey and also reflected the CSS philosophy of democratic, locally oriented reform. The stress on the school as the site of reform was underscored by his suggestions on the role the NCA should play in developing the program. Acknowledging that the central leadership by the Commission was vital, Romine cautioned that the NCA authority be "established and exercised so as to grow out of and feed back into the committee in each state." In part, the slow, cautious pace and the focus on the school reflected the uncertainty and lack of knowledge among both junior high school administrators and NCA figures. Conversely, since so many respondents reported using various policies and criteria, the NCA also needed to study existing accreditation and appraisal programs. A final observation touched upon the influence of outside factors on the survey findings. Romine claimed that the "unrest and tension of today probably influenced respondents." Though he did not expand upon this point, the enhanced stress probably was caused by the cold war, the growing civil rights movement, the new directions indicated by the Kennedy campaign, the continuing suburbanization movement, the need to accommodate the huge influx of African-American migrants into the cities and the urban schools, and the ongoing flux in educational circles.

To begin developing junior high accreditation, Romine recommended the NCA convene regional meetings for representatives from each state to "draft plans for the basic deliberation and study essential to the development of a regional accreditation program."[39] At its summer 1962 meeting, the Administrative Committee appointed a committee to study junior high school accreditation. In creating the committee, the Administrative Committee insisted that "whatever policies and criteria might be needed in developing a program of accrediting junior high schools will be formulated cooperatively by junior high school principals and teachers in the NCA region." The composition of the committee put this promise into practice. Everett V. Samuelson, director of the University of Colorado Bureau of Educational Research and Service, was named chair. Other members included: Gene Maybee, principal of Tappan Junior High School in Ann Arbor, Michigan; Glenn Rose, principal of Drake Junior High School in Arvada, Colorado; Donald Stout, director of secondary education in Cedar Rapids, Iowa; and Richard Wedel, principal of Lincoln Junior High School in Rockford, Illinois.[40]

By the end of 1962, considerable progress had been made. The state chairs had conducted meetings with junior high administrators "to assess the sentiments and obtain suggestions regarding the accreditation of junior high schools." In addition, the committee presented its plan. Samuelson provided a constitutional basis for undertaking the accrediting of the junior high schools, observing junior high accreditation was "a natural outgrowth of Article 2 of the NCA Constitution which states in part: 'The object of the Association shall be the development and maintenance of high standards of excellence for...secondary schools.'"[41] The next item covered the important issue of definition. In its early years, defining levels of education had been a major priority of the Association. A prerequisite to accreditation was defining just what was being accredited. Reflecting the variations in organization, the committee defined the junior high as a school that included grade seven through nine or any combination of two of these grades. This definition is important because while the grade designation reflected conditions in the early 1960s, the seventh-to-ninth-grade span eliminated another popular configuration that combined grades six through eight in a school. In addition, the growing trend towards middle schools led to a readjustment of the junior high accrediting program in 1970 to accommodate the movement toward middle schools.[42] A more enduring definition described NCA junior high school accreditation as "the process whereby any junior high school, within the NCA geographical region, voluntarily applies for membership in the Association, is evaluated on adopted procedure and criteria, and is approved by membership in the Association on the basis of having met the policies and criteria as stated."

Samuelson saw two purposes of junior high accreditation. The first was the traditional NCA rationale of fostering self-evaluation by goals of the school. Interestingly, the committee added the phrase "provided that such goals are consistent with the goals of the community and the nation." This addition recognized the influence of outside forces on education, apparently seeking greater compatibility among educational efforts, the local community needs, and the nation's objectives. The second purpose probably reflected the desires of the junior high administrators in that the NCA was "to provide leadership in helping achieve such goals in a junior high school."

The development followed the CSS philosophy of local, democratic action and the needs of this pioneering program. The committee asserted, "The creative efforts of the principals themselves must provide the leadership." The committee representation helped realize this goal. The committee advised that developing accrediting criteria would take over two years, explaining it "must come through cooperative action among junior high school principals and teachers of each state in the NCA." The program followed the reforms in modernizing accrediting generally. Institutional self-appraisal was basic to the process, and an evaluation instrument was needed to guide the schools. A potential solution was an *Evaluative Criteria* for junior high schools that the National Study on Secondary School Evaluation had scheduled for publication 1963.[43]

Samuelson outlined the advantages of junior high accreditation and identified concerns previously noted by junior high administrators. Accreditation would help schools improve their educational programs, and the NCA would act as a "source of information and leadership through research studies and consultative help." NCA membership helped articulation by promoting a closer relationship among the various precollegiate levels, particularly the high schools. Accreditation enhanced the status of junior high schools. In addition, the NCA facilitated experimentation and research. As for potential pitfalls, the possibility existed that the NCA would impose policies and criteria "without the involvement of those with sufficient background—namely—junior high oriented persons." The danger existed of "super-imposing adapted senior high school criteria on junior high schools." The statements of the Administrative Committee and the report of the NCA junior high accrediting committee addressed this danger. Other concerns included unnecessarily duplicating reportage, the costs of the program, and the potential loss of flexibility on a school's operations.[44]

The junior high accreditation committee plan addressed many of the pitfalls. The first phase had state committees conduct the area and state meetings to ascertain the opinions of principals regarding accreditation during the 1962–1963 school year. The next stage focused on the *Evaluative Criteria* for junior highs. After distributing copies for review, the committee launched a pilot program to test the *Criteria* in seventy schools. In addition, tentative policies and criteria were developed cooperatively and submitted to junior high administrators for "reactions, suggestions, modifications, and changes" that were incorporated in the final recommendations.[45]

By 1965, Donald Stout had replaced Samuelson as committee chair. He reported that a pilot test of the *Evaluative Criteria* had showed it needed much revision. As a result, the committee was working "on the development of principles and standards consistent with the purposes of the junior high school; on an organizational basis for carrying on junior high accreditation; and on procedures to be followed in accrediting these schools."[46]

Myrle E. Hemenway. Professor of education at the University of Colorado, Hemenway was associate director for junior highs and a leader in the development of accreditation standards for junior high schools.

The following year, assistant chair Myrle Hemenway of the University of Colorado reported that the program was almost finished. Hemenway recommended that each state appoint a liaison person or associate chair to attend a summer meeting. He also noted the committee was preparing a final statement. In 1967, the Commission approved the committee's accreditation program. To facilitate implementation, the CSS instituted an interim pilot program that expanded the state committee to include three junior high school representatives, with one to be an associate chair. The annual meeting also featured a training session for thirty-five junior high administrators. In addition, the "Policies, Principles and Standards for Approval of Junior High Schools" became available to schools on June 15, 1967.[47] After five years of careful, studied development, junior high school accreditation became part of the NCA operations. In 1968, the NCA welcomed eighteen junior high school members from seven states. Colorado, Iowa, and Indiana had three or more new members. The first, but hardly the last, significant expansion of school membership in over seventy years of accreditation had occurred.

By 1974, the Commission on Secondary Schools had developed accreditation programs for adult and occupational high schools and special function schools. The following year, the CSS began accrediting elementary schools. The ability to accommodate different levels of education and different kinds of schools was due to a variety of factors. The local, democratic philosophy provided a basis for expansion that required involvement by those schools seeking accreditation, thereby ensuring that the policies and criteria developed were pertinent to their operations. This collaborative method also facilitated acceptance of the programs. Equally important, the reformed accrediting program based on self-study and revisitation proved remarkably flexible and compatible to the decentralized school orientation of the Commission. Also paralleling the policy of the higher commission, the CSS was committed to a single commission because "education is better served by the conjoining of efforts of all educators than by a proliferation of specialized and fragmented commissions." Though committed to functional specialization, the CSS had defined that specialization broadly enough to encompass almost all of precollegiate education. Reflecting this expansion, on July 1, 1974, the CSS officially changed its name to the Commission on Schools.[48]

DEPENDENTS' SCHOOLS AND THE UNIQUE GOVERNMENT RELATIONSHIP

One of the most interesting expansion efforts involved the federal government and arose due to the international situation after World War II. As the growing cold war split the world into two armed camps, the United States defined its sphere of influence through various treaties and alliances. A pivotal aspect of this territorial imperative was the creation of military bases throughout the world. The U.S. had a military presence in the defeated nations of Germany, Italy, and Japan, as well as Great Britain, Spain, Turkey, South Korea, Thailand, and the Philippines, Panama, and Cuba. In the last two nations, American military presence predated the war.[49] New, overseas American communities evolved around these bases to serve the military personnel and their families. A central part of these communities was the school, and that is where the NCA became involved.

In May 1946, the U.S. Army organized the Dependents' School Service for U.S. bases in Germany. Besides educating the children of base personnel, the schools provided a model for German educators to use in their efforts to democratize and reform the German educational system. The impetus behind changing the German system was a foreign policy initiative by the U.S. to ensure the schools were purged of all traces of Nazism. An irony of this development was that the German system was a major prototype for American educators at the turn of the twentieth century—forty-five years later these roles were reversed.

On October 14, 1946, the Dependents' School Service opened thirty-eight elementary and five high schools for two thousand American children from forty-eight states. The enrollment rose to 3,000 by the end of the school year. Initially, the facilities were less than ideal. Classes were held in houses, barracks, and prewar school buildings. In addition, during the first year, a shortage of American teachers led to the hiring of some German instructors.[50] However, military officials recognized the role good schools played in building the morale of Americans stationed overseas and sought to ensure their quality. As NCA Commission on Secondary Schools secretary Edgar G. Johnston commented in 1950, "it was very important for the army in recruiting clientele for the theaters of operation that they be able to give their people who are invited to come over there, the assurance that their children would have school facilities comparable to those with which they felt familiar in the United States."[51] To ensure the quality of the schools, the military sought NCA accreditation in early 1947.

As Johnston later reported, the Army request for accreditation of dependents' schools was quite unusual. "It was rather an unprecedented action," he recalled. "To my knowledge, it is the first time that the Association had accredited any schools outside the twenty states comprising its territory." At the June 23–24, 1947, meeting of the Administrative Committee in Chicago, the government request generated much discussion. There were no constitutional conflicts, since the addition of New Mexico and Arizona forty years earlier had led to amendments allowing expansion without regard to regionalism. A proposal to consult with the other regional associations before taking any action was rejected because the situation required a quick decision. In the end, two factors led the NCA Executive Committee to approve the Army's request. They felt "this represented a service to a group of young people, many of whom came from schools in the North Central territory and have returned to colleges in the North Central territory." In addition, the commitment would not be long-term. Johnston explained, "Because the United States had a responsibility which would be a temporary one, but would exist for several years in the occupied countries, the schools were admitted." Actually, the schools in Berlin, Frankfurt, Heidelberg, Munich, and Nurnberg, Germany, were approved only after being visited by superintendent Virgil Rogers of Battle Creek, Michigan. Rogers had been in Germany as part of an assignment from the War Department and had agreed to the NCA request that he examine the schools. The accreditation was for one year and continuation of NCA membership depended upon filing the required annual report.

To administer the program, the Administrative Committee created the Reviewing Committee for Dependents' Schools, later called the Committee on Dependents' Schools. The CSS secretary served as chair. Other initial members included Illinois state chair Lowell Fisher and Missouri state chair John Rufi. It was agreed that the dependents' schools undergo the same accrediting procedures as those in the United States. However, the Administrative Committee believed that three areas deserved special scrutiny. The Commission expressed concern over taking "unusual care in the selection of teachers," providing well-equipped libraries, and instructional materials.[52]

NCA officials considered the accrediting of overseas schools an emergency, short-term measure. They also realized that the overseas school system would grow, requiring an appropriate response from the secondary commission. For example, in June 1948, the NCA not only expanded its operations in Germany, but also began accrediting schools in Japan and the Philippines, becoming involved with the U.S. Air Force in the process.[53] However, even as the CSS accommodated growth overseas, questions

Lowell B. Fisher. Illinois State Director, NCA
Commission on Schools, 1947–72; Chair of
the Commission on Schools, 1954–55; President of the Association in 1958.

arose about its authority to accredit the schools. The Commission
considered it important to confer with other regional associations
to explain "the status of the dependents' schools, the emergency
character of our action, and the continuing nature of the problem." Edgar Johnston pursued this for eighteen months. Johnston
suggested logistical problems prohibited getting together, even
though, given the eventual outcome, the other regionals may have
wanted to avoid the issue.

At the annual meeting of the Association of School Administrators, Johnston met with representatives of the New England and
Middle States associations and Director of Secondary Education
Galen Jones, of the U.S. Office of Education. The decisions made at
this meeting set the policy of the regional accrediting associations
regarding the dependents' schools. As reported at the March 19,
1950, meeting of the Administrative Committee, "It was the unanimous feeling of the group present in Atlantic City that accrediting
of these schools should be carried out by one association only and
that the North Central Association was in the best position to

assume this responsibility." Apparently, the NCA was in the best position because few others volunteered to help. Johnston observed that the Middle States Association had no interest. The Northwest Association had accredited schools in Japan, but showed little willingness to continue.

At a subsequent meeting on November 25 and 26, 1950, at the Middle States Association annual meeting in Atlantic City, representatives of all the regionals and several military personnel agreed upon both the need for accrediting the dependents' schools and on having the NCA perform this activity. In return, the other regionals would abide by any NCA decisions.[54] These decisions changed the ad hoc commitment of the NCA into the official accrediting policy for the dependents' schools. In the process, the nature of the Association's secondary accreditation was transformed, though on a very narrow plane. In one sense, NCA accrediting became national accrediting, because all those involved in institutional accreditation agreed to follow its dictates. Even though the Administrative Committee passed a resolution limiting overseas involvement to schools under military aegis, the secondary commission still admitted schools located around the globe. As a result, NCA membership assumed international dimensions.

Yet, the entry of the CSS onto the national and international scene did not follow the normal, studied pattern of decision making. Rather, a quick response to an emergency led to a cooperative resolution that the Association accepted with little discussion or dissent. Since the CSS did not exploit this opportunity for expansion, but adhered strictly to the narrow plane of activity, few jurisdictional problems arose. But the precedent was set for action outside the region and into other domestic areas, such as the later accrediting of Native American schools.

In addition, the secondary schools commission established a unique relationship with the federal government on several levels. The very accrediting of the overseas schools implied support for U.S. foreign policy on a very basic level. As Herman Search, supervisor of Army schools in France and Germany, explained in 1956, "The giving of support to our governmental program in Europe. This objective, in our analysis, becomes our biggest objective."[55] What was true in Europe applied around the globe. In many cases, the military bases and the dependents' schools accredited by the NCA were the only direct points of contact between the United States and the people of other nations. The quality of the schooling provided American children outside the nation exemplified the American way of life during a period of intense competition between the U.S. and the Soviets. The schools helped create a positive image of the United States during the cold war.

NCA officials had another reason for accrediting overseas schools. It was a unique opportunity to serve America's youth. "When you visit as many as several of these schools and find these bright-eyed Americans who are going to school all over the world in American environments, but still in a situation of another world," CSS chair Floyd Miller commented, observing,

> when you see the stars in their eyes because they are fine, American kids,...when you think of the extreme difficulties they have in providing educational opportunities,...and then when you stop and think that one of the major reasons why they are having excellent educational opportunities...because the North Central Association saw fit to take another responsibility upon itself, that of sponsoring and accrediting the Dependents' schools.

He concluded, expressing great pride in the Commission's work abroad. Herman Search also cited the service to youth, claiming, "To lose their accreditation and the support of the North Central Association would endanger the educational welfare of approximately 500 high school young men and young women."[56]

Recognizing that the overseas schools were becoming a long-term commitment, the Commission adjusted its perceptions and practices. At the June 24, 1954, meeting of the Administrative Committee in Chicago, Secretary Alva Gibson reported, "In the beginning it was thought that this [Dependents' School] Committee was an emergency or temporary setup, and that the Dependents' Schools would soon fade out of the picture. However, it now appears that there will be Dependents' Schools for some time to come." In response, the Administrative Committee reorganized the Dependents' School Committee. The membership was expanded to five, including the CSS secretary who remained committee chair. Other members served two-year terms and could not succeed themselves. The committee tenure was staggered to provide experience and continuity as one member was to be the retiring chair of

Alva J. Gibson. West Virginia state director
of the NCA Commission on Schools and
secretary of the Commission on Secondary
Schools, 1953–62.

the Commission and two others were recruited from individuals
who had participated in the last visits overseas. One member was
elected at large.[57]

The purpose of the reorganization was to put the committee
"on a more or less permanent basis, somewhat in line with the
State Committees." In 1957, Edgar Johnston waxed enthusiastically over the Dependents' School Committee work, acknowledging its permanence and unique character. "I sometimes wonder if
we should not include that as possibly the twentieth state in the
North Central Association." While not constitutionally considered
part of the Commission, in practice, the Dependents' School Committee was an integral part of CSS operations whose responsibilities
grew as the number of schools increased. By 1957, an estimated
one hundred thousand American youth attended school overseas.
Only a small minority were enrolled in NCA-accredited schools,
but expansion was also evident here. From five high schools in one
nation at the beginning of the program, the NCA had accredited

forty-one schools in twelve countries, Puerto Rico, and Guam on four continents by 1957. Germany had fifteen schools and Japan eight, while France and Italy had three each, Puerto Rico, French Morocco, and England had two, and there was one each in Guam, the Azores, Turkey, Libya, Spain, and the Philippines. These schools contained a total enrollment of 13,255 pupils and employed 760 teachers. The largest school was in Agana, Guam, and had 1,996 students, while the smallest was in Leghorn, Italy, with 38 students.[58]

As the Commission involvement became a more organized and professional effort, the NCA relationship with the federal government experienced some twists and turns that broke new ground regarding the connection between the government and a voluntary association. Unlike the situation in higher education, the sanctioning power rested with the NCA, but the Commission initially seemed reluctant to exercise its authority. In the early years of accreditation, the committee and the government administrators of the overseas school program recognized the situation was unique and required innovative solutions.

The first challenge arose at the end of the first year of accrediting with the expansion into Japan. Some of the Japanese schools were very small and thus could not individually meet all the NCA standards. In consultation with R. B. Patin, the director of these schools, Edgar Johnston reported, "We worked out a provision for these schools somewhat similar to that carried out in certain of your states where…a branch high school may be just a small school, depending upon an accrediting relation with another school." The solution was to combine several schools under one administrative superintendent who would supervise the entire group.[59] In this instance, cooperation followed by innovative adaptation of a domestic practice effectively addressed a vexing issue. Many military bases were small, sometimes remote outposts. The attached schools drew from an equally small population base and had proportionate facilities. The accrediting responsibility required accommodating these schools, rather than dismissing them out of hand.

A different problem arose in Europe in 1952 when NCA visiting teams reported on "problems and deficiencies" in some schools as a result of budget cuts. After a meeting of the Dependents'

School Committee with Army and Office of Education personnel, Edgar Johnston reported there was "excellent cooperation of the Armed Services in taking steps to correct deficiencies." Selected military personnel later attended the NCA annual meeting and met with the reviewing committee to explain the Army program and its problems. However, the problems in Europe went unsolved and similar difficulties arose in Asia. NCA Commission on Research and Service member Paul Harnly had visited Asian schools. Responding to a letter sent the CSS by director Patin that reported a congressional appropriation of $200 per child, Harnly angrily wrote the Commission to complain that the Army was taking out its economy drive on the schools. "I do not see how satisfactory education can be supplied for this amount in the scattered areas," he noted. "It provides only the barest necessities of textbook-centered instruction, and I do not see how it can be comparable to that offered by even the poorest North Central Association schools in America." The Commission directed Johnston to write to the Special Assistant to the Secretary for Education of the Department of the Army to express its concern over the reduced support of the overseas schools.[60]

But conditions did not improve. In October 1952, Edgar Johnston reported that the situation in Europe was critical. He warned that some schools might lose their accreditation. The Commission chair was directed to write the Secretary of the Army informing him of the situation and expressing the "hope that steps will be taken to correct the situation and continue the membership of schools in the Association." By March of the following year, however, the areas of concern had been addressed satisfactorily. Johnson praised the determination of the headquarters of the European command to meet NCA requirements. He also reported that they were conducting a search for a new administrator to head up the new Dependents' Education Organization. The revised government organization divided the responsibilities between a civilian educator who directed educational operations and a colonel who handled logistics. Previously, a colonel had directed all aspects of the program. In this regard, growth and budgetary restraints probably combined to create the crisis. However, the military acknowledged the NCA authority and responded favorably. As a sign of good faith, government officials attended the NCA annual meeting.[61]

Unfortunately, budget cuts and growth continued to plague the operation of the schools, forcing the Commission into more drastic action. In 1964, CSS secretary Gordon Cawelti reported that funding limitations had led to warnings and advisements to more schools for insufficient offerings and teacher preparation deficiencies. He also noted that the dependents' schools program was being reorganized so the Army would administer all schools in Europe, Asian schools would be under the Air Force, and the Navy would manage the Atlantic area. The following year, Cawelti explained that funding restrictions had created more problems. He observed, "Some of the smaller schools are unable to provide a comprehensive offering because of the limited number of teachers that are allocated to them; the inadequacy of instructional equipment and supplies poses another problem." Again, some schools received advisements and warnings on problems related to accrediting, and one school was dropped. The Commission chair also testified before the Defense Appropriations Committee in Congress in April 1965. In 1966, overcrowding was a major problem and had apparently been a concern of the NCA for the previous five years. As enrollments had risen, no accompanying expansion of facilities had occurred. No schools were dropped, but Cawelti noted, "A number of warnings were recommended this year." Again, the Commission chair was scheduled to testify before Congress.[62] Interestingly, these CSS actions occurred during a period when the relationship between the NCA and the overseas schools had not been formalized. It was not until 1970 that an amendment to the *Rules of Procedure* was passed that formally integrated the Dependents' Schools into the Commission administration.[63]

The informal and improvisational nature of the Dependents' School experience along with the continuing need for the CSS to address the recurring problems with the schools that arose from budgetary actions underscored the unique quality of the overseas accrediting experience. In essence, the government—the Army, Navy, and Air Force—became members of a voluntary association and agreed to follow the policies and procedures of the Association. In return, they received the benefits of membership, including the services of the CSS in improving their educational programs. When certain schools fell below required standards, they received warnings, advisements, or were dropped. But, because the problems arose from the actions of a different branch of the government, the CSS chair went to Congress as an advocate for the schools, seeking the funds needed to resolve the difficulties. The Commission thus played two different roles with the federal government at the same time. The government relationship, along with the agreement of the other regional associations to abide by NCA decisions, and the very accrediting of schools scattered around the planet, made the Dependents' Schools accrediting program as the most unusual and intriguing episode in the Association's hundred-year history.

DEMOCRACY OF MASS REFORM IN A FUNCTIONAL ORGANIZATION

In examining the histories of the secondary and higher commissions between 1945 and approximately 1975, one conclusion is readily apparent. The immensity of the tasks involved in administering the reformed accrediting programs combined with the expansion of memberships represented the greatest transformation of the NCA since the advent of accrediting. In a short period of time, the Association changed from a narrowly defined, elite group to an incredibly diverse, mass organization encompassing most levels of education. Interestingly, both commissions based their operations on accrediting by objectives using the self-study and periodic visits for evaluation and improvement efforts. In neither case did the addition of a professional staff headed by an executive secretary lead to a shift in the distribution of power and responsibility. Rather, it added an administrative layer to enhance coordination and implementation of programs. However, the underlying philosophies and processes of change differed. Though both favored a participatory-democracy reform strategy, the higher commission was highly centralized. The secondary commission was more locally oriented and decentralized.

In the final analysis, the democratic philosophy and decentralized structure of the NCA secondary commission served its purposes as well as the equally democratic, though centralized approach did for the higher commission. Both allowed the NCA accrediting commissions to accommodate the needs of their constituencies during a period of revolutionary change in education. But their success created stresses and strains in the Association that led to the fourth re-creation of the NCA.

NOTES

1. John Stanavage, "The Membership Assesses the Present and Future of the NCA Schools Commission," *North Central Association Quarterly* 44 (Spring 1971): 319, 323.

2. *Statistical Abstracts of the United States* (Washington, D.C.: GPO), vol. 83 (1962), 111; vol. 91 (1970), 104; vol. 113 (1993), 147.

3. Arthur S. Link and William B. Catton, *American Epoch: A History of the United States since 1900,* vol. 3: *1946–1973,* 4th ed. (New York: Alfred A. Knopf, 1974), 74.

4. Gordon Cawelti, "Trends in Secondary Schools," *North Central Association Quarterly* 40 (Fall 1965): 229. See also, O. K. Garretson, "Statistical Summary of Annual Reports from Secondary Schools, 1945–46,"*North Central Association Quarterly* 21 (January 1947): 327–38.

5. Maurice McGlasson, chair of NCA Junior High School Accreditation Committee, cited in John A. Stanavage, "I. Report of the Commission," in "Proceedings of the Commission on Secondary Schools," *North Central Association Quarterly* 45 (Summer 1970): 65.

6. Diane Ravitch, *The Troubled Crusade* (New York: Basic Books, 1983), xi, 10–11, 16–17; Minutes, Administrative Committee meeting, November 14, 1947, Chicago, Illinois.

7. Geiger, *Voluntary Accreditation,* 111.

8. Herbert W. Schooling, "Constructive Changes in Education," in "Association Notes and Editorial Comment," *North Central Association Quarterly* 37 (Winter 1963): 217; Donald C. Manlove, "Self-Study and Visitation for Member Schools," *North Central Association Quarterly* 39 (Winter 1965): 234. This topic is explored in the last chapter of this book.

9. Maurice M. McGlasson, "I. Report of the Commission," in "Proceedings of the Commission on Schools," *North Central Association Quarterly* 49 (Summer 1974): 91.

10. Stephen Romine, "What Member Schools Think of the N.C.A.," *North Central Association Quarterly* 29 (January 1955): 299–300. Other findings focused on improved public relations, greater member participation on review committees, the practice of annual reports, altering the meeting schedules, and the need for closer relations between the secondary and collegiate institutions. The forging of closer ties between the two levels of education was the rationale behind founding the NCA in the first place. It proved an illusory quest for a variety of reasons, including different patterns of development and the varying influences on accrediting. On the expression of the need for better relations, see "Committee on Accreditation Procedures Appointed," *North Central Association Today* 7 (November-December 1962) by Maurice McGlasson cited in John A. Stanavage, "I. Report of the Commission," in "Proceedings of the Commission on Secondary Schools," *North Central Association Quarterly* 48 (Summer 1973): 93.

11. Stephen Romine, "A Look Ahead at Accreditation in the Secondary School," *North Central Association Quarterly* 30 (April 1956): 339, 341–42.

Other trends included a more active role for boards of education in the NCA, closer cooperation between high schools and colleges and universities, and improved public relations. Of these three, only the last was realized in practice.

12. "Secondary Fee Committee to Report," *NCA Today* 6 (November-December 1961).

13. Both accounts appeared in the Association newsletter, but were separated by five months. The first statement comes from "Committee of Fees Appointed," *NCA Today* 5 (May 1961), and the second from "Secondary Fee Committee to Report," ibid. (November-December 1961). An article in the *NCA Quarterly* repeated the second version, see "Fee Committee to Report to Secondary Commission," *North Central Association Quarterly* 36 (Winter 1962): 245.

14. Cited in Alva J. Gibson, "I. The Report of the Commission," in "Proceedings of the Commission on Secondary Schools," *North Central Association Quarterly* 37 (Summer 1962): 56.

15. Administrative Committee minutes, June 23, 1961; "Fees Raised for NCA Members," *NCA Today* 6 (May 1962).

16. "Commissions Appoint New Personnel: Cawelti and Davis join NCA Staff," *North Central Association Today* 7 (November-December 1962). Though the sources indicate Cawelti was the first full-time professional secretary, this is open to debate. He certainly was not the first paid employee. In the 1961–1962 fiscal year, his predecessor, Alva Gibson of West Virginia, had received an annual salary of $6,300, and assistant Sara McDermott earned $4,000. Whether they were employed full-time is not mentioned. Minutes, Administrative Committee meeting, March 19, 1961, Chicago, Illinois.

17. Cited in *NCA Today* 6 (May 1962).

18. Donald C. Manlove, "Self-Study and Visitation for All Member Schools," *North Central Association Quarterly* 39 (Winter 1965); Alva J. Gibson, "I. Report of the Commission," in "Proceedings of the Commission on Secondary Schools," *North Central Association Quarterly* 37 (Summer 1962): 55. If no breaks were taken, and this is unlikely, each volunteer reviewed just over one report per hour.

19. Minutes, Sixteenth Annual Conference of the Administrative Committee and State Chairman, Little Rock, Arkansas, October 17–20, 1962. These minutes were prepared by Gordon Cawelti from notes taken by Carrie Williams. As such, they provide the temper of the proceedings but some conclusions drawn here are speculative since few members are identified as to the opinions expressed in the various discussions, nor is a time frame of the meetings noted. Interestingly, no mention was made in the minutes of the higher commission's program of self-study and visitation.

20. "Committee on Accreditation Procedures," *NCA Today* 7 (November-December 1962); Gordon Cawelti, "I. Report of the Commission," in "Proceedings of the Commission on Secondary Schools," *North Central Association Quarterly* 38 (Summer 1963): 50.

21. Manlove, "Self-Study and Visitation for All Member Schools," 233. Revision of CSS accreditation policies and criteria had been the charge of a committee chaired by L. V. Van Dyke created in the late 1950s that largely had completed its work by 1962. (Alva J. Gibson, "I. Report of the Commission," in "Proceedings of the Commission on Secondary Schools," *North Central Association Quarterly* 33 (July 1958): 54; ibid. 34 (July 1959): 41; 36 (July 1961): 46–47: "Secondary Schools to be Given Final Voice on Far-Reaching Revision of Policies and Criteria," *NCA Today* 4 (May 1959).

22. "Policies and Criteria," *North Central Association Quarterly* 39 (Summer 1964): 147; Manlove, "Self-Study and Visitation for All Member Schools," 233. On the lack of application of the *Evaluative Criteria*, see above.

23. Stephen Romine, "The North Central Association—A Look to the Future," *North Central Association Quarterly* 35 (October 1960): 178.

24. Manlove, "Self-Study and Visitation for All Member Schools," 234; Minutes of the Eighteenth Annual Conference of the Administrative Committee and State Chairmen, September 23–25, 1964; "NCA Commissions Plan Review of Institutions," *NCA Today* 8 (May 1964); "NCA Member High Schools to Be Reevaluated," *NCA Today* 9 (May 1965); Gordon Cawelti, "I. Report of the Commission," in "Proceedings of the Commission on Secondary Schools," *North Central Association Quarterly* 40 (Summer 1965): 59.

25. Minutes, Administrative Committee meeting, Chicago, Illinois, June 24–25, 1965.

26. Elmer Weltzin, "Report to the Association," *North Central Association Quarterly* 40 (Summer 1965): 14; Manlove, "Self-Study and Visitation for All Member Schools," 235–36.

27. NCA Member High Schools to Be Reevaluated," *NCA Today* 9 (May 1965); Manlove, "Self-Study and Visitation for All Member Schools," 234. The Committee on Accreditation Procedures had undergone some personnel changes by this time. Lawrence Simpson had left the committee in 1964 and was replaced by Hazlett Wubben of the University of Colorado. In addition, Principal Don R. Gill of Hastings High School in Michigan had joined the committee. "Foreword," *Evaluation Guide for Secondary Schools* (Chicago: NCA, 1965), reprinted in *North Central Association Quarterly* 39 (Spring 1965): 324.

28. Weltzin, "Report to the Association," 14; Minutes, Administrative Committee meeting, Chicago, Illinois, June 24–25, 1965. At that meeting the question arose about who could authorize a school to use something besides the *Evaluative Criteria*. It was decided that the Administrative Committee should perform this function.

29. *Evaluation Guide for Secondary Schools*, 325–37.

30. Charles Edwards, *"Evaluative Criteria*—Let's Improve Our Use of It," *North Central Association Quarterly* 39 (Winter 1965): 238–41.

31. *Evaluation Guide for Secondary Schools*, 327.

32. "H.S. Reevaluation Program Underway," *NCA Today* 10 (November 1965).

33. Minutes of the Administrative Committee meeting, June 24–25, 1965, Chicago, Illinois; June 23–24, 1966, Chicago, Illinois; Gordon Cawelti, "I. Report of the Commission," in "Proceedings of the Commission on Secondary Schools," *North Central Association Quarterly* 41 (Summer 1966): 53.

34. Minutes of the Administrative Committee, March 23–24, 1968, Chicago, Illinois; Gordon Cawelti, "I. Report of the Commission," in "Proceedings of the Commission on Secondary Schools," *North Central Association Quarterly* 43 (Summer 1968): 61. On the Commission Training program, see, Minutes of the Administrative Committee meeting, September 28, 1966; "Helpful Materials for High School Self-Evaluation," *NCA Today* 12 (December 1967); Gordon Cawelti, "I. Report of the Commission," in "Proceedings of the Commission on Secondary Schools," *North Central Association Quarterly* 42 (Summer 1967): 56–57. The training program went on hiatus in 1969–1970, and apparently was not resumed. During this period, John Stanavage replaced Gordon Cawelti as CSS executive secretary, and this change may have contributed to the end of the program. John A. Stanavage, "I. Report of the Commission," in "Proceedings of the Commission on Secondary Schools," *North Central Association Quarterly* 44 (Summer 1969): 65.

35. "Changes Proposed in High School Criteria," *NCA Today* 11 (May 1967); "Proposed H. S. Criteria under Consideration," *NCA Today* 12 (December 1967); "NCA High Schools to Vote on Proposed Criteria," *NCA Today* 12 (May 1968); "New High School Criteria Effective Sept. 1969," *NCA Today* 13 (May 1968); Gordon Cawelti, "I. Report of the Commission," in "Proceedings of the Commission on Secondary Schools," *North Central Association Quarterly* 42 (Summer 1967): 56; *North Central Association Quarterly* 43 (Summer 1968): 61; John A. Stanavage, "I. Report of the Commission," in "Proceedings of the Commission on Secondary Schools," North Central Association Quarterly 39 (Summer 1969): 65.

36. "NCA Accrediting Commissions Step Up Activities," *NCA Today* 10 (May 1966); Minutes of the Administrative Committee meeting, March 28, 1966, Chicago, Illinois.

37. "The Junior High School Years," *North Central Association Quarterly* 35 (October 1960): 172; "Junior High Schools Survey," *NCA Today* 5 (May 1961); Stephen Romine, "Opinions about North Central Association Accreditation of Junior High Schools," *North Central Association Quarterly* 36 (Fall 1961): 193.

38. Ibid., 195–99, 201. Another interesting finding was that two-thirds of the principals reported the use of policies, criteria, and guidelines developed for junior high schools. Romine did not indicate what these were used for, however, making it difficult to determine whether they were evaluation, improvement, or some other type of instruments.

39. Ibid., 195–96.

40. "State Groups Consider Jr. H.S. Accreditation," *NCA Today* 7 (November-December 1962); Everett V. Samuelson, *North Central Association Quarterly* 37 (Winter 1963): 233–34.

41. "State Groups Consider Jr. H.S. Accreditation," *NCA Today* (November-December 1962); Samuelson, "The Accreditation of Junior High Schools by the North Central Association of Colleges and Secondary Schools," 234.

42. Stanavage, "I. Report of the Commission," in "Proceedings of the Commission on Secondary Schools," North Central Association Quarterly 40 (Summer 1970): 65.

43. Samuelson, "The Accreditation of Junior High Schools by the North Central Association of Colleges and Secondary Schools," 235. The National Study on Secondary School Evaluation was the permanent organization that developed out of the Cooperative Study.

44. Ibid.

45. "Plan to Accredit Junior High Schools Approved," *NCA Today* 7 (May 1963); Weltzin, "Report of the Association," 13–14; Gordon Cawelti, "I. Report of the Commission," in "Proceeding of the Commission on Secondary Schools," *North Central Association Quarterly* 38 (Summer 1963); "Jr. H.S. Accreditation Committee Holds Meeting," *NCA Today* 8 (December 1963); Samuelson, "The Accreditation of Junior High Schools by the North Central Association of Colleges and Secondary Schools," 235.

46. Cawelti, "I. Report of the Commission," in "Proceeding of the Commission on Secondary Schools," *North Central Association Quarterly* 40 (Summer 1965): 59.

47. Cawelti, "I. Report of the Commission," in "Proceeding of the Commission on Secondary Schools," *North Central Association Quarterly* 41 (Summer 1966): 55, and 42 (Summer 1967): 57; "Junior High Schools to be Accredited," *NCA Today* 11 (May 1967).

48. "NCA Commission on Schools Voted into Existence," *NCA Today* 48 (May 1974).

49. Walter LaFeber, *America, Russia, and the Cold War*, 3d ed. (New York: John Wiley and Sons, 1976), xvi–xvii, 13–14. See also, Thomas G. Paterson, "The Origins of the Postwar International System," in *Major Problems in American History since 1945*, ed. Robert Griffith (Lexington, Massachusetts: D. C. Heath, 1992), 14–15. Excerpted from Thomas G. Paterson, *On Every Front: The Making of the Cold War* (New York: W. W. Norton, 1979).

50. Herman Search, supervisor of U.S. Army schools of France and Germany; speech, reproduced in Minutes of the Administrative Committee meeting, "Report of the American Dependents' Schools," April 3, 1957, Chicago, Illinois.

51. Edgar G. Johnston, "Committee Report on American Dependents' Schools," in "Proceedings of the Commission on Secondary Schools," March 23, 1950, Chicago, Illinois.

52. Ibid., minutes of the Administrative Committee meeting, June 26–27, 1947, Chicago, Illinois.

53. Minutes, Administrative Committee meeting, June 24, 1948, in Chicago, Illinois. The new schools accredited were in Wiesbaden, and Bremen, Germany; Gifu, Kokura, Kyoto, Nagoya, Osaka, Yokohama, and Johnson Air Base, Japan; and Clark Air Force Base in the Philippines.

54. The military figures attending included: R. B. Patin, director of Dependents' Schools in Asia; Charles DeWitt, former superintendent of German Dependents' Schools; Arthur D. Robertson, educational consultant, Air Force Educational and Information Branch; Paul W. Weikel, deputy chief of staff for personnel for the Air Force Educational and Information Branch. Minutes, Administrative Committee meetings, March 26, 1951, June 28–29, 1951, Chicago, Illinois; Johnston, "Committee Report on American Dependents' Schools," March 23, 1950.

55. Search, in "Report of the American Dependents' School Committee," April 13, 1957.

56. Floyd Miller, quoted in Minutes, Administrative Committee meeting, April 11, 1956, Chicago, Illinois; Herman Search in "Report of the American Dependents' School Committee," April 13, 1957.

57. Alva J. Gibson, "Report of the American Dependents' School Committee," April 13, 1957.

58. Johnston, "Committee Report on American Dependents' Schools," March 23, 1950.

59. Minutes, Administrative Committee meetings, March 30, 1952, June 26, 1952, Chicago, Illinois.

60. Minutes, Administrative Committee meetings, October 23, 1952, March 23, 1953, Chicago, Illinois; Herman Search, in "Report of the American Dependents' Schools Committee," April 3, 1957.

61. Gordon Cawelti, "I. Report of the Commission," in "Proceedings of the Commission on Secondary Schools," *North Central Association Quarterly* (1964): 54 (1965): 60 (1966): 55–56.

62. Ibid.

63. Johnston, cited in "Report of the American Dependents' Schools Committee, April 3, 1957; *Rules of Procedure* amendments, cited in John A. Stanavage, "I. Report of the Commission," in "Proceedings of the Commission on Secondary Schools," *North Central Association Quarterly* 45 (Summer 1970): 70.

Chapter Seven

Ties That Bind and Divide

*There has been a tendency for separatism to
develop within the Association. The three Commissions and the Executive Committee have been
the functioning groups of the Association, each in
its small corner, and the Association in none. The
fingers of the left hand have been blissfully
unaware as to how much or how little the fingers
of the right hand have been getting burned.*

—Carl G. F. Franzen

CARL G. F. FRANZEN SERVED as Indiana state director for the NCA
Commission on Schools from 1928 to his retirement in 1957.
Midway into his NCA career, at the 1941 annual meeting, Franzen
commented on the increasing separation of the organization, the
growing lack of communication and cooperation, and the growing
animosity among those connected with the three Commissions,
His observations contributed to the hostile feelings. He castigated
the higher Commission standards revision project, calling it "a
star-chamber, inner circle study." Conversely, he praised the CSS
development of new accrediting criteria. Franzen also questioned
the existence of the third Commission, declaring, "It is difficult for
those of us of the Secondary Commission to see any other excuse
for this Commission than as a service agency of the other two." He
concluded that most members knew only one side of the Association, and that the membership was divided into two distinct constituencies, and "for each of these two groups the Association and
the Commission are one and the same."[1] He recommended
expanding the membership of all three Commissions to foster
democracy.

   The Indiana state director was not the first NCA official to
question the value of the third Commission, or to note the erosion
of the Association as an organizational entity in the face of the

growing strength of the separate Commissions. The question of what to do about the Association was periodically raised after the 1916 constitution revisions decentralized the organization. The debate intensified in the late 1930s, leading to extended discussion of the problem in 1937 and 1938.

Charles Judd spearheaded the effort that culminated in 1942 with revisions to the NCA constitution that aimed to unify the Association. The reform initiative began at a Commission on Secondary Schools session at the 1937 annual meeting. Judd opened a symposium on how the three Commissions could cooperatively study mutual problems. In discussing the rationale for decentralized organization, he explained, "It is one of the penalties of great size and complexity of problems that we have found it necessary to subdivide our operations and assign the duties of the operations to three commissions." But he also suggested that since conditions raise questions pertinent to all Commissions, "we come together from time to time for the discussion of perfectly definite, specific problems, and set up, if necessary, the agencies between the commissions that will bring us suggestions with regard to the solution of these problems."

Judd deplored the fact that the Commissions met separately at the annual meeting and came together as an Association only for the presentation of reports. He suggested bunching the reports together in a morning session, and then getting all members together in two general meetings to discuss intellectually appealing topics. Bringing all the members of the Association together for a deliberative session would correct a mistake made when the NCA was reorganized into three Commissions. At that time, no provision was made for annually binding the Commissions together. He closed with a dim view on the state of the two Commissions: "We are at the point in American education where somebody has to be inventive.... I am interested in finding somebody who will lift the secondary. I realize I am talking to your Commission, but I mean somebody who will lift it out of the morass. Then I would like the colleges associated with you long enough to get out of their bog also." Thus, even amid the transformation of the accrediting programs and the various curriculum projects, Judd acknowledged that more educational reform was needed, and that the NCA was not fostering better relations between high schools and colleges.[2]

His recommendation for general discussions harkened back to the debating society format of the initial Association meetings.

Rudolph D. Lindquist of Ohio State University delivered the second paper in the 1937 symposium. He represented the curriculum Commission, the one that was supposed to provide common ground for members of the other two. Lindquist affirmed that all three Commissions sought the improvement of education by methods that imposed conditions, rather than encouraged, stimulated, and guided activity. He noted changes in education bode well for reform, particularly the increasing stress on subjective factors and the trend toward a more functional approach to instruction. To promote a functional type of education, he called for the three Commissions to unite by approaching their sphere of activity and any program from three basic questions. The first question asked if the activity better met the needs of students, prompting schools "to reformulate institutional objectives more in harmony with their student body needs and with demands of changing social and economic conditions." The next inquiry was whether scholarship and the development of programs to meet institutional objectives were encouraged. The third question focused on evaluating any proposed action by the reformulated objectives and the stimulation of further progress. Lindquist proposed undertaking separate, but highly coordinated, action to better address areas of mutual concern, but he offered no ideas on how the Commissions might work together.[3]

University of Arizona professor Oliver K. Garretson represented the Commission on Secondary Schools. He noted it was easy to offer criticism but difficult to propose solutions. He particularly decried the attacks on the Association by high school principals, quoting one member of a state committee from a large high school who commented, "We do not attach any great importance to membership in the North Central Association. It is largely an honorary organization." Garretson suggested that the prevalence of criticism reflected the lack of Association philosophy regarding secondary education and a corresponding absence of initiative in addressing problems. "This, I believe, is due less to lack of ideas and desire," he explained, "than to the somewhat peculiar framework of organization within which we must work." He reiterated Judd's comments on separation of efforts dictated by the structure of the

Association and the appalling lack of communication within the NCA. "Our present organization must have been carefully designed to make cooperative endeavor needlessly difficult," he concluded. Garretson recommended a system of interlocking memberships on the three Commissions that structurally facilitated communication and cooperation by having one-third of the membership of the secondary Commission come from the higher Commission, and vice versa. He also stressed the importance of the third Commission in the study of mutual problems. In closing, Garretson called for change, stating, "*I believe* the Association needs a major operation."[4]

The symposium prompted NCA president E. H. Kemper McComb to call a special conference on the issue of the Commissions and their role in the Association. Eight questions guided the discussion, but the most ominous was number three: "Is the Association tending to become more and more three different Associations (Commissions)?" The various answers to this question of differentiation influenced the organizational re-creation of the third Commission and the Association level of operations from the revision of the constitution in 1942 to changes instituted in the mid-1970s. While the initial thrust was to strengthen the Association and the three-Commission structure, later efforts asserted the supremacy and autonomy of the accrediting Commissions, leading to the demise of the third Commission and the weakening of the Association level.

THE LANGER CASE

The 1937 conference on the future of the Association produced fourteen suggestions on such topics as initiating research projects to better coordinate activities, developing membership, and educational policies. It also "recommended that the Executive Committee make a thorough study of the functions of the Association and of the scope of its activities."[5] However, in the midst of these discussions, a crisis arose from outside the Association that threatened its very foundations.

At the same annual meeting where NCA secretary Arthur Clevenger reported on the conference recommendations to improve the Association, the CIHE dropped North Dakota Agricultural College from the list of institutions approved by the NCA. The

Arthur W. Clevenger. High school visitor, University of Illinois, Clevenger was Illinois state director, 1928–43, NCA secretary, 1931–38, and NCA president in 1939; he was an active participant in the Association for more than thirty years.

removal of accredited status followed the recommendation of the Board of Review and resulted from an investigation into charges of political interference with the institution's administration. Apparently, several administrators and faculty at the agricultural college had been dismissed without any apparent explanation, and the president, Dr. J. H. Sheppard, had resigned for unspecified reasons.

NCA secretary George Works learned about the changes at the North Dakota college from an article in the April 21, 1937, issue of *School and Society*. He sought unsuccessfully to gain information on the dismissals from Dr. West, the new acting president of the Agricultural College. The NCA became officially involved on September 8, 1937, when Works received a formal protest from one of the people dismissed. A. H. Parrott, the former registrar, requested an

NCA investigation into the matter. Correspondence between West and Works failed to resolve the issue, resulting in a meeting of the NCA Board of Review on January 20 and 21, 1938, attended by West. A committee of inquiry consisting of Iowa State Agricultural College president Friley, President Barrows of Lawrence College, and Dean A. J. Brumbaugh of the University of Chicago visited the North Dakota college on March 10, 1938.

From April 3 to 5, 1938, the NCA Board of Review met to hear the committee's report and rebuttals from officials of the North Dakota Agricultural College. The inquiry committee had found no just cause for any of the dismissals, concluding that the North Dakota Board of Administration, the college's governing body, gave false or misleading reasons for firing the faculty and administrators. The committee recommended the removal of the college's accreditation for several reasons. "Undue interference by the board of Administration in the internal administration of the College" had lowered the morale of the faculty to "the point where the quality of instruction was seriously jeopardized." In addition, North Dakota's administration of the college and other state higher education institutions did not "provide a sufficient degree of autonomy to the individual institutions to guarantee a satisfactory level of performance." To preserve academic and institutional freedom in the face of political intrusion, the Board of Review accepted the committee's findings, recommending that the CIHE drop the institution from its accredited list.

In response to the unfavorable NCA action, on April 8, 1938, President West wrote Works, requesting an advisory committee review the situation at the Agricultural College. He also petitioned for reinstatement of the college. Works replied, explaining that West's petition did not follow the Association's procedures and informed the North Dakota Agricultural College president of the NCA policy in this regard. But the NCA received no formal appeal. Instead, on May 10, 1938, Governor William Langer filed suit against the NCA in the District Court of the United States for the Eastern District of Illinois. The complaint offered several charges against the North Central Association. The most damaging charge was that the NCA had usurped powers belonging to the state, and, following this logic, the suit asserted "that the accrediting of schools, upon the theories and principles on which the Association was founded and on which it has proceeded, unconstitutionally and arbitrarily deprived State institutions of North Dakota of the power of control which rightfully belonged to them under the State law and the Constitution of the State."[6]

The potential consequences of a court ruling in favor of Governor Langer were readily recognized. The lawsuit not only threatened the very existence of accreditation and the NCA; it also attacked the role and status of voluntary associations in a democratic society. The editors of *The School Review* called the action "unique in the history of voluntary standardizing associations."[7] The NCA defense was handled by NCA presidents E. H. Kemper McComb and A. W. Clevenger along with CIHE secretaries George A. Works and his successor A. J. Brumbaugh. The NCA legal defense was conducted by F. B. Leonard of the firm Leonard, Meyer, and Franklin of Champaign, Illinois, ably assisted by Sveinbjorn Johnson, professor of law and legal counsel for the University of Illinois. On June 16, 1938, Judge Walter C. Lindley denied the North Dakota motion. His ruling was later upheld in appellate court. The NCA had successfully weathered its first legal challenge and, in the process, gained a legal precedent for its action.

Lindley's decision established the legal status and rights of voluntary associations: "Voluntary associations, have the right to make their own regulations as to admission or expulsion of members and one who becomes a member, by its membership, assents to the Constitution and rules of procedure adopted by such an Association." The judge explained, "The Constitution, by-laws, and rules, knowingly assented to, become in effect, a civil contract between the parties, whereby their rights are fixed and measured."[8] The compact principle upon which the Association was founded thus gained legal sanction. The legal decision in the Langer case strengthened the organization and profoundly influenced the deliberations of a committee created in October 1938 to revise the NCA constitution.

RE-CREATING THE CONSTITUTION

The Langer case and the discussion on the nature and functioning of the Association prompted the appointment of Clevenger, E. B. Stouffer, and Association secretary George W. Rosenlof to the constitutional revision committee. They presented a draft of their revisions at the 1942 annual meeting. Though extensively altered, only a few constitutional changes are relevant to this discussion. An important alteration was the significant expansion of the objectives of the Association. Until 1942, the original goal of improving relations between secondary schools and higher education had remained the sole purpose of the NCA. In addition to stating the advisory nature of Association decisions, the new objective listed four goals that reflected the changes in accrediting: (1) developing and maintaining high standards of educational excellence; (2) employing a scientific, professional approach to continually improve educational programs and instructional effectiveness; (3) establishing cooperative relationships between secondary and higher education; and (4) maintaining working relationships with other educational organizations.

The provision on the advisory character of NCA decisions was expanded into a new, separate section in the membership article. The impact of the Langer decision was evident here. Using language strikingly similar to that of Judge Lindley, the constitution offered this disclaimer:

> It shall be understood that membership in the Association for universities, colleges, and secondary schools is strictly voluntary. Although all decisions of the Association bearing upon the policy and management of universities, colleges, and secondary schools are advisory in character, it shall be understood that the Association has the right to establish requirements for membership, to develop and establish criteria for the evaluation of universities, colleges, and secondary schools, and to establish and maintain all regulations and conditions for continued membership in the Association.

By stating these policies, the NCA established the organizational compact on a firmer legal basis. Perhaps also reflecting the Langer case, the appeals process was altered and made more specific.

The Association level of operation was strengthened by expanding the responsibilities of the Executive Committee. The pre-1942 constitution noted that the Executive Committee received the approved lists of institutions from the Commissions and then published them. The revision called for the Committee "to pass upon such lists and submit them to the Association for final approval." Having the Association provide final approval showed institutions that they were accredited by the NCA and not by a Commission. In addition, under the section on meetings, the Executive Committee, with the approval of the Association, gained the right to call other meetings of the Association or any Commission, besides the annual meeting. Despite the calls for greater cross-representation, no changes occurred in the membership of the accrediting Commissions to increase communication and coordination of efforts.[9]

The constitutional revisions allowed the NCA to adopt an active approach to reform that stressed scientific, functional ideas. To validate the more active stance, the compact was concretely defined, probably to eliminate future legal entanglements. The place and status of the NCA in education was also better established. The revisions indicated that the previous building of relationships between educational levels had a new methodology, namely, cooperation. The changes also showed that the NCA had expanded its influence to the national arena.

The final major revision concerned the third Commission, retooled and renamed, the Commission and Research on Service, hereafter known as CRS.

THE COMMISSION ON RESEARCH AND SERVICE CHARTS ITS COURSE

The official NCA description of the previous Commission on Curricula of Secondary Schools and Institutions of Higher Education was sketchy, offering little insight into its role and purpose. Beyond describing its membership and stating that the Commission would elect its own officers, the constitution vaguely noted it was to "plan and carry forward research relating to the curricula of the secondary schools and institutions of higher education within the Association." This narrow mandate reflected the Commission's growth out of the pre-1916 committee on unit courses and curriculum. At that time, the need was for defining these educational aspects and providing more uniformity to the curriculum. Changing conditions required a more expansive research effort and a different thrust. The revisions in accreditation had created a greater need for member services, in part, to help institutions adapt to the new system. The orientation of the accrediting reforms also initiated a greater effort to help institutions learn how to change themselves, a foundation policy of the research Commission.

As a result, the new Commission on Research and Service had expanded responsibilities and received a more detailed description in the 1942 NCA constitution. The previous membership requirements were retained. The CRS had twenty-four members, twelve from each of the two accrediting Commissions. Reflecting the new emphasis on the Association, all CRS members served subject to Association approval. The Commission officers included a chair, vice chair, and secretary elected in accordance with the CRS policies and regulations. In addition, a steering committee provided another layer of bureaucracy, though its responsibilities were not detailed. Every activity was subject to the approval of the Executive Committee.

The mandate of the Commission was quite diverse, but revolved around conducting research and providing services. Subject to Executive Committee approval, the Commission could initiate activities or respond to requests from the accrediting Commissions. The Commission reported its findings to the Commissions or Association. In this way, the CRS was to "furnish leadership in interpreting its research findings and in focusing attention on those problems which are in need of consideration." The role the CRS played as a link between the other two Commissions was not stated, or even implied, except in the membership section.[10]

The activities of the Commission on Research and Service filled an important functional void in the Association and its operating policies seemed compatible with the accrediting reforms. In many cases, institutions participating in the various projects performed the work, while the CRS committee provided administration and guidance. Though never explicitly stated as such, the underlying philosophy was that problem solving was best done by the institutions in a cooperative, collaborative setting. The Commission's grassroots approach promoted active member involvement and strengthened connections among institutions whose participation in projects often called for sharing ideas and findings with others.

Over three decades, the CRS conducted numerous short- and long-term projects of incredible diversity. The content of the activities changed over time, but two constants were teacher education and experimental projects. At least thirty-one committees and subcommittees were established by the CRS. They addressed a wide range of issues, including teacher education, articulation of high schools and colleges, guidance and counseling, vocational-technical education, junior and community colleges, foreign affairs, instructional technology, curriculum issues, and, lastly, the two examples covered in this chapter, liberal arts education and superior and talented students.[11]

THE LIBERAL ARTS EDUCATION PROJECT

One of the first projects to help institutions learn to change themselves was the long-lived Liberal Arts Education Study (LAS). The Study began in 1938 and ended in the early 1970s, when the committee was reorganized under a different name. In his 1954 assessment of CRS operations, W. Fred Totten explained, "The end results

W. Fred Totten. President of Flint Junior College (Mich.), Totten was a member of the NCA Executive Committee, and he was active in the Commission on Research and Service in the 1950s.

of all research efforts and services must be evaluated in terms of real projects for real reasons." The first project that met this criterion was the Liberal Arts Study. Totten described the LAS as "one of the most enduring cooperative studies in the history of higher education." He noted its influence on institutions, concluding, "Strong educational advances on many campuses during the past fourteen years testify to the dynamic character and notable effectiveness of this service."[12]

The Study began modestly in 1938, when the Committee on Teacher Education reported its investigation into "the Subject Matter Preparation of High School Teachers" required further inquiry. The curriculum Commission created several subcommittees, including one on the preparation of high school teachers in liberal arts colleges, chaired by George A. Works of the University of Chicago. The narrow focus on this type of college reflected its important role in teacher education. In 1942, the secretary of the liberal arts college subcommittee, political science professor Russell Cooper of Cornell College in Mt. Vernon, Iowa, observed that liberal arts colleges prepared "almost as many high school teachers as all other agencies combined."[13]

During the autumn of 1940, Cooper surveyed twelve liberal arts colleges: Bethany College, West Virginia; Hanover College, Indiana; Hastings College, Nebraska; Hope College, Michigan; Kenyon College, Ohio; Knox College, Illinois; Lawrence College, Wisconsin; Lindenwood College, Missouri; Saint Olaf College and the College of St. Catherine, Minnesota; Simpson College, Iowa; and Yankton College, South Dakota. He spent three to five days at each institution and was assisted by faculty from neighboring institutions, who spent one day at the college. Following these visits, on January 18, 1941, the subcommittee members and representatives from the twelve colleges met in Chicago. The subcommittee presented its findings in a twenty-page mimeographed report. Because of the interest generated by the survey, the subcommittee secured a grant from the General Education Board to continue their investigation.[14]

The subcommittee sponsored ten two-day conferences to identify issues for future study. Between February 7 and April 19, 1941, a total of 1,345 college faculty members and high school teachers attended meetings in Illinois, Missouri, Ohio, Indiana,

Kansas, Nebraska, Minnesota, and Iowa. The conference format mixed general presentations with group sessions. The opening paper was usually by a high school administrator on the question, "What Do We Expect from the Colleges?" An educational psychologist delivered the other general paper on "Learning Problems at the College Level." The strong academic stress of the LAS and its focus on the subject-matter professor was reflected in the group sessions that lasted for six hours and covered the following topics: natural science, social science, language, literature, fine arts, and personnel. Cooper noted that two to three high school teachers participated in each conference, facilitating communication between educational levels and adding another dimension to the discussions. The assignment of the opening address to a high school administrator also reflected the awareness of the connection of teacher education to the secondary level.

The conferences identified eight issues for further study. Showing the wide-ranging concerns of the teacher training component of a college education, they included how to broaden the education of prospective teachers, educational practices in the classroom, ways of making student thinking more scholarly and creative, the importance of subject-matter professors in teacher education, guidance programs, the unique contribution of liberal arts colleges to teacher education, and the impact of the world situation on education.[15]

The ten regional conferences generated even more interest than the initial survey, leading the subcommittee to design a pilot project. Eighty institutions applied for the pilot study, but only twenty-eight liberal arts colleges from fourteen states were admitted. Thirteen were affiliated with a religious denomination, and they ranged in size from two hundred to fifteen hundred students. Four of the participants were not NCA members. As a prerequisite for taking part in the pilot program, each college appointed a local director and granted that person release time to do the required work. In the summer of 1941, the local directors met in a six-week leadership training and project planning workshop at the University of Minnesota. Following the workshop, they returned to their campuses to develop their individual reform efforts.

Project coordinator Russell Cooper visited the participating colleges. He reported that eighteen colleges had reexamined their total purpose and the effectiveness of their educational program to see if it met student needs. Over half the participants had assessed their general education component, and two-thirds had investigated their guidance programs. Faculty instructional practices were another area of scrutiny at most of the colleges. Other points of inquiry included broadening student interests and deepening their insights, extracurricular activities, and professional education courses.[16] A 1945 report entitled *Better Colleges—Better Teachers* chronicled the experience of the twenty-eight participating colleges. Cooper noted that "in response to the requests of many colleges," the subcommittee was expanding its work.[17] The timing of the pilot phase of the Liberal Arts Study showed that even in the midst of global conflict, educational reform continued.

By the end of the pilot phase, the Liberal Arts Study had developed its goals and operating procedures. The Study would be a grassroots effort that stressed local autonomy while seeking institutional cooperation in solving problems. This strategy differed significantly from past efforts that often produced a single solution for schools to use as they desired, such as the curriculum guide of the 1920s; or initiatives that invoked Association mandates to solve problems, as had occurred with athletics in the 1930s. Russell Cooper explained the LAS strategy:

> Each institution [must] determine its own program without domination from this North Central Committee. The policy throughout this program has been one of complete local autonomy, each college determining for itself the problems to be studied and the procedures to be employed.... There has been no attempt to press a common program or even common studies upon cooperating institutions.

He suggested that this approach fostered greater institutional diversity, concluding, "All may be better."

The success of the LAS depended upon building a reciprocal relationship between the NCA staff and the participating institutions. Each party had to understand clearly its particular duties and responsibilities. Using contractual terms, Cooper outlined the staff obligations and participant contributions. In the process, he identified the LAS's components. The staff consisted of administrative coordinators, "approximately one for every twenty-five institutions." The number of coordinators ranged from five to seven academic professors. Their "obligations" included developing two four-week summer workshops, visiting each participating college, facilitating "inter-campus faculty visitations," and establishing "a clearing house for distributing materials developed in the cooperating colleges." As the project developed, other workshops and conferences were added and the clearinghouse function became more complex, but the basic structure of the LAS remained the same. In return, a participating college had to "have a genuine interest in analyzing and improving its program," and in sharing the results with others. Each institution contributed $100 for administrative costs and paid $125 tuition per delegate attending the summer workshops. At least one representative from each college had to attend a workshop.[18]

Another major innovation was the emphasis on academic faculty instead of the administration. "It is important that the subject-matter professors assume active leadership in the enterprise," Cooper advised. "There is great value in having the educational initiative flow from the classroom professor rather than be handed down by the administration." The rationale behind this approach was that "classroom professors...are the only ones who can effect and carry through educational improvements."[19] But this strategy also was quite risky. In many colleges, relations between the faculty and administration ranged from contentious to hostile, a state of affairs that worked against the cooperative philosophy of the LAS. In addition, there was the problem of providing effective training to academicians, many of whom found participation in the LAS a new experience. In her 1951 assessment of the LAS, Anne C. Greve of Bethany Peniel College in Oklahoma observed, "Each institution chose a local director of studies,...and this director was typically a professor in some academic field who was a recognized faculty leader. Usually he was untrained in educational research but was known to be vitally interested in educational problems."[20] Obviously, initiative, both personal and institutional, played a major role in the success of the LAS.

But willingness needed to be paired with expertise. The LAS helped the colleges fulfill their obligations in two ways. By 1950, the LAS had adapted the 1930s accrediting reform idea of using the self-study to stimulate institutional improvement to LAS's purposes, providing a method for identifying and solving problems. In addition, the summer workshops trained local directors to perform their tasks. Cooper called these workshops "the most important single contribution of the program." Greve suggested they were "the most central part of the North Central Study program."[21] In his 1945 report, Cooper described the four-week workshops held that summer. Each workshop attracted approximately fifty participants. "Moreover each group included professors from nearly every department of learning." He explained:

> The following thirty interests were represented at one or both of the places:
>
> Agriculture, Bible, Biology, Business manager, Chemistry, Dean, Dean of Men, Dean of Women, Economics, Education, English, French, German, Greek, History, Journalism, Latin, Librarian, Mathematics, Music, Personnel, Philosophy, Physical Education, Political Science, President, Psychology, Registrar, Sociology, Spanish, and Vice President.[22]

The workshops followed the pattern developed for the pilot phase and apparently their organization changed little over the years. They were structured around a mix of general sessions, seminars, and informal gatherings. Representatives from each college came to the workshop with a definite problem, used the time at the workshop to develop solutions, and returned to their institutions "with a number of concrete proposals." The NCA committee provided "facilities for stimulation,...and then to render every possible assistance when help was requested." To facilitate the individualized, cooperative, problem-solving thrust of the LAS, the project followed a pragmatic approach. "The emphasis has been upon analysis and research rather than the promulgation of any educational theory," Cooper commented. He stressed, "The committee has assiduously avoided any proposal of standard educational pattern."[23] As a result, the workshops did not try to develop common programs or studies, even though they offered opportunities for cooperation. The context of the collaboration was working together to meet individual goals, drawing upon the experience and expertise of others, but not necessarily involving the same problem or coming to a common solution.

However, results depended upon institutional preparation. In 1951, Anne Greve reported the findings of a survey of participating schools. She suggested that those institutions complying with the requirements of the LAS experienced greater satisfaction because they had identified problems in advance and sent their representatives to develop specific solutions. Only one-half of the colleges surveyed had conducted "long-range planning of projects for local study and development." As a result, "Too frequently these projects were selected following the workshop rather than preceding it." Apparently, this deficiency did not preclude taking advantage of the workshop experience, because only one-sixth of the colleges responding to the survey failed to report any results occurring during the school year following the summer workshop.[24]

The Study's effectiveness was enhanced by a one-to-two-day follow-up visit by a NCA coordinator during the academic year. In addition to discussing various trends and issues in education with faculty, the coordinator met with the individuals and committees working on particular problems identified in the workshop, often sharing ideas and programs from other campuses. The coordinator did not visit a campus as an educational expert, Russell Cooper explained, "but rather as a person who is himself confronted with similar problems on his own campus and who, through visitation of many other colleges, has become familiar with promising attempts at solutions."[25] Casting the coordinator as a fellow seeker of solutions—not a superior outside expert—strengthened the cooperative character of the LAS.

The workshop component also was expanded. In 1948, a five-day summer workshop for college presidents was added. This effort later developed into a three-day "President's Workshop" held in Chicago just prior to the NCA annual meeting. In 1953, seventy college presidents attended the LAS conference. The format was a roundtable discussion on various topics, sometimes focusing on a single broad issue. For example, in 1953, the topic was "What is the role of the liberal arts college in the next decade?" Initially, the president's workshop was also open to deans, but by 1959, a separate workshop for the latter had been established.[26] The creation of different meeting venues for various administrators facilitated communication and collaboration horizontally among faculty, deans, and presidents. But the functional organization of the workshops did not allow for vertical communication and cooperation among these often contentious groups.

In addition to the summer workshops, the LAS subcommittee sponsored regional conferences in various states, often in collaboration with state educational associations. The one-to-two-day meeting featured a mix of lectures and group work sessions for faculty unable to attend the summer workshops, and provided another opportunity to analyze educational problems and share ideas on solutions. One of the more successful efforts was in Arkansas, where an annual conference on higher education was initiated in 1949. Among the topics discussed were "Adopting College Programs to Everyday Needs" in 1952, and "Evaluation of Current Purposes of Higher Education" in 1954. Annual meetings were also held in Oklahoma, Ohio, and West Virginia. The inaugural effort in Oklahoma in 1952 discussed "The Goals of Liberal Education."[27]

The expansion of the workshop component created problems for the NCA staff. In her 1951 appraisal of the LAS, Anne Greve identified a serious difficulty, "the enlistment of adequate and stimulating leadership for the seminars and special interest groups." The cooperative, institutionally oriented direction of the project meant that "occasionally it took a staff member a considerable time to catch the democratic spirit of the program." Those used to lecturing had to learn how to become better facilitators. Another issue was expertise, particularly when representatives with previous Study experiences returned to the workshop. The returnees needed more advanced seminars and staff members, requiring more training for workshop leaders. As late as 1958, no solution had been found for the problem of recruiting competent staff. Coordinator Lewis B. Mayhew of the University of Michigan reported, "The study now relies on faculty members from liberal arts colleges for its coordinating staff. They are successful, but more training should be provided." Mayhew suggested two possible solutions: Have potential staff participate in "some of the consultant workshops to be sponsored by the Commission on College and Universities," or secure financial support for the LAS to offer its own staff-training workshops.[28]

The changing focus of the LAS showed the NCA willingness to adapt to changing conditions, but exacerbated the problem of skilled staff. In 1950, the project shifted its focus, seeking "to relate the research needs of the liberal arts colleges to the research resources of university graduate schools." In this instance, the subcommittee acted as a "liaison agency enabling graduate students and colleges to get together to carry on studies for their mutual benefit." The proliferation of graduate programs, particularly at the masters level, in the immediate post–World War II years probably led the LAS into this area of research needing resources. Another contributing factor was a change in the content of the workshops from "the abstract discussion of institutional objectives to concrete studies of student needs that need to be served."[29] In 1954, Cooper's report showed a further drift toward more pragmatic problem solving, reflected in "a desire for scientific local research on the problems" identified in the workshops.[30] The ability to adjust its program to fit the changing needs of its constituency contributed to the LAS's longevity and also showed a strong commitment to serving the needs of institutions.

The cooperative aspects also contributed to its long tenure, particularly the sharing of experiences by participants. Beyond discussions at meetings, each college submitted written documents to show the results of the various projects. The Study collected and disseminated these materials through its clearinghouse function. The idea of having the NCA act as an information clearinghouse dated back to at least 1911, when Charles Judd proposed such a service. Over the following decades, the publication of numerous studies and the *North Central Association Quarterly* partially performed this function. The LAS pursued a more active course by distributing a monthly newsletter and packet during the academic year to present and former participants. The LAS Committee also created a resource file and library that loaned materials upon request. In this way, the Liberal Arts Study apprised colleges of the progress of projects on other campuses, facilitated the sharing of experiences, and helped the colleges accumulate their own resource collections.

The monthly *News Bulletin* was part of a post-1945 Association commitment to expand publishing activities. The eight- to ten-page mimeographed newsletter included "information concerning the general progress of the LAS, a popular section designated 'What's Happening on the Campuses,' personnelograms about workshop participants, book reviews of important publications, and other matters of general interest." At least one issue detailed the history of the LAS.[31] By 1950, the mailing list included five hundred names. The mailing of the *Bulletin* was bundled with "a packet of materials submitted by the cooperating colleges each month." These packets contained "the syllabi of new courses, personnel suggestions, the results of studies, and other items which may prove suggestive to faculty committees in member institutions." By 1949, sixty such packets containing over a thousand items had been distributed.[32]

The expansion of operations required substantial funding and consistent leadership. Between 1941 and 1948, Anne Greve estimated, "more than $50,000 was expended for central activity, and more than $25,000 is known to have been expended by the participating colleges in local activities." In 1948, the LAS received a three-year grant for $21,000 from the Carnegie Foundation to employ a full-time director. Dr. Clarence Lee Furrow, biology professor at Knox College in Illinois, became project director. He was assisted by six part-time coordinators, who apparently donated their time. The temporary professionalization of the staff helped the LAS expand its activities, but also required raising fees for participants. In 1945, each college paid a $100 administrative fee. In 1954, they paid $150, and four years later, the annual fee was $200. In addition, by 1953, the Association was contributing $600 annually to the LAS to help meet committee meeting expenses.[33]

Despite the increase in fees and Association contributions, costs often exceeded revenues. A 1957 report noted, "For the past several years the study has operated on deficits in the neighborhood of $1500," meaning the LAS reserves were being used to balance the budget. The shortfalls hampered "initiating new projects and rendering greater service to the participating schools."[34] In response, the LAS actively pursued grants for new projects. In the early 1960s, concerns arose over the preparation of new college teachers. In 1964, the LAS sponsored a pilot seminar for college teachers just entering the classroom. To continue the program for another year, the committee secured a grant from the Danforth Foundation.[35]

The grant program of the Liberal Arts Study was part of a larger Commission on Research and Service funding initiative. The costs of many studies, particularly those extending over long periods of time, far exceeded the budgetary resources of the Commission. But the mission of the CRS made cutting back on the number of projects impossible. As Clyde Vroman, chair of the CRS, explained in 1962, the Commission "is to receive suggestions concerning the new problems and new needs in education, and then to formulate and initiate new study and action programs to help resolve these problems and meet these needs." Vroman noted that there were twelve active subcommittees in 1962. Of these, one-half "have grants from various foundations and external sources which make it possible to carry on their work." Interestingly, one of the new initiatives was a collaborative project with the American Association for Higher Education on improving the supply and quality of college teachers that was initially funded by a small grant from the Lilly Endowment.[36]

Clyde Vroman. Director of admissions at the University of Michigan, Vroman was NCA president in 1965.

After three fruitful decades, the Liberal Arts Study was reorganized under a new name, the Committee on Undergraduate

Education, indicating its functions were expanded. In its thirty-plus years of existence, the LAS exemplified the new NCA direction of helping institutions learn to solve their own problems and thus change themselves. It also had established a pattern of project development followed by other CRS projects.

THE SUPERIOR AND TALENTED STUDENTS PROJECT

The Guidance and Motivation of Superior and Talented Secondary-School Students project arose in response to changing societal needs and an educational controversy sparked by a Ford Foundation–funded project on early admission to college. The Ford initiative raised a protest in secondary school circles, leading first to Commission on Schools involvement and then to the development of the CRS effort.

In 1951, Edgar Johnston, secretary of the CSS, reported on a grant of $1.2 million provided by the Fund for the Advancement of Education (Ford Foundation) "to four universities—Chicago, Columbia, Wisconsin, and Yale—to admit in September 1951, with scholarship aid, two hundred boys under sixteen-and-a-half years of age who would have completed the sophomore year of high school." Later, the grant was extended to other institutions of higher education, including "Louisville, Utah, Fisk, Goucher, Lafayette, Shimer, and Oberlin colleges." Johnston commented that the program elicited a swift response from the National Association of Secondary School Principals. The NASSP circulated a letter that largely condemned the project. The Administrative Committee of the Commission on Schools and the NCA Conference of State Chairmen discussed the matter at their meetings in June and October 1951. The Conference of State Chairmen placed the Ford project on the agenda at their October 1951 session. As a result, the CSS appointed a special committee to survey members and report at the 1952 annual meeting. Robert L. Fleming, principal of South High School in Youngstown, Ohio, chaired the committee.[37]

The survey asked whether the problem created by the Ford program was important enough to merit a Commission response, and if the Ford initiative was truly experimental. Most of the several hundred replies criticized the Ford project, particularly regarding its experimental status, prompting the Commission to adopt a motion supporting the condemnation by the National Association of Secondary Principals. The CSS also opposed "any plan which will result in the curtailment of secondary education youth even though it may be on a limited basis," promising to "use every means at our command to present to all educational community, and other meetings, the implications of the unsound practices of curtailing secondary education and the subsequent admission of students to college before graduation."[38]

In a unique context, the long-standing issue of the length of secondary education had reemerged. The controversy over the Ford project had less to do with the question of experimentation than with the integrity of secondary education. On this issue, and with prominent NCA higher education members participating, the secondary Commission strongly voiced its opposition. Apparently the project continued despite the protests, showing there were limits to the power of voluntary associations. However, the idea behind the Ford project stimulated interest in an ironic situation in American education. In his paper at a general session at the 1952 NCA annual meeting, T. R. McConnell of the University of Buffalo observed, "Secondary education is more widely available in the United States than in any other country of the world.... But we have been more successful in extending educational opportunity than in individualizing it."

Though college enrollment had increased tremendously, one group of students had not taken advantage of available opportunities in higher education. "In a time when highly trained intelligence is so necessary," McConnell explained, "half of the young people in the highest 10 percent of scholastic aptitude do not attend college."[39] The Educational Policies Commission (EPC) had earlier commented on the gravity of this situation. In its 1950 study, *Education of the Gifted*, the EPC noted that the stage of the nation's democracy and the tense world situation made intellectual accomplishment and leadership pivotal to America's future.

The post–World War II era was a time of international crisis. The cold war and the red scare of the early 1950s heightened the anxiety of Americans, who faced the threat of nuclear holocaust should armed conflict break out. The anxiety level of American school-age youth, in particular, was raised considerably by the tense atmosphere. The paranoid, anxious mood of the people also influenced the development of education. In his paper at the 1959

NCA annual meeting, James B. Conant, former president of Harvard University, explained how changing public moods affected education. He noted that in the 1930s the threats of Nazism, Fascism, and Communism had raised public concerns that stimulated a movement for citizenship education that aimed at "establishing a continuing basis for a free society, for understanding the American way of life." During World War II, the goal of winning the conflict in the shortest time possible had created the need for "scientists, engineers, mathematical people with aptitudes." Referring to the postwar era, Conant explained, "And now, a mood increasing since the end of World War II, recognizes the grim struggle we are in with the Soviet Union, and that we live in a deeply divided world marked by atomic weapons and intercontinental missiles." This postwar mood had stimulated interest in gifted students, leading Conant to conclude, "As a consequence people are anxious about whether or not all the potential academic talent is being found and developed."[40]

In the early 1950s, the academic potential of many students was not being realized. The question of what to do about the gifted students in the age of expanding, democratic education frequently arose during the decade. Several factors contributed to the low percentage of top students attending college, particularly, economics. T. R. McConnell noted that maintaining a gifted program was expensive for schools. In addition, many parents could not afford a college education. Financial considerations probably contributed to the scholarship provisions of the Ford grant. But McConnell suggested that even if various aid programs had removed the economic problems, other obstacles remained. Motivation played an important role in whether or not a student pursued a college education. Some students were uninterested and other students had not considered a higher education. McConnell suggested the schools were partly to blame for the lack of student motivation. He criticized educators for being concerned solely with intellect, and for not including "social, emotional, and healthful development" in their curriculum. Interestingly, the objectives of 1920s NCA curriculum reorganization effort had focused on these nonacademic aspects of student development.

A variety of difficulties plagued the education of gifted students. Five NCA panels between 1954 and 1956 discussed various aspects of gifted education, identifying many problems and showing the increasing importance of the issue. Though most panelists agreed that these students needed special attention, they also believed that "in too many of our schools our talented youth are being discriminated against." A major stumbling block was defining the term *gifted*. "There is some confusion as to terminology," observed Evanston, Illinois, Township High School superintendent Lloyd S. Michael at a 1956 NCA panel. He noted, "In some studies, 'gifted' pupils have been considered as those in the upper one or two percent in intellectual ability." He thought this definition was too confining and suggested that demonstrated academic excellence in the classroom was another indicator of exceptional ability.[41]

General conditions in the schools also worked against gifted education. Large class sizes in many schools made individual attention impossible. The instructional program also made it difficult to meet the needs of gifted students. The inflexibility of the curriculum and methods of teaching presented "a formidable barrier to the development of exceptional students." Inadequate materials exacerbated the poor state of affairs. In addition, few gifted programs existed and those that did were usually of low quality. Most efforts focused on identification of talented students, but offered little follow-up on guidance and motivation through what the NCA called action programs. Funding also was in short supply and often short-term, supporting the initiation of experimental programs but not their continuation.[42]

In 1958, the NCA took action through the Commission on Research and Service. On March 24, the CRS announced it had received funds from the Carnegie Corporation to develop a two-year Superior and Talented Students (STS) project. The grant was for $174,000. The spark for the project was an event of astronomical proportions. As the NCA report announcing the STS project (as it was called) explained, "The events of the past year and the current concern and differences of opinion about how best to use our human and ěducational resources bring into clearer focus the urgency for a major service program of research and action by the Association." The Soviet launch of the first space satellite, Sputnik, accelerated efforts to develop a project on gifted students, just as it thrust education generally into the limelight. In this respect, societal and education forces combined to stimulate NCA action. The procurement of outside funds followed the tradition established in the 1930s.

The STS project aimed to increase the number of talented and superior students attending college. Another goal was to "develop practical ways by which America can make a major increase in its pool of educated and trained manpower in all fields necessary for the maintenance and defense of our country and its way of life." The STS goals showed how the cold war mentality had affected education and NCA activities. Beyond preparing young people to become productive citizens and fulfilled individuals, education in the 1950s played a crucial role in the competition between the American capitalist and the Soviet communist ways of life.

Following the philosophy of helping institutions learn how to change themselves, the STS project would not develop a single program for use in all schools. Instead, participating schools would design their own pilot programs and test them for two years. To enhance communication and cooperation, participants also had "to share ideas and materials with other participating schools." Project staff would help schools develop their pilots, facilitate the sharing of ideas and techniques, and evaluate progress.

The STS project followed a new, collaborative direction initiated by the research Commission after World War II. The project was a joint effort of the NCA and a private, educational company, Science Research Associates (SRA) of Chicago. SRA provided the project headquarters and probably the office staff to handle the administrative tasks, relieving the NCA of this responsibility. The connection with SRA followed a similar relationship with the company on another NCA effort inspired by the cold war, the Foreign Relations Project. In addition, J. Ned Bryan, the director, came from outside the NCA. Bryan had served as director of the Academically Talented Pupil Project of the NEA. In this capacity, he worked with NCA member schools in West Virginia. The associate director was NCA schools Commission state chair for Indiana, Bruce Shertzer, who also was the director of the Division of Guidance and Pupil Personnel in the Indiana State Department of Public Instruction. To oversee the STS project, the Commission on Research and Service formed a subcommittee headed by Clyde Vroman of the University of Michigan.

The response of the schools to the STS program was over-whelming. The original plan limited participation to fifty schools, but after seven hundred schools applied for the project, the number of participants was increased to one hundred.[43]

Each school's pilot program had to address three areas. After identifying students whose intellect and talent indicated they should attend college, the schools were to analyze student plans regarding college attendance by studying "the factors which are significant in affecting their motivation for a college education." Special emphasis was placed on discovering why some students with college aptitude did not plan to attend college and on devising ways "to make it possible and desirable for them to go to college." In addition, the pilots had to develop ways to stimulate general interest in attending college, not only to motivate students, teachers, and parents, but to build support in the community. The project description explained, "Special study will be made of the role and influence of non-school groups and persons, communities and scholarships. Nearby colleges may cooperate and aid individuals in many aspects of the Project."[44] Hopefully, the extended outreach effort would sell the idea of a college education to a community that may have been unaware of its value. Gaining the cooperation of the community and local colleges fit the STS goal of altering the public's mind-set regarding higher education to ensure that the best and the brightest youth availed themselves of an opportunity to realize their fullest potential.

Because the burden of work fell heavily on the participants, many of whom had little or no experience with gifted programs, the STS project required a major commitment by the school and ample training by the NCA. To prepare participants, the NCA staff conducted five five-day workshops in the summers of 1958 and 1959. In 1958, these workshops were held at universities scattered throughout the region. Each was led by a NCA member of the STS project staff. Nationally known experts on superior and talented students also assisted in the presentations at the various seminars. On June 23–27, Clyde Vroman led the workshop at the University of Michigan in Ann Arbor. Frank Endicott led the July 7–11 session at Northwestern University, while James Harlow did the same at the University of Oklahoma in Norman from July 14 to July 18. Workshops were also held at the University of Minnesota from July

Frank S. Endicott. Director of placement at Northwestern University, Endicott was vice chair of the Commission on Colleges in 1960 and chaired the Committee on Current Educational Problems in 1961.

28 to August 1, and at the University of Colorado in Boulder August 4–8. Russell Cooper led the Minnesota session and Stephen Romine performed this task in Boulder. The grant provided two hundred scholarships of $50 each for workshop participants to help defray travel and subsistence costs. Each school sent a team consisting of the principal and a counselor or teacher to a workshop. Though the content of these orientation conferences was not detailed, they probably familiarized attendees with the project and provided information and ideas on setting up a program at their school.[45]

In 1959, Charles Boardman, secretary for the Association, reported that the STS project had targeted two areas of concern, providing guidance and counseling to gifted students and offering "stimulating and challenging situations and educational experiences for them." He praised the project for making great strides in a short period of time and applauded the quick action taken by the participants. "There is evidence that the participating schools have made rapid progress in integrating this program into the overall program of the school," he explained. To facilitate the work, five brief pamphlets on project activities had been published. Two promoted the STS project. The workshop procedures and a summary of the 1958 workshop proceedings were explained in two more bulletins. The remaining pamphlet was titled, *Identifying Superior and Talented Students*. Articles in various journals, combined with a flood of requests for project staff to give reports and speeches at various organizational meetings, demonstrated that the STS project "has stimulated national interest." In closing his report, Boardman reiterated his belief that the project was proceeding successfully. He also observed that the Carnegie funding would run out in a year, noting, "It is our hope that funds will be found to extend the study until 1962."[46]

In 1960, the Carnegie Corporation provided a $150,000 supplement to continue the STS project through 1961. The success of the project certainly helped in obtaining the extension. By 1960, "All told 30,000 talented high school students have been identified by the project for special programs of guidance and motivation in the participating schools." In addition, a book was published. *Working with Superior Students: Theories and Practices* contained a series of articles on identification, guidance, motivation, and other "major dimensions of dealing with superior students," including instructions on developing a program.[47] The extension grant allowed the STS to expand its activities to other regions. Invitations were sent to the other regional accrediting associations, leading to the addition of eighteen more schools to the project. Of these, four were in California, three in Georgia, two each in Washington and Kentucky, and one each in Idaho, Oregon, Massachusetts, Vermont, Florida, South Carolina, and Connecticut. Following the original procedure, teams of two from each school attended a one-week workshop at Northwestern University from June 26 to July 1, 1960. They heard presentations from national experts on superior students, discussed the various phases of developing a superior student program, and developed and evaluated an action program for their respective schools. During the following school year, the STS staff visited these new participants. Plans called for including even more schools, while materials also were disseminated nationally.[48]

On August 31, 1961, the Carnegie grant expired and the STS staff disbanded. However, the project continued under the auspices of the NCA-STS Committee and the Liaison Committees of the cooperating regional associations. The project headquarters moved to the new NCA offices in Chicago. The STS Committee asked participating schools to use the success of the previous three years to "continue your present interest and activities at the highest possible level. The outcomes of the next two years can result in the most significant contributions of this five-year plan."

During the latter phase of the project, the major activity was national dissemination of the results, primarily through workshops and publications. Both the New England and Southern Associations sponsored STS seminars in 1962. NCA members Clyde Vroman and J. Fred Murphy along with former project director J. Ned Bryan participated in the New England workshops. Vroman also appeared at a Southern Association workshop at the University of Alabama in September 1962. Within the NCA region, a Continuation Planning Conference was held in Chicago on July 8 and 9, 1962 for NCA Commission of Schools state chairs. At the meeting, each state chair formulated a tentative dissemination plan to present to his state committee for revision and implementation. NCA state dissemination conferences informed secondary and higher education members of "the activities and outcomes of the STS Project and their implications for the improvement of education." The NCA-STS Committee also surveyed participants on various problems encountered.[49]

The publication component of the dissemination phase continued with the sale of various materials. By 1966, fourteen different titles were available that covered a wide variety of topics on the STS project and programs. Several publications focused on development of a school program for superior students, but others discussed more general topics. For example, for ten cents, a pamphlet on "Cues to Successful Study" was available. Vance Packard's *Do Your Dreams Match Your Talents* and Robert F. DeHaan's *Guidelines for Parents of Capable Youth* cost sixty cents each. A kit containing all thirteen titles cost $10. One of the more interesting studies focused on Memphis, Tennessee. Its description indicates that participating schools might have represented large districts, and that

Robert J. Keller. Professor at University of Minnesota, Keller chaired the NCA Committee on Publications and Information Services, and he was NCA interim secretary in 1960.

the resulting programs were actually districtwide. *The Memphis Story* was published in 1965.[50]

To determine interest in gifted education, the *North Central Association Quarterly* analyzed the various orders for its publications in 1964. Administrators favored two recent publications. One was *Problems, Practices, Procedures: Experiences of 62 Project Schools*, a compilation of reports from original participants that described the difficulties encountered and the most successful practices and procedures employed in their STS programs. The other administrator's choice was *Building a Program for Superior and Talented High School Students* by J. Ned Bryan. The *Quarterly* reported that "counselors have expressed their enthusiasm for 'Cues to Successful Study' and Frank S. Endicott's 'Guiding Superior and Talented Students' which contains a checklist of evaluative criteria for guidance programs." The DeHann pamphlet that provided guidelines for parents was popular with schools and PTAs.[51] The different preferences of different groups indicated that the NCA-STS project was reaching virtually everyone interested in educating the best students. The comprehensiveness of the target audience also signified a concerted effort to increase NCA control over its environment.

The STS project succeeded in a number of ways. It alerted the American people and educators to the need for special programs to make qualified students aware of the opportunity a college education afforded. The number of schools participating and the eventual popularity of the publications indicated the STS initiative stimulated the development of successful programs that actually increased college attendance. In this respect, the project addressed the need for better-qualified people by offering a solution to an educational problem. By contributing to the improvement of education, the STS initiative also fulfilled the NCA goal of promoting cooperation with other groups, and, given the scope of the project, establishing better relations between secondary and higher education. Regarding the Association, the STS and Liberal Arts Study projects show that the CRS was a vehicle for reform, taking action on needs expressed in the sessions of both accrediting Commissions at annual meetings.

THE DECLINE AND FALL OF THE THIRD COMMISSION

A third Commission that focused specifically on research and service to enhance the ability of members to manage change was a major NCA innovation. But, the methods and philosophy of the curriculum Commission were quite different from those of the Commission on Research and Service after World War II.

As it developed, the CRS served a number of prescribed and possibly unperceived purposes. Constitutionally, the Commission was to conduct research and provide services, either by initiating activities or responding to requests from the other Commissions, subject to Executive Committee approval. The Liberal Arts Study was largely a self-initiated program carried over from the former third Commission, while the Superior and Talented Students project came to the CRS from the secondary Commission. The Commission also acted as a vital structural link, bonding the two accrediting Commissions together through its membership. Each accrediting Commission provided one-half of the CRS members. In addition, some activities brought individuals associated with the secondary or collegiate Commission together in a working relationship. At an annual workshop in 1974, several speakers noted the CRS acted as a bridge between the other two Commissions. Speaking for the Association, NCA president Richard Burkhardt observed, "The Commission on Research and Service may help to remind us of our relationships within the North Central Association—indeed of our dependency on each other." He suggested that the equality of secondary and collegiate membership on the Commission underscored the interdependent nature of the organization. Representing the schools Commission, David Wilkerson observed that the CRS was "the one arena in which both accreditation commissions join their efforts in worthy educational pursuits." Thomas Keating, the CRS representative, agreed with the other two speakers, asserting that the research Commission "has proved an element of strength and a medium of coordination."[52]

The Commission on Research and Service also forged links among the NCA members, though on a very different level than was true of the accrediting Commissions. The Liberal Arts Study brought institutional representatives together to seek solutions to problems and thereby contribute to the improvement of education. The LAS and the Superior and Talented Students project also demonstrated how the CRS activities helped build relationships with other organizations, either for funding or for collaborative purposes. The expansion of the STS project to include representatives of the other regional associations was one example. The grant funding that often provided the means for CRS activities to proceed represented a different kind of cooperation. Through these and other activities, the CRS addressed societal concerns. For example, reflecting the increasing importance of current events in American schools and society, the CRS Committee on Experimental Units published pamphlets on "Practical Politics" and "A Study of India, Pakistan, and Southern Asia" in the mid-1950s.[53] Recognizing the growing influence of technology in education, the Commission established a committee on television. Responding to a call from teacher organizations and the growing importance of foreign policy, the Commission overrode a commitment not to become involved in curriculum development and created the Foreign Relations Project to provide materials for social studies teachers. The foreign relations initiative also taught American educators about the world during the volatile cold war era.

The Commission on Research and Service also performed unexpected, but welcome functions. The CRS provided a training ground for educational reformers and NCA leaders. "The activities of the Research and Service Commission have through the years produced many able individuals who have contributed to the prestige and work of the Association," noted Herbert Schooling in

Herbert W. Schooling. Dean of faculties at the University of Missouri, Schooling was NCA president in 1968.

1975. "These individuals have been a part of the solid base of concerned educational leaders who have supported, interpreted, and defended the North Central Association and the accreditation process." In addition, the third Commission assumed responsibilities the two other Commissions were unable to handle because accreditation consumed all their energies.[54]

Despite the praise often accorded the CRS, a rising tide of criticism led to its demise in 1975. At a workshop that year, the members of the Commission on Research and Service approved a plan that ended sixty years of the three-Commission structure by dissolving the CRS. The workshop report listed a number of reasons for taking such drastic action. The research Commission was isolated from the mainstream of accrediting Commission concerns. Misunderstandings existed over the meaning of research in its name and the selection and role of CRS commissioners in terms of their relationship to their accrediting Commissions. The CRS policy of establishing ad hoc committees created auditing and evaluation problems. Confusion existed over the relationship between the CRS and the Committee on Research Projects of the Association created in 1969, though the rationale behind the creation of the latter committee and its mandate never were made clear and it died in 1976.[55]

While calling for the dissolution of the third Commission, the workshop report acknowledged the need for a research arm of the Association, but recommended downgrading its status from a separate and equal Commission to an inferior council. On January 1, 1977, the ill-fated Council on Research and Service Projects was officially established. Three years later, in 1980, the Council was dissolved, thus ending the long and innovative NCA tradition of a separate research arm.[56]

MAINTAINING THE ASSOCIATION COMPACT

The rapid decline and end of the Commission on Research and Service raises several questions, but the major one is: After weathering numerous and serious threats over the previous sixty years, why did the crisis of the 1970s so drastically change the organizational structure of the Association? The NCA had previously survived the aborted 1916 rebellion of high school principals; effectively responded to serious criticisms of accreditation in the 1930s; emerged triumphant from the first legal challenge to Association authority in 1938; and had adapted to the increasing divisiveness caused by the functional, Commission structure by revising the constitution in 1942. In each of these cases, the NCA emerged stronger and more effective, while maintaining the unique three-Commission organization. The events of the 1970s represented just another in a long line of crisis situations that required a significant response. However, the proposed solution was not an innovative response, but a reactionary action, involving a cutback that was well in tune with the retrenchment ideas of the times.

But there was more to the change in structure than the end of the research Commission. A larger issue involved the nature of the

Association. While the accrediting Commissions had transformed themselves to meet the changing times and had emerged stronger in terms of the compact between them and their members, the same was not true at the Association level. Here, the compact appeared so severely strained that the organization seemed headed toward dissolution. The comments made by Franzen at the beginning of the chapter regarding the tendency for separatism also applied in the 1970s. However, where the late 1930s reforms led to a strengthening of the organization at the Association level, initially the opposite occurred in the seventies. The story of how the Association emerged stronger is told in the following chapter. The purpose here is to discuss the strains that threatened the integrity of the Association and led to another NCA re-creation that reduced the organization to two autonomous accrediting Commissions connected by a symbolic Association level.

From the early forties to the middle seventies, the question of the future often revolved around adherence to the compact that served as the reason for the Association's being. Initial efforts strengthened the Association level. The creation of the Commission on Research and Service to enhance activities in those two areas and to structurally create links of communication and coordination was one such initiative. The mid-1950s reorganization movement increased the effectiveness of the Association level of operations. The appearance of the *NCA Today* quarterly newsletter provided regular communications with members and among Commissions and the Association. Enhanced public relations efforts, including the publication of the *Know Your NCA* brochure, keep educators and the public better informed about the organization and its activities. In 1961, the hiring of Norman Burns as executive secretary of the NCA and the opening up of a central office in the Shoreland Hotel in Chicago professionalized the Association staff and centralized operations. By 1963, the Association and the two accrediting Commissions were housed under one roof, theoretically facilitating communication and coordination. By removing final approval from the Executive Committee, an intermediary step in the accrediting process was eliminated, streamlining operations and freeing the Executive Committee to concentrate on other matters.[57] In the early 1960s, the development of the Association climaxed with the incorporation of the Association as a nonprofit

Harlan C. Koch. Associate dean of the graduate school at University of Michigan, Koch
was editor of the *NCA Quarterly* for twenty
years (1941–61); he served on the NCA
Executive Committee and chaired the Committee on Public Relations.

organization. As a result, bylaws replaced the constitution and the
Executive Committee became the Board of Directors.[58] Finally, the
legal status of the Association, established by the *Langer* case, was
reconfirmed by the *Parsons* decision.

During the same period, when efforts were made to
strengthen the organizational integrity of the NCA at the Association level, internal and external forces were working to counter
these moves. Norman Burns' view of the NCA executive secretary
position as honorary both helped and hurt the Association. In
some ways, this eliminated potential problems. Since he also
served in a similar capacity for the higher Commission, the issue of
being able to perform his duties effectively was probably a consideration. The psychological factor of having someone from higher
education as the top administrator was possibly another concern.
Unlike the tradition of having a secondary and higher education
representative alternatively assume the presidency, there was no

such provision regarding the top professional position in the NCA. Conversely, because he did not actively assume the position of NCA secretary, the Association did not have a strong, full-time administrator working to improve coordination, communication, and cooperation among the three Commissions and the Association. Instead, the administration rested with the volunteer Board of Directors and a small staff. Equally important, the Commission on Research and Service was denied any professional staff until 1969, and even then its secretary was a part-time employee. The Association and the CRS remained in the older, voluntary mold and did not develop an administrative structure equal to the accrediting Commissions. As a result, an imbalance existed between the central organization and its parts that favored the accrediting Commissions.

Not only did the power and authority devolve to the higher and secondary Commission, but they followed divergent paths in their development. The higher Commission moved toward greater centralization and increased national involvement. Conversely, the secondary Commission maintained a decentralized structure and a local orientation. Not surprisingly, tensions arose between the two Commissions. The CSS, in particular, viewed the nationalizing tendencies of the CIHE with alarm. In 1972, the Administrative Committee of the Commission on Secondary Schools discussed "the new forces impinging upon the North Central Association." The first topic was the establishment of an office in Washington, D.C., by the Federation of Regional Associations of Commissions of Higher Education. The Committee complained that the office "would impose increasingly severe financial demands on the resources of the North Central Association." But the real reason for its concern was that "the surge for centralization now apparent in FRACHE seemingly traverses those principles of decentralization and local control so integral to the rationale, structure, and operations of the Secondary Commission."[59] Though not cited in this context, the Administrative Committee members certainly knew that Norman Burns strongly advocated a greater national presence for the higher Commission. Different accrediting programs also created difficulties. The higher Commission combined accreditation and evaluation for improvement while the secondary Commission separated the two.

In the 1970s, the Association faced a crisis. Many of the existing tensions became exacerbated by outside forces. At a 1971 workshop sponsored by the Commission on Research and Service, a number of speakers voiced grave concerns over the future. Albert Pugsley suggested that the NCA was only one of many educational groups focusing on contemporary problems. He claimed, "There is a power struggle in education in which extreme elements, often boring from within, are attempting to discredit and overthrow the decision-making structure." The Association stood at a crossroads and was "required to respond to a 'deterioration of public trust in our mission.'" Reporting on the results of a survey of 290 high school principals, Richard Klahn noted a general uneasiness among the respondents because "public criticism seems more general than does public support." Norman Burns suggested criticisms of education were criticisms of accrediting, too. "The very survival of all sorts of voluntary accrediting is now at stake with the general public raising important issues," he noted. Virtually all workshop participants suggested that the public image of the Association had created many problems. Two actions were proposed: to correct "policies and procedures which are inconsistent between the Commissions or give basis for just criticism, and to improve public understanding of the Association's functions."[60]

Given the violence and turbulence of the times both at home and abroad, the increase in tension in the Association was understandable. School and college campuses were major centers of the turbulence that rocked the nation in the late sixties and early seventies. In addition, a palpable change was evident in the general state of education. The "Golden Age" of the previous twenty-five years rapidly gave way to a transitional period characterized by calls for accountability amid dwindling resources. The focus on retrenchment by advocates of accountability intensified the resource drain. A corollary movement aimed at certifying the quality of education by assessing the product, namely student achievement. A financial dimension slanted this assessment approach so the central question became whether students and parents were getting their money's worth for the education received. Because they were seen as guarantors of quality in education, accrediting associations came under intense scrutiny. In 1972, schools Commission chair Wilbert Mick observed that just as the NCA demanded accountability from member schools, so the public was demanding the same of the Association.[61] Unfortunately, misunderstandings existed over what accrediting was and what it did. The NCA idea of evaluation of the institution as a whole clashed with the public and government desires for assessing return on investment.

Two different responses developed in the NCA to address the various issues and problems that had emerged. On one hand, there were calls for greater cooperation and unity. In 1970, at the close of his term as schools Commission representative to the Commission on Colleges and Universities, Curtis Howd called for closer cooperation between the two Commissions to "present a more united front in these troubled times."[62] The following year, CSS chair Neil Aslin issued a similar call. He suggested that external threats made close working relationship between schools and colleges imperative. Aslin also reaffirmed the secondary Commission's commitment "to maintain the integrity of the Association and of regional accreditation, despite some strong centripetal forces now working in the nation." However, the other response supported the divisive tendencies. Aslin's successor, Wilbert Mick, suggested that if the NCA could not refute the criticisms lodged against it, "we should indeed cease to exist."[63]

By 1974, the separate schools of thought had developed strong opinions on the future of the Association. At a workshop that year sponsored by the Commission on Research and Service, NCA president Richard Burkhardt described the situation, "It is no secret...that there are those in our nation, indeed in the 19 states that are served by the NCA, who doubt the efficacy of the North Central Association. There are those who would abandon it entirely, or so modify its programs or blunt its effectiveness that it would no longer be the standard bearer of quality education." He claimed that many who called for the end of the NCA desired a federal accrediting program. Within the Association, Burkhardt observed, "There are those who doubt the usefulness of the Association as currently structured. [They ask:] Why does the Commission bother with the Association? We would be better off to operate independently. Who needs 'The Association'?" Burkhardt answered these critics, "No one of the Commissions could be as powerful independently as it is being a part of the Association."[64]

In the end, the workshop participants' changes were needed and the Association had to be preserved. The Commission on Research and Service was an easy lamb to sacrifice. Its demise was the first in a series of actions that re-created the NCA for the fourth time. This last re-creation culminated with the constitutional revisions of the early 1980s that provided each accrediting Commission with virtual autonomy, reducing the Association to a symbolic shell. The NCA still remained more than the sum of its parts, but the power rested with the Commissions. While the members agreed that the compact that held the organization together had to be maintained, they demanded that the Association be decentralized to reflect the functional nature of the Commission operations. As such, the integrity of the NCA remained intact, but in a very different form.

NOTES

1. Carl F. G. Franzen, "Some Observations and Remarks concerning the Aims and Purposes of the North Central Association," *North Central Association Quarterly* 16 (October 1941): 172, 175.

2. Charles H. Judd, "I. As Seen from the Viewpoint of the Commission on Institutions of Higher Education," "How the Commission Can Undertake Cooperatively the Study of Problems of Mutual Concern—As Symposium," *North Central Association Quarterly* 12 (July 1937): 318, 323.

3. Rudolph D. Lindquist, "II. As Seen from the Viewpoint of the Commission on Curricula of Secondary Schools and Institutions of Higher Education," ibid., 323–24.

4. Oliver K. Garretson, "III. As Seen from the Viewpoint of the Commission on Secondary Schools," ibid.: 324–30. The italics are mine. Interestingly, the presence of higher and secondary education members on each other's Commissions met Garretson's suggested ratio.

5. Arthur W. Clevenger, "The Association—Some Suggestions for a Continued Program of Service," *North Central Association Quarterly* 13 (October 1938): 183–84. Clevenger presented this paper before the Association at the 1938 annual meeting.

6. Arthur W. Clevenger, "A Review of the Governor Langer Suit," *North Central Association Quarterly* 13 (April 1939): 505–17. The article included a reprint of the final decree of the court.

7. "Judicial Vindication of a Regional Association," *The School Review* 46 (October 1938): 566–67.

8. Cited in Clevenger, "A Review of the Governor Langer Suit," 513.

9. "The Proposed Revision of the Constitution of the Association," *North Central Association Quarterly* 16 (April 1942): 362–63, 365–67, 369, 374.

10. Ibid., 372–73.

11. Stephen Spangehl, "The North Central Association's 'Third Commission,'" *North Central Association Quarterly* 68 (Fall 1993): 341–57.

12. W. Fred Totten, "Research and Service Needed by Both the Commission on Colleges and Universities and the Commission on Secondary Schools," *North Central Association Quarterly* 29 (October 1954): 167–68. For reasons of clarity, the project will be called the Liberal Arts Study, or LAS, in this discussion.

13. On the committee structure, see, "Committees of the Commission of Curricula and of the Commission on Institutions of Higher Education," *North Central Association Quarterly* 16 (July 1941): 30. Also see, Russell Cooper, "Liberal Arts Colleges Study Teacher Preparation," *North Central Association Quarterly* 16 (January 1942): 262.

14. Ibid., 263; Russell Cooper, "Working with Liberal Arts College Faculties on Teacher Education, *North Central Association Quarterly* 16 (April 1942): 396–97; Russell Cooper, "The Liberal Arts College Study Goes On," *North Central Association Quarterly* 20 (July 1945): 162; Anne C. Greve,

"Appraisal of the Liberal Arts College Study," *North Central Association Quarterly* 25 (April 1951): 364. Regarding the members of the subcommittee, in 1940 and 1941, in addition to Works, the other members were University of Chicago professor of English Clarence A. Faust, Waldo H. Furgason of the University of Missouri School of Education, Coe College president Harry M. Gage, University of Nebraska Teachers College dean Frank R. Henzlik, and professor of education Edgar B. Wesley of the University of Minnesota.

15. Cooper, "Working with Liberal Arts College Faculties," 397.

16. Ibid., 397.

17. Cooper, "The Liberal Arts College Study Goes On," 162; Russell Cooper, "The Liberal Arts College Faces Its Contemporary Problems," *North Central Association Quarterly* 24 (January 1950): 284; Greve, "Appraisal of the Liberal Arts College Study," 364.

18. Cooper, "The Liberal Arts College Study Goes On," 165.

19. Ibid.; Cooper, "The Liberal Arts College Faces Its Contemporary Problems," 284.

20. Greve, "Appraisal of the Liberal Arts College Study," 365.

21. Cooper, "The Liberal Arts College Faces Its Contemporary Problems," 285; Greve, "Appraisal of the Liberal Arts College Study," 368.

22. Cooper, "The Liberal Arts College Study Goes On," 164.

23. Cooper, "The Liberal Arts College Faces Its Contemporary Problems," 285; Cooper, "The Liberal Arts College Study Goes On," 165.

24. Greve, "Appraisal of the Liberal Arts College Study," 368.

25. Cooper, "The Liberal Arts College Faces Its Contemporary Problems," 285.

26. Greve, "Appraisal of the Liberal Arts College Study," 365; Cooper, "The Liberal Arts College Faces Its Contemporary Problems," 285; Cooper, "Liberal Arts Education," *North Central Association Quarterly* 28 (October 1953): 167; Cooper, "Report of the Subcommittee on Liberal Arts Education," *North Central Association Quarterly* 28 (April 1954): 355; Cooper, "Report of the Subcommittee on Liberal Arts Education," *North Central Association Quarterly* 29 (January 1955): 238; Cooper, "North Central Activities in Teacher Education, *North Central Association Quarterly* 33 (April 1959): 286.

27. Cooper, "The Liberal Arts College Faces Its Contemporary Problems," 285–86.

28. Greve, "Appraisal of the Liberal Arts College Study," 368; Lewis B. Mayhew, "Report of the Committee on Liberal Arts Education," *North Central Association Quarterly* 32 (April 1958): 289.

29. Cooper, "The Liberal Arts College Faces Its Contemporary Problems," 286, 287. In discussing the switch in focus, Cooper wryly observed, "The growing interest in the individual student, strangely enough, occurs at a time when enrollments are bulging and mass education is a continual threat to the realization of these objectives." Perhaps the conditions he cited created the need to focus on the individual, particularly at liberal arts

colleges that stressed the teaching mission. As noted in the discussion of the STS project, a similar reaction prompted attention on gifted students.

30. Cooper, "Report of the Subcommittee on Liberal Arts Education," 379. In the late 1950s, as concerns over testing arose, the LAS met a growing need by cosponsoring conferences with the Educational Testing Services. "Report of the Committee on Liberal Arts Education," *North Central Association Quarterly* 29 (January 1955): 288–89.

31. Greve, "Appraisal of the Liberal Arts College Study," 369. The *North Central News Bulletin of the Committee on Liberal Arts Education* 15 (October 1954), reprinted in "Let's Have a Wider Audience for the Liberal Arts Study," *North Central Association Quarterly* 30 (October 1955): 176–77.

32. Cooper, "The Liberal Arts College Faces Its Contemporary Problems," 286; The *North Central News Bulletin of the Committee on Liberal Arts Education* 15.

33. "Subcommittee on Liberal Arts Education, *North Central Association Quarterly* 24 (January 1950): 252. The grant was later extended for another three years at the same level of $7,000 per year. Furlow retired from the executive director position in that year. Russell Cooper, "Report of the Subcommittee on Liberal Arts Education," *North Central Association Quarterly* 28 (April 1954): 355; Russell Cooper, "Report of the Subcommittee on Liberal Arts Education," *North Central Association Quarterly* 29 (January 1955): 239. Both these reports appeared in the *North Central Association Quarterly* the year following their presentation at the annual meeting. The dates reflect their date of publication, not their presentation. See also, Greve, "Appraisal of the Liberal Arts College Study," 365.

34. Mayhew, "Report of the Committee on Liberal Arts Education," 291.

35. John Hollenbach, "Seminar for New College Teachers," *North Central Association Quarterly* 39 (September 1965): 318–21. Hollenbach was chair of the Committee of Liberal Arts Education.

36. Clyde Vroman, "The Role of the North Central Association: Improving Education through the Accreditation Process," *North Central Association Quarterly* 37 (Summer 1962): 23, 24. His report was one of several made at the 1962 annual meeting.

37. "Proceedings of the Commission on Secondary Schools, *North Central Association Quarterly* 27 (July 1952): 61, 65.

38. Letter, May 4, 1951, from the National Association of Secondary Principals to the NCA Commission on Secondary Schools, reprinted in ibid., 69.

39. T. R. McConnell, "Some Unresolved Problems of Secondary Education," *North Central Association Quarterly* 27 (January 1953): 260. This is a reprint of his address before the NCA membership. McConnell based much of his argument on the following publication of the Educational Policies Commission, *Education of the Gifted* (Washington, D.C.: Educational Policies Commission, 1950).

40. James B. Conant, "Development of Talent in Europe and the United States," *North Central Association Quarterly* 34 (April 1960): 270–71. This is a reprint of his NCA address.

41. McConnell, "Some Unresolved Problems of Secondary Education," 260–62. Lloyd Michael, in "Commission on Research and Service Panel Discussions: VI. 'What are the Features and Implications of the Experimental Program, Which Permits High School Students to Enter Colleges with Advanced Standing,'" *North Central Association Quarterly* 30 (April 1956): 364. The panel discussed a project funded by the Ford Foundation called the Kenyon Plan, after the Ohio liberal arts college. Though listed under CRS panels, actually the higher education Commission sponsored this panel. See also "Summaries of Conferences Arranged by the Commission on Research and Service," *North Central Association Quarterly* 29 (January 55): 267. Besides the two panels cited above, the others were: "Proceedings of Commission Conferences: Commission on Research and Service: Conference No. 3: How can we improve our program for our talented youth?" *North Central Association Quarterly* 31 (April 1957): 335–37, synopsis of the 1956 annual meeting session; "Conferences Conducted by the Commission on Research and Service: Conference No. 6: How can we effectively guide and motivate superior and talented high school students?" *North Central Association Quarterly* 33 (October 1958): 192–94, from a session at the 1958 annual meeting and focusing on a NCA project; "Conferences Conducted by the Commission on Secondary Schools: Conference No. 2: How can students be grouped to provide the most effective instruction?" *North Central Association Quarterly* 33 (January 1959): 254. At the 1959 annual meeting, three panels discussed gifted-student topics, "Summaries of Group Discussion at the Sixty-Fourth Annual Meeting," *North Central Association Quarterly* 34 (April 1960): 301–2, 305.

42. McConnell, "Some Unresolved Problems of Secondary Education," 260–62.

43. "A New Research and Action Service Project: The Guidance and Motivation of Superior and Talented Secondary-School Students," *North Central Association Quarterly* 32 (April 1958): 286–87; Charles W. Boardman, "Report of the Secretary of the Association," *North Central Association Quarterly* 34 (July 1959): 13.

44. "A New Research and Action Service Project: The Guidance and Motivation of Superior and Talented Students," 287.

45. Ibid., 287–88.

46. Boardman, "Report of the Secretary of the Association," 13–14; "Five Important Bulletins," *North Central Association Quarterly* 33 (April 1959): 278.

47. Item, in *North Central Association Quarterly* 35 (July 1960): 20; "Working with Superior Students: New STS Project Book," *North Central Association Quarterly* 35 (October 1960): 170.

48. "STS Activities beyond the NCA Region," *North Central Association Quarterly* 35 (October 1960): 218; "Report of the Secretary of the Association, *North Central Association Quarterly* 36 (Summer 1961): 15.

49. "STS Project Begins Dissemination Phase," *North Central Association Quarterly* 37 (Fall 1962): 168.

50. Item, in *North Central Association Quarterly* 40 (Summer 1965): 18; "Publications of the North Central Association, *North Central Association Quarterly* 41 (Summer 1966): 172–73.

51. "STS Project Publications Are Widely Distributed, *North Central Association Quarterly* 39 (Fall 1964): 174.

52. Cited in William N. Atkinson, secretary, "Report of the 1974 Workshop: Commission on Research and Service, January 7–8. 1974, Kansas City, Missouri. Interestingly, the only speaker at the conference who did not cite the CRS for providing essential links between the other two Commissions was the CIHE representative, Norman Burns.

53. Totten, "Research and Service Needed by Both the Commission on Colleges and Universities and the Commission on Secondary Schools," 169. Other published accounts misrepresent the publications record of the Commission during World War II. John Emens' report on activities in 1945 cited Calvin Davis' history of the NCA on ten similar publications. In his 1993 article on the CRS, CIHE associate director Stephen Spangehl cites Emens on the same information. However, Davis tells a somewhat different story in that his account refers mostly to the period before 1942, meaning he was writing about the earlier curriculum Commission and not the CRS. What the CRS did was to continue publishing the earlier materials and also to expand the list. See, John Emens, "History, Current Activities, and Future Services of the Commission on Research and Service," *North Central Association Quarterly* 20 (July 1945): 154–55; Spangehl, "The North Central Association's 'Third Commission,'" 343; Davis, *A History of the North Central Association*, 89–92.

54. Herbert Schooling, "Musing about the North Central Association and the Commission on Research and Service in Particular," in "Minutes of the Commission on Research and Service: Attachment B-1," December 12, 1975, St. Louis, Missouri. In 1969, Schooling had authored a CRS self-study. Minutes of workshop of Commission on Research and Service, May 1–2, 1971.

55. "Minutes of the Commission on Research and Service: Attachment B-1," December 12, 1975.

56. Spangehl, "The North Central Association's 'Third Commission,'" 351–52.

57. Minutes, Executive Committee meeting, November 20, 1953.

58. The idea of incorporation had been proposed first by James Armstrong in his pivotal 1915 presidential address.

59. Stanavage, "I. Report of the Commission," *North Central Association Quarterly* 42 (Summer 1972): 74.

60. "Report of 1971 Workshop: Commission on Research and Service."

61. Stanavage, "I. Report of the Commission" (Summer 1972): 82.

62. Stanavage, "I. Report of the Commission," *North Central Association Quarterly* 40 (Summer 1970): 67.

63. For Aslin's comments, see Stanavage, "I. Report of the Commission," *North Central Association Quarterly* 41 (Summer 1971): 73, 74; for those of Mick, see Stanavage, "I. Report of the Commission," *North Central Association Quarterly* 42 (Summer 1972): 82.

64. "Report of 1974 Workshop: Commission on Research and Service."

Chapter Eight

Past, Present, and Future

"At the Crossroads" implies choice. It also sug-
gests that there are poor choices and good
choices.... At this crossroads we are not struggling
to keep moving. At this crossroads we need to
maintain our momentum.

—Thurston E. Manning, 1991[1]

IN THE EARLY 1990S, the idea of being at a crossroads was so much
on the minds of NCA leaders that the staff of the Commission on
Institutions of Higher Education selected "Regional Accreditation
at the Crossroads" as its theme for the 1991 annual meeting. Later,
the Commission published a collection of papers on the subject.[2]
The crossroads imagery illuminates NCA history and provides an
apt metaphor for the way the Association has re-created itself periodically to meet changing times. The decision of the NCA to abandon the deliberative format in favor of a more active posture led to
its re-creation as an accrediting organization between 1901 and
1916. Beginning in the late 1920s and continuing over the next
four decades, the Association again re-created itself, developing
and implementing a new theory of accrediting based on qualitative
measures. In the process, the thrust of the NCA changed from
enforcing standards to stimulating improvement by helping institutions learn how to change themselves. The third re-creation
occurred in the 1970s and early 1980s when the Association abandoned the three-Commission structure and granted autonomy to
the accrediting Commissions. The Association level was reduced to
a symbolic shell, but the organization survived a serious threat to
its existence.

The crossroads decisions that the NCA confronted between
the early 1970s and the midnineties differed from those encountered previously. As Ted Manning suggested, this last crossroads has

325

been dynamic. Instead of standing at a juncture and choosing a straight path to follow, the Association has traveled a road where each decision made almost immediately raised other crossroads choices. The momentum never stopped; if anything, it accelerated. In addition, the choices available were not always clear-cut. The traditional fork-in-the-road image does not describe the NCA situation. CIHE director Patricia Thrash characterized the NCA crossroads "as a very crowded intersection on a busy highway: traffic signals are out, horns are honking, and everyone is trying to get someplace fast." She concluded that the choices at the crossroads were not simple and more than one decision was needed to make a difference.[3] Her description underscores the frenetic pace of development and shows that a variety of forces have contributed to the multidimensional, dynamic character of the crossroads highway the NCA has sped along over the last two-and-one-half decades.

Patricia Thrash. Executive director of CIHE, 1988 to 1996.

Internally and, more importantly, externally, the influences on the NCA have multiplied and become more complex since the early seventies. The tangled web of relationships in which the NCA currently operates reflects the greater integration of education and accreditation into governmental and societal affairs. The closer connection to government and society triggered an ongoing attempt by a variety of outside forces and the Association to redefine accreditation and the NCA to fit the changing environment. Throughout its history, the ability of the North Central Association to survive and prosper has depended upon how well it changed itself to meet the altered conditions of a specific time. At no time in the last hundred years has this need been greater than in the last twenty-five years. Though the two accrediting Commissions are largely autonomous, in many respects they faced similar pressures and issues that produced analogous responses. But the sources of these influences were often different, pulling the two Commissions in different directions.

REFORM AND ACCOUNTABILITY

In a sense, the hundred-year history of the North Central Association has come full circle. Both its founding in 1895 and its centennial in 1995 occurred in the midst of major reform movements stimulated by periods of phenomenal growth and large-scale, deep-rooted transformations of American education. The rise of institutions such as the public high school and the modern university in the late nineteenth century, combined with the spread of the elective system, established the basic model of American education in the twentieth century. In the thirty years following World War II, the expansion of graduate education; the emergence of the occupationally oriented, postsecondary sector; and the coming of age of the middle schools combined with the notions of mass and universal education to expand the roles and purposes of education. In both eras, the reform movements attempted to create orderly development by controlling the processes of change to instill more order into the ongoing developments. In each case, the ultimate goal was improving the quality of education. Another similarity was that voluntary associations and government were major agencies of reform in both periods.

Despite the general similarities of the educational changes and reforms of the late nineteenth and late twentieth centuries, profound differences also existed. The educational reforms of the

Centennial. Phil LeBeau (left), Minnesota state director, and Robert Mills, COS chair (1994–95) display a banner for the centennial meeting of the Association in 1995.

late 1800s were part of a much larger initiative, known as Progressivism, that continued into the early 1900s and affected virtually every aspect of society. Child labor, food processing, urban blight, assimilation of immigrants, and corruption in business and government were just a few of the areas targeted by Progressive reformers. Conversely, the post-1970 educational reforms have been an independent development. The perspective roles played by government also differed. In the Progressive era, municipalities, sometimes working with local associations, were the primary engines of reform. While municipalities have contributed to contemporary initiatives, the federal government has dominated, followed closely by the states.[4]

Perhaps the greatest difference between the Progressive and contemporary reforms has been their underlying thrusts. Following the general motivation behind Progressivism, late-nineteenth-century educational reformers aimed at instilling order into chaotic conditions, often seeking uniformity or at least agreement on common attributes. The 1890s Committee of Ten report attempted to order the curriculum. The early NCA discussions on institutional definitions pursued a similar goal for high schools and colleges while the initial motivation behind accreditation was to coordinate college admission programs. The post-1970 reforms sought a different kind of control and order. Accountability has been at the core of recent initiatives, but the term has been defined in various ways. On one hand institutions should be accountable to students, parents, government, and the public for the quality of education delivered, typically gauged by the competence of their students. Under this definition, reformers have developed programs to create state and national curricula and standards to coordinate instruction better and to provide data for assessing the outcomes of instruction. Such efforts fit within the historic tradition that dates back to the Committee of Ten and other efforts developed over the last century to transform American education from a loose collection of disparate parts into a cohesive whole.

Following a strict economic orientation, accountability also means using a financially inspired, either-or balance sheet method to assess education. The financial orientation of accountability arose from the idea that the student was a consumer and education was part of the American market economy. "An educational institution is, among its many attributes, a business enterprise from which services are purchased," explained William A. Goddard, secretary of the National Association of Trade and Technical Schools Accrediting Commission, at a 1978 conference on accreditation and student consumer protection. Following this line of reasoning, Goddard identified a primary thrust of educational reform in the seventies, explaining, "The era of consumerism has reached the educational marketplace.... Students are entitled to equal protection in the American marketplace."[5]

In turn, the consumer idea was a response to serious financial problems that emerged in the early 1970s. The widespread expansion of federal eligibility programs and the resulting postsecondary education explosion in the late 1960s and early 1970s created greater opportunities for educational fraud, including the reemergence of a seemingly insoluble problem, the degree mill.[6] The ease of obtaining charters and other legal restrictions hampered policing efforts. In 1971, Anne Stameshkin, associate secretary of the NCA, noted that some states had little legal recourse to stopping the spread of degree mills. In Ohio, a nonpublic school just needed a license to open its doors.[7]

The problem of fraudulent institutions took its toll on the government, the public, and many students. In 1977, Executive Deputy Commissioner of Education John Ellis tied the issue to student loans and educational opportunity. "The Congress and other people are deeply concerned about some of the fraudulent and abusive practices that are emerging in the student loan program," he explained, offering some costly and deplorable examples. "We've also had institutions mushroom, offer courses to pupils, and then disappear from sight, with the Federal Government being asked to hold the guarantee on the loan, and with the consumers wondering where in the world their education went."[8]

Charles Chambers, a Council of Postsecondary Accreditation staff member, approached the fraudulent institution issue from a different perspective. Writing in 1983, Chambers suggested, "An unfortunate consequence of the fact that accrediting bodies are nongovernmental is that purveyors of fraudulent education are able to contrive their own accrediting groups to 'accredit' their own 'diploma mills.'" He claimed two such organizations existed in 1982, but did not state whether these two groups had been approved by the U.S. Department of Education to certify educational quality as part of the federal funding eligibility program.[9] Much as accreditation provided a threshold for institutions to seek federal funds, so the Department of Education approval performed a similar function for accreditation agencies. How the government administered its gatekeeping program affected the integrity of accreditation and influenced the accrediting community's ability to ensure institutional quality.

The second problem was the difficulty the U.S. Office of Education met in administering the federal funding programs. In 1975, U.S. Commissioner of Education Terrell H. Bell remarked that an "enormous tangle of legislation," resulting from the passage of nine different laws in the previous ten years, had created serious problems in student aid programs. A 1969 act opened participation to almost every type of institution, quadrupling the dollar volume of the Guaranteed Student Loan program from $2.2 to $8.8 billion. By 1975, five million students in eighty-seven hundred institutions had secured federally guaranteed loans from nineteen thousand lenders. Bell commented that the expansion of the funding programs had put the U.S. Office of Education in "the loan business in every city and town in the United States." But he also noted that while the workload had increased substantially, not until 1974 was his staff expanded from fifty to two hundred people. Further complicating the administrative nightmare, the Office of Education had little regulatory power until 1972.[10]

THE CHANGING WORLD OF HIGHER EDUCATION ACCREDITING

The NCA and other organizations also faced a tremendous expansion of their communities that created numerous difficulties. In this case, numbers were less a problem than the growing diversity of institutions that sought accrediting to become eligible for federal funding. In 1979, Council on Postsecondary Accreditation (COPA) president Richard Millard reported, "Accreditation is now expected to evaluate and assure the educational quality of everything from a one-man school of welding to a statewide system of postsecondary education, from a hospital offering degrees by examination, from institutions that operate campuses across the world to institutions that have no campuses at all."[11]

Because so many institutions were new, they were unfamiliar with the idea of voluntary accreditation and the accrediting organizations. The viability of peer review evaluation of educational institutions depended on members having a clear and common conception of accreditation, and on their support of the practice through active participation. As a natural consequence of the growth and expansion tied to admitting new and different institutions, misperceptions arose in the accrediting community about the nature and purpose of the self-evaluation process that bound institutions and accrediting agencies together.

Due to the mass dimensions of accreditation, government officials and the public also became more involved with accreditation, but they, too, were unclear about accrediting's purpose and methodology. Prior to World War II, the narrow range of membership and the small portion of the population seeking a college education meant that accreditation's public comprised a minority of the American population. The postwar democracy-of-education movement drastically altered the composition of accrediting's public. Describing the situation the NCA and other organizations faced, Patricia Thrash commented, "The exploding postsecondary universe and the chain reaction of events that followed pushed accreditation agencies into new and more complex relationships with their institutions and programs, the states, the federal government, students, and the public—each with a different set of expectations for accreditation." Associations such as the NCA had to contend with various new "publics," as they were called, that depended upon it for a variety of reasons. One author identified nine different "publics" involved in some fashion with accreditation. Assess-

Helen Levin and William Nault. First two public members of CIHE (1976–80): Helen Levin, civic leader and former treasurer, U.S. League of Women Voters; and William Nault, executive vice president of Field Enterprises Education Corp.

ing the impact of the proliferation of the accrediting "publics," University of California at Santa Barbara chancellor Barbara Uehling concluded, "So long as the users were contained within the academy, there were few problems. It was the extension of the use of these self-regulatory procedures for other purposes that began to create some of the dilemmas confronting accreditation today."[12] Misperceptions regarding what they did and what functions they performed have continued to plague accrediting associations, including the NCA, into the 1990s.

The consumer protection issue shows how the expansion of publics created conflicting perceptions of accreditation. Barbara Uehling observed, "Consumer protection interests of students and employers led to the use of accreditation information by both prospective students and the employers who might hire graduates." In addition, she continued, "The importance of the wise expenditure of public information and the appropriate education of youth as a protection for the future of the nation led to the use of accreditation information by state and federal governments." As a consequence, accreditation meant different things to different people and groups. Gordon K. Davies, director of Virginia's State Council of Higher Education, explained, "Historically, accreditation has been a means of institutional self-improvement.... I think the general public now views it as a consumer protection device."[13] Some federal government officials agreed with the public's view. Accrediting organizations, conversely, considered the states as the proper guardian of the educational consumer's interests, and voiced this opinion continuously for twenty-five years with little effect.

THE TRIAD OF EDUCATIONAL OVERSIGHT

The problem of conflicting viewpoints is important because, following passage of the Higher Education Act of 1965, the idea arose of a triad to oversee the federal postsecondary educational funding programs. The three components were the accrediting agencies, the states, and the federal government. Each triad member performed a function related to its normal operations. Based upon the self-study and peer review visit, accrediting groups, such as the NCA, certified institutional quality. Building upon constitutional interpretation and various statutes, the states chartered institutions. Since possessing a state charter was a requirement for accreditation, the complementary mix of functions was already built into the system. Officials in Washington were responsible for administering the aid programs. The idea of a triad based on performance of complementary, though distinct functions made sense. Effective implementation, however, required that all parties agree on certain basic aspects of the relationship. Each triad member had to make the commitment to participate fully. Lackluster participation would doom the venture since the triad depended upon the interworking of its parts. In addition, misperceptions played a role in this aspect, and the members had to agree on the parameters of each sector's responsibilities. Confusion or differences over functions and responsibilities would create controversies and disputes that hampered performing tasks effectively and the blending of these distinct elements into a cohesive, effective system.

In terms of commitment, the federal government, educational institutions, and the accrediting associations recognized the mutual benefits they gained from the triad arrangement. Initially, accrediting groups were recruited into the eligibility program because the Office of Education did not possess the technological expertise or resources to perform the task of certifying institutions for funding. In this respect, the employment of accrediting agencies followed the general, post–World War II federal government policy of using private groups in certain capacities. The government also acknowledged the important role played by accreditation organizations in eligibility and the development of American education.[14] Accredited institutions and programs depended on accrediting organizations to work with the federal government because that made members eligible for federal funds, and the loss of funding could doom many to oblivion. In addition, longtime student of accreditation Fred Harcleroad observed that working for the government gave accreditors "a visibility and clout they have never had before."[15]

Disagreement over roles was the stumbling block. The necessary symbiosis between the three parts was never reached because no consensus was reached on the proper boundaries of responsibility and relations. Federal officials, in particular, failed to recognize that just as a geometry of interest bound their triad together, even stronger ties bonded the accrediting associations and their members into a slightly different configuration. "If government agencies do not recognize the limitations and the appropriate role of accreditation," explained Harcleroad, "it cannot retain its voluntary character and at the same time serve government purposes."[16]

Initially, few problems arose. As the eligibility triad developed in the late 1960s, the federal government requested changes to facilitate educational growth and expansion. The CIHE agreed with the trend of expansion and was already accrediting increasingly diverse types of institutions. So the Commission adjusted its membership requirements to provide for more categories preparatory to full accreditation. However, led by the always forward-looking Norman Burns, the regional accrediting Commissions involved in the triad soon recognized that the evolving national dimensions of higher education required an equally national approach by them. The founding of Federation of Regional Accrediting Commissions of Higher Education (FRACHE) provided the CIHE and others with a national umbrella organization based in Washington, D.C., to represent their interests.

Burns' foresight was confirmed in the late 1960s and early 1970s, when rising concerns over fraud led accountability advocates to attack the performance of the eligibility triad and its components. Accrediting organizations were criticized for a variety of abuses. Critics wanted to reduce the independence and autonomy of accrediting agencies by increasing their accountability to the government and the public. Though rising fraud had focused attention on the triad and its components, most attacks on the accrediting community targeted their status and power rather than their specific performance in guaranteeing institutional quality.[12]

Simultaneously at conferences and in reports sponsored by the U.S. Office of Education, accrediting agencies were roundly condemned. At a 1970 meeting on "Accreditation and the Public Interest," James Koerner's keynote speech strongly criticized regional associations. He called them "old-fashioned trade associations piously pretending to represent the public interest," but claimed they abused this privilege by protecting the status quo and using nonscientifically based standards. Koerner suggested the assertions of being voluntary were misleading and that accrediting operations were secretive. He also castigated the organizations for failing to supply students with guides to institutions that offered comprehensive and comparative information. The following year, Stanford University professor Frank Newman chaired a task force commissioned by Secretary of Health, Education, and Welfare Elliot Richardson to examine accreditation's role in institutional eligibility. The Newman team also concluded that accreditation had no accountability, and the associations wielded monopolistic power that stifled competition while protecting selected educational practices and standards. The task force recommended clarifying the federal role regarding institutional eligibility and accreditation by establishing a new system to protect educational consumers and support different accrediting mechanisms. The Newman report established a pattern evident in later critiques that hardly clarified matters. Though questioning the effectiveness of the accreditation system and Washington's reliance upon it, "the Newman task force continued to endorse the very process which it believed was not susceptible to reform."[18]

The attacks on accreditation reached a peaked in 1974 with a massive report entitled *Private Accreditation and Public Eligibility.* Funded by the Office of Education and prepared by the National Academy of Public Administration Foundation and the Brookings Institution, this two-volume, 576-page study was written primarily by Harold Orlans. Though it received more negative than positive reviews, the Orlans report raised issues that generated much discussion. Perhaps the most damaging criticism was the claim that "accreditation is a reliable indicator neither of institutional integrity nor viability." The report recommended less reliance on accreditation in determining funding eligibility, in part because of the inability of the accrediting organizations to change. "The attempt of some OE [Office of Education] officials to plant consumer protection in the accrediting process is as promising as a crop of Arctic coconuts," Orlans sarcastically concluded. Since his report appeared during the period when student loan defaults, dropout rates, and school closings had raised what U.S. Office of Education official Ronald Pugsley called a "chorus of alarm," accreditation was thrust into the public spotlight.[19]

The strident criticisms by Koerner, the Newman Task Force, and Orlans struck a nerve among Office of Education officials, who believed that the complaints lodged against the accreditors indicated flaws in the government administration of the eligibility program. In 1976, Ronald Pugsley explained that if accrediting organizations were a conservative force working against innovation and experimentation, the federal government was supporting such a policy in its distribution of funds. If accrediting standards were not valid or reliable indicators of quality, than the government was employing a similarly flawed "benchmark" for providing aid. If accrediting groups made decisions based on elitist values, the government was endorsing those values. As a result, a crisis of confidence arose in the Office of Education regarding its "gatekeeping" function of accrediting agency recognition. The Office of Education response was to launch an unsuccessful, twenty-five-year campaign to make the informal triad into a more effective system of educational oversight. In the process, it tried to change the CIHE to better meet federal needs.[20]

The effort to transform the higher education commissions of voluntary accrediting associations started almost two decades after the NCA and other organizations began working with the eligibility program. In early 1972, the USOE staff drafted a set of revised eligibility criteria for accrediting organizations. In April, the Office of Education submitted its proposals for review to the chief executive officers of accrediting groups, state boards of higher education, state education agencies, consumer groups, and institutions. A second and then a third draft were produced and similarly studied, and the revisions took into account the comments of the various reviewers. Two years later, on April 20, 1974, the revised criteria became effective. The entire process was punctuated by bitter debates and sometimes bad feelings that strained relations between the Office of Education and the NCA higher Commission.[21]

The new criteria included substantive changes designed to address various criticisms. According to Ronald Pugsley, "The revised criteria placed increased emphasis upon accrediting agencies' responsibility to the public interest and their reliability of operations." More specifically, consumer items were included to better define and clarify accrediting procedures. In addition, to be recognized by the USOE, accrediting agencies needed clearly defined policies of awarding or denying accredited status. They had to involve the public in Association administration. The government also required a detailed program of reviewing complaints, including written procedures and due process in proceedings. Each accrediting group was to develop an evaluation program to assess standards and to establish policies to guard against conflicts of interest in decision making.[22]

On April 5, 1974, Norman Burns sent John R. Profitt, director of the Accreditation and Institutional Eligibility Staff (AIES), a new CIHE policy statement outlining its relations with the AIES. The CIHE reaffirmed its "desire to work co-operatively with the United States Office of Education." Reacting to the new burdens placed on it by the criteria, however, the Commission set out the parameters of this cooperation. After agreeing generally to an AIES review, the Commission added a proviso that stated that the Commission rejected liability for any problems or violations arising "when it has not been permitted to carry out its procedures which were originally accepted as the basis for the United States Commissioner's recognition." Most importantly, the position paper closed with a request, jointly issued with FRACHE, for a conference with Office of Education personnel to establish the procedures the AIES would use in reviewing accrediting organizations and "handling complaints and grievances." If changes were to be made, the NCA wanted to be part of the process so it could state its opinion and defend its interests. Collaboration in the making of policy and procedures also promised to strengthen the triad, since all parties involved would contribute to the rules guiding its operation.[23]

Soon after the CIHE position paper appeared, the Commission underwent a review by the Office of Education to maintain its status as a recognized accrediting body. The process extended over 1974 and part of 1975. During this period, the Commission experienced a significant transition of power. Norman Burns retired and Joseph Semrow temporarily held the position of director until Thurston Manning assumed the post. In May 1975, the CIHE received a two-year extension of recognition, but the new terms showed the government had tightened its control of the eligibility program. U.S. Commissioner of Education Terrell Bell explained the two-year period "is based upon a desire to review the Commission's effort in implementing revised policies and procedures," in response to a petition by the Michigan Community College Association and a study by Stephen Romine. He also suggested that the Commission needed to improve its program regarding occupational education, citing the dissatisfaction that existed "among certain vocational institutions and State directors of vocational education within the North Central Region."[24]

Thurston Manning. Director of CIHE, 1975–87.

The CIHE acceptance of the new criteria and the government's renewal of NCA participation in the eligibility triad masked severe, seemingly irreconcilable differences between Washington officials and accrediting groups over the purpose of accrediting and the nature of their relations. These problems typically flared up when government regulations were changed or legislation concerning funding higher education was considered. But the polarized positions of the accreditors and the government made relations tense, even in cooperative undertakings, as a 1970s collaborative project showed.

In 1977 the U.S. Office of Education Division of Eligibility and Agency Evaluation (successor to the AIES), relevant commissions of the NCA, Western Association, New England Association, and the American Institute of Research (AIR) collaborated on a project to improve the consumer protection programs of accrediting associations. The AIR developed a self-study instrument on consumer protection issues. The resulting Institutional Self-Study Form (ISSF) was field-tested in nine institutions. On November 20 and 21, 1978, an invitational conference was held to assess the AIR product. The

NCA higher Commission played a pivotal part in this project. In addition to being a project cosponsor, three NCA member institutions field-tested the questionnaire, and the CIHE staff arranged the conference attended by 119 officials from educational and accrediting associations, state and federal government, and learning institutions. The Commission also published and distributed the summary report of the meeting.[25]

The collaborative thrust of the project showed the willingness of all triad members to address mutual problems. In commenting upon the project, CIHE associate director Charles Cook noted the Commission staff and administrators at the institutions participating in the field test had learned much from the experience. He also suggested that the NCA was considering using a shorter survey based on the AIR instrument as part of the annual report turned in by member institutions.

However, the response to the AIR questionnaire and the conference discussions brought up fundamental disagreements that showed why solving problems proved so difficult. The arguments against integrating student consumer protection into the accrediting process indicated that strong opposition to the idea, itself, threatened any solution. Ted Manning called student consumer protection an ill-defined and expanding field, "an uncharted wilderness," and suggested that accrediting groups had no insight into how it would affect their operations. Another question was whether accrediting organizations were equipped to take on the consumer protection task. They could judge educational quality, but were not ready to enforce regulations. Regulation was outside the traditional purview of accrediting, and conflicted with their voluntary association status. Associations did not have the necessary resources. Their sole sanction of loss of membership was too harsh a punishment. Many participants opposed integrating consumer protection on a regulatory basis into the accrediting procedures, because they considered protecting the consumer a function of the states.[26] As a result, the AIR effort may have been in vain because no matter how it was received, the rationale behind its production was still a hotly debated topic.

The experience of the 1970s demonstrated that misperceptions over status, roles, and responsibilities largely hamstrung efforts to improve the effectiveness of the triad. Despite all the difficulties, the commitment to the triad idea remained strong. As Western Illinois University education professor Virginia Helms explained, all three members of the triad tried to make the relationship work. "During the 1970s," she observed, "a core group of selected, influential leaders in each section of the triad participated in various workshops, conferences, and seminars designed to assess the problem(s) of the eligibility triad and to devise one or more solutions." Problems were identified, but no solutions were developed because of disagreements over each participant's role and function.[27] What was true in the 1970s unfortunately characterized relations during the 1980s and 1990s.

In the late 1980s, another crisis indicated that little progress had occurred over the last decade. The major obstacle in this instance was the process of development. The request by the NCA in the early 1970s to be involved in the deliberations on revisions was ignored by federal officials, creating a confrontational situation. On September 8, 1987, the U.S. Department of Education published its proposal for new regulations for recognizing accrediting agencies that placed a greater stress on outcomes and assessment. Commission chair Sister Mary Janet McGilley outlined the CIHE's objections. She criticized the content of the regulations and their method of development. The content issue was more a matter of degree than anything else. The new Department of Education proposals were characterized as a case of overregulation. McGilley supported making institutions accountable and acknowledged the importance of student outcomes and assessment. But the Commission questioned whether student achievement was the sole determinant of institutional effectiveness, noting that "institutions of higher education also serve many other intellectual and civic purposes, particularly in areas of basic research and community service." Besides, NCA policies and practices already included outcomes measures in its criteria for candidacy and accreditation.

The process of developing the new regulations also ran counter to the cooperative philosophy and practice of the triad. There was no communication and collaboration in the early stages of planning. "We can only express concern that the U.S. Department of Education has chosen to conduct a discussion with the accrediting community primarily through promulgation of new regulations," McGilley complained, noting that several of the new proposals "come as a complete surprise to us." Another issue concerned who should set policy for the accrediting community. The CIHE chair emphasized that the Council on Postsecondary Accreditation was the appropriate body to determine "interagency policies on accreditation, not the federal government." Again, the problem of misperception and the appalling lack of progress in determining proper roles and responsibilities was made apparent. McGilley also attacked the intrusion into NCA and institutional affairs the new regulations promised. The CIHE claimed that the development of outcomes assessment measures took time and assessing outcomes was most effective when done by *"the people within the institution."* She stressed, "We are not ready to require the use of nationally normed tests or other competency exams simply to produce some outcome scores."[28]

By March 1988, many of the difficulties with the Department of Education regulations had been resolved to the satisfaction of the CIHE. Following the public review policies generally employed by the federal government, the accrediting associations were brought into the deliberative process as commentators on the new regulations and they succeeded in revising the new regulations substantially. The new CIHE director, Patricia A. Thrash, noted in her first annual report to the NCA higher education members that the new regulations were acceptable for the most part.[29]

The conflict over the Department of Education regulations that flared up in the late 1980s offers great insight into the lack of progress made in forging the triad into a system of oversight. The ongoing, seemingly insoluble problem of differing conceptions over roles, status, and responsibilities complicated matters. In addition, as McGilley's letter indicated, the triad construction had become more complicated. The accrediting associations had added another layer of bureaucracy, and another player, to represent their interests. While FRACHE had originally provided the regional with a presence and voice in Washington, the Council on Postsecondary Accreditation was a profoundly different organization. Though a national umbrella group, COPA had an expansive membership that included two distinct camps of accreditors, the regionals focusing on institutions, and the nationally organized professional groups focusing on one department or program within an institution. While this comprehensive membership provided more power and status, it also created some difficulties. COPA had to reconcile any diverging views held by its diverse members to represent them effectively.

A similar situation faced the CIHE. Its membership was equally diverse. The diversity of membership meant that, from the accrediting perspective, the geometric construction was incredibly complex and cannot be accurately described as a triad. Rather, it was a collection of various configurations that were grouped, at the most general level, around the accrediting, state, and federal government levels. The organizations that stood where the triad angles met did not possess the independence or autonomy to make the arrangement a simple meeting of three parties. The U.S. educational agency, the accrediting organizations, and the state agencies were the visible parts of a hidden, intricately structured geometry of relationship and representation that exerted various pressures and influences on the respective triad members. The U.S. Department of Education, for example, was subject to influences from all three branches of the federal government as well as the public.

The idea of expanding accrediting publics contributed to many of the long-standing misconceptions and disputes between the federal government and associations such as the NCA. Each public, whether it be the institutional members, the students at these institutions and their parents, the federal officials, the public, or numerous other groups, possessed its own definition of what accrediting was and how the accrediting organizations worked. The perceptions of these publics influenced their ideas as to whom accrediting was primarily accountable. Few acknowledged that the voluntary nature of accrediting groups dictated that their primary allegiance and accountability were to the institutions that formed the organization. The strength of the Association compact that determined the existence of the organization depended upon member support and involvement. The decisions made and the courses of action were determined by the members. Conflicts arose when the other "publics" sought action by the NCA that went against the interests of Association members.

Different decision-making procedures also created problems between the federal government and the voluntary accrediting associations. In 1988 and at other times when a dispute occurred, a major obstacle was not the ultimate aim of the issue but the process of development. In the federal government, decisions were made at the top by Congress or high executive department officials and agencies were mandated to implement the decisions. In the NCA, decision making moved in the opposite direction, up from the members to the Commission and then to the professional staff for implementation. These two contrasting styles produced conflicts. When the government officials tried to impose their will on the NCA, the Association seldom submitted, because CIHE officials considered government mandates cavalier and beyond the bounds of CIHE's relationship with Washington. But reaching a satisfactory compromise was also inevitable because the goal of maintaining the triad superseded any difficulties.

THE HIGHER EDUCATION ACT REAUTHORIZATION

In 1988, Ted Manning resigned from the CIHE and Patricia A. Thrash was named director of the Commission. The first woman to head the Commission's professional staff, Thrash had been a dean at Northwestern University before joining the Association in 1972. Having worked with Norman Burns and Manning, she was experienced in Commission affairs.

In 1990, a crisis arose as student loan defaults reached $2.5 billion. A Department of Education study published the following year reported that 178 institutions faced loss of funding eligibility because of high student loan default rates. Each had recorded over 35 percent default totals in 1987, 1988, and 1989. Of these, 155 were proprietary, 14 were public, and 9 were private, nonprofit institutions. Eleven were NCA members, but most of these had mitigating circumstances. Three of the NCA members were tribal or minority institutions and so were exempt from the possible funding loss. Five were community colleges in urban areas with high minority and, presumably, low income enrollments. Only one NCA institution was proprietary.[30] Though the NCA record differed from the general default trends, the Department of Education did not distinguish the situations of its members from others facing loss of funding. Nor did there appear to be any attempt to rate various accrediting associations as to their membership rates of default or to provide separate governing policies. Rather, all were subjected to the same criticisms and, ultimately, the same regulations. The regular cycle of reauthorization of the Higher Education

Act of 1965 (HEA) provided the opportunity to address the loan default issue.

In her early statements as director, Thrash accurately described the CIHE situation and identified the major points of contention that later fueled the crisis surrounding the HEA reauthorization. Speaking at the 1988 NCA annual meeting, she introduced the idea of the CIHE as an "uncommon alliance." Thrash identified three related and sometimes contradictory aspects of this coalition. In her opinion the defining quality of the alliance was the Commission's commitment to its members, manifested "by demanding excellence and encouraging improvement." But, Thrash also identified other, important sides of the relationship, including the eligibility triad and the federal government where connections were less clear. Noting the need to "reemphasize the complementary roles of the triad," she also cited the necessity to "continue our vigilance in seeing that federal recognition requirements for accrediting agencies are legal and reasonable."

In her first annual report to CIHE members, Thrash identified a challenge the Commission faced that puts the increasing importance of government relations and their impact in perspective: "We must continue to rethink accreditation in the context of changing societal realities, attempting to discover and refine appropriate purposes for a voluntary institutional accrediting Commission in providing public assurance of institutional quality and assisting institutions in their improvement."[31] Though evident in some fashion throughout its history, the integration of the NCA into the public sector was complete by the late 1980s. Accreditation served public as well as educational and Association purposes. Still at issue, however, was the question of whether providing public assurances meant serving government interests. Because officials in Washington viewed the accrediting community very differently than the accreditors perceived themselves, the CIHE operated in an environment characterized by a tangled web of relationships and conflicting loyalties. As the reauthorization incident showed, the Commission walked along a tightrope marked by increasingly frequent crossroads that offered several different choices.

As was true of prior periods of strife, during the reauthorization of the HEA, the federal government tried to transform the CIHE into a quasi-governmental regulatory agency. The longevity of the crisis is due to its division into two phases. The first stage involved the debate over the proposed legislation reauthorizing the HEA and lasted from approximately 1989 to the passage of the bill in 1992. The second stage focused on the CIHE opposition to the Department of Education program to implement the amended Act that began following the bill's passage in 1992 and ended in 1994. Ironically, the effort to tie the CIHE more closely to the government and channel its efforts into areas desired by Washington officials had the opposite effect. The HEA reauthorization incident actually strengthened the role of the CIHE as the representative of its members in Washington.

Many of the proposed amendments to the legislation and later draft regulations prepared by the Department of Education stimulated strong negative reactions by the CIHE and members. Two proposed solutions for the default issue threatened the status of the accreditation community in the triad. The first was to eliminate the accrediting leg entirely and reconfigure the new geometry to enhance state roles. This notion gave way to a related program of creating State Postsecondary Recognition Entities (SPRE) to deal with consumer protection issues. Related provisions aimed at transforming accrediting agencies into quasi-governmental, regulatory arms by providing for federal micromanagement of accreditation, and forcing accreditors to intrude into institutions in ways that affected their autonomy.

Faced with hostile action by the federal government, the CIHE followed the set pattern of meetings and deliberations with federal officials and COPA (until its dissolution in March 1993) seeking removal of the offensive amendments and, later, policies. The debate over the education act produced substantial changes in the legislation, but the incident of the early 1990s was marked by some significant out-of-the-ordinary measures and results. The calling of emergency meetings in late 1993 by Patricia Thrash and Commission chair Jack Bottenfield, then president of Iowa Central Community College, to inform members of the problem areas of the proposed new federal regulations was a major CIHE departure that may have profound ramifications on future activities. Hastily called and arranged, the session on December 21, 1993, at the O'Hare Hilton in Chicago was attended by over 250 representatives from approximately 180 institutions. It examined the "Potential

Impact of the Department of Education's Proposed Recognition Requirements" from the perspective of higher education associations based in Washington and the NCA. The discussion covered three major areas of concern: (1) state oversight by the SPREs; (2) the first explicit attempt by the Department of Education to regulate accreditation; and (3) federal eligibility and certification. The emergency session ended with a panel that offered "short-term strategies for responding to the proposed regulations and long-term strategies for dealing with the final regulations."[32]

The coming together of so many NCA member institutions in literally a matter of days was just one of many indications that the HEA reauthorization episode was a watershed in CIHE history. The experience of the early 1990s also triggered profound changes in the positions of the Commission and the U.S. Department of Education regarding the triad. Buttressed by strong support from members, the Commission adjusted its role in the triad toward greater advocacy of member and accreditation needs. In her June 1995 report to the membership, Patricia Thrash observed that the CIHE remained committed to the triad relationship, but had hardened its stance regarding advocacy of member and Association positions. "While acknowledging the Commission's responsibilities to work cooperatively and productively with Department of Education and state agencies as the new law and regulations were implemented, I emphasized that we would be mindful and faithful to our historical role of service to our members."[33]

Thrash based her comments on CIHE responses to government actions, including the idea of the SPREs and the provisions on unannounced reviews of institutions. Though initially unsuccessful in removing provisions for the SPREs from the HEA, on Patricia Thrash's advice, the Commission continued its opposition by refusing to help set up the new agencies. While the strong movement to downsize the federal government and curtail regulation exerted a much greater influence, the refusal of the NCA and other accrediting organizations to support the SPREs contributed to their apparent demise in 1995. The Commission has also adopted a cautious, watchful attitude regarding unannounced inspection visits to institutions, and so far, its opposition has already produced changes in the policy. Though the visits remain part of the law, thirty days' notice will be provided by the Department of

Education before conducting reviews of an institution's financial aid programs.

The steadfast opposition of the NCA and other accrediting agencies influenced the U.S. Department of Education to soften its positions on regulation and the role of accreditation in the triad. The Department of Education convened a meeting on May 10, 1995, to discuss improving communication among the triad members. U.S. Department of Education director of Institutional Participation and Oversight Service Marianne Phelps admitted that some of the 1992 amendments to the HEA were "overkill." She also explained the government agency's position in regulation, covering several issues raised by the CIHE over the last two decades. She commented, "We want to regulate to the extent that we have to, but not regulate more than we have to...to ensure accountability while creating incentive for improved performance, reducing institutional burdens, and providing a clearer role for partners in the Triad."[34]

A major casualty of the HEA reauthorization experience was the demise of COPA. Regional association officials had voiced dissatisfaction with COPA before the reauthorization crisis, but the complaints grew more strident as the education act situation became more tense. The regionals noted that the diverse membership created an incompatibility of interests that made it impossible "to develop an effective set of organizational activities." Following the resignation of the regional associations and after twenty years of a turbulent existence, The COPA board voted on April 7, 1993, to disband the organization effective December 31, 1993.[35] The decline of COPA was surprisingly quick. As late as 1988, the CIHE had voiced its strong support for the umbrella organization, commending the Council on Postsecondary Accreditation for its action in the dispute over new government regulations.

The problems the regional associations had with COPA did not lessen support for a national umbrella organization. In June 1993, officials of the regionals and Washington-based higher education associations formed a National Policy Board on Higher Education Institutional Accreditation. CIHE chair Glenn Niemeyer, provost and vice president of academic affairs at Grand Valley State University in Michigan, noted, "The critical concern seemed to be the need to shore up accreditation against federal intrusion and lack of accountability and credibility."[36] Thus, reflecting the Commission position, a primary drive behind the national organization was greater advocacy of accreditation interests in Washington.

THE CIHE ADAPTS TO MEET CHANGING CONDITIONS

As part of and exclusive from its efforts to forge a more effective triad of educational oversight, the Commission has adjusted its policies and practices to meet the changes of the last twenty-five years. For example, a combination of factors have created greater opportunities for women and minorities in the CIHE. The enduring influence of the civil rights movement and the women's movement played a role, as did the increasing presence and power of women and minorities in higher education at all levels. In addition, federal and NCA policies mandated a commitment to diversity and equity. As a result, women in particular have become much more populous and prominent in Commission affairs. Greater minority involvement also has occurred but on a smaller scale. Executive Director Patricia Thrash made diversity a hallmark of her tenure, especially in the hiring of staff members.

Over the last two decades, the CIHE has consistently pursued a change of direction in membership policies, tightening its requirements significantly. In 1981, the Commission developed the idea of general institutional requirements (GIRs) to be met by all those seeking NCA membership.[37] One of the major provisions was the reaffirmation of the general education component. In the early 1990s, a critical issues committee, organized by Commission chair Roland Dille, discussed membership requirements. Morton Weir, then chancellor of the University of Illinois at Urbana, advocated raising the floor on admission to include only degree-granting institutions. The passage of this provision in 1993 eliminated schools offering certificates or some other terminal award from membership.[38] The action reversed an expansionist trend in Association post–World War II membership practices that had aimed at accommodating the growth of higher and postsecondary education. Basically, the CIHE stated that—as its name implied—its community was limited to higher education, and higher education was defined as degree-granting institutions. The Commission could not be all things to all institutions. In tightening its membership requirements, the CIHE has followed a reform thrust for higher standards in education generally.

John Kemp (left), NCA president (1992–93) and Illinois State Director, COS, presents honorary membership to Morton Weir, chancellor of the University of Illinois and former NCA president (1991–92)

The service role of the CIHE and the continuing drive to help institutions change themselves also has been substantially altered The continuing demands on institutions for assessment and outcomes, among other things, has dictated that they improve existing efforts in these areas or develop new programs. In either case, the growing technical aspects of the many aspects of accreditation and funding eligibility have created a need to educate not only institutional officials but also the Commission's Consultant-Examiners. In response, the CIHE component of the annual meeting has become dedicated to providing training for Association consultant-examiners and institutional representatives. In the early 1980s, Commission chair Ronald Roskens recommended the annual meeting be improved and established a committee to review the CE (consultant-examiner) process. The committee suggested that CE orientation and professional development be integrated into

Incoming NCA president (1989–90) Ronald Roskens (right), president of the University of Nebraska system, congratulated by outgoing president (1988–89) Emeral Crosby, principal of Pershing High School in Detroit, 1989 Annual Meeting.

the annual meeting. The Commission staff also has become more actively involved in the educational efforts. As the drive for assessment became stronger and more pervasive in the late 1980s, staff members presented workshops and published collections of papers on assessment and other topics of concern to members.[39] The Commission also required all institutions to submit plans for assessing student achievement by June 30, 1995.

The new focus on member advocacy and on the workshops and publications indicates a possible future path for the Commission. Whether externally generated by government or society or internally motivated by the CIHE or the institution, higher education is likely to feel increasing pressure to improve all areas of performance, especially undergraduate instruction and occupational training. Making the necessary changes may prove difficult because funding constraints are a fact of life in higher education. The mix of these factors increases the importance of accurately assessing program and institutional effectiveness, and that is where the future of the CIHE comes into play. In responding to the needs of members, the CIHE may subtly transform itself into a service association that does accreditation, instead of the other way around.

While predicting the future is difficult, one trend appears certain to continue. Much as the major influence on CIHE development since the early 1970s has been the interplay between governmental, societal, and educational forces, which will likely continue for the foreseeable future, the same appears true for the Commission on Schools. The interaction between similar forces, though with a slightly different thrust, affected the development of the NCA schools Commission over the last twenty-five years. The schools Commission also experienced changes in its relations with government. Here, the impetus from the reform movement was stronger and more direct, often preceding government efforts. In addition, the focus of government interaction was on the states, where the parameters of the relationships differed profoundly from those of the CIHE and Washington. Not surprisingly, the process of change and the results were very different from those of the CIHE.

THE SCHOOLS AS TARGETS OF CRITICISM AND REFORM

In the 1980s, virtually every aspect of the American school enterprise came under attack and was targeted for reform. The quality of instruction was given special attention. A major turning point occurred in 1983, when the National Commission on Excellence, a federal study group, published *A Nation at Risk*. This report strongly criticized the schools, suggesting that low standards had led to rising illiteracy rates and had contributed to the lagging performance of American students in comparison to those of other industrialized nations. The situation was so severe that many companies had been forced to establish on-the-job, remedial education programs for their workers. *A Nation at Risk* unleashed a tidal wave of studies denouncing the state of American education.

The federal government was a major source of criticism. For example, humanities instruction was scrutinized in several studies funded by the National Endowment for the Humanities. A 1986 survey of high school juniors showed an appalling lack of historical knowledge. Two-thirds of the students surveyed were over fifty years off in dating the Civil War. A similar proportion could not identify the Reformation or the Magna Carta. Three years later, an NEH-funded study of college seniors indicated that 25 percent could not differentiate the words of Winston Churchill from those of Joseph Stalin, or those of Karl Marx from the U.S. Constitution. Over half the students surveyed showed no comprehension of the purpose of the Emancipation Proclamation or the Federalist Papers.[40]

A variety of nongovernmental efforts also identified major gaps in student knowledge and understanding in other subjects. In 1988, a National Geographic Society study reported that a majority of high school graduates could not locate Ohio, Michigan, or New Jersey on a map. Nor could they identify Chile, Argentina, or Peru. A 1982 international mathematics survey ranked American seniors second to last among the fifteen nations surveyed in advanced algebra. Seven years later, the Educational Testing Service (ETS) announced that American students had finished last in an international math competition. ETS officials reported, "Only 9% of Americans showed an understanding of basic principles of measurement and geometry." Regarding science, *Newsweek* claimed in 1990 that only 7 percent of American seventeen-year-olds possessed the advanced science skills needed to "perform well in college-level courses."[41]

Some critics suggested that the structure of the curriculum was a major part of the problem. *A Nation at Risk* called for the return of the core course of study, echoing the proposal offered almost a century before in the Committee of Ten report. The NEH supported this idea, attacking the undergraduate curriculum for its omissions. In a 1987 report entitled *Humanities in America: A Report to the President, the Congress, and the American People*, the Endowment claimed that, in 1989, a student could graduate from over 80 percent of the nation's institutions of higher education without a course in American history. Almost 40 percent of the colleges and universities required absolutely no history for graduation; 45 percent did not require an American or English literature course, and 77 percent had no foreign language requirement.

The government was not the only critic of the curriculum. In 1987, two best-selling books castigated the courses of study in American schools. In *The Closing of the American Mind*, University of Chicago philosophy professor Allan Bloom claimed that higher education had failed democracy by abandoning sound liberal arts study for what he called trendy and relevant subjects. His book topped the *New York Times* nonfiction list and was the number one seller in Chicago, Los Angeles, and Boston. One of Bloom's major competitors in the book market was *Cultural Literacy* by E. D. Hirsch. A professor of English at the University of Virginia, Hirsch complained the schools were creating a generation of cultural illiterates because of the stress on skills development.[42]

While some critics espoused a more Western approach, others attacked this idea, calling the American humanities curriculum sexist, racist, and Eurocentric. They desired a more multicultural, gender-equitable course of study to reflect the diversity of the American people. Multiculturalism was not a new idea; its contemporary roots dated back to the National Defense Education Act of the late 1950s. But it created much controversy in the 1980s and 1990s as multicultural and conservative forces clashed. In 1994, the publication of the *National Standards for American History* by a group funded by the NEH raised the temperature of this debate, leading some to advocate the end of the endowment.[43]

The above examples represent the tip of the iceberg of criticism directed at all levels of American education, but they show the controversy generated by conflicting ideas. The validity of these attacks is less important here than the fact they precipitated a very rapid reform response that proved just as massive and just as diverse. Professional associations, federal and state governments, foundations, colleges, and schools came forth with ideas to improve the schools. Among others, the National Council for the Social Studies, the National Council of Teachers of Mathematics, the National Council for Geographic Education, the National Endowment for the Humanities, and various states launched numerous curriculum reform projects. In the mid-1990s, reform efforts are focused on developing standards for various subject areas such as the controversial set for history and a less criticized model for geography.

State and local governments also have taken a much closer interest in school improvement, initiating programs to monitor instruction and administration. In cities like Chicago, local school councils were organized to administer schools, actively bringing the community into the reform equation. In 1995, the city of Chicago assumed control of the Chicago public schools following the passage of state legislation authorizing such a move.[44]

THE RISE OF OUTCOMES ACCREDITATION

One particular idea has dominated the various reform initiatives: assessing outcomes. The product of education, particularly regarding student achievement, became the focus of reform. In a 1985 NCA *Quarterly* article, Northwestern professor of education John Wick traced the origins of the outcomes focus to the reaction to *A Nation at Risk*, particularly the more proactive, aggressive stance of the states. In Illinois, he explained, the response was the appointment of a Commission on School Reform in 1984. This Commission concluded, "The quality of schools should be judged first and foremost on the basis of student learning." Wick considered the stress on outcomes a logical turn because the "parent focuses on the college entrance scores."[45] Illinois later developed a comprehensive school reform initiative that included yearly testing of students in various subjects and the issuing of school report cards that informed the public of the test results. These report cards generate much interest and discussion in school communities.

Arizona State University professor emeritus and Commission on Schools research consultant Robert Armstrong traced the origins of outcomes to two other related sources. He saw the notion arising out of a combination of the accountability movement and the later mastery education reform idea. In a more general sense, outcomes represented a synthesis of the criticisms of those seeking accountability and the reform solutions generated by these critiques. And the late 1970s and early 1980s witnessed the appearance of a plethora of ideas and programs. Reform initiatives most relevant to outcomes were the mastery effort that aimed at improving student command of subject matter, the effective schools program, and outcomes-based education. The effective schools initiative focused on identifying such schools and analyzing their common characteristics, particularly as they differed from those considered ineffective. Armstrong suggested this idea produced inconsistent results because effective characteristics differed in various schools. Outcomes-based education focused on using results, or outcomes, in curriculum design.[46]

As reform turned toward the quality of education, determined largely by student achievement, both NCA Commissions launched major programs on assessing outcomes.

An irony of the outcomes movement in the Commission on Schools (COS) is that it occurred soon after the membership had voiced very strong support for the existing accrediting program. In 1982, the schools Commission surveyed a significant portion of its membership to assess the effectiveness of its standards in improving the quality of the school's educational program. Though other questions were asked, the survey basically required an answer to one question applied to all the standards: "To what extent do you believe the specified quality of the measure affects directly and positively the quality of the school's program of education?" The four answers were: no, little, considerable, or significant effect. To ensure a representative sampling, the survey targeted the three primary membership classifications: elementary, junior high/middle school, and secondary; and three major school personnel types: teacher, principals, and superintendents.

The respondents rated the COS standards extremely high in terms of satisfaction and effectiveness. Overall, 89 percent of the respondents agreed that the standards had had considerable or significant effect on their schools' educational program. Questions on topics related to outcomes also received high scores. At all levels of schooling and from all three personnel categories, approximately nine of every ten respondents answered considerable or significant effect to questions on the value of the self-study and team visit, and the development of a school improvement plan within a year after the study and visit. The standards received the same high approval rating on the need for an effective working relationship between the principal and the staff, and on gathering information in a variety of areas, including student achievement.[47]

The following year, the COS appointed a Task Force on Student Success to review the national reports being published at the time and the Commission accrediting program to determine if its policies, standards, and procedures needed modification. Comprised of educators from all school levels, including college and NCA personnel, the task force reported its findings in 1985.

The task force report covered two areas. First, it defined a successful student was one who was aware of and sought to attain "universals characteristic of productive, satisfied, and educated persons." The universals were organized into general categories—knowledge, skills, personal values, and personal qualities—and subcategories. Second, the report made recommendations regarding appropriate school characteristics. Again there were general areas, program, school climate, learning process, personnel, and organization and time, which were broken down into specific attributes. According to John Kemp, then Illinois state director, "One of the major recommendations for the Commission that surfaced early in the discussion—was the need for the Commission to be focusing more on the outcomes of the educational process."[48]

The interest in outcomes was in tune with prevailing reform trends, but the NCA had no need to rely on contemporary ideas in planning an outcomes accrediting approach. The notion was not new in the mid-1980s. In his keynote speech at the ninety-first NCA annual meeting in 1991, University of Kentucky professor of education Thomas R. Guskey traced the origins of outcomes to Ralph Tyler's 1949 book, *Basic Principles of Curriculum and Instruction*. Outcomes had also been discussed in the 1930s, during the accrediting modernization initiatives, and had resurfaced in the 1960s.[49] However, the published NCA literature indicates more recent reform ideas exerted a much stronger influence on the outcomes accreditation program than its long, though episodic NCA history. Armstrong noted that the effective schools program of identifying superior characteristics offered ideas for outcomes accreditation school plans. Linda Petros of Mount Clemens High School in Michigan reported that her school staff researched the effective schools literature as part of their outcomes accreditation (OA) experience. Consciously or not, the COS OA model represented a culmination of sorts of contemporary reform trends, some long-standing NCA ideas, and the existing school accrediting system.

COS executive director John Vaughn spearheaded the outcomes initiative by introducing the idea of outcomes accreditation in 1983.[50] The Commission on Schools officially launched its outcomes initiative in 1984 with the appointment of an OA steering committee. Three related, but distinct, projects made up the OA program. At the 1985 annual meeting, the Commission approved a developmental pilot project for the design of procedures that involved thirty-eight schools. Simultaneously, the Committee on Research developed "outcomes-oriented standards" to integrate this component into the accrediting system. The Committee on Theory and Practice of School Evaluation also developed a handbook to guide schools through the OA process. The handbook's primary author was professor William R. Shirer of the University of Wisconsin. He was assisted by Ken Gose of the University of Arizona and Robert Armstrong of Arizona State University.[51]

The handbook authors criticized contemporary definitions of student outcomes for being too narrow. Generally, student outcomes were defined as "cognitive information students gain from information." Since cognitive data were the easiest to assess, state departments of education, publishers, various organizations, and schools had devised tests "to measure cognitive outcomes." Building upon the work of the successful student task force, the handbook expanded the definition of student outcomes to include personal qualities and values. But, the authors claimed, "The affective outcomes of schooling must also be considered because they represent an equally important sphere of expectations for American schools."

Regarding outcomes accreditation, schools had two OA options. They could assess district or school student outcomes or focus on the instructional program's outcomes in various subject areas. Both options involved the cooperative working of administrators and faculty, particularly the latter, in a committee structure. In either case, the general procedure was basically the same. After identifying school district or instructional program objectives and targeting areas of improvement, baseline data on these areas were gathered. The information was then disaggregated, or broken down according to the specific areas of improvement. For each area, an action plan was developed using the revised objectives and then implemented. Data obtained from posttesting were compared with the disaggregated information to assess the plan's effectiveness. Following analysis of the results and possibly developing revisions for the plan, a new cycle of assessment of different areas was begun.[52]

Outcomes accreditation was not so much a totally new direction as an adaptation of the existing self-study/team visit to changing needs. The core remained the self-study, but the emphasis shifted from process to product and required revising the procedures. Because the outcomes focus dictated the collection of comparative baseline data, the workload increased and the time commitment was greater. According to John Wick, the effort was well worth it. He called outcomes accreditation a "triple-win situation," explaining that "it addresses the legitimate needs of the educator to focus on process, responds to the legitimate concern of the public to address outcomes, and can significantly improve the performance levels of the students." He also stressed the compatibility of the traditional process-oriented approach and the new stress on outcomes. "Outcomes are a function of the process," he explained. "The emphasis on the former increases interest in the latter because improvement involves changing aspects of how things are done."[53]

Wick voiced his opinions in 1985, when the COS outcomes program was just getting started. In 1993, John C. Pennoyer, who had extensive experience with the program's early development, supported Wick's claims. Pennoyer had been curriculum coordinator at one of the original pilots—Lyons Township, Illinois high school. He later served as a team chair on two OA school visits. He described the traditional self-study/visit program as resource-oriented. In assessing the strengths of outcomes evaluation, Pennoyer observed that the careful and thorough identification of resources helped school officials remember the importance of the resource base in effective education. As a preparatory step for outcomes accreditation, he advised schools to use the traditional accrediting program to carefully catalog resources to diagnose programs that could be changed. His suggestions showed that the two accrediting approaches were not only compatible, but strengthened each other.

Pennoyer saw outcomes accreditation as an "outstanding opportunity" to improve schools, because it promised to revitalize and energize the staff as well as to transform the school culture by refocusing its purpose to student learning possibilities. Outcomes accreditation accomplished these things by empowering faculty and administrators "to take charge of the school improvement program." Thomas Guskey of the University of Kentucky School of Education claimed the Commission's outcomes accrediting program was "the most powerful and significant reform effort taking place in our country today."

Guskey omitted the modifier "potential." As he noted in his keynote address at the 1991 NCA annual meeting, and other authors also have recognized, some big obstacles stood in the way of realizing the full potential of the OA model. Guskey suggested the greatest stumbling block was the strong support for traditional, basic beliefs about learning and education that conflicted with the stress on outcomes. Contributing to the problem was the frustration that accompanied the lack of knowledge about the new program. But he acknowledged such frustration was a normal part of change. Much more important, he warned, was the prospect of having these factors rob OA of its vitality, leading educators to believe that outcome accreditation was "a mere sequence of activities to perform and mark off on a checklist."[54]

Pennoyer's warning could be applied to any transitional phase, but it contained a striking irony, too. Many of the same criticisms had been voiced before, helping stimulate the reforms of the 1930s and the early 1960s. Similar claims about the revitalizing character and continual improvement aspects of earlier reforms were repeated almost verbatim in the OA literature. The recurring admonitions to guard against a lackluster effort identified an endemic problem that, over time, threatened any innovations. After the idea and promise of the "new" energized and excited people, this mood slowly dissipated as what was once novel became routine, resulting in apathy.[55]

Initially, the OA program did offer schools a realistic chance at renewal, as the experience of Mount Clemens High School in Michigan showed.[56] For Principal Wayne C. Ries, the NCA outcomes accreditation program was an opportunity to implement ideas he had long held regarding school administration. "Several years ago, I had begun my tenure as a high school principal with a number of lofty goals," he explained, "including the use of participative management." His beliefs had been nurtured throughout his education. As an engineering student, Ries studied industrial psychology and became familiar with the work of Norman Meier at two Michigan companies. His graduate work in educational administration and his later professional development allowed Ries to develop his ideas on participatory management. But during his tenure as a principal, Ries met strong resistance when he tried to apply what he had learned by seeking to involve department chairs in decision making. Typically, he received two negative responses. The first was: "Why don't you make the decision? You're the principal." The second showed a marked resistance to change: "We're doing okay; if it ain't broke don't fix it." This latter answer came in response to Ries' efforts to become involved with the effective schools movement.

In the late 1980s, a fortunate confluence of developments finally provided Ries with the opportunity to practice his theories. Following a pattern evident in many other places, the Mount Clemens school district underwent a complete reorganization that included the hiring of a new superintendent, deputy superintendent, and business manager. According to Ries, these changes caused "considerable anguish" among the staff. Teacher Linda Petros suggested the impact was much greater: "Mount Clemens High School was a school in need of a massive dose of improvement and morale enhancement for students and staff in the fall of 1988." By chance, 1988 also was near the end of the NCA visitation cycle, meaning the school was to engage in a year of self-study in preparation for a team visit. In preparation for the task, Ries asked his NCA team cochairs to go to the state NCA conference. While there, they attended a session on outcomes accreditation that became, in Petros' opinion, "the spark which led to a three-year renewal of school and staff." Ries recalled that cochairs Petros and G. Douglas Sutherland returned very excited about the OA opportunity, but showed some hesitation because it would be led by the teachers and driven by the staff. Such ideas fit well with Ries' beliefs, and those of new superintendent Blanche Fraser, who had begun the effective school process districtwide. Seeing connections to the OA process, she agreed to support the effort.

The first step involved increasing the knowledge of the staff and administration to gain support for participating in an OA school improvement program. To make the decision, the Mount Clemens faculty needed to know about OA, the effective schools program, and outcomes-based education. Six staff members conducted research on "effective Schools, agenda planning, team building, and conflict resolution training." Five half-day information sessions were held to build support and ensure commitment. Fraser provided one half-day per month to work on the program. In addition, staff members gave up either a preparation hour or devoted time before or after school to learn about OA. Equally important, the administration accepted site-based decision making, while the staff agreed it was accountable for the process. During this preparatory phase, the steering committee made a number of independent decisions, because of the lack of a "cookbook." For example, building upon successful past experience, the committee changed the recommended NCA sequencing to small groups and presentations.

The OA process was organized into a series of interrelated phases, beginning with identification and organization. Small group brainstorming sessions identified school strengths and weaknesses. A list was produced and distributed to teachers, facilitating the move to planning improvements. Next, the list of possible outcomes contained in the NCA handbook was distributed to the staff. Each member chose five outcomes they wanted to include in the assessment. Petros noted the results were predictable, as the choices included reading, writing, mathematics, courtesy, and respect. The work was then organized into various committees. Staff members selected three non-ranked committee assignments from the five target areas and two more options, student profile and mission. Committee staffing took account of "departments, race/ethnicity, gender, enthusiastic people, and staff members who tended to be obstructionists." A steering committee member acted as a liaison to each working committee.

A pivotal part of the OA process is the establishment of target goals. The Mount Clemens staff experienced difficulties with this phase. They probably started the process too early and exhibited some confusion over the distinction between goals and objectives. Once the student profile committee provided the information it had collected, the task became easier. Having a more accurate idea of student performance allowed the committees to draft a "simple goal statement, rationale, and objectives." Petros reported the discussion during this period was "interesting." Her mention of the use of conflict resolution techniques to reach a consensus indicates "heated" more accurately described the discussions.

After the goals were set and a NCA team approved the progress made at Mount Clemens, the focus shifted to building an information base to use in developing the plan. Establishing baseline data was the first task. Capitalizing on a staff member's computer expertise and Ries' statistical background, a program was developed to disaggregate the data in common terms. Using this information, the goals and objectives of each committee were revised to reflect conditions more accurately. During this period, each committee conducted a statewide library search for pertinent literature. Copies of the research materials were attached to each committee's strategy page to enhance the general and specific knowledge of the staff. This practice also built a large and accessible resource library of sorts.

The development of the plan revolved around organizing the findings of the various committees. Each committee presented a report that included its top priorities. The steering committee modified the priorities and integrated them into an overall plan. Implementation began with reading and then moved to writing and mathematics. Each stage of the implementation featured in-service and follow-up activities.

In assessing the OA experience, Ries, Sutherland, and Petros showed how the new program could affect a school. Ries explained that his role evolved into that of a facilitator and colleague, thus allowing realization of his long-stymied ideas on administration. In reflecting upon the criterion for OA, he explained, "The venture is dependent on the ownership found through working together as colleagues towards common goals." Sutherland supported Ries, likening school improvement to football. Both required teamwork, some taking of risks, and time to build a strong program. Sutherland also commented on the need to accept the inevitability of change, calling the "'If-it-ain't-broke-don't-fix-it' mentality...complacency at its worst." In concluding, he noted, "Once the need for change is accepted by educators, then the planning, the risk taking, the restructuring, and the retraining will come about through public education. School improvement will result."

Where Ries and Sutherland focused more on the results, Petros probed into the process. She described the Mount Clemens experience as "a roller coaster ride through a maze," involving much revisiting and revising of work that "helped establish ownership." Though confronting many obstacles and setbacks, the staff confidence and possession of the outcomes assessment process grew stronger as reform proceeded and knowledge grew. She also highlighted the key role played by planning. "We have come to realize that creating the plan to fit our school, staff, and community was the reason for our initial success." Petros concluded the OA provided the motivation behind the effort.

Further development of the COS accreditation program continued in the early 1990s. In conjunction with the American College Testing service, the Commission developed a transitions accreditation model to measure student success as they make the transition from one school level to another or from school to work. Full implementation at all school levels was expected to occur in 1996.[57]

THE COMMISSION ON SCHOOLS–STATE GOVERNMENT RELATIONSHIP

The outcomes accreditation program arose during a period of greater state involvement in education, particularly regarding student achievement. But, the development of the OA accreditation model was influenced less by state pressure than by the trends in school reform. Beginning in the late 1980s and early 1990s, however, state departments of education, often propelled by legislative mandates, became much more involved in what were traditionally NCA activities. The intrusion of the state agencies did not lead to acrimonious conflicts as had occurred at the higher education level. In virtually every instance, friendly, frequently close cooperation characterized the relations between the state and the Commission on Schools. Still, the COS did experience a transformation in its role, its status, and, to a lesser extent, its relationship with the states. The Commission became more integrated into the public realm, and so was subject to outside influences in a much greater and more sustained way than in the past. Because the COS situation was profoundly shaped by historical forces and long-standing traditional relationships, the Commission on Schools experience was unique.

Historical events dating back to the nation's earliest days affected school accreditation. Based on the recognition that a republic required a literate, informed citizenry, the Founding Fathers of the United States had provided for public education even before the adoption of the Constitution. The Land Ordinances of the 1780s firmly established the state as the legal authority for the administration of the schools, and the federal government as the power that supplied the wherewithal to create a public education system through land grants. Constitutional interpretations of the tenth amendment reserved all powers for the states not specifically delegated to the national government, further supporting the policy of education as the state's domain.[58] The idea of local autonomy, whether applied to state relations with the federal government, or communities in their interaction with the states, initially evolved as a practical necessity. As public education developed in the nineteenth century, logistics of transportation and communication required leaving much of the daily responsibility for running the schools to local communities.

Autonomy on the local level did not always mean lack of state interest in the schools, though oversight policies varied from state to state. In Michigan, the influence of the French model led to the idea of a unified system capped by a state university that had the responsibility for overseeing the schools. In the 1870s, the issue of college admissions prompted the University of Michigan to develop the certificate program. Secondary schools could gain university admission for their graduates by having university inspectors visit them and then certify their quality. The certificate system spread quickly through the West and offered an alternative to the college-admission-by-examination program popular along the eastern seaboard.[59]

The early actions by the government, the states, and the universities set the pattern in which the COS as an independent arm of a voluntary association later functioned. The inspection of schools for college admission or for other reasons paved the way for accreditation. The NCA accrediting system was largely grafted onto existing inspection programs operated by universities or state departments of education. A major consultant to the original NCA schools accreditation effort was University of Michigan inspector Allen S. Whitney. An early NCA president was George Aiton, state inspector of high schools for Minnesota. The final version of the first NCA standards acknowledged the Association's debt to contemporary inspection efforts, and set up the partnership that later grew between the COS and the states. The last standards explained that NCA inspectors would be individuals employed in that capacity by the state university or state government. Only where no state inspection authority existed would the Association appoint an inspector. The use of state inspectors also identified the points of contact between the NCA and the states while showing the variations that existed in inspection programs. In Michigan and Illinois, for example, state university faculty inspected schools. In Minnesota, inspection was the responsibility of the state department of education.

The historical development of public education, inspection, and eventually the NCA accrediting connection followed a different path than was true of voluntary association-government relations. After World War II, the relationship between many voluntary associations and government changed. It largely revolved around new uses of such organizations by the federal government, though increasing activism by the states also affected some associations, including the NCA. But the NCA accreditation of schools exhibited a different pattern, both in terms of longevity and interaction. The Association relied on the states to perform organizational functions. From the beginning, then, the relationship had quasi-public, quasi-governmental implications. In conjunction with the ongoing development of the NCA schools accreditation program, school inspectors became Commission on Schools state directors. These individuals actually had a dual employment status. They not only worked for the COS; they also held symbolic or real positions in a state university or state education agency, with their paychecks coming from the state or the university.

In 1995, thirteen NCA state directors are sponsored by universities, with the director enjoying a faculty or administrative position. Missouri state director Robert Shaw is employed as a faculty member by the University of Missouri, with 50 percent of his time going to NCA duties. In Illinois, Jerry Loyet works out of the University of Illinois at Urbana Office of Academic Policy Analysis. His official title is University Coordinator of School and College Relations/NCA State Director, but most of his duties are related to the NCA. State education departments sponsor the remaining seven NCA offices and employ the state director, whose Association responsibilities are part of the overall job description. For example, Nebraska state director Gerald Jordan's NCA appointment is part of the job description of his position with the state's department of education.[60]

An intriguing aspect of the school Commission state director-
ship is that universities and state agencies bid for sponsorship and
the Commission makes the final decision. In a sense, the state
serves the Association. In practice, however, the situation is less
clearly defined.[61] Most NCA state directors agree that the Commission enjoys a collaborative relationship with the states. The hous-
ing of the office and the employment status of the director
institutionalize the cooperative relationship. The type of relationship also creates very different stances regarding the role and function of the Commission, providing a system of checks and balances
to ensure that neither the state nor the university representatives
move beyond the established boundaries of the relationship.
Robert Shaw observed that directors in state education departments often assume a more regulatory approach, often attempting
to have the NCA follow the policies of their state. Conversely, uni-
versity-based directors advocate the nonregulatory stances supported by their institutions and the Association. Solving any
problems that arise typically involves clarifying roles that might
become confused due to the nature of employment. Many potential problems are alleviated, because all parties recognize the
supremacy of the state in educational matters. Unlike at the higher
education level, the NCA acknowledges the authority of the state
to regulate education, and also asserts that the Association will not
perform such services. Because the same person often represents
the state and the Association, and due to the long, historical tradition of cooperation, fewer disputes arise.[62]

State actions can, however, threaten the viability of the NCA.
Increased activism in the 1960s led the Commission to consider
leaving accrediting functions to the states. In the last few years, the
impact of educational reform has created vexing problems for
some state offices. Before 1987, accreditation in Indiana was almost
totally the purview of the NCA. Following a general trend of
greater state activism as part of the reform movement, the state
introduced its own accrediting program that led many schools to
question the value of NCA membership. The issue, as state director
Nancy Carey explained, was the resulting overlap of doing two separate self-studies for two different agencies that involved a great
deal of time and energy. Since the Indiana state office was univer-
sity-based, the institutional tie with the state was less firm. Carey

noted her state committee had "weathered the storm" by designing a self-study process that met the needs of the state and the NCA. The new process was developed collaboratively by Carey and the director of state accreditation during the 1992–1993 school year. In addition, to enhance communication and cooperation, the Indiana state accrediting director now serves on the NCA state committee.[63]

West Virginia faced a similar situation. In the state committee's 1991 self-study, the long relationship with the West Virginia Department of Education was called "a major strength to both organizations." In the 1980s, court rulings followed by legislative and administrative state actions created a separate government accrediting process. School principals expressed their frustration because of the increased time and effort required to comply with two separate accrediting processes. However, strong NCA support did not threaten membership, as had happened in Indiana. As happened in Indiana, the West Virginia NCA state committee and state education department cooperatively developed a common and mutually acceptable program.[64] In both Indiana and West Virginia, as well as in other states, the Commission on Schools drew upon long-standing ties with state agencies to devise acceptable solutions to the intrusion of state government on traditional Association activities. Interestingly, the same collaborative process characterized responses from NCA offices in universities and state agencies.

Other developments in Indiana and West Virginia show that funding issues pose serious threats to the NCA and presage hard times. As part of the budget cutbacks evident throughout higher education, Indiana University dropped all service functions in 1992, leaving the NCA state office without a sponsor. Indiana State University successfully bid for the sponsorship, but the question of adequate funding in a time of reduced resources remains a problem. For offices in state education departments, similar difficulties have arisen. The shrinking support for the state education agency in West Virginia translated into reduced funding for the NCA state office. NCA state director Philip Thornton explained that his office no longer performed its functions adequately, but solving the funding dilemma seemed an impossible task. He noted that budget deficits in many school districts eliminated the option of raising dues and fees, since the end result would be reduced membership. As of June 1994, no solution to the shortfall had been proposed.[65]

The above discussion indicates that the Commission on Schools had little trouble acclimating to the changing role and nature of voluntary associations. The Commission's institutionalized relations with the state governments eliminated the stressful adjustments the CIHE experienced. What was new and different for some voluntary associations was historical and traditional for the Commission on Schools. Other factors also eased the transition. The decentralized structure of education and the COS determined that responses were local and flexible, rather than national and strictly conforming as was true in higher education. Within the context of NCA policies and procedures, the COS could respond differently to the needs of each state and its schools rather than try to accommodate all parties with a single program. The public, educational, NCA, and governmental consensus on the supremacy of the state also eliminated a major controversy over authority.

Still, the future poses serious problems to the cooperative relationships enjoyed by the COS and the states. The decline in funding threatens the ability of schools, the NCA state offices, and the states to perform their functions satisfactorily, particularly in the face of various reform initiatives, including those mandated by referendum, legislation, or the courts. Cooperation may lessen some difficulties, but facing budget restraints is likely to vex all concerned with education in the future. The dominance of questions over answers in the present and the seemingly overnight changes in attitudes indicates that the only certainty about the immediate future is its uncertainty. For example, in April 1993, North Dakota state director Ronald Stastney warned that increased federal funding to the states probably meant more state reforms and more regulation from Washington.[66] Two years later, Congress seems to be moving in the opposite direction, cutting education funding and eliminating federal regulation. Whether the same trend will prevail two years from now is open to conjecture.

EPILOGUE

Gazing back over the last one hundred years of the North Central Association, it certainly seems a long, strange, and often remarkable trip. Amid all the turbulence, the strident criticism, the internal and external pressures trying to pull the organization in various directions, and the numerous crises, the NCA has not only survived, but even thrived, and grown stronger. The Association's organizational fortitude has been most remarkable. And that, of course, begs the question, Why?

Past presidents at 1966 Annual Meeting. (standing, l. to r.) Norman Burns, Association Secretary; Stephen A. Romine, 1961; T. H. Broad, 1959; Marvin C. Knudson, 1966; R. Nelson Snider, 1947; Irwin J. Lubbers, 1963; J. Fred Murphy, 1962; Clyde Vroman, 1965; L. A. Van Dyke, 1967; (sitting, l. to r.) J. Edgar Stonecipher, 1956; John R. Emens, 1948; Edgar G. Johnston, 1955.

One way to make sense of the NCA experience is to focus on recurring themes that unfolded throughout its history. One major theme has been the continuing need of the Association to confront change. From accrediting's inception in the early 1900s to the present, all of the theories and practices of NCA accreditation have revolved around the quest to make continual change an integral part of accrediting and its organizational development. The goal was to maintain the organization's relevance and effectiveness by keeping up with the continually developing state of educational thought and practice. This underlying notion of the dynamic character of education and the Association found early expression in the NCA debates over the nature of education generally and the process orientation of problem solving, in particular. "Whoever thinks that any educational problem is permanently solved deludes himself and misleads others," advised Charles A. Thurber

of the University of Chicago in 1898, "for problems of education...
are, and always must be in process of solution."[67] The history of
the NCA has revolved around the belief that problem solving is a
continuing process. In this regard, the Association's success in
keeping up with changes in education has made it an organization
always in tune with, if not ahead of, its time.

Accepting change as a desirable constant has raised stiff challenges to the organization, even though it sought to accommodate
such a belief. Maintenance of policies, norms, and values over
time, as well as the development of an administrative structure and
procedures, among other things, requires stability. The pursuit of
change can severely destabilize or doom even the strongest organization. At several times in its history, the NCA has stood at a crossroads where its existence was hotly debated.

The Association's ability to surmount the various difficulties
that emerged was due to another recurring theme, its strong continuity with the past. Continuity has had more to do with a sense of
tradition than with history or memory. New generations of NCA
activists have often seized upon seemingly fresh and bold solutions
that, unbeknownst to them, had been proposed by their forebears,
sometimes more than once. For example, outcomes evaluation is
an old notion revived to meet current needs, though few current
advocates, if any, are fully aware of its heritage. At the centennial
meeting, a brief booklet enumerating the firsts of the NCA was distributed. Many attending the celebration who read the accounts,
taken from Calvin Davis' history of the NCA's first fifty years, were
surprised by the Association's past accomplishments.

While the historical record is largely unknown to NCA members, the same is hardly true of the Association's tradition. Century-
old, fundamental beliefs and principles that comprise the NCA tradition have steadfastly guided the Association on its hundred-year
journey through turbulent times. Though the environment grew
more complex and expanded, the tradition remained circum-
scribed and stable, offering clear and surprisingly narrow direction.
The NCA philosophy that saw change as a constant and problem
solving as a process dictated the impermanence and imperfection
of all policies and actions, stimulating the organization to adapt
several times and re-create itself to meet commitments to members. How the Association serves its members has changed over

Bill Clinton. Then governor Clinton was keynote speaker at two NCA Annual Meetings.

time, but the principle of commitment has resisted all pressures to alter the organization's primary allegiance, including the potent calls of the government. A cornerstone of member commitment is the principle of the full participation of members in decision making. The NCA is a unique hybrid that combines egalitarian republican and participatory democratic government practices. While representatives develop plans and make decisions, their actions are often guided by surveys and other means of receiving feedback from the general membership.

Underlying the philosophy of change and the commitment to members are the two purposes of the North Central Association. Initially, the explicit goal was to improve relations between secondary schools and colleges. This original purpose was actually a means to meet the implicit goal of improving the quality of education. The confusion of college admission requirements that created chaos in the curriculum was connected to inadequate relations that, in turn, were seen as negatively affecting the constructive development of education. The NCA founders focused on relations because the first step in instilling some order into the chaos—and thereby improving the quality of education—was founding an organization that enhanced communication and cooperation by bringing secondary school and college figures together to discuss issues of common concern. Once the dialogue started, the emphasis quickly shifted to action, leading to accreditation that sought improvement of educational institutions.

Currently, the explicit NCA purpose remains improving education.[68] Conversely, the bettering of relations is now an implied goal, and relates not only to educational institutions but to the Association's Commission as well. A recent survey of Colorado COS members underscored the need for a strong school-college relationship. Of the twelve suggestions for the future, eight involved schools and universities working together. In some cases, the context was NCA activities, but other survey respondents mentioned teacher education and identifying high school students with graduate education possibilities.[69]

Commission relations have also improved. Officials in both NCA accrediting groups have recognized the need to improve communications and have collaborated on several projects. NCA president Charles Lindly, the Wyoming state director, began the process by calling a meeting for December 6 and 7, 1990, on school-college relations attended by representatives of both Commissions.[70] In the early 1990s, annual planning conferences brought the NCA board of directors and higher education and schools Commission representatives and professional staff together to discuss issues of mutual concern. Held in Scottsdale, Arizona, November 1993, the first planning conference examined peer review. The topic of the November 1994 session in Albuquerque, New Mexico, was legal issues facing accreditation organizations.[71] Planning for the NCA centennial was another cooperative undertaking that reminded members why the NCA exists. The centennial planning committee chaired by Dean Mary Ann Carroll of Indiana State University was composed of representatives of both Commissions and professional staff members.

The commitment of various Association members and the professional staffs of the Commissions to the Association strengthened the cooperative efforts, including the centennial celebration. Kenneth Gose, executive director of the COS, and Patricia Thrash, executive director of the CIHE, have devoted much time and

Charles Lindly. Wyoming state director,
NCA Commission on Schools, Lindly was
president of the Association, 1990–91.

energy to better relations. Former Illinois state director and NCA president John Kemp worked closely with the CIHE staff on centennial matters. Perhaps the most active figures working for cooperation were Susan Van Kollenburg, CIHE associate director for programs and member services, and Cathy Baird, COS assistant executive director. They planned the various activities geared to bringing the Commissions together.

The complementary mix of change and continuity has been the dynamic behind the development of the NCA. From this perspective, the history of the organization has revolved around the attempt to improve the quality of education by bettering relations between schools and colleges. The Association's development has been guided by an immutable tradition of member commitment and a philosophy of the constancy and desirability of change that has allowed the organization to re-create itself in order to to maintain its relevancy and effectiveness. In part, success depended on balancing the pressures for change with those seeking continuity.

But change and continuity do not fully illuminate the NCA story. Another recurring theme that predates the organization's founding has also been at work. This book opened with the notion that the tendencies toward individuality and similarity drove the development of education after the Civil War, creating the problems that the NCA was founded to solve. These tendencies did not just disappear after 1895. Rather, they continued to spark criticism and reform. The criticism in the early 1970s suggesting that accreditation raised obstacles to experimentation was a familiar refrain. It was raised at the initiation of accrediting, and similar complaints in the twenties stimulated the reforms that developed the self-study-based reforms of the following decade. Perhaps the most repeated statement made by NCA officials over the years has been that the Association is dedicated to preserving institutional individuality—another unchanging organization principle.

What was originally an external condition has been internalized into the fabric of NCA life. The stresses created by the commitment to individuality and the need for similarity have contributed the difficulties the organization has encountered, though often they have become manifest in strikingly different ways. Where, at times, the Association has been attacked for inhibiting institutional individuality, it emerged as a champion of the right of institutions to freely develop during the most recent crisis with the federal government. At a different level, the increasing functional structure of the Association, particularly the current autonomy of the accrediting Commissions, has worked against the cohesiveness of the organization. Virtually everyone interviewed for this book made the same comment in almost exactly the same words, "The commissions are very different. The work they do is so different."

Since the Association has been robbed of all power and exists solely as symbol of unity, why maintain it? Tradition plays a role, as does name recognition status, and the respect the NCA commands. But there are two more underlying principles that have bonded the organization together. The first tenet precipitated the creation of the organization. Much as the problems of that time required concerted action by schools and colleges, so the difficulties arising one hundred years later also need cooperative action. The second tenet was initially stated by William Rainey Harper in 1896 when he welcomed the delegates attending the first NCA annual meeting. Noting the increasing individuality evident in education, he also observed that all the individual institutions sought the same thing. That message resonates today and was repeated at the hundredth annual meeting by incoming president Mary Ann Carroll. The pursuit of a common goal explains why the Association was formed and why it remains a vital force in education today. As the book opened with Harper's original statement of this recurring theme, so Mary Ann Carroll's version one hundred years later provides a good place to end:

> Schools and Colleges share common purposes, too, and thus could be stronger and more effective if a closer alliance were formed between all levels of formal education. It does not matter that our commissions function differently; it does not matter that our learners are of different ages; it does not matter that the curricular content of our educational units is different. What matters is that we share a common goal.[72]

Mary Ann Carroll. Director of Governmental Relations and Assistant to the President at Rose-Hulman Institute in Indiana, Carroll was a member of the CIHE Commission, chair of the Centennial Committee, and president of the Association, 1995–96.

NOTES

1. Manning, "Regional Accreditation at the Crossroads: Challenges and Directions for the Future," 108. In 1991, Manning was president of the Council on Postsecondary Accreditation.

2. Allan O. Pfnister, "Regional Accreditation at the Crossroads: A Historical Perspective," in ibid., 108. Pfnister noted a similar crossroads situation existed in 1917 and was the subject of an earlier article. See Allan O. Pfnister, "Regional Accrediting Agencies at the Crossroads," *Journal of Higher Education* 42 (October 1971). The crossroads theme was covered in the 1991 collection of papers that contained the articles by Manning, Pfnister, and others.

3. Patricia Thrash, "Regional Accreditation at the Crossroads," 1991 NCA Annual Meeting announcement (1990).

4. On the role of municipalities in Progressive reform, see George E. Mowry, *The Era of Theodore Roosevelt and the Birth of Modern America, 1900–1912* (New York: Harper & Row, 1958), 59–106; and Bradley R. Rice, *Progressive Cities: The Commission Government Movement* (Austin: University of Texas Press, 1977).

5. William A. Goddard, in *Summary Report on Invitational Conference on Accreditation and the Protection of the Student as Consumer* (Washington, D.C.: U.S. Office of Education, 1978). The NCA was one of the cosponsors of this conference.

6. In May 1971, John R. Proffitt, director of the Accreditation and Institutional Eligibility Staff of the U.S. Office of Education, wrote Norman Burns about "the increasingly troublesome problem which degree mills are presenting." Letter, John R. Proffitt to Norman Burns, May 6, 1917. Apparently, the rapid and uncontrolled proliferation of postsecondary education had created favorable conditions for unscrupulous people to exploit the demand for educational services.

7. Regarding the publication of degree mills, Stameshkin cited a future *NCA Quarterly* article as an example, explaining that the authors could only list common traits of bogus institutions, since providing names, places, and dates could lead to libel suits, even if the claims were accurate. Letter, Anne Stameshkin to Edward Carr, February 2, 1971.

8. John Ellis, cited in the Advisory Committee on Accreditation and Institutional Eligibility and the Division of Eligibility and Agency Evaluation, *The Federal Government's Relationship to the Nationally Recognized Accrediting Agencies* (Washington, D.C.: GPO, 1977), 3. This publication contains the proceedings of a conference held June 14 and 15, 1977. Ellis offered the keynote speech.

9. Charles N. Chambers, "Characteristics of An Accrediting Body," in Kenneth E. Young, Charles M. Chambers, H. R. Kells, and Associates, *Understanding Accreditation* (San Francisco: Jossey-Bass Publishers, 1983), 138.

10. Short statement by Terrell Bell, U.S. Commissioner of Education before the Permanent Subcommittee on Investigations, Committee on Government Operations, U.S. Senate, November 20, 1975; copy in NCA archives. Ellis' statement in 1977 indicated the problem continued to grow. Developments in the late 1980s and early 1990s also show that little progress was made in solving the student loan default problem.

11. Richard M. Millard, "Postsecondary Education and 'The Best Interests of the People of the States,'" *Journal of Higher Education* 50 (March/April 1979): 134. While the NCA community was not this expansive, chapter 5 showed that its membership also expanded greatly.

12. Patricia Thrash, "Accreditation: A Perspective," *Journal of Higher Education* 50 (March/April 1979): 118; Ronald S. Pugsley quoted Richard Millard as listing nine publics. See Ronald S. Pugsley, "The Consumer Interest in Voluntary Accreditation, *North Central Association Quarterly* 51 (Spring 1977): 354; Barbara Uehling, "Accreditation and the Institution," *North Central Association Quarterly* 62 (Fall 1987): 352.

13. Uehling, "Accreditation and the Institution," *North Central Association Quarterly* 62 (Fall 1987): 352; Gordon K. Davies, "Accreditation and Society," *North Central Association Quarterly* 62 (Fall 1987): 384. See also Pugsley, "The Consumer Interest in Voluntary Accreditation," Goddard, *Summary Report on Invitational Conference on Accreditation and the Protection of the Student as Consumer.*

14. See Proffitt and Binker, "The U.S. Office of Education's Role in Supporting Accreditation in the United States"; and the statement of John Ellis in the Advisory Committee on Accreditation and Institutional Eligibility and the Division of Eligibility and Agency Evaluation, *The Federal Government's Relationship to the Nationally Recognized Accrediting Agencies*, 2.

15. Thurston E. Manning, "Are the Secretary's Intentions Honorable?" *Academe* (July-August 1988): 13; Fred Harcleroad, "Accreditation: Voluntary Enterprise," in Young et al, *Understanding Accreditation*, 50. On the use of private associations to perform public tasks, see David Sills, "Voluntary Associations: Sociological Aspects," 375; Harland Bloland, *Higher Education in a Decentralized State*, 28–30, and the discussion in this book's preface.

16. Harcleroad, "Accreditation: Voluntary Enterprise," 51.

17. Pugsley, "The Consumer Interest in Voluntary Accreditation," 354–56, 359–60. The 1976 court case was *Marlboro Corporation d/b/a Emery School v. Association of Independent Colleges and Schools.*

18. James D. Koerner, "Who Benefits from Accreditation: Special Interests or the Public?" in *Seminar: Accreditation and the Public Interest* (Washington, D.C.: U.S. Office of Education and the National Commission on Accrediting, 1970). The draft copy of the Newman report on "Accreditation and Institutional Eligibility" was not published though Ronald Pugsley claimed it was widely circulated privately. The contents of the article and the interpretation are taken from Pugsley, "The Consumer Interest in Voluntary Accreditation," 355–56. The economic aspects of accreditation are explored in detail in Erika Georges, "The Economics of Accreditation,

unpublished Ph.D. dissertation, UCLA, 1977. Georges' analysis, like those of other critics, often adopted an extremely narrow focus that made its conclusions highly questionable.

19. Harold Orlans, cited in Pugsley, "The Consumer Interest in Voluntary Accreditation," 359.

20. Ibid., 357–58. In 1972, 47 such agencies had secured USOE recognition. Interestingly, Ronald Pugsley noted the criticisms of accrediting had largely ignored the gatekeeping function.

21. Semrow, *In Quest of Quality*, 122.

22. Pugsley, "The Consumer Interest in Voluntary Accreditation," 357–58.

23. Letter, Norman Burns to John Proffitt, April 5, 1974, with attached "Commission Position on Relations with the Accreditation and Institutional Eligibility Staff."

24. Letters Terrell H. Bell to Joseph Semrow, November 5, 1974; Terrell H. Bell to Ted Manning, June 23, 1975; Ted Manning to Terrell H. Bell, July 11, 1975.

25. *Summary Report on Invitational Conference on Accreditation and the Protection of the Student as Consumer.*

26. See, for example, Pugsley, "The Consumer Interest in Voluntary Accreditation," 361; Richard Millard, "Role of Accreditation to the States and the Federal Government," *North Central Association Quarterly* 62 (Fall 1987): 374; N. Edd Miller, "Synthesis," during the recent crisis with the federal government, *Recognized Accrediting Agencies*, 57. See the comments of Thurston Manning in *Summary Report on Invitational Conference on Accreditation and the Protection of the Student as Consumer.* A 1977 conference on the relationship of the federal government to accreditation raised similar issues, showing wide disagreement over many aspects of the triad relationship.

27. Virginia Helms, "What Is the Eligibility Triad and What Is It Doing to Accreditation?" *North Central Association Quarterly* 57 (Spring 1983): 401. A partial list of the numerous meetings is included in Proffitt and Binker, "The U.S. Office of Education's Role in Supporting Accreditation in the United States." See also the conference report, *The Federal Government's Relationship to the National Recognized Accrediting Agencies.*

28. Letter, Sr. Mary Janet McGilley to Ted Manning, October 1, 1987, reprinted in *Briefings* 5 (November 1987): 3. The italics are in the letter. At the time, McGilley was president of St. Mary's College.

29. Patricia A. Thrash, "Annual Report," special insert to *Briefings* 6 (March 1988): 4. See also, "Proposed USDE Regulations: A Progress Report," ibid., 5.

30. "Agency Reports: The Regionals," *Briefing* 8 (November 1990): 9; Patricia A. Thrash, "Notes from the Executive Director: Current Federal Concerns," *Briefing* 9 (Fall 1991): 6.

31. Patricia A. Thrash, "An Uncommon Alliance," *Selected Papers from the 1988 Annual Meeting: Special Insert to the July 1988 Briefing*, *Briefing* 6

(July 1988): 5; Patricia A. Thrash, "Annual Report of the Executive Director," *Special Insert to the March 1989 Briefing, Briefing 7* (March 1989): 6.

32. Meeting packet for "Forum on the Potential Impact of the Department of Education's Proposed Recognition Requirements," December 21, 1993, Chicago, Illinois.

33. "Challenges to Higher Education Act and Proposal to Create a New Organization for Accreditation Reach Critical Stages," *Briefing* 13 (June 1995):1; Patricia Thrash, "Report from the Executive Director," ibid., 7.

34. "USDE Triad Coordinating Group Meets in Washington, D.C.," ibid., 1.

35. "Regionals Issue Statement of Intent to Form Independent Organization," *Briefing* 11 (May 1993): 2; "A Statement of Intent by the Directors of the Nine Regional Accrediting Commissions," ibid., 3; interview, Patricia Thrash, Chicago, Illinois.

36. Glenn Niemeyer, "Sustaining a Tradition of Excellence," Selected Papers from the 1995 Annual Meeting of the North Central Association, insert to *Briefing* 13 (June 1995): 5.

37. The General Institutional requirements were considered the threshold requirements for membership eligibility. They were supplemented by Criteria for Accreditation that were met to gain or maintain membership. Semrow, *In Search of Quality,* 128–29.

38. "Commission Appoints Committee on Critical Issues," *Briefing* 9 (Fall 1991): 1, 4; "Critical Issues Committee Report," *Briefing* 10 (March 1992): 1, 3; Interviews, Glenn Niemeyer and Morton Weir, March 18, 1993, Chicago, Illinois.

39. See, for example, the annual volumes of NCA Commission on Institutions of Higher Education, *A Collection of Papers on Self-Study and Institutional Improvement,* 1992, 1993, 1994. In addition, the following issues of the *North Central Association Quarterly* were devoted solely to assessment. "Sharpening the Focus on Assessment: The Regional and the NCA States," *North Central Association Quarterly* 65 (Fall 1990), and "Assessing Student Academic Achievement," *North Central Association Quarterly* 66 (Fall 1991). Patricia Thrash credits Roskens for transforming the annual meeting, Letter, Patricia Thrash to author, June 27, 1995.

40. The results of the high school survey were published in Diane Ravitch and Chester E. Finn, Jr., *What Do Our 17-Year-Olds Know?* (New York: Harper & Row, 1987). The college survey was conducted for the NEH by the Gallup Organization. See *A Survey of College Seniors: Knowledge of History and Literature* (Princeton, N.J.: The Gallup Organization, 1989), 33–57).

41. *Geography: An International Gallup Survey,* conducted for the National Geographic Society (Princeton, N.J.: The Gallup Organization, 1988), 43; Sharon Begley, "Scratch 'n' Sniff Science," *Newsweek,* special issue, 116 (September 1990): 28.

42. Lynne V. Cheney, *Humanities in America: A Report to the President, the Congress, and the American People* (Washington, D.C.: National Endowment for the Humanities, 1988); Allan Bloom, *The Closing of the American Mind*

(New York: Simon & Schuster, 1987); E. D. Hirsch, *Cultural Literacy* (Boston: Houghton Mifflin, 1987). Hirsch's thesis was supported by Carnegie Foundation president Ernest Boyer. In *College: The Undergraduate Experience*, published in 1986, Boyer complained that higher education had confused goals, disjointed career programs, and lacked a liberal arts core curriculum. See Ernest Boyer, *College: The Undergraduate Experience* (New York: Harper & Row, 1987).

43. A good introduction to multiculturalism in the larger context is in *Social Education* 56 (September 1992). The whole issue is devoted to multicultural education.

44. See, for example, Curriculum Task Force for the National Commissions on Social Studies in the Schools, *Charting a Course: Social Studies for the 21st Century* (1989). This project was jointly conducted by the American Historical Association, Carnegie Foundation for the Advancement of Teaching, National Council for the Social Studies, and Organization of American Historians.

45. John W. Wick, "Including Assessment of Student Outcomes in the School Accreditation and Evaluation Process," *North Central Association Quarterly* 59 (Spring 1985): 363–64.

46. Robert Armstrong, "OBE, Effective Schools and NCA's OA: Romance or Feud," *North Central Association Quarterly* 66 (Winter 1992): 522, 523–26; Robert Armstrong, "Review of Literature," ibid., 539. See also Linda L. Petros, "Outcomes Accreditation Motivates Improvement," ibid., 516.

47. "An Evaluation of the Accreditation Standards of the NCA Commission on Schools—By Teachers, Principals, and Superintendents," *North Central Association Quarterly* 57 (Spring 1983): 410, 416, 420, 421, 425, 426, 431.

48. Letter, John Kemp to author, June 6, 1995.

49. Armstrong, "OBE, Effective Schools and NCA's OA: Romance or Feud," 523–26; Linda L. Petros, "Outcomes Accreditation Motivates Improvement," ibid., 516; Thomas R. Guskey, "The Importance of Focusing on Student Outcomes," *North Central Association Quarterly* 66 (Winter 1992): 507. Reprint of his keynote speech. See also chapter 4, 123 and chapter 6, 235–36.

50. Letter, John Kemp to author, June 6, 1995.

51. "Assessing Student Outcomes: A Part of the School Self-Study," *North Central Association Quarterly* 60 (Summer 1985): 14.

52. Ibid., 15–20; Armstrong, "OBE, Effective Schools and NCA's OA: Romance or Feud?" 525.

53. Wick, "Including Assessment of Student Outcomes in the School Accreditation and Evaluation Process," 368–69.

54. John C. Pennoyer, "Combining the Strengths of the Old with the OA Model," *North Central Association Quarterly* 67 (Winter 1993): 361–63; Thomas Guskey, "The Importance of Focusing on Student Outcomes," 508.

55. See the pertinent discussions in chapters 4, 5, and 6.

56. The following account is taken from a series of three brief articles published under the heading "Outcomes Accreditation—Three Down Home Perspectives," in the *North Central Association Quarterly* 66 (Winter 1992). The articles are: G. Douglas Sutherland, "An Analogy," 513–15; Linda L. Petros, "Outcomes Accreditation Motivates Improvement," 516–18; and Wayne C. Ries, "A View from the Dugout," 519–21.

57. Letter, John Kemp to author, June 6, 1995.

58. For an early NCA affirmation of state authority, see George Carman, "Presidential Address."

59. See chapter 2 for details of the University of Michigan program.

60. Interviews, Robert Shaw, Chicago, Illinois, April 5, 1993; Gerald Jordan, Chicago, Illinois, April 6, 1993.

61. Following a recommendation of the 1970s suggesting the COS headquarters be on a university campus to take advantage of its facilities and personnel, the Commission was relocated on the Arizona State University campus in Tempe in 1989.

62. Interview, Robert Shaw.

63. Mail survey response, Nancy Carey, December 23, 1993.

64. West Virginia NCA State Committee, "Self-Study, Section I: Historical Perspective" (1991), included with mail survey response, Philip Thornton, West Virginia state director, June 15, 1994.

65. Mail survey responses, Nancy Carey, Philip Thornton.

66. Interview, Ronald Stastney, April 6, 1993, Chicago, Illinois.

67. NCA *Proceedings*, 1898, 38.

68. Regarding the implied goal of improving education, see A. F. Nightingale, "Presidential Address," NCA *Proceedings*, 1898, 7. The CIHE mission statement and the draft COS Vision are, respectively, in "The Culture of the Commission: The North Central Association's Commission on Institutions of Higher Education," December 1994; and draft "Vision, Mission, and Beliefs" statement, July 1995, enclosure in letter, Ken Gose to Patricia Thrash, July 7, 1995.

69. Kathryn Kirkpatrick and Edward Brainard, "Images for the NCA's Future: Perceptions in One State," *North Central Association Quarterly* 69 (Fall 1994 and Winter 1995): 331.

70. Cited in "Agency Reports: The Association," *Briefing* 9 (Spring 1991): 8.

71. "Voluntary Peer Review for the 21st Century: Keeping It on Track," NCA Board of Directors Planning Conference packet, Scottsdale, Arizona, November 11–13, 1993; "Legal Issues in Accreditation: Policy Implications for the Association and Its Commissions," NCA Board of Directors Fall Conference packet, Albuquerque, New Mexico, November 3–4, 1994.

72. Mary Ann Carroll, "Toward a Second Century," presidential address at the 1995 NCA Annual Meeting, March 29, 1995, reprinted in "Selected Papers from the 1995 Annual Meeting," 5.

Bibliography

THE MOST VALUABLE SOURCES consulted in the writing of this book were the publications or files of the North Central Association of Colleges and Schools. The chapter endnotes contain specific references for the NCA *Proceedings,* the *North Central Association Quarterly,* the *NCA Today, Briefings,* and numerous other documents. The two previous histories of the NCA also proved helpful. They are Calvin O. Davis, *The History of the North Central Association* (Ann Arbor: NCA, 1945), and Louis G. Geiger, *Voluntary Accreditation: A History of the North Central Association, 1945–1970* (Menasha, Wisconsin: George Banta Company for the North Central Association, 1970)

Outside works consulted are listed below.

ARCHIVES

Andrew Draper. Papers. University of Illinois (Urbana).
William Rainey Harper. Papers. University of Chicago.
Thomas Holgate. Papers. Northwestern University.
Charles H. Judd. Papers. University of Chicago.
North Central Association. Files. University of Illinois (Urbana) and University of Chicago.

BOOKS AND REPORTS

The Advisory Committee on Accreditation and Institutional Eligibility and the Division of Eligibility and Agency Evaluation. *The Federal Government's Relationship to the Nationally Recognized Accrediting Agencies.* Washington, D.C.: GPO, 1977.

Allen, Frederick Lewis. *Only Yesterday: An Informal History of the 1920s.* 1931. Reprint, New York: Harper & Row, Publishers, 1959.

Angell, James B. *Reminiscences.* Freeport, N.Y.: Books for Libraries Press, 1971, originally published 1911.

Bloland, Harland. *Associations in Action: The Washington D.C. Higher Education Community.* ASHE-ERIC Higher Education Report number 2.

Washington, D.C.: Association for the Study of Higher Education, 1985.

Bloland, Harland. *Higher Education Associations in a Decentralized Education System.* Berkeley: University of California Center for Research and Development, 1969.

Bloom, Allan. *The Closing of the American Mind.* New York: Simon & Schuster, 1987.

Boyer, Ernest. *College: The Undergraduate Experience.* New York: Harper & Row, 1987.

Brubacher, John S., and Willis Rudy. *Higher Education in Transition.* Rev. ed. New York: Harper & Row, 1968.

Bryce, Lord James. *The American Commonwealth.* Vol. 2. 1888. Rev. ed. New York: Macmillan, 1933.

Burstall, Sara. *Impressions of American Education in 1908.* London: Longmans, Green and Co., 1909.

Butler, Leslie A. *The Michigan Schoolmasters' Club.* Ann Arbor: University of Michigan, 1957.

Butler, Nicholas Murray, ed. *Education in the United States.* Albany, New York: J. B. Lyon, 1900.

Carnegie Commission on Higher Education. *Continuity and Discontinuity: Higher Education and the Schools.* Berkeley: Carnegie Commission on Higher Education, published by McGraw-Hill, 1973.

Chafe, William H. *The Unfinished Journey: America since World War II.* 2d ed. New York: Oxford University Press, 1991.

Cheit, Earl F. *The New Depression in Higher Education: A Study of Financial Conditions at 41 Colleges and Universities, A Report by the Carnegie Commission on Higher Education.* Berkeley: Carnegie Commission on Higher Education, 1972.

Cheney, Lynne V. *Humanities in America: A Report to the President, the Congress, and the American People.* Washington, D.C.: National Endowment for the Humanities, 1988.

Cowley, Malcolm. *Exile's Return.* New York: Viking Press, 1951.

Cremin, Lawrence. *The Transformation of the School: Progressivism in American Education, 1876–1957.* New York: Alfred A. Knopf, 1961.

Cronon, William. *Nature's Metropolis: Chicago and the Great West.* New York: W. W. Norton, 1991.

Curriculum Task Force for the National Commissions on Social Studies in the Schools. *Charting a Course: Social Studies for the 21st Century.* Washington, D.C.: National Council for the Social Studies, 1989.

Curti, Merle, and Roderick Nash. *Philanthropy in the Shaping of American Higher Education.* New Brunswick, N.J.: Rutgers University Press, 1965.

Dexter, Edwin G. *History of Education in the United States*. New York: Burt Franklin, 1906.

Drake, St. Clair, and Horace Cayton. *Black Metropolis: A Study of Negro Life in a Northern City*. Rev. ed. New York: Harper & Row, 1962.

Flink, James J. *The Car Culture*. Cambridge, Mass.: MIT Press, 1975.

Fosdick, Raymond B. *Adventure in Giving: The Story of the General Education Board*. New York: Harper & Row, 1962.

Ginger, Ray. *Six Days or Forever? Tennessee v. John Thomas Scopes*. Boston: Beacon Books, 1958.

Graham, Hugh. *The Uncertain Triumph: Federal Education Policy in the Kennedy and Johnson Years*. Chapel Hill: University of North Carolina Press, 1984.

Grossman, James R. *Land of Hope: Chicago, Black Southerners, and the Great Migration*. Chicago: University of Chicago Press, 1989.

Handlin, Oscar, and Mary Handlin. *The American College and American Culture*. Berkeley: Carnegie Commission on Higher Education, published by McGraw-Hill, 1970.

Harcleroad, Fred. *Voluntary Organizations in American and the Development of Educational Accreditation*. Washington, D.C.: Council on Postsecondary Accreditation, 1980.

Hawkins, Hugh. *Banding Together: The Rise of National Associations in American Higher Education, 1887–1950*. Baltimore: The Johns Hopkins University Press, 1992.

Hawley, Ellis. *The Great War and the Search for a Modern Order: A History of the American People and Their Institutions, 1917–1933*. 2d ed. New York: St. Martin's Press, 1992.

Henry, David D. *Challenges Past, Challenges Present: An Analysis of American Higher Education since 1930*. Berkeley: Carnegie Council on Policy Studies in Higher Education, published by Jossey-Bass Publishers, 1975.

Hirsch, E. D. *Cultural Literacy*. Boston: Houghton Mifflin, 1987.

International Encyclopedia of the Social Sciences. 1968.

Israel, Jerry, ed. *Building the Organizational Society*. New York: The Free Press, 1972.

Jackson, Kenneth T. *The Ku Klux Klan in the City, 1915–1930*. New York: Oxford University Press, 1967.

Kimberly, John. *The Organizational Life Cycle*. San Francisco: Jossey-Bass Publishers, 1982.

Kluger, Richard. *Simple Justice: The History of Brown v. Board of Education and Black America's Struggle for Equality*. New York: Alfred A. Knopf, 1976.

Krug, Edward. *The Shaping of the American High School*. Vol. 1, *1880–1920*. New York: Harper & Row, 1964.

———. *The Shaping of the American High School.* Vol. 2, *1920–1940.* Madison: University of Wisconsin Press, 1972.

Kursh, Harry. *The United States Office of Education: A Century of Service.* Philadelphia: Chilton Books, 1965.

Leuchtenberg, William. *The Perils of Prosperity, 1914–1932.* Chicago: University of Chicago Press, 1958.

Levine, David O. *The American College and the Culture of Aspiration, 1915–1940.* New York: Cornell University Press, 1986.

Ling, Peter J. *America and the Automobile: Technology, Reform, and Social Change.* New York: Manchester University Press, 1990.

Link, Arthur S., and William B. Catton. *American Epoch: A History of the United States since 1900.* Vol. 3, *1946–1973.* 4th ed. New York: Alfred A. Knopf, 1974.

Lynd, Robert S., and Helen Merrell Lynd. *Middletown: A Study of Modern American Culture.* New York: Harcourt, Brace & World, 1929.

MacDonald, J. Fred. *Don't Touch That Dial!* Chicago: Nelson-Hall, 1979.

Marchand, Rolland. *Advertising the American Dream: Making Way for Modernity, 1920–1940.* Berkeley: University of California Press, 1985.

Marsden, George M. *Fundamentalism and American Culture: The Shaping of 20th Century Evangelicalism, 1870–1925.* New York: Oxford University Press, 1980.

Mayhew, Lewis B., Patrick J. Ford, and Dean L. Hubbard. *The Quest for Quality: The Challenge for Undergraduate Education in the 1990s.* San Francisco: Jossey-Bass Publishers, 1990.

Miles, Matthew, ed. *Innovation in Education.* New York: Teachers College, Columbia University, 1964.

Mowry, George E. *The Era of Theodore Roosevelt and the Birth of Modern America, 1900–1912.* New York: Harper & Row, 1958.

———., ed. *The Twenties: Fords, Flappers & Fanatics.* Englewood Cliffs, N.J.: Prentice-Hall, 1963.

Nash, Roderick. *The Nervous Generation: American Thought, 1917–1930.* Chicago: Rand McNally, 1970.

Nivens, John F. *A Study of the Organization and Operation of Voluntary Accrediting Agencies.* Washington, D.C.: Catholic University Press of America, 1959.

Oleson, Alexandra, and John Voss. *The Organization of Knowledge in Modern America, 1860–1920.* Baltimore: Johns Hopkins University Press, 1979.

Olson, Keith W. *The G.I. Bill, the Veterans, and the Colleges.* Louisville: University of Kentucky Press, 1974.

Pace, Vernon, and Donald C. Manlove. *The First Fifty Years: Five Decades of Service to Education.* Falls Church, Virginia: National Study of School Evaluation, 1983.

Peckham, Howard H. *The Making of the University of Michigan, 1817–1967.* Ann Arbor: University of Michigan Press, 1967.

Ravitch, Diane. *The Troubled Crusade: American Education, 1945–1980.* New York: Basic Books, 1983.

Ravitch, Diane, and Chester E. Finn, Jr. *What Do Our 17-Year-Olds Know?* New York: Harper & Row, 1987.

Reisman, David. *On Higher Education: The Academic Enterprise in an Era of Rising Student Consumerism.* San Francisco: Jossey-Bass Publishers, 1980.

Rice, Bradley R. *Progressive Cities: The Commission Government Movement.* Austin: University of Texas Press, 1977.

Rudolph, Frederick. *The American College and the American University.* New York: Alfred A. Knopf, 1962.

Savage, Howard J. *Fruit of an Impulse: Forty-Five Years of the Carnegie Foundation.* New York: Harcourt, Brace, 1953.

Selden, William K. *Accreditation: A Struggle over Standards in Higher Education.* New York: Harper & Brothers, 1960.

———. *Accreditation and the Public Interest.* Washington, D.C.: Council on Postsecondary Accreditation, 1976.

Sklar, Robert. *Movie-Made America: A Cultural History of American Movies.* Rev. ed. New York: Vintage Books, 1994.

Stout, John Erle. *The Development of High School Curricula in the North Central States from 1860 to 1918.* 1921. Reprint, New York: Arno Press & New York Times, 1969.

Summary Report on Invitational Conference on Accreditation and the Protection of the Student as Consumer. Washington, D.C.: U.S. Office of Education, 1978.

Susman, Warren I. *Culture as History: The Transformation of American Society in the Twentieth Century.* New York: Pantheon Books, 1973.

Trivett, David R. *Accreditation and Institutional Eligibility.* Washington, D.C.: American Association for Higher Education, 1971.

Veysey, Laurence. *The Emergence of the American University.* Chicago: University of Chicago Press, 1965.

Warren, Donald R. *To Enforce Education: A History of the Founding Years of the United States Office of Education.* Detroit: Wayne State University, 1974.

Wesley, Edgar B. *NEA: The First Hundred Years.* New York: Harper & Brothers, 1957.

Williams, Roger L. *The Origins of Federal Support for Higher Education: George W. Atherton and the Land-Grant College Movement.* University Park, Penn.: Pennsylvania State University Press, 1991.

Young, Kenneth E., Charles M. Chambers, H. R. Kells, and Associates, with the assistance of Ruth Cargo. *Understanding Accreditation.* San Francisco: Jossey-Bass, 1983.

Accreditation and the Public Interest. Washington, D.C.: U.S. Office of Education and the National Commission on Accrediting, 1970.

Geography: An International Gallup Survey. Princeton, N.J.: Gallup Organization, 1988.

A Survey of College Seniors: Knowledge of History and Literature. Princeton, N.J.: Gallup Organization, 1989.

PERIODICALS

Arnstein, George. "Bad Apples in Academe." *American Education* 10 (September 1974).

Begley, Sharon. "Scratch 'n' Sniff Science." *Newsweek*, special issue, 116 (September 1990).

Butts, William H. "National Uniformity in Secondary Instruction." *The School Review* 3 (February 1895).

Brooks, Stephen D. "The Work of a High School Visitor." *The School Review* 9 (January 1901).

Capen, Samuel P. "College Efficiency and Standardization: Certain Fundamental Principles." *Bulletin of the Association of American Colleges* 1 (1915).

―――. "The Principles Which Should Govern Standards and Accrediting Practices." *Educational Record* 12 (April 1931).

Carrothers, George. "The Cooperative Study in Action." National Association of Secondary School Principals *Bulletin* 26 (April 1942).

Collins, Robert G. "Notes on the Parsons Experience." *Education Digest* 33 (January 1968).

Flanagan, Maureen. "Gender and Urban Political Reform: The City Club and the Woman's City Club of Chicago in the Progressive Era," *American Historical Review* 95 (October 1990).

Galambos, Louis. "The Emerging Organizational Synthesis in Modern American History." *Business History Review* 64 (Autumn 1970).

Gibson, Raymond C. "The Scholarch of Parsons and the NCA." *Phi Delta Kappan* 49 (June 1968).

Holmes, Kenneth. "The Fixing of Standards in Higher Education." *School and Society* 27 (March 31, 1928).

Horwill, Herbert. "A National Standard in Higher Education." *Atlantic Monthly* 90 (September 1902).

Judson, Harry Pratt. "Dangers of the Standardization Movement." *The Educational Record* 2 (July 1921).

McConn, Max. "Academic Standards and Individual Differences—The Dilemma of Democratic Education." *The School Board Journal* (December 1935).

Millard, Richard M. "Postsecondary Education and 'The Best Interests of the People of the States.'" *Journal of Higher Education* 50 (March/April 1979).

Pfnister, Allan O. "Regional Accrediting Agencies at the Crossroads." *Journal of Higher Education* 42 (October 1971).

Proffitt, John R. "The Federal Connection for Accreditation." *Journal of Higher Education* 50 (March/April 1979).

Stevens, W. LeConte. "College Standardization." *Popular Science Monthly* 73 (December 1908).

Terreberry, Shirley. "The Evolution of Organizational Environments." *Administrative Science Quarterly* 12 (March 1968).

Thrash, Patricia. "Accreditation: A Perspective." *Journal of Higher Education* 50 (March/April 1979).

Trow, Martin. "American Higher Education: Past, Present, and Future." *Educational Researcher* 17 (April 1988).

Tyler, Ralph W. "The Federal Role in Education." *The Public Interest* 34 (Winter 1974).

Waugh, Frank A. "A Standardized World, *School and Society* 16 (November 4, 1922).

White, Richard Grant. "The Public School Failure." *North American Review* 170 (December 1880).

Whitney, Allen S. "Methods in Use of Accrediting Schools, *The School Review* 11 (February 1903).

Wiley, Mary Glenn, and Mayer N. Zald. "The Growth and Transformation of Accrediting Agencies: An Exploratory Study in Social Control of Institutions." *Sociology of Education* 41 (Winter 1968).

Zook, George F. "The Movement toward Standardization of Colleges and Universities." *School and Society* 16 (December 23, 1922).

NEWSPAPERS

Chicago Tribune.

GOVERNMENT PUBLICATIONS

Commissioner of Education. *Report of the Commissioner of Education for the Year 1872–1873*. Washington, D.C.: GPO, 1873.

Commissioner of Education. *Report of the Commissioner of Education for the Year 1893–1894*. Washington, D.C.: GPO, 1894.

Judd, Charles H. *Research in the United States Office of Education.* Advisory Committee of Education Staff Study Number 19. Washington, D.C.: GPO, 1939.

Judd, Charles H. *A Study of the Colleges and High Schools of the North Central Association.* U.S. Bureau of Education *Bulletin* 6 (1916).

Lykes, Richard. *Higher Education and the United States Office of Education, 1867–1953*. Washington: GPO, 1975.

Statistical Abstract of the United States. Vols. 83, 91, 113. Washington, D.C.: GPO, 1962, 1970, 1993.

DISSERTATIONS

Georges, Erika. "The Economics of Accreditation." Ph.D. diss., UCLA, 1977.

Harper, William S. "A History of 'Extra-Legal' Accrediting of Higher Education in the United States from 1890 to 1970." Ph.D. diss., University of Missouri, Columbia, 1972.

Mehl, Bernard. "The High School at the Turn of the Century." Ph.D. diss., University of Illinois, 1954.

Paulsen, Russell C. "The North Central Association: Its Change Agent Role on Administrative Practices, Policies, and Procedures in Wisconsin Technical Institutes." Ph.D. diss., University of Wisconsin, Madison, 1974.

Ziemba, Walter J. "Changes in the Policies and Procedures of the Accrediting Process of the Commission on Colleges and Universities of the North Central Association of Colleges and Secondary Schools." Ph.D. diss., University of Michigan, 1966.

INTERVIEWS

All interviews were conducted in Chicago, Illinois, by the author.

Bottenfield, Jack. 4 April 1993.
Brooks, Robert. 6 April 1993.
Bushaw, William. 5 April 1993.
Carroll, Mary Ann. 5 April 1993.
Felton, Geraldine. 4 April 1993.
Jordan, Gerald. 6 April 1993.
Kolenbrander, Harold. 4 April 1993.
Matesich, Sr. Mary Andrew. 4 April 1993.
Neimeyer, Glenn. 4 April 1993.
Sampson, Patsy. 4 April 1993.

Shankel, Delbert. 5 April 1993.
Shaw, Robert. 5 April 1993.
Stastney, Ronald. 5 April 1993.
Thrash, Patricia. 14 December 1994.
Wee, David, 5 April 1993.
Weir, Morton. 5 April 1993.

MAIL SURVEYS

Selected NCA figures were sent a mail survey that asked pertinent questions about their professional and Association experiences. The following responses were received.

Ballowe, James. 6 January 1994.
Bass, Emma. 7 January 1994.
Bauer, Otto F. 31 January 1994.
Berg, Kenneth. 3 January 1994.
Carey, Nancy. 23 December 1993.
Christensen, George C. 6 January 1994.
Gram, Christine. 21 January 1994.
Hemenway, Myrle. 25 January 1994.
Holmes, Deborah S. 13 December 1993.
Humphrey, Kenneth. 31 January 1994.
Klein, Harriet. 20 January 1994.
Leigh, Howard W. 22 December 1993.
McGilley, Sr. Mary Janet. 17 January 1994.
Reinert, Paul C., S.J. 21 December 1993.
Roskens, Ronald. 14 December 1993.
Roush, Donald C. 19 January 1994.
Thornton, Philip. 15 June 1994.
Vale, Richard L. 8 January 1994.
Whitmore, Richard F. 11 April 1994.

Index

Note: Locaters in *italics* indicate photographs.

Curtin, Chester, 155 n.15
Curtis, Chester B., 108

Daugherty, Newton, 7
Davies, Gordon K., 333
Davis, Calvin O., 42, 93, *94,* 123,
    156 n.23
DeHaan, Robert F., 307-8
deliberative process, 57
democratic process
    of CSS, 235-36, 252, 270-71
    and CSS fee structure, 239
    and educational goals, 166
    of NCA, 43, 57, 62
    and accreditation standards, 88
    bureaucracy and, 62, 71
    transformed by commission struc-
        ture, 137, 181
    vs. standardization movement, 78
    rise of education and, 3-4, 6
    rise of voluntary associations and,
        17
Denney, James V., 93
DePauw University, 33, 134
Dependents' School Service, 2610-70
Detroit, Michigan, 145
Detroit High School, 33
Dewey, John, 36, 106
Dille, Roland, 349
Dougherty, Newton C., 22, 35
Drake Junior High School (Colorado),
    256
Draper, Andrew, 27, *29,* 32-35, 40-41,
    45, 47-48, 66, 69-71
    chaired founding meeting, 30
Dressel, Paul, 215

Edmonson, James, 145
educational oversight, 333-44
Educational Testing Service (ETS), 165,
    353
Edwards, Charles, 249
Eells, Walter, 150
Eikenberry, D. H., 107
Eisenhower, Dwight D., 229
elective system, and curricular develop-
    ment, 7-10
elementary education, defined, 39-40
Eliff, James, 93
Eliot, Charles, 8, 21, 25

Ellis, John, 330
Emens, John R., 223 n.64, *370*
Endicott, Frank S., 304, *305*
England, 267
Englewood High School, 35, 59, 92
Enlightenment period, rise of educa-
    tion and, 5
entrance requirements. *See also* admis-
    sion policies.
    examinations, 44
    higher education, 10
evaluative criteria, 142-44, 148-49
    educational thermometers, 142-44
    Evaluative Criteria pamphlets, 151
    pattern (profile) map, 142-43, 194-
        95
    self study, 178-81, 183-91, 358-59
    vs. regulation, 238-39
Evanston Township High School, 302

Faculty, and LAS report, 292
faculty development, at universities, 8-
    10
Federal Council of Churches, xv
federal eligibility and certification, 347
federal government. *See* U.S. Govern-
    ment.
Federation of Regional Accrediting
    Commissions of Higher Education
    (FRACHE), 211-12, 315, 335
Field Enterprises Education Corp., 332
First District Normal School of Mis-
    souri, 81
Fisher, Lowell B., 262, *263*
Fisk College, 299
fit-for-life education, 39, 106
Fleming, Robert L., 299
Flint Junior College, 288
Florida, 306
Forbes, Stephen A., 59-63
Forbes Plan, for accreditation, 59-63
Ford, J. W., 41
Ford Foundation, and STS, 299-300
France, 267
Franzen, Carl F. G., 146, 278, 313
Fraser, Blanche, 361-62
French Morroco, 267
Frieze, Henry S., 10
Fund for the Advancement of Educa-
    tion. *See* Ford Foundation.

INDEX

Reeves, Floyd W., 126-27, 132-33, 139
regional certification, 24
Reinert, Paul C., S.J., 190
religious training, in antebellum colleges, 4
research universities, development of, 8
Rhemus, Paul, 149
Richardson, Elliott, 335
Ries, Wayne C., 360-61, 363
Roberts, Millard G., 207
Rockefeller General Education Board.
    See General Education Board
Roemer, Joseph, 146
Rogers, Henry Wade, 11, 26, *26*, 27, 35, 42-48, 50-51, 56 n.68, 58, 95
Rogers, Virgil, 262
Romine, Stephen A., 199, 214, 233, *235*, 236, 240, 243, 255, 305, 338, *370*
Rose, Glenn, 256
Rosenlof, George W., 151-52, 284
Roskens, Ronald, 190, 350, *351*
Rudolph, Frederick, 5
Rufi, John, 262
Russell, John Dale, 127, 132, 134, 139, 163

Saint Louis (Missouri) meeting, 147-48
Saint Louis University, 190
Saint Olaf College, 289
Samuelson, Everett V., 256-57
Sante Fe Indian School, *227*
Schaeffer, Charles A., 31, 34, 41, 48
Schooling, Herbert W., 231, 311, *311*
Science Research Associates (SRA), 303
scientific-technological developments, and liberal education, 5-9, 17, 125, 140
Search, Herman, 264-65
secondary education, 66, 72-78, 144-53, 231-71
    accreditation, 72-78, 144-53
    adult high schools, 228
    changing face of, 226-31
    college cooperation, 17
    criteria
        for defining, 38-40, 48
        vs. regulation, 238-39, 340
    curriculum reorganization project, 110-18
    educational thermometers, 142-44

secondary education (*continued*)
    extracurricular development, 114
    junior high schools, 228, 254-55
    middle schools, 228
    modernization, 239-53
    NEA *Cardinal Principles of Secondary Education*, 110 ff.
    overseas dependents' schools, 228, 260-70
    and population increase, 1920-40, 105
    postwar reform, 229ff.
    qualitative *vs.* quantitative objectives, 113-16, 237-38, 252-53
    racial integration, 230
    self study, 237, 339
    and social change, 256
    standards, 69-76, 144-53
    and State Boards of Education, 236-37
    vocational-technical schools, 228
    self-study
        consumerism programs, 339
        Evaluation Guide for Secondary Schools, 245-50
        Evaluative Criteria, 242-44
        in secondary education, 237, 331
    self-study consultants, 183-91
    self-study/visitation program, in secondary education, 244-53
Semrow, Joseph, 215, 338
Shaw, Robert, 366-67
Sheppard, J. H., 282
Shertzer, Bruce, 303
Shimer College, 299
Shoreland Hotel (Chicago), 199, 313
Shurtleff College, 134
Sifert, Earl, *230*
Sills, David, xii
Silverman, Bob, xix
Simpson, Lawrence, 274 n.27
Simpson College, 289
Slocum, William F., 46
Snider, Nelson, *370*
sociology, antebellum changes in U.S., 10
South Carolina, 306
South Dakota, 92, 149, 253, 289
South High School (Ohio), 299